ALEXANDER POPE

SELECTED WORKS

ALEXANDER POPE

SELECTED WORKS

EDITED, WITH AN INTRODUCTION,

BY LOUIS KRONENBERGER

THE MODERN LIBRARY · NEW YORK

*I should like to express my sincere thanks
to Saxe Commins who has lightened and
brightened my task at every turn.*   L. K.

CONTENTS

Introduction

EVEN today, even after two hundred years, Pope's name continues to be ringed with controversy, as Chatterton's with pathos or Byron's with scandal. Moreover, the world goes on loudly and heatedly disputing not only how good Pope was as a poet but how bad he was as a man. It goes on playing the detective at least as zestfully as it plays the critic; and whatever conclusions it arrives at, it goes on being fascinated. Great poet or very special poet or no poet at all, Pope—it will nowhere, I think, be denied—charged his couplets with intense and insistent life; aggressor or victim, demi-devil or child of pain, Pope everywhere still makes his presence passionately felt.

Like Chatterton, like Byron, Pope boasts a "story" as well as an achievement: indeed, his character was so devious and his career so dazzling that they have often shifted the limelight from the poetry to the poet, and made the "little monster" who hobnobbed with dukes rather more of a figure than the author of *The Dunciad* and the *Epilogue to the Satires*. Furthermore, the "story" and the achievement have forcibly affected each other. Thus some of the Victorians, quite sure that very little about Pope was creditable, went on to wonder how much of him could be great; and today there are those who act as if white-washing his character was a *sine qua non* to appreciating his art.

Today, at any rate, Pope's goodness is far more in question than his greatness: his greatness, I think it might even be ventured, is no longer in question at all. Classicism has only needed a friendly hearing for so famous a classicist to be once more acclaimed. Abuse has only needed to be considered as "poetic" as, say, eulogy, for the most telling of our satirists to exert on the twentieth century some of the force he exerted on the eighteenth. It is even possible that Pope may become too fashionable for a time, though not that he will ever be-

come widely popular. (For some reason, a Pope or a Dryden
is usually recommended to the public as a "change" from
Keats or Shelley: but the great mass of readers don't want a
change from Keats and Shelley.) Meanwhile the man—and
no one can care much about the poet without coming to be
interested in the man—continues to be wrangled over, and I
suspect that any jury chosen to pass judgment on him would
wind up failing to agree. *Were* his provocations greater than
his revenges? Do his handicaps on the whole excuse his faults?
Was he more sinned against than sinning—and quite as much
the victim of his age as of his ailments? Or was he most of all
the victim of a succeeding age—of Victorian smugness and
self-righteousness and of that Victorianism which, resenting
its repressions, so frequently managed to be cruel while it
pretended to be moral?

Alexander Pope was born in London on the 21st of May,
1688. Both his parents were then past forty and both (his
father by conversion) Roman Catholics. Both were also of
what we should now describe as middle-class origin; for Pope's
claims that on his father's side he descended down some cir-
cular staircase from an earl were long ago disposed of. Pope's
father had prospered as a linen draper and was able, soon
after the poet's birth—it was also (a matter of some importance to papists) soon after the Revolution—to retire from
business and quietly remove to the country. The boy received
a very jumbled and discontinuous schooling, hardly so much
at school as among priests and tutors, and in later life could
claim with some accuracy to be largely self-taught. He made
a good-looking child who at ten had a "plump, pretty face"
and a "fresh complexion"; but soon after—and as the tale
runs through "perpetual application"—Pope began to suffer
from ill-health and in particular from a tuberculous infection
that in time caused him to be deformed. Condemned to be a
hunchback not five feet tall, tormented with headaches and
other recurring ailments, the youth was early set apart from

most of his kind as much by his disabilities as by his genius; and was also to bear the burden of his religion at a time when it could be particularly heavy.

Shut off by his faith from many callings, and by his health from many others, and by his appearance moreover from some of the primary gratifications of life, the young Pope was yet not altogether unfortunate. He could be what alone he seems ever to have wanted to be; he could be a poet. As yet, as we all remember—

> *As yet a child, nor yet a fool to fame,*
> *I lisp'd in numbers, for the numbers came.*

Fortunately, too, his parents raised no objections—indeed, his father so far encouraged him as to be critical of his "rhimes"; and there was the family purse to give substance to the family blessing.

Thus Pope was started on a grown-up career at an age when even most serious boys are satisfied with collecting coins. It is possible that, as he in later life maintained, Pope saw Dryden kinging it at Will's Coffee House: Pope was just twelve when Dryden died. It is certain that by his middle teens—there were "intellectual" and influential country neighbors to introduce him about—he had begun to know a number of established writers. Before he was seventeen, Pope was exchanging letters with the ageing Wycherley; and it was about then that he received from the poet Walsh a piece of very famous advice. "He . . . used to tell me, that there was one way left of excelling: for though we had several great poets, we never had any one great poet that was correct, and he desired me to make that my study and aim." Both Walsh and Congreve, moreover, sufficiently admired Pope's youthful *Pastorals* to bring them to the attention of the well-known bookseller—we should say publisher—Jacob Tonson; and in 1708, when Pope was twenty, Tonson published them in one of his Miscellanies. Now Pope was really launched; another five years and, having published both the *Essay on Criticism* and *The Rape of the Lock*, he would be really famous.

Yet another five years, which brings us to Pope at thirty, and he had not only become the most celebrated poet of his age, he had also revolutionized the poet's place in the world. He was something much rarer, for a poet, than illustrious; he was independent. He had made, or would very soon have made, well over five thousand pounds from his translation of the Iliad—which is much like making over $100,000 in America today. This was the pivotal, the decisive, thing in Pope's life. It saved him from ever having to be a hack. It enabled him to regard the lords he moved among as friends rather than patrons. It made it possible for him to settle down for the rest of his life at Twickenham, where he might busy himself with his garden and his grotto, care for his mother, receive his guests, polish his verse, touch up his letters, nurse his feuds and amplify his fame.

It can only be because Pope is so extremely notorious for his enmities that he is not remarkably famous for his friendships. Few men, certainly, have had more glittering connections—and these include connections with writers. The greatest writer of the age, Dean Swift, was very nearly Pope's greatest friend. Gay, Congreve, Prior, Thomson, Steele—the literary list could be much further enlarged though not much further embellished—were all men with whom Pope moved on easy or affectionate terms. One sentence from a letter of Pope's written when he was twenty-nine, and rather on the threshold than at the apex of his glory, will aptly enough convey how well he did in the great world: "After some attendance on my Lord Burlington, I have been at the Duke of Shrewsbury's, Duke of Argyle's, Lady Rochester's, Lord Percival's, Mr Stonor's, Lord Winchelsea's, Sir Godfrey Kneller, who has made me a fine present of a picture, and Duchess Hamilton's." To each of these moreover he had gone, not as one might reasonably imagine, for dinner, but for a visit of "some days."

Pope followed his translation of the Iliad with his edition of Shakespeare and his translation of the Odyssey. These three undertakings—and while they were performing, he did only very minor work besides—bring us to 1726 and to Pope at thirty-eight. It is to be noted that though for a number of years he had been easily the first poet of the age, of the poetry for which we really value him today he had written nothing but *The Rape of the Lock* and some scattered verses. It is to be noted further that though Pope, long before 1726, had become the center of numerous feuds, he had almost never retorted upon his enemies in print. Barring some early pieces, there was only—and at its first appearance it fell upon barren ground—the "Atticus" portrait of Addison. Indeed, Pope's career as a satirist, which is in the vital sense his career as a poet, was only now to begin. From the first version of *The Dunciad* in 1729 to the final version of *The Dunciad* in 1743, Pope produced a body of work, a succession of masterpieces, which do something to justify the existence of malice in this world, and which include, so far as that goes, not simply the vitriol Pope threw so unerringly in the faces of his personal enemies, but a massive onslaught against mediocrity, incompetence and dullness. In the design and much of the detail of *The Dunciad*; in the Moral Essays; and most of all in the Satires and Epistles, Pope brought his genius to its fullest flower.

Life, all in all, had perhaps not grown sunnier as it grew more distinguished. The Prince of Wales might come to visit Pope at Twickenham and the Queen of England hint that she would like to come; and every year Pope might make the circuit of patrician country houses, as too he might enjoy the devotion of his friends and that final homage, the quaking terror of his enemies. Still, there was a good deal amiss. Though the hump might grow no bigger on Pope's back, it loomed larger and larger in Pope's mind. From the outset of his career he had never been allowed to forget his appearance; he had had to endure such taunts in print as Dennis' about "a young, squab, short Gentleman . . . the very bow of the God of Love." Even more painfully, he had had to endure the common fate of the misshapen, becoming in the eyes of the other sex an object of pity when he was not an outright object of scorn. The story goes—and the hardness of the age, not to speak of the hardness of the lady, tends to support it— that upon Pope's declaring his feelings for Lady Mary Montagu, she was seized with laughter. The story of his love for Martha Blount has doubtless been much embroidered, lacking solid facts to build on; but very possibly Pope did love her, and if so, loved in vain.

All this, as time went on, could have made Pope no happier: nor must we forget that he was chronically ill as well as deformed, and that there is no great exaggeration in his celebrated reference to "that long disease, my life." The little fellow who used to pad out his rickety legs with three pairs of stockings, used too to need a servant within call, for whom he might have to ring a dozen times a night. From boyhood the headaches had been agonies, and as life wore on there were more serious ailments as well. Then, too, one after another of his closest friends began dropping away: Gay died, and Arbuthnot; Atterbury was sentenced to exile, and Swift, after a time, sentenced himself. Doubtless the enmities remained more fixed. There had always been dunces to flay, and Dennises to be flayed by. There was to the very end— Pope died of a dropsy when he was fifty-six—the need and the ability to have the last word.

The need to have the last word is a common enough and never very engaging trait; and though the source of it is occasionally pride, it is infinitely oftener vanity. Pope was one of the vainest and hence one of the touchiest men who ever lived. Edith Sitwell, the most ardent champion of Pope to have yet appeared, says that vanity was "the one grave fault in his character." This in a sense is quite true, but hardly redeems Pope so much as Miss Sitwell fancies. After all, vanity is the one grave fault in most people's characters; being, surely, the *fons et origo* of almost everything unpleasant or evil in their actions. Nevertheless, even though Miss Sitwell shuts her eyes to the enormity of Pope's misbehavior, it is good to find her understanding the nature of it. It keeps Pope altogether human; it quite disproves him a monster. And it explains, without necessarily justifying, much that Pope's own age found inexplicable and the Victorian age found shocking.

All the same, we need not pretend that the world of his time was the prettier for having Pope in it. His talent for getting in the last word must have made him loom a perpetual menace; just about what a vastly malicious columnist of brilliant gifts and immense reputation—who had little to fear from the laws of libel—would be today. For it was very evident that because of Pope anybody might wake up of a morning to find himself infamous. Pope, moreover—it is one of the most devastating things about him as an artist, but most damning as a man—seldom lashed out in the heat of anger; he knew how to bide his time, how to age his resentments. One thing was certain: whoever stepped on his toes could not sidestep his anger. As I am perhaps too fond of saying, it was Pope's instinct to take offense, and he made it his trade.

But Pope was not just vindictive. His vanity demanded that he preen as well as protect himself; that he lose no chance of appearing as generous or kindhearted or wise or rakish or precocious* or indifferent to fame as possible. He went to great lengths that people (and posterity) should think so, and to even greater lengths lest they think otherwise. His

---

* He pretended, for example, to have written a great many poems earlier than he actually wrote them, "so that he might be admired as a prodigy."

desire to seem nobler than he was;* his indulgence in what
Dr. Johnson, and not Dr. Johnson alone, would have termed
cant; his carefully limelighted admiration for the good life, are
much harder to bear than his malice. Vanity, moreover, made
Pope fantastically devious, involving him in almost as much
conspiracy as cant. As Lady Bolingbroke once remarked,
the little man couldn't have resisted playing the politician
with cabbages and turnips. The key to much of Pope's life
is the character of many of Pope's letters. He not only wrote
a vast number, full of fancy sentiments, in a ceremonious
style; he not only used the same ones more than once: but
later in life he tried wherever possible to get his letters back,
that he might ink out what was injurious and touch up what
was not. And all this was merely preliminary to Pope's real
object: getting his letters published. But, it being impossible
for Pope to do this in a forthright manner—or even, as someone has said, for him to be normally arch and pretend that
he was giving in to the urgings of "friends"—Pope cooked up
the most elaborate of plots. I have not the space, and am by
no means certain that I have the skill, to set forth the famous
"P.T." saga in all its detail. Very briefly, however, Pope—to
quote Macaulay—"robbed himself of his own letters, and
then raised the hue and cry after them." Pope, that is, invented a person named P.T. who, through a flesh-and-blood
intermediary of Pope's hiring, surreptitiously supplied a piratical publisher, Edmund Curl, with a good many Pope letters. These being in due course published, Pope now stepped
forth to denounce the correspondence as unauthorized and
inaccurate; and soon after brought out, in "self-defense," the
authorized version that had been his object from the first.

---

* Which rubs us the wrong way in even the most polished of his
moralizings; for example:

> *When Truth or Virtue an affront endures,*
> *The affront is mine, my Friend, and should be yours . . .*
> *Mine, as a Friend to every worthy mind,*
> *And mine as Man, who feels for all Mankind.*

Using much the same tactics, he pursued much the same stratagems with some of his best friends, notably Swift.

It need not surprise us that a man who from vanity could trick his closest friends should from pique, or genuine pain, contrive harsh revenges against his enemies. Once, for example, Pope pretended to seal a reconciliation with Curl by "civilly" drinking sack with him: shortly afterwards, the bookseller was griped by the emetic Pope had dropped into his wine. Usually, however, Pope chose to pay off old scores with from a couplet's worth to a column's worth of verse. Sometimes, as with Hervey or Lady Mary, the repayment went on, in this poem and that, for years; sometimes, as with Theobald—or Cibber, who displaced him—the victim of Pope's displeasure became the very hero of his poem. Sometimes, as with many of the dunces, the victims had sinned not so much against Pope as against poetry, and the thwacking was administered in the name of Art. But whatever the provocation, and whether mere concentrated venom or sheer malicious magic—

> *Pox'd by her love or libelled by her hate*

or

> *Silence, ye wolves! while Ralph to Cynthia howls*
> *And makes night hideous—Answer him, ye owls!*

or

> *Beauty that shocks you, Parts that none will trust,*
> *Wit that can creep, and Pride that licks the dust*

—the punishment always more than fits the crime.

Diligent in implying the best about himself, Pope shrank—more than a satirist strictly needs to do—from owning up to his more questionable impulses. Having anonymously published something licentious or sharp-toothed, Pope did not merely deny having written it when asked; with a pious look he would deny having written it unasked, and would sometimes go so far as to abuse the poem or "identify" the anonymous author.

Such duplicity, though there may have been an element of self-protection in it, was chiefly grounded in a nature that had to throw dust in people's eyes, had to mislead, had to lie. The letters are filled with pointless lying, often in the form of needlessly fervent or solemn assertions; the life is a tissue of ambiguities and falsifications. Having lied like many another man about his ancestry, Pope proceeded to lie, like very few others, about almost everything else. Professor Sherburn, the foremost living authority on Pope, is indignant that Leslie Stephen should have characterized Pope as "the most untruthful man of his age." It is indeed a whopping indictment, for the age of Pope, furious with faction and intrigue, was outrageously untruthful, outstandingly treacherous. All the same, if Pope was not "the most untruthful man of his age," I do not know who could have been except the man Pope saluted (in the phrase he coined for the occasion) as his "guide, philosopher and friend"—Lord Bolingbroke.

There were other very disagreeable and discreditable qualities—petty plagiarisms, rather shabby dealings with collaborators, a snide withholding of full credit from people who helped Pope as a matter of business or of friendship, a tendency toward smirking and even nasty-mindedness. Yet even to ask the question today, *Was Pope a bad man?* is obviously to beg it. Doubly to beg it: for on the one side there juts up all that tends to redeem Alexander Pope, and on the other, all that helps to explain him. We must seek as much of a medical as of a moral judgment for a man who nearly all his life had a sick crooked body and hence a sick crooked mind. Nor need we be sanctimonious about a man who, endowed with an incomparable talent for vituperation, was prodded time and again into making use of it. We must see Pope, furthermore, in relation to his age: he was enormously sensitive, and the age was coarse; incredibly vain, and the age was cruel. But all the same we must deplore a general lack of forbearance and an almost utter lack of charity in Pope who, be it noted, put into polished form virtually every cliché of morality except *Love thine enemies*, and who considered the ability "to forgive" as not human but "divine."

The Victorians—most notably the Rev. Whitwell Elwin, who grew so abusive he had to be disbarred from completing what is still the standard edition of Pope's works—went at Pope all wrong. Men so very respectable, and so very repressed, got an almost pathological enjoyment out of being scandalized; and in Pope's endless mendacities, in his overflowing malice, in his habitual and sometimes smirking indecencies, there was much to scandalize them. Moreover, the Victorians railed against Pope as a man during an era when it was safest to depreciate him as an artist. And railed with little restraint: the Rev. Whitwell Elwin displays almost all of Pope's venom without any of his verve. Today the pendulum has rather swung to the other extreme. Since Elwin, who attempted to crucify him, Pope's most biased biographer is Miss Sitwell, who did all she could to make him out a martyr.

But he was even less a martyr than he was a monster. His hateful qualities are very glaring indeed: there is simply no means of arguing them away, and not much reason to suppose that had other people been habitually sympathetic, Pope would have been habitually sweet. His provocations were sometimes great, but in the perspective of a lifetime his revenges seem highly disproportionate. Yet, and not at all from any desire to soften an indictment or throw a sop, it must be made very clear that, beyond a gay and witty side, Pope had a charming side, a kindly side, even a truly loyal and generous side. It was once the custom, after painting Pope at full length as a fiend, to concede that he had been good to his family. We can do better than that. The extremely affectionate and devoted son was, toward a surprising number of people, an extremely affectionate and devoted friend. He was deeply and generously attached to Martha Blount. His flattery (as manifested in his letters) can be degrading; but Pope had a good deal of social grace; and as a talker and host must have had a good deal of personal charm. No doubt, like all the other writers of his age, and most writers in every age, Pope was a climber and a snob; yet from a very early period of his career he was certainly as much sought after as seeking; nor would great lords have annually solicited the honor of housing a difficult semi-invalid had it not been a pleasure as well.

The man knew how to please almost as artfully as he knew how to wound. The best of his compliments are very different from his habitual flatteries—in fact, they do not rank too far below the best of his barbs. And if Pope loved a lord, it was not without gallantry: for his loyalties were, on the whole, very much less toward lords in power than toward lords in opposition, or in retirement, or even in disgrace. Pope was not at all put off by unpopular causes—you may say, but I think in this case injudiciously, that a satirist cannot afford to be—and he was not upset by a worse than unpopular, by a downright unsafe, religion. More than one friend bade Pope mend his faith lest it might mar his fortune; but first and last, and as the real victim of some of its slighter and the potential victim of some of its severer disabilities, Pope remained an avowed Roman Catholic. He remained one, moreover, despite being by temperament pretty much a skeptic and by conviction pretty much a deist. It holds true, I think, that for all that was sick in Pope, and deceitful, and done for effect, and almost fiendishly rancorous, he had a quite impressive amount of character. "That long disease, my life" was spent, not in a bed, but on a battlefield.

II

The Pope we have so far discussed as though he were a rather fascinating character in a novel happened to be a great poet. He happened to be the greatest master of rhymed vituperation in the history of letters; so that even to prick him with a pin was a sure if not very choice way of achieving immortality. He was also the greatest master of the heroic couplet in the English language; and he was, finally, a great master of words, in sound and in sense, in combination and in opposition: indeed, so much and so mainly an artist that, though spectacularly unlike them in his vision of the world, Pope is commonly grouped with such other pre-eminent artists as Spenser, Milton, Keats and Tennyson.

How then, we may ask, can there have raged so long and shrill and *à outrance* a conflict over whether this thrice-great poet was a poet at all? How came he, for something like a century, to be so often disparaged or damned with faint praise: was this most conspiratorial of writers himself the victim of a long-drawn-out conspiracy?

I am beginning to give the air of a mystery melodrama to what, after all, is one of the most celebrated reversals of judgment and reflections on shifting taste in literary annals; but there is even now something dramatic, as well as ironical and instructive, about Pope's being toppled from the heights where he reigned so long. Yet, up to a point, what happened to Pope was bound to happen. "Every hero," Emerson remarked, "at last becomes a bore"; and if heroes, how much more readily heroic couplets. People got fed up with heroic couplets, particularly when written by other hands than Pope's; people got fed up with "correctness," particularly when not reinforced by skill; people got fed up with the eighteenth century, particularly if they happened to be living in the nineteenth. It was time an old age was out: poetry, like music, was now to have a darker, dreamier, lusher and in many ways grander orchestration.

In the new age, unfortunately, Pope was not merely condescended to for writing unfashionable poetry; he was all but ostracized for not writing poetry at all. For he made no appeal to the feelings, or to the senses, or to the soul. One could read him for hours without breathing a larger air, or issuing upon a more glowing landscape; all too often Pope's adjectives were opprobrious, and his figures of speech downright objects of revulsion. To a century hardly less exalted by Arnold's doubts than by Wordsworth's affirmations, a century equally entranced by the visions of Coleridge and the music of Swinburne, Pope seemed frivolous, mundane, besmirched—and as far removed from poetry as Scott seemed adjacent to it.

All this is so very old a story that it doubtless seems an outmoded one as well. But it is really not: the business of abusing Pope may have stopped, but the business of appreciating him again has scarcely started. His poetry remains a stumbling-block; which is to say that while it is safe to call Pope great—in fact very unsafe to call him anything less—the usual yardsticks will never confirm his greatness; nor will a sincere lover of poetry necessarily be a lover of Pope. If he quite reasonably seeks in Pope something that appeals to the feelings or the senses or the soul, he will almost never find it. It is important to state, and even to stress, what Pope was not; and it could possibly be maintained that, in a very restricted and Romantic view, he was not a poet. But there is no view by which it could possibly be maintained that he was not a great genius; and on those grounds Matthew Arnold's dictum that Pope is not a classic of our poetry but a classic of our prose will not hold up. For Arnold clearly meant to demote him to a lower level, and the most that anyone may permissibly do is to exclude him at a corresponding one. At the very least he is a classic—and a great classic—of our literature.

In the wake of Arnold's calling Pope a classic of our prose, his admirers have been at some pains to exhibit him as—*by Arnold's standards*—a classic of our poetry. They have quoted, over and over, such lines as

> *Die of a rose in aromatic pain*

or

> *Lo! where Maeotis sleeps, and hardly flows*
> *The freezing Tanais thro' a waste of snows.*

And no doubt, had he cared to, Pope might have written, quite consummately, more of Arnold's—or the average poetry lover's—kind of poetry. But what he happened to write on "poetical" subjects was most of it conventional and even counterfeit, and we are much better off to face the fact. His real glory lies in a different sphere.

That sphere is not, again, the part of Pope that comes readiest to men's lips or bulks largest in Bartlett. Literally anybody who can quote anything can quote (or misquote) Pope:

> *A little learning is a dangerous thing;*
>
> *To err is human; to forgive divine;*
>
> *For fools rush in where angels fear to tread.*

It was in giving so sharp a turn to the better explored truths of life that the twenty-three-year-old Pope achieved his first important success, the *Essay on Criticism*; and of this side of him there is little to add to his own nine-word précis of the subject:

> *What oft was thought, but ne'er so well expressed.*

He reclothed clichés of thought so vividly that they long ago became clichés of language; he became as great an aphorist and expounder of worldly wisdom as any Poor Richard in prose. At its own level all this is remarkable; but all this plainly never made Pope great, or a poet.

What made him both, of course, was his satire—a body of work in which he mingles autobiography and abuse, is equally master of the scalpel and the poisoned dart, and proves himself the most brilliant student of manners of the age, and the most artful scandalmonger. His is not the noblest tradition of satire; chastising evildoers interested him far more than reforming them. He is often very malicious and sometimes very unjust; but he can be as lynx-eyed as any Saint-Simon, as worldly as LaRochefoucauld, as witty as Voltaire, as con-

scientious an artist as Flaubert and (in his own field) as con-
summate a one as Virgil.

The artist, indeed, is the important thing about the satirist.
Though Pope's stock-in-trade was the famous figures of his
day, as a social historian he can seldom be trusted: he has
LaRochefoucauld's worldliness without his disinterestedness,
Saint-Simon's sharp eyesight without his honesty. And though
he may very often happen to be speaking the truth, once we
cease to count on his doing so, we can approach his satires,
and come to value them, as works of art.* The grudges that
start off in Pope as goads wind up as catalysts, converting
flawed eighteenth-century figures into flawless characters of
fiction. Pope's Sporus is no more Lord Hervey than Dickens'
Harold Skimpole is Leigh Hunt: Sporus is a good deal more
wicked and immeasurably more wonderful. Yet it is not quite
true that Pope always had to invent or exaggerate or un-
scrupulously "arrange" his portraits in order to triumph: the
resemblance between Atticus and Addison, for example, is
uncomfortably close.

---

* The point of many of Pope's jibes is now quite lost, and the point
of many others depends on a detailed knowledge of Pope's era. A full
appreciation of Pope's work is possible only to someone up to his neck
in the social and political, the literary and artistic, history and gossip
of seventeenth- and eighteenth-century England and Europe, with a
further very ripe background of antiquity; and—since Pope "imitated"
on an immense scale—with a solid knowledge of four or five literatures
to boot. The perfectly equipped reader of the Satires or *The Dunciad*,
effortlessly catching the point of each reference as he reads along, is
indeed to be envied; but the non-scholar cannot achieve the same experience by boning up, by constantly grappling with footnotes. It is
better, on the whole, to miss many of Pope's allusions than, by fussing
over them, to miss any of Pope's art. Footnotes, in something like the
scholarly Twickenham Edition of Pope's poetry, are both fascinating
and indispensable; but in an edition for the general reader, once they
go beyond being really necessary signposts, they are in danger of becoming ubiquitous billboards that disfigure and even obscure the landscape. I have therefore cut footnotes to a minimum; and included, at
the back of the book, a few facts about the most prominent or interesting
"characters" in Pope's work.

Moreover, though Pope took revenge in print—and superb revenge—upon his enemies, it was his essential self as much as particular circumstances that made a great satirist of him; which is to say that it came quite as naturally to him to be abusive as to feel abused. Consider his portrait of Narcissa:

> *Narcissa's nature, tolerably mild,*
> *To make a wash, would hardly stew a child;*
> *Has even been proved to grant a lover's prayer,*
> *And paid a tradesman once to make him stare;*
> *Gave alms at Easter, in a Christian trim,*
> *And made a widow happy, for a whim.*

"Narcissa" may be a sobriquet for somebody Pope disliked; but we feel here a malice—if malice it be—that has been so completely aërated into sheer wit, we feel here so much greater an impulse to create a portrait than to destroy a person, that no animus seems involved.

Pope furthermore proves himself quite as brilliant a satiric artist when pure worldling as when pure wasp: it is the hundreds upon hundreds of lines in the style and at the level of

> *A saint in crape is twice a saint in lawn*

or

> *Proud to catch cold at a Venetian door*

that are most representative of Pope's skill and most indicative of his temperament. He had a "sophisticated" knowledge of the world that contained much truth, even if too much cynicism: indeed, so easily wounded by particular men that he could never be very wise about them, Pope was wisest about mankind in the mass.

Mankind for Pope—the mankind, at any rate, that Pope has any first-hand understanding of—is chiefly the society world, whose follies feel the cold hard glare of his wit:

> *Pleasure the sex, as children Birds, pursue,*
> *Still out of reach, yet never out of view . . .*

> *At last, to follies Youth could scarce defend,*
> *It grows their Age's prudence to pretend . . .*
> *As Hags hold Sabbaths, less for joy than spite,*
> *So these their merry, miserable Night;*
> *Still round and round the Ghosts of Beauty glide,*
> *And haunt the places where their Honour died.*
> *See how the World its Veterans rewards!*
> *A Youth of Frolics, an old Age of Cards;*
> *Fair to no purpose, artful to no end,*
> *Young without Lovers, old without a Friend;*
> *A Fop their Passion, but their Prize a Sot;*
> *Alive, ridiculous, and dead, forgot!*

Now and then, as in his great parody that comes so close to being great poetry, Pope—and not just because Pope's Homer is reverberating in our ear—manages to transform the tarnished social spectacle into a kind of fairyland of regret, to give things a true moral coloration, to bring them to a delicate emotional pitch:

> *Oh! if to dance all night, and dress all day*
> *Charm'd the small-pox, or chas'd old-age away;*
> *Who would not scorn what housewife's cares produce,*
> *Or who would learn one earthly thing of use?*
> *To patch, nay ogle, might become a saint,*
> *Nor could it sure be such a sin to paint.*
> *But since, alas! frail beauty must decay,*
> *Curl'd or uncurl'd, since locks will turn to grey;*
> *Since painted, or not painted, all shall fade,*
> *And she who scorns a man, must die a maid;*
> *What then remains, but well our pow'r to use,*
> *And keep good-humour still whate'er we lose?*
> *And trust me, dear! good-humour can prevail,*
> *When airs, and flights, and screams, and scolding fail.*

Here we have a sensibility apprehended through the gauze of worldly wit that is one of the finest things about Pope. And let us note in passing another fine thing about him.

That Pope's war against the dunces was fundamentally a Holy War in the service of art is so beyond serious dispute as to have become a critical commonplace; but I think it is very far from well known generally. Unfortunately, the "little monster" squirting his poison at his Grub-Street ill-wishers has quite effaced the fiery poet brandishing his sword in a great cause. Yet Pope's sniping at his very large circle of enemies, and even his deplorable sneering at those "sons of a day," the starveling hacks, is incidental to his grand mock-epic design of attacking dullness and incapacity. Pope's record in the matter of appraising his contemporaries would do credit to the most disinterested and distinguished of professional critics: whom Pope abandoned, few subsequent critics have defended; and whom Pope praised—though here the record is far less remarkable—usually deserved to be praised. He was "moral" about writers, *qua* writers, because he was passionate about literature.

As a moralist about life, Pope seems to me to have infinitely less importance. Until quite recently, in fact, it would scarcely have occurred to me to discuss the point. But it was no doubt inevitable that one kind of excess about Pope should be followed by another; that he should come to be acclaimed, as he had formerly been assailed, on quite the wrong grounds; and that, while we were most of us absolving Pope of a number of his sins and labeling the rest of them sickness, some few should actually find him a moral poet in as grave and positive a sense as Dr Johnson is. For a particularly earnest example of this sort, turn to a recent published lecture, *The Moral Poetry of Pope*, by Geoffrey Tillotson. Professor Tillotson labors to show, not only that Pope's was a "sound morality," but that when he moralized in couplets he produced genuine poetry. Now Pope, like other mixed and malignant beings, possessed intense moral sensibility and saw all that was beautiful in virtue; he was quite as "moral" as the next man who aims high but only fitfully practices what he preaches. And no doubt what Pope preached was sound enough: but sound preaching is a very different matter from sound poetry. Out-and-out didactic verse has poetic impact, as a rule, only to the extent that it has personal impact, whether of vision or of style. Pope, borrowing and embroidering the standard texts—Pope, producing "what oft was thought but ne'er so well expressed"—quite fails to write good poetry, though he frequently writes good epigrams. Even Dr Johnson's second-best manner, even

> *Still raise for good the supplicating voice,*
> *But leave to Heaven the measure and the choice*

has an accent that Pope quite lacks. It required, not a moral philosopher, but a great poet like Homer to raise Pope to a "poetically" serious level (and even there, Pope is neat where Homer is spacious):

> *But since, alas! ignoble age must come,*
> *Disease, and death's inexorable doom,*
> *The life which others pay, let us bestow,*
> *And give to fame what we to Nature owe.*

The poet usually slumbers in Pope when he is formulating moral laws, and only comes broad awake when he can single out who broke them; when he can tag Addison as

> *Willing to wound, and yet afraid to strike*

or dub Bacon

> *The wisest, brightest, meanest of mankind.*

Professor Tillotson's praise of Pope as a moral poet seems to me the kind of thing from which Pope—and particularly now, when he is being restored to much of his former glory—must be saved. Exactly as Matthew Arnold insisted that it is not in his moral effusions but in the roaring bestiality of *The Jolly Beggars* that Burns achieves superb poetry, so we may insist that Pope being moral usually writes smooth couplets, but Pope being malicious usually writes glorious verse. It is much to be hoped that Pope will not come back in style as a sort of tarnished saint, or an Interesting Mind. Ours is an age with, critically, a greater capacity to analyze than to appreciate. It is an age very good at reducing a work of art to its social and political, or its religious and psychological elements; an age very apt at telling us what a given work of art signifies, or symbolizes, or suggests; or whence it derives or toward what it is moving. It is just not a very splendid age for telling us what a work of art *is*; what it, so to speak, tastes like. And with Pope, even though he palpably derives from dozens of earlier poets and tremendously influenced dozens of later ones, the only very important thing is the poetry itself. Compared with what there is to appreciate in him, there is little to analyze. Technically, yes: Pope's metrics will repay endless study; but his "meaning" demands almost none. Goethe said of Byron, "Whenever he thinks, he is a child"; and it might be as fairly said of Pope, "Whenever he thinks, he is a plagiarist." His works are a sort of anthology of other men's thoughts and beliefs and moral sentiments; only the language is Pope's, only the language really mattered to him, and only the language, for the most part, need matter for us. On the other hand, and it involves nothing contradictory, Pope is enormously cerebral as an *artist*.

In almost every way, in fact, he is one of the most astounding technicians, one of the most astounding artists, in the whole history of verse. (It is to be hoped that our many distinguished critic-poets—one or two of whom, like Mr Auden, have already written well but too briefly of Pope—will give Pope a good deal of their attention.) He scarcely needed to think, or to appeal very strongly to the feelings or the senses or the soul, in order to be great; and whoever doubts that a supreme gift for verse and vituperation adds up to greatness, had better steer clear of Pope. Deliberately I have left to the very end mention of certain qualities of Pope which one would sometimes gather are beneath notice in literature, but which

I am bound to think are above praise—his great energy, gaiety, verve. They are the qualities that keep Pope—and all literature—fresh; that make Pope—and all literature—fun.

Louis Kronenberger

ALEXANDER POPE

SELECTED WORKS

ℂ Spring

THE FIRST PASTORAL,

DAMON

FIRST in these fields I try the sylvan strains,
Nor blush to sport on Windsor's blissful plains:
Fair Thames, flow gently from thy sacred spring,
While on thy banks Sicilian Muses sing;
Let vernal airs thro' trembling osiers play,
And Albion's cliffs resound the rural lay.
You, that too wise for pride, too good for pow'r,
Enjoy the glory to be great no more,
And carrying with you all the world can boast,
To all the world illustriously are lost!
O let my Muse her tender reed inspire,
Till in your native shades you tune the lyre:
So when the Nightingale to rest removes,
The Thrush may chant to the forsaken groves,
But, charm'd to silence, listens while she sings,
And all th' aërial audience clap their wings.

Soon as the flocks shook off the nightly dews,
Two Swains, whom Love kept wakeful, and the Muse,
Pour'd o'er the whitening vale their fleecy care,
Fresh as the morn, and as the season fair:
The dawn now blushing on the mountain's side,
Thus Daphnis spoke, and Strephon thus reply'd.

DAPHNIS

Hear how the birds, on ev'ry bloomy spray,
With joyous musick wake the dawning day!

Why sit we mute when early linnets sing,
When warbling Philomel salutes the spring?
Why sit we sad when Phosphor shines so clear,
And lavish nature paints the purple Year?

STREPHON

Sing then, and Damon shall attend the strain,
While yon' slow oxen turn the furrow'd Plain.
Here the bright crocus and blue vi'let glow;
Here western winds on breathing roses blow.
I 'll stake yon' lamb, that near the fountain plays,
And from the brink his dancing shade surveys.

DAPHNIS

And I this bowl, where wanton Ivy twines,
And swelling clusters bend the curling vines:
Four figures rising from the work appear,
The various seasons of the rolling year;
And what is that, which binds the radiant sky,
Where twelve fair Signs in beauteous order lie?

DAMON

Then sing by turns, by turns the Muses sing,
Now hawthorns blossom, now the daisies spring,
Now leaves the trees, and flow'rs adorn the ground,
Begin, the vales shall ev'ry note rebound.

STREPHON

Inspire me, Phœbus, in my Delia's praise
With Waller's strains, or Granville's moving lays!
A milk-white bull shall at your altars stand,
That threats a fight, and spurns the rising sand.

Daphnis

O Love! for Sylvia let me gain the prize,
And make my tongue victorious as her eyes;
No lambs or sheep for victims I 'll impart,
Thy victim, Love, shall be the shepherd's heart.

Strephon

Me gentle Delia beckons from the plain,
Then hid in shades, eludes her eager swain;
But feigns a laugh, to see me search around,
And by that laugh the willing fair is found.

Daphnis

The sprightly Sylvia trips along the green,
She runs, but hopes she does not run unseen;
While a kind glance at her pursuer flies,
How much at variance are her feet and eyes!

Strephon

O'er golden sands let rich Pactolus flow,
And trees weep amber on the banks of Po;
Blest Thames's shores the brightest beauties yield,
Feed here my lambs, I 'll seek no distant field.

Daphnis

Celestial Venus haunts Idalia's groves;
Diana Cynthus, Ceres Hybla loves;
If Windsor-shades delight the matchless maid,
Cynthus and Hybla yield to Windsor-shade.

Strephon

All nature mourns, the Skies relent in show'rs,
Hush'd are the birds, and clos'd the drooping flow'rs;
If Delia smile, the flow'rs begin to spring,
The skies to brighten, and the birds to sing.

Daphnis

All nature laughs, the groves are fresh and fair,
The Sun's mild lustre warms the vital air;
If Sylvia smiles, new glories gild the shore,
And vanquish'd nature seems to charm no more.

Strephon

In spring the fields, in autumn hills I love,
At morn the plains, at noon the shady grove,
But Delia always; absent from her sight,
Nor plains at morn, nor groves at noon delight.

Daphnis

Sylvia 's like autumn ripe, yet mild as May,
More bright than noon, yet fresh as early day;
Ev'n spring displeases, when she shines not here;
But blest with her, 't is spring throughout the year.

Strephon

Say, Daphnis, say, in what glad soil appears,
A wond'rous Tree that sacred Monarchs bears:
Tell me but this, and I 'll disclaim the prize,
And give the conquest to thy Sylvia's eyes.

Daphnis

Nay tell me first, in what more happy fields
The Thistle springs, to which the Lily yields:

And then a nobler prize I will resign;
For Sylvia, charming Sylvia, shall be thine.

DAMON

Cease to contend, for, Daphnis, I decree,
The bowl to Strephon, and the lamb to thee:
Blest Swains, whose Nymphs in ev'ry grace excel;
Blest Nymphs, whose Swains those graces sing so well!
Now rise, and haste to yonder woodbine bow'rs.
A soft retreat from sudden vernal show'rs,
The turf with rural dainties shall be crown'd,
While op'ning blooms diffuse their sweets around.
For see! the gath'ring flocks to shelter tend,
And from the Pleiads fruitful show'rs descend.

☾ Summer

THE SECOND PASTORAL,

OR

ALEXIS

A SHEPHERD'S Boy (he seeks no better name)
Led forth his flocks along the silver Thame,
Where dancing sun-beams on the waters play'd,
And verdant alders form'd a quiv'ring shade.
Soft as he mourn'd, the streams forgot to flow,
The flocks around a dumb compassion show,
The Naiads wept in ev'ry wat'ry bow'r,
And Jove consented in a silent show'r.
Accept, O GARTH, the Muse's early lays,
That adds this wreath of Ivy to thy Bays;
Hear what from Love unpractis'd hearts endure,

From Love, the sole disease thou canst not cure.
    Ye shady beeches, and ye cooling streams,
Defence from Phœbus', not from Cupid's beams,
To you I mourn, nor to the deaf I sing,
The woods shall answer, and their echo ring.
The hills and rocks attend my doleful lay,
Why art thou prouder and more hard than they?
The bleating sheep with my complaints agree,
They parch'd with heat, and I inflam'd by thee.
The sultry Sirius burns the thirsty plains,
While in thy heart eternal winter reigns.

    Where stray ye, Muses, in what lawn or grove,
While your Alexis pines in hopeless love?
In those fair fields where sacred Isis glides,
Or else where Cam his winding vales divides?
As in the crystal spring I view my face,
Fresh rising blushes paint the wat'ry glass;
But since those graces please thy eyes no more,
I shun the fountains which I sought before.
Once I was skill'd in ev'ry herb that grew,
And ev'ry plant that drinks the morning dew;
Ah wretched shepherd, what avails thy art,
To cure thy lambs, but not to heal thy heart!

    Let other swains attend the rural care,
Feed fairer flocks, or richer fleeces shear;
But nigh yon' mountain let me tune my lays,
Embrace my Love, and bind my brows with bays.
That flute is mine which Colin's tuneful breath
Inspir'd when living, and bequeath'd in death;
He said: Alexis, take this pipe, the same
That taught the groves my Rosalinda's name:
But now the reeds shall hang on yonder tree,
For ever silent, since despis'd by thee.
Oh! were I made by some transforming pow'r
The captive bird that sings within thy bow'r!
Then might my voice thy list'ning ears employ,

And I those kisses he receives, enjoy.

And yet my numbers please the rural throng,
Rough Satyrs dance, and Pan applauds the song:
The Nymphs, forsaking ev'ry cave and spring,
Their early fruit, and milk-white turtles bring;
Each am'rous nymph prefers her gifts in vain,
On you their gifts are all bestow'd again.
For you the swains the fairest flow'rs design,
And in one garland all their beauties join;
Accept the wreath which you deserve alone,
In whom all beauties are compris'd in one.

See what delights in sylvan scenes appear!
Descending Gods have found Elysium here.
In woods bright Venus with Adonis stray'd,
And chaste Diana haunts the forest-shade.
Come, lovely nymph, and bless the silent hours,
When swains from shearing seek their nightly bow'rs,
When weary reapers quit the sultry field,
And crown'd with corn their thanks to Ceres yield.
This harmless grove no lurking viper hides,
But in my breast the serpent Love abides.
Here bees from blossoms sip the rosy dew,
But your Alexis knows no sweets but you.
Oh deign to visit our forsaken seats,
The mossy fountains, and the green retreats!
Where'er you walk, cool gales shall fan the glade;
Trees, where you sit, shall crowd into a shade;
Where'er you tread, the blushing flowers shall rise,
And all things flourish where you turn your eyes.
Oh! how I long with you to pass my days,
Invoke the Muses, and resound your praise!
Your praise the birds shall chant in ev'ry grove,
And winds shall waft it to the pow'rs above,
But would you sing, and rival Orpheus' strain,
The wond'ring forests soon should dance again;
The moving mountains hear the pow'rful call,

And headlong streams hang list'ning in their fall!
   But see, the shepherds shun the noonday heat,
The lowing herds to murm'ring brooks retreat,
To closer shades the panting flocks remove;
Ye Gods! and is there no relief for Love?
But soon the sun with milder rays descends
To the cool ocean, where his journey ends.
On me love's fiercer flames for ever prey,
By night he scorches, as he burns by day.

☾ Autumn

THE THIRD PASTORAL,

OR

HYLAS AND ÆGON

BENEATH the shade a spreading Beech displays,
Hylas and Ægon sung their rural lays,
This mourn'd a faithless, that an absent Love,
And Delia's name and Doris' fill'd the Grove.
Ye Mantuan nymphs, your sacred succour bring;
Hylas and Ægon's rural lays I sing.
   Thou,* whom the Nine with Plautus' wit inspire,
The art of Terence, and Menander's fire;
Whose sense instructs us, and whose humour charms,
Whose judgment sways us, and whose spirit warms!
Oh, skill'd in Nature! see the hearts of Swains,
Their artless passions, and their tender pains.
   Now setting Phœbus shone serenely bright,
And fleecy clouds were streak'd with purple light;
When tuneful Hylas with melodious moan,

* Wycherley, to whom "Autumn" was dedicated.

Taught rocks to weep, and made the mountains groan.
  Go, gentle gales, and bear my sighs away!
To Delia's ear, the tender notes convey.
As some sad Turtle his lost love deplores,
And with deep murmurs fills the sounding shores;
Thus, far from *Delia*, to the winds I mourn,
Alike unheard, unpity'd, and forlorn.
  Go, gentle gales, and bear my sighs along!
For her, the feather'd quires neglect their song;
For her, the limes their pleasing shades deny;
For her, the lilies hang their heads and die.
Ye flow'rs that droop, forsaken by the spring,
Ye birds that, left by summer, cease to sing,
Ye trees that fade when autumn-heats remove,
Say, is not absence death to those who love?
  Go, gentle gales, and bear my sighs away!
Curs'd be the fields that cause my Delia's stay;
Fade ev'ry blossom, wither ev'ry tree,
Die ev'ry flow'r, and perish all, but she.
What have I said? where'er my Delia flies,
Let spring attend, and sudden flow'rs arise:
Let op'ning roses knotted oaks adorn,
And liquid amber drop from ev'ry thorn.
  Go, gentle gales, and bear my sighs along!
The birds shall cease to tune their ev'ning song,
The winds to breathe, the waving woods to move,
And streams to murmur, e'er I cease to love.
Not bubbling fountains to the thirsty swain,
Not balmy sleep to lab'rers faint with pain,
Not show'rs to larks, nor sun-shine to the bee,
Are half so charming as thy sight to me.
  Go, gentle gales, and bear my sighs away!
Come, Delia, come; ah, why this long delay?
Thro' rocks and caves the name of Delia sounds,
Delia, each cave and echoing rock rebounds.
Ye pow'rs, what pleasing frenzy sooths my mind!

Do lovers dream, or is my Delia kind?
She comes, my Delia comes!—Now cease my lay,
And cease, ye gales, to bear my sighs away!

  Next Ægon sung, while Windsor groves admir'd;
Rehearse, ye Muses, what yourselves inspir'd.

  Resound, ye hills, resound my mournful strain!
Of perjur'd Doris, dying I complain:
Here where the mountains less'ning as they rise
Lose the low vales, and steal into the skies:
While lab'ring oxen, spent with toil and heat,
In their loose traces from the field retreat:
While curling smokes from village-tops are seen,
And the fleet shades glide o'er the dusky green.

  Resound, ye hills, resound my mournful lay!
Beneath yon' poplar oft we past the day:
Oft' on the rind I carv'd her am'rous vows,
While she with garlands hung the bending boughs:
The garlands fade, the vows are worn away;
So dies her love, and so my hopes decay.

  Resound, ye hills, resound my mournful strain!
Now bright Arcturus glads the teeming grain,
Now golden fruits on loaded branches shine,
And grateful clusters swell with floods of wine;
Now blushing berries paint the yellow grove;
Just Gods! shall all things yield returns but love?

  Resound, ye hills, resound my mournful lay!
The shepherds cry, "Thy flocks are left a prey"—
Ah! what avails it me, the flocks to keep,
Who lost my heart while I preserv'd my sheep.
Pan came, and ask'd, what magic caus'd my smart,
Or what ill eyes malignant glances dart?
What eyes but hers, alas, have pow'r to move!
And is there magic but what dwells in love?

  Resound, ye hills, resound my mournful strains!
I'll fly from shepherds, flocks, and flow'ry plains.—
From shepherds, flocks, and plains, I may remove

Forsake mankind, and all the world—but love!
I know thee, Love! on foreign Mountains bred,
Wolves gave thee suck, and savage Tigers fed.
Thou wert from Ætna's burning entrails torn,
Got by fierce whirlwinds, and in thunder born!
   Resound, ye hills, resound my mournful lay!
Farewell, ye woods! adieu the light of day!
One leap from yonder cliff shall end my pains,
No more, ye hills, no more resound my strains!
   Thus sung the shepherds till th' approach of night,
The skies yet blushing with departing light,
When falling dews with spangles deck'd the glade,
And the low sun had lengthen'd ev'ry shade.

☾ Winter

THE FOURTH PASTORAL,

OR

DAPHNE

TO THE MEMORY OF MRS. TEMPEST

LYCIDAS

THYRSIS, the music of that murm'ring spring,
Is not so mournful as the strains you sing,
Nor rivers winding thro' the vales below,
So sweetly warble, or so smoothly flow.
Now sleeping flocks on their soft fleeces lie,
The moon, serene in glory, mounts the sky,
While silent birds forget their tuneful lays,
Oh sing of Daphne's fate, and Daphne's praise!

Thyrsis

Behold the groves that shine with silver frost,
Their beauty wither'd, and their verdure lost.
Here shall I try the sweet Alexis' strain,
That called the list'ning Dryads to the plain?
Thames heard the numbers as he flow'd along,
And bade his willows learn the moving song.

Lycidas

So may kind rains their vital moisture yield,
And swell the future harvest of the field.
Begin; this charge the dying Daphne gave,
And said; "Ye shepherds, sing around my grave!
Sing, while beside the shaded tomb I mourn,
And with fresh bays her rural shrine adorn."

Thyrsis

Ye gentle Muses, leave your crystal spring,
Let Nymphs and Sylvans cypress garlands bring;
Ye weeping Loves, the stream with myrtles hide,
And break your bows, as when Adonis died;
And with your golden darts, now useless grown,
Inscribe a verse on this relenting stone:
"Let nature change, let heav'n and earth deplore,
Fair Daphne 's dead, and love is now no more!"
'T is done, and nature's various charms decay,
See gloomy clouds obscure the cheerful day!
Now hung with pearls the dropping trees appear,
Their faded honours scatter'd on her bier.
See, where on earth the flow'ry glories lie,
With her they flourish'd, and with her they die.
Ah what avails the beauties nature wore?
Fair Daphne 's dead, and beauty is no more!
For her the flocks refuse their verdant food,

Nor thirsty heifers seek the gliding flood.
The silver swans her hapless fate bemoan,
In notes more sad than when they sing their own;
In hollow caves sweet Echo silent lies,
Silent, or only to her name replies;
Her name with pleasure once she taught the shore,
Now Daphne 's dead, and pleasure is no more!

   No grateful dews descend from ev'ning skies,
Nor morning odours from the flow'rs arise;
No rich perfumes refresh the fruitful field,
Nor fragrant herbs their native incense yield.
The balmy Zephyrs, silent since her death,
Lament the ceasing of a sweeter breath;
Th' industrious bees neglect their golden store;
Fair Daphne 's dead, and sweetness is no more!

   No more the mounting larks, while Daphne sings,
Shall list'ning in mid air suspend their wings;
No more the birds shall imitate her lays,
Or hush'd with wonder, hearken from the sprays:
No more the streams their murmur shall forbear,
A sweeter music than their own to hear,
But tell the reeds, and tell the vocal shore,
Fair Daphne 's dead, and music is no more!

   Her fate is whisper'd by the gentle breeze,
And told in sighs to all the trembling trees;
The trembling trees, in ev'ry plain and wood,
Her fate remurmur to the silver flood;
The silver flood, so lately calm, appears
Swell'd with new passion, and o'erflows with tears;
The winds and trees and floods her death deplore,
Daphne, our grief! our glory now no more!

   But see! where Daphne wond'ring mounts on high
Above the clouds, above the starry sky!
Eternal beauties grace the shining scene,
Fields ever fresh, and groves for ever green!
There while you rest in Amaranthine bow'rs,

Or from those meads select unfading flow'rs,
Behold us kindly, who your name implore,
Daphne, our Goddess, and our grief no more!

LYCIDAS

How all things listen, while thy Muse complains!
Such silence waits on Philomela's strains,
In some still ev'ning, when the whisp'ring breeze
Pants on the leaves, and dies upon the trees.
To thee, bright goddess, oft a lamb shall bleed,
If teeming ewes increase my fleecy breed.
While plants their shade, or flow'rs their odours give,
Thy name, thy honour, and thy praise shall live!

THYRSIS

But see, Orion sheds unwholesome dews,
Arise, the pines a noxious shade diffuse;
Sharp Boreas blows, and Nature feels decay,
Time conquers all, and we must Time obey.
Adieu, ye vales, ye mountains, streams and groves,
Adieu, ye shepherd's rural lays and loves;
Adieu, my flocks, farewell ye sylvan crew,
Daphne, farewell, and all the world adieu!

❰ Windsor Forest

THY forests, Windsor! and thy green retreats,
At once the Monarch's and the Muse's seats,
Invite my lays. Be present, sylvan maids!
Unlock your springs, and open all your shades.
GRANVILLE commands; your aid, O Muses, bring!
What Muse for GRANVILLE can refuse to sing?
    The Groves of Eden, vanish'd now so long,
Live in description, and look green in song:
These, were my breast inspir'd with equal flame,
Like them in beauty, should be like in fame.
Here hills and vales, the woodland and the plain,
Here earth and water seem to strive again;
Not Chaos-like together crush'd and bruis'd,
But, as the world, harmoniously confus'd:
Where order in variety we see,
And where, tho' all things differ, all agree.
Here waving groves a chequer'd scene display,
And part admit, and part exclude the day;
As some coy nymph her lover's warm address
Nor quite indulges, nor can quite repress.
There, interspers'd in lawns and op'ning glades,
Thin trees arise that shun each other's shades.
Here in full light the russet plains extend:
There wrapt in clouds the blueish hills ascend.
Ev'n the wild heath displays her purple dyes,
    And 'midst the desert fruitful fields arise,
That crown'd with tufted trees and springing corn,
Like verdant isles the sable waste adorn.
Let India boast her plants, nor envy we
The weeping amber or the balmy tree,
While by our oaks the precious loads are born,
And realms commanded which those trees adorn
Not proud Olympus yields a nobler sight,

Tho' Gods assembled grace his tow'ring height,
Than what more humble mountains offer here,
Where, in their blessings, all those Gods appear.
See Pan with flocks, with fruits Pomona crown'd,
Here blushing Flora paints th' enamel'd ground,
Here Ceres' gifts in waving prospect stand,
And nodding tempt the joyful reaper's hand;
Rich Industry sits smiling on the plains,
And peace and plenty tell, a STUART reigns.

Not thus the land appear'd in ages past,
A dreamy desert, and a gloomy waste,
To savage beasts and savage laws a prey,
And kings more furious and severe than they;
Who claim'd the skies, dispeopled air and floods,
The lonely lords of empty wilds and woods:
Cities laid waste, they storm'd the dens and caves,
(For wiser brutes were backward to be slaves:)
What could be free, when lawless beasts obey'd,
And ev'n the elements a tyrant sway'd?
In vain kind seasons swell'd the teeming grain,
Soft show'rs distill'd, and suns grew warm in vain;
The swain with tears his frustrate labour yields,
And famish'd dies amidst his ripen'd fields.
What wonder then, a beast or subject slain
Were equal crimes in a despotic reign?
Both doom'd alike, for sportive Tyrants bled,
But while the subject starv'd, the beast was fed.
Proud Nimrod first the bloody chase began,
A mighty hunter, and his prey was man:
Our haughty Norman boasts that barb'rous name,
And makes his trembling slaves the royal game.
The fields are ravish'd from th' industrious swains,
From men their cities, and from Gods their fanes:
The levell'd towns with weeds lie cover'd o'er:
The hollow winds thro' naked temples roar;
Round broken columns clasping ivy twin'd;

O'er heaps of ruin stalk'd the stately hind;
The fox obscene to gaping tombs retires,
And savage howlings fill the sacred quires.
Aw'd by his Nobles, by his Commons curst,
Th' Oppressor rul'd tyrannic where he durst,
Stretch'd o'er the Poor and Church his iron rod,
And serv'd alike his Vassals and his God.
Whom ev'n the Saxon spar'd the bloody Dane,
The wanton victims of his sport remain.
But see, the man who spacious regions gave
A waste for beasts, himself deny'd a grave!
Stretch'd on the lawn his second hope* survey,
At once the chaser, and at once the prey:
Lo Rufus, tugging at the deadly dart,
Bleeds in the Forest like a wound'd hart.
Succeeding monarchs heard the subjects' cries,
Nor saw displeas'd the peaceful cottage rise.
Then gath'ring flocks on unknown mountains fed,
O'er sandy wilds were yellow harvests spread,
The forests wonder'd at th' unusual grain,
And secret transport touch'd the conscious swain.
Fair Liberty, Britannia's Goddess, rears
Her cheerful head, and leads the golden years.

Ye vig'rous swains! while youth ferments your blood,
And purer spirits swell the sprightly flood,
Now range the hills, the gameful woods beset,
Wind the shrill horn, or spread the waving net.
When milder autumn summer's heat succeeds,
And in the new-shorn field the partridge feeds,
Before his lord the ready spaniel bounds,
Panting with hope, he tries the furrow'd grounds;
But when the tainted gales the game betray,
Couch'd close he lies, and meditates the prey:
Secure they trust th' unfaithful field beset,

* Richard duke of Bernay, said to have been killed by a stag in the New Forest.

'Till hov'ring o'er 'em sweeps the swelling net.
Thus (if small things we may with great compare)
When Albion sends her eager sons to war,
Some thoughtless Town, with ease and plenty blest,
Near, and more near, the closing lines invest;
Sudden they seize th' amaz'd, defenceless prize,
And high in air Britannia's standard flies.

See! from the brake the whirring pheasant springs,
And mounts exulting on triumphant wings:
Short is his joy; he feels the fiery wound,
Flutters in blood, and panting beats the ground.
Ah! what avail his glossy, varying dyes,
His purple crest, and scarlet-circled eyes,
The vivid green his shining plumes unfold,
His painted wings, and breast that flames with gold?

Nor yet, when moist Arcturus clouds the sky,
The woods and fields their pleasing toils deny.
To plains with well-breath'd beagles we repair,
And trace the mazes of the circling hare:
(Beasts, urg'd by us, their fellow-beasts pursue,
And learn of man each other to undo).
With slaught'ring guns th' unwearied fowler roves,
When frosts have whiten'd all the naked groves;
Where doves in flocks the leafless trees o'ershade,
And lonely woodcocks haunt the wat'ry glade.
He lifts the tube, and levels with his eye;
Straight a short thunder breaks the frozen sky:
Oft, as in airy rings they skim the heath,
The clam'rous lapwings feel the leaden death:
Oft, as the mounting larks their notes prepare,
They fall, and leave their little lives in air.

In genial spring, beneath the quivering shade,
Where cooling vapours breathe along the mead,
The patient fisher takes his silent stand,
Intent, his angle trembling in his hand:
With looks unmov'd, he hopes the scaly breed,

And eyes the dancing cork, and bending reed.
Our plenteous streams a various race supply,
The bright-ey'd perch with fins of Tyrian dye.
The silver eel, in shining volumes roll'd,
The yellow carp, in scales bedropp'd with gold,
Swift trouts, diversified with crimson stains,
And pikes, the tyrants of the wat'ry plains.

Now Cancer glows with Phœbus' fiery car:
The youth rush eager to the sylvan war,
Swarm o'er the lawns, the forest walks surround,
Rouse the fleet hart, and cheer the opening hound.
Th' impatient courser pants in every vein,
And, pawing, seems to beat the distant plain:
Hills, vales, and floods appear already cross'd,
And ere he starts, a thousand steps are lost.
See the bold youth strain up the threat'ning steep,
Rush thro' the thickets, down the valleys sweep,
Hang o'er their coursers' heads with eager speed,
And earth rolls back beneath the flying steed.
Let old Arcadia boast her ample plain,
Th' immortal huntress, and her virgin train;
Nor envy, Windsor! since thy shades have seen
As bright a Goddess, and as chaste a Queen;*
Whose care, like hers, protects the sylvan reign,
The Earth's fair light, and Empress of the main.

Here too, 't is sung, of old Diana stray'd,
And Cynthus' top forsook for Windsor shade:
Here was she seen o'er airy wastes to rove,
Seek the clear spring, or haunt the pathless grove;
Here arm'd with silver bows, in early dawn,
Her buskin'd Virgins trac'd the dewy lawn.

Above the rest a rural nymph was fam'd,
Thy offspring, Thames! the fair Lodona nam'd;
(Lodona's fate, in long oblivion cast,
The Muse shall sing, and what she sings shall last).

* Queen Anne.

Scarce could the Goddess from her nymph be known,
But by the crescent and the golden zone.
She scorn'd the praise of beauty, and the care;
A belt her waist, a fillet binds her hair;
A painted quiver on her shoulder sounds,
And with her dart the flying deer she wounds.
It chanc'd, as eager of the chase, the maid
Beyond the forest's verdant limits stray'd,
Pan saw and lov'd, and, burning with desire,
Pursued her flight; her flight increas'd his fire.
Not half so swift the trembling doves can fly,
When the fierce eagle cleaves the liquid sky;
Not half so swiftly the fierce eagle moves,
When thro' the clouds he drives the trembling doves;
As from the god she flew with furious pace,
Or as the god, more furious, urg'd the chase.
Now fainting, sinking, pale, the nymph appears;
Now close behind, his sounding steps she hears;
And now his shadow reach'd her as she run,
His shadow lengthen'd by the setting sun;
And now his shorter breath, with sultry air,
Pants on her neck, and fans her parting hair.
In vain on father Thames she calls for aid,
Nor could Diana help her injur'd maid.
Faint, breathless, thus she pray'd, nor pray'd in vain;
"Ah, Cynthia! ah—tho' banish'd from thy train,
Let me, O let me, to the shades repair,
My native shades—there weep, and murmur there."
She said, and melting as in tears she lay,
In a soft, silver stream dissolv'd away.
The silver stream her virgin coldness keeps,
For ever murmurs, and for ever weeps;
Still bears the name* the hapless virgin bore,
And bathes the forest where she rang'd before.
In her chaste current oft the goddess laves,

* The river Loddon.

And with celestial tears augments the waves.
Oft in her glass the musing shepherd spies
The headlong mountains and the downward skies,
The wat'ry landscape of the pendant woods,
And absent trees that tremble in the floods;
In the clear azure gleam the flocks are seen,
And floating forests paint the waves with green,
Thro' the fair scene roll slow the lingering streams,
Then foaming pour along, and rush into the Thames.
    Thou, too, great father of the British floods!
With joyful pride survey'st our lofty woods;
Where tow'ring oaks their growing honours rear,
And future navies on thy shores appear.
Not Neptune's self from all her streams receives
A wealthier tribute than to thine he gives.
No seas so rich, so gay no banks appear,
No lake so gentle, and no spring so clear.
Nor Po so swells the fabling Poet's lays,
While led along the skies his current strays,
As thine, which visits Windsor's fam'd abodes,
To grace the mansion of our earthly Gods:
Nor all his stars above a lustre show,
Like the bright Beauties on thy banks below,
Where Jove, subdued by mortal Passion still,
Might change Olympus for a nobler hill.
    Happy the man whom this bright court approves,
His Sov'reign favours, and his Country loves:
Happy next him, who to these shades retires,
Whom Nature charms, and whom the Muse inspires:
Whom humbler joys of home-felt quiet please,
Successive study, exercise, and ease.
He gathers health from herbs the forest yields,
And of their fragrant physic spoils the fields:
With chymic art exalts the min'ral pow'rs,
And draws the aromatic souls of flow'rs:
Now marks the course of rolling orbs on high;

O'er figur'd worlds now travels with his eye;
Of ancient writ unlocks the learned store,
Consults the dead, and lives past ages o'er:
Or wand'ring thoughtful in the silent wood,
Attends the duties of the wise and good,
T' observe a mean, be to himself a friend,
To follow nature, and regard his end;
Or looks on heav'n with more than mortal eyes,
Bids his free soul expatiate in the skies,
Amid her kindred stars familiar roam,
Survey the region, and confess her home!
Such was the life great Scipio once admir'd:—
Thus Atticus, and Trumbal thus retir'd.

Ye sacred Nine! that all my soul possess,
Whose raptures fire me, and whose visions bless,
Bear me, O bear me to sequester'd scenes,
The bow'ry mazes, and surrounding greens:
To Thames's banks, which fragrant breezes fill,
Or where ye Muses sport on Cooper's Hill.
(On Cooper's Hill eternal wreaths shall grow,
While lasts the mountain, or while Thames shall flow.)
I seem thro' consecrated walks to rove,
I hear soft music die along the grove.
Led by the sound, I roam from shade to shade,
By god-like Poets venerable made:
Here his first lays majestic Denham sung;
There the last numbers flow'd from Cowley's tongue.
Oh early lost! what tears the river shed,
When the sad pomp along his banks was led?
His drooping swans on every note expire,
And on his willows hung each muse's lyre.

Since fate relentless stopp'd their heavenly voice,
No more the forests ring, or groves rejoice;
Who now shall charm the shades where Cowley strung
His living harp, and lofty Denham sung?
But hark! the groves rejoice, the forest rings!

Are these reviv'd? or is it Granville sings?
'T is yours, my Lord, to bless our soft retreats,
And call the Muses to their ancient seats;
To paint anew the flow'ry sylvan scenes,
To crown the forests with immortal greens,
Make Windsor-hills in lofty numbers rise,
And lift her turrets nearer to the skies;
To sing those honours you deserve to wear,
And add new lustre to her silver star!

Here noble Surrey felt the sacred rage,
Surrey, the Granville of a former age:
Matchless his pen, victorious was his lance,
Bold in the lists, and graceful in the dance:
In the same shades the Cupids tun'd his lyre,
To the same notes, of love, and soft desire:
Fair Geraldine, bright object of his vow,
Then fill'd the groves, as heav'nly Mira now.

Oh wouldst thou sing what heroes Windsor bore,
What Kings first breath'd upon her winding shore,
Or raise old warriors, whose ador'd remains
In weeping vaults her hallow'd earth contains!
With Edward's acts adorn the shining page,
Stretch his long triumphs down through every age,
Draw monarchs chain'd, and Cressi's glorious field,
The lilies blazing on the regal shield:
Then, from her roofs when Verrio's colours fall,
And leave inanimate the naked wall;
Still in thy song should vanquish'd France appear,
And bleed for ever under Britain's spear.

Let softer strains ill-fated Henry mourn,*
And palms eternal flourish round his urn.
Here o'er the martyr-king the marble weeps,
And, fast beside him, once-fear'd Edward sleeps:**
Whom not th' extended Albion could contain,

* Henry VI.
** Edward IV.

From old Belerium to the northern main,
The grave unites; where e'en the great find rest,
And blended lie th' oppressor and th' opprest!

　Make sacred Charles's tomb for ever known
(Obscure the place, and uninscrib'd the stone),
Oh fact accurst! what tears has Albion shed,
Heav'ns, what new wounds! and how her old have bled!
She saw her sons with purple deaths expire,
Her sacred domes involv'd in rolling fire,
A dreadful series of intestine wars,
Inglorious triumphs and dishonest scars.
At length great Anna said, "Let Discord cease!"
She said! the world obey'd, and all was Peace!

　In that blest moment from his oozy bed
Old father Thames advanc'd his reverend head.
His tresses dropp'd with dews, and o'er the stream
His shining horns diffus'd a golden gleam:
Grav'd on his urn appear'd the moon, that guides
His swelling waters and alternate tides;
The figur'd streams in waves of silver roll'd,
And on their banks Augusta rose in gold.
Around his throne the sea-born brothers stood,
Who swell with tributary urns his flood;
First the fam'd authors of his ancient name,
The winding Isis, and the fruitful Thame:
The Kennet swift, for silver eels renown'd;
The Loddon slow, with verdant alders crown'd;
Cole, whose dark streams his flowery island lave;
And chalky Wey, that rolls a milky wave:
The blue, transparent Vandalis appears;
The gulfy Lee his sedgy tresses rears;
And sullen Mole, that hides his diving flood;
And silent Darent, stain'd with Danish blood.

　High in the midst, upon his urn reclin'd
(His sea-green mantle waving with the wind),
The god appear'd: he turn'd his azure eyes

Where Windsor-domes and pompous turrets rise;
Then bow'd and spoke; the winds forget to roar,
And the hush'd waves glide softly to the shore,
   Hail, sacred peace! hail, long-expected days,
That Thames's glory to the stars shall raise!
Tho' Tiber's streams immortal Rome behold,
Tho' foaming Hermus swells with tides of gold,
From heav'n itself though sev'nfold Nilus flows,
And harvests on a hundred realms bestows;
These now no more shall be the Muse's themes,
Lost in my fame, as in the sea their streams.
Let Volga's banks with iron squadrons shine,
And groves of lances glitter on the Rhine,
Let barb'rous Ganges arm a servile train;
Be mine the blessings of a peaceful reign.
No more my sons shall dye with British blood
Red Iber's sands, or Ister's foaming flood:
Safe on my shore each unmolested swain
Shall tend the flocks, or reap the bearded grain;
The shady empire shall retain no trace
Of war or blood, but in the sylvan chase;
The trumpet sleep, while cheerful horns are blown,
And arms employ'd on birds and beasts alone.
Behold! th' ascending Villas on my side
Project long shadows o'er the crystal tide.
Behold! Augusta's glitt'ring spires increase,
And Temples rise, the beauteous works of Peace.
I see, I see, where two fair cities bend
Their ample bow, a new Whitehall ascend!
Their mighty Nations shall inquire their doom,
The World's great Oracle in times to come;
There Kings shall sue, and suppliant States be seen
Once more to bend before a BRITISH QUEEN.
   Thy trees, fair Windsor! now shall leave their woods,
And half thy forests rush into thy floods,
Bear Britain's thunder, and her Cross display,

To the bright regions of the rising day;
Tempt icy seas, where scarce the waters roll,
Where clearer flames glow round the frozen Pole:
Or under southern skies exalt their sails,
Led by new stars, and borne by spicy gales!
For me the balm shall bleed, and amber flow,
The coral redden, and the ruby glow,
The pearly shell its lucid globe infold,
And Phœbus warm the ripening ore to gold.
The time shall come, when, free as seas or wind,
Unbounded Thames shall flow for all mankind,
Whole nations enter with each swelling tide,
And seas but join the regions they divide;
Earth's distant ends our glory shall behold,
And the new world launch forth to seek the old.
Then ships of uncouth form shall stem the tide,
And feather'd people crowd my wealthy side,
And naked youths and painted chiefs admire
Our speech, our colour, and our strange attire!
O stretch thy reign, fair Peace! from shore to shore,
Till Conquest cease, and Slav'ry be no more;
Till the freed Indians in their native groves
Reap their own fruits, and woo their sable loves,
Peru once more a race of kings behold,
And other Mexico's be roof'd with gold.
Exil'd by thee from earth to deepest hell,
In brazen bonds shall barbarous Discord dwell;
Gigantic Pride, pale Terror, gloomy Care,
And mad Ambition, shall attend her there:
There purple Vengeance bath'd in gore retires,
Her weapons blunted, and extinct her fires:
There hateful Envy her own snakes shall feel,
And Persecution mourn her broken wheel:
There Faction roar, Rebellion bite her chain,
And gasping Furies thirst for blood in vain.
    Here cease thy flight, nor with unhallow'd lays

Touch the fair fame of Albion's golden days:
The thoughts of gods let Granville's verse recite,
And bring the scenes of op'ning fate to light.
My humble Muse, in unambitious strains,
Paints the green forests and the flow'ry plains,
Where Peace descending bids her olives spring,
And scatters blessings from her dovelike wing.
Ev'n I more sweetly pass my careless days,
Pleas'd in the silent shade with empty praise;
Enough for me, that to the list'ning swains
First in these fields I sung the sylvan strains.

ℂ Ode on Solitude

HAPPY the man whose wish and care
  A few paternal acres bound,
Content to breathe his native air,
        In his own ground.

Whose herds with milk, whose fields with bread,
  Whose flocks supply him with attire,
Whose trees in summer yield him shade,
        In winter fire.

Blest, who can unconcern'dly find
  Hours, days, and years slide soft away,
In health of body, peace of mind,
        Quiet by day,

Sound sleep by night; study and ease,
  Together mixt; sweet recreation;
And Innocence, which most does please
        With meditation.

Thus let me live, unseen, unknown,
  Thus unlamented let me die,
Steal from the world, and not a stone
        Tell where I lie.

❡ The Dying Christian to His Soul

I

VITAL spark of heav'nly flame!
Quit, oh quit this mortal frame:
Trembling, hoping, ling'ring, flying,
Oh the pain, the bliss of dying!
Cease, fond Nature, cease thy strife,
And let me languish into life.

II

Hark! they whisper; Angels say,
Sister Spirit, come away.
What is this absorbs me quite?
Steals my senses, shuts my sight,
Drowns my spirits, draws my breath?
Tell me, my Soul, can this be Death?

III

The world recedes; it disappears!
Heav'n opens on my eyes! my ears
  With sound seraphic ring:
Lend, lend your wings! I mount! I fly!
O Grave! where is thy Victory?
  O Death! where is thy Sting?

❦ An Essay on Criticism

'T is hard to say, if greater want of skill
Appear in writing or in judging ill;
But, of the two, less dang'rous is th' offence.
To tire our patience, than mislead our sense.
Some few in that, but numbers err in this,
Ten censure wrong for one who writes amiss;
A fool might once himself alone expose,
Now one in verse makes many more in prose.

'T is with our judgments as our watches, none
Go just alike, yet each believes his own.
In Poets as true genius is but rare,
True Taste as seldom is the Critic's share;
Both must alike from Heav'n derive their light,
These born to judge, as well as those to write.
Let such teach others who themselves excel,
And censure freely who have written well.
Authors are partial to their wit,* 't is true,
But are not Critics to their judgment too?

Yet if we look more closely, we shall find
Most have the seeds of judgment in their mind:
Nature affords at least a glimm'ring light;
The lines, tho' touch'd but faintly, are drawn right.
But as the slightest sketch, if justly trac'd,
Is by ill-colouring but the more disgrac'd,
So by false learning is good sense defac'd:
Some are bewilder'd in the maze of schools,
And some made coxcombs Nature meant but fools.
In search of wit these lose their common sense,
And then turn Critics in their own defence:
Each burns alike, who can, or cannot write,
Or with a Rival's, or an Eunuch's spite.

* The word 'wit' is said to be used in Pope's Essay on Criticism in
seven different senses. [Bain.]

All fools have still an itching to deride,
And fain would be upon the laughing side.
If Mævius scribble in Apollo's spite,
There are who judge still worse than he can write.
   Some have at first for Wits, then Poets past,
Turn'd Critics next, and prov'd plain fools at last.
Some neither can for Wits nor Critics pass,
As heavy mules are neither horse nor ass.
Those half-learn'd witlings, num'rous in our isle,
As half-form'd insects on the banks of Nile;
Unfinish'd things, one knows not what to call,
Their generation 's so equivocal:
To tell 'em, would a hundred tongues require,
Or one vain wit's, that might a hundred tire.
   But you who seek to give and merit fame,
And justly bear a Critic's noble name,
Be sure yourself and your own reach to know,
How far your genius, taste, and learning go;
Launch not beyond your depth, but be discreet,
And mark that point where sense and dulness meet.
   Nature to all things fix'd the limits fit,
And wisely curb'd proud man's pretending wit.
As on the land while here the ocean gains,
In other parts it leaves wide sandy plains;
Thus in the soul while memory prevails,
The solid pow'r of understanding fails;
Where beams of warm imagination play,
The memory's soft figures melt away.
One science only will one genius fit;
So vast is art, so narrow human wit:
Not only bounded to peculiar arts,
But oft in those confin'd to single parts.
Like kings we lose the conquests gain'd before,
By vain ambition still to make them more;
Each might his sev'ral province well command,
Would all but stoop to what they understand.

First follow Nature, and your judgment frame
By her just standard, which is still the same:
Unerring NATURE, still divinely bright,
One clear, unchang'd, and universal light,
Life, force, and beauty, must to all impart,
At once the source, and end, and test of Art.
Art from that fund each just supply provides,
Works without show, and without pomp presides:
In some fair body thus th' informing soul
With spirits feeds, with vigour fills the whole,
Each motion guides, and ev'ry nerve sustains;
Itself unseen, but in th' effects, remains.
Some, to whom Heav'n in wit has been profuse,
Want as much more, to turn it to its use;
For wit and judgment often are at strife,
Tho' meant each other's aid, like man and wife.
'T is more to guide, than spur the Muse's steed;
Restrain his fury, than provoke his speed;
The winged courser, like a gen'rous horse,
Shows most true mettle when you check his course.
    Those RULES of old discovered, not devis'd,
Are Nature still, but Nature methodiz'd;
Nature, like liberty, is but restrain'd
By the same laws which first herself ordain'd.
    Hear how learn'd Greece her useful rules indites,
When to repress, and when indulge our flights:
High on Parnassus' top her sons she show'd,
And pointed out those arduous paths they trod;
Held from afar, aloft, th' immortal prize,
And urg'd the rest by equal steps to rise.
Just precepts thus from great examples giv'n,
She drew from them what they deriv'd from Heav'n.
The gen'rous Critic fann'd the Poet's fire,
And taught the world with reason to admire.
Then Criticism the Muses handmaid prov'd,

To dress her charms, and make her more belov'd:
But following wits from that intention stray'd,
Who could not win the mistress, woo'd the maid;
Against the Poets their own arms they turn'd,
Sure to hate most the men from whom they learn'd.
So modern 'Pothecaries, taught the art
By Doctor's bills to play the Doctor's part,
Bold in the practice of mistaken rules,
Prescribe, apply, and call their masters fools.
Some on the leaves of ancient authors prey,
Nor time nor moths e'er spoil'd so much as they.
Some drily plain, without invention's aid,
Write dull receipts how poems may be made.
These leave the sense, their learning to display,
And those explain the meaning quite away.

You then whose judgment the right course would steer,
Know well each ANCIENT's proper character;
His fable, subject, scope in ev'ry page;
Religion, Country, genius of his Age:
Without all these at once before your eyes,
Cavil you may, but never criticize.
Be Homer's works your study and delight,
Read them by day, and meditate by night;
Thence form your judgment, thence your maxims bring,
And trace the Muses upward to their spring.
Still with itself compar'd, his text peruse;
And let your comment be the Mantuan Muse.

When first young Maro* in his boundless mind
A work t' outlast immortal Rome design'd,
Perhaps he seem'd above the critic's law,
And but from Nature's fountains scorn'd to draw:
But when t' examine ev'ry part he came,
Nature and Homer were, he found, the same.
Convinc'd, amaz'd, he checks the bold design;

* Virgil.

And rules as strict his labour'd work confine,
As if the Stagirite o'erlook'd each line.
Learn hence for ancient rules a just esteem;
To copy nature is to copy them.
　　Some beauties yet no Precepts can declare,
For there's a happiness as well as care.
Music resembles Poetry, in each
Are nameless graces which no methods teach,
And which a master-hand alone can reach.
If, where the rules not far enough extend,
(Since rules were made but to promote their end)
Some lucky Licence answer to the full
Th' intent propos'd, that Licence is a rule.
Thus, Pegasus, a nearer way to take,
May boldly deviate from the common track;
From vulgar bounds with brave disorder part,
And snatch a grace beyond the reach of art,
Which without passing thro' the judgment, gains
The heart, and all its end at once attains.
In prospects thus, some objects please our eyes,
Which out of nature's common order rise,
The shapeless rock, or hanging precipice.
Great wits sometimes may gloriously offend,
And rise to faults true Critics dare not mend.
But tho' the Ancients thus their rules invade,
(As Kings dispense with laws themselves have made)
Moderns, beware! or if you must offend
Against the precept, ne'er transgress its End;
Let it be seldom, and compell'd by need;
And have, at least, their precedent to plead
The Critic else proceeds without remorse,
Seizes your fame, and puts his laws in force.
　　I know there are, to whose presumptuous thoughts
Those freer beauties, ev'n in them, seem faults.
Some figures monstrous and mis-shap'd appear,

Consider'd singly, or beheld too near,
Which, but proportion'd to their light, or place,
Due distance reconciles to form and grace.
A prudent chief not always must display
His pow'rs in equal ranks, and fair array.
But with th' occasion and the place comply,
Conceal his force, nay seem sometimes to fly.
Those oft are stratagems which error seem,
Nor is it Homer nods, but we that dream.

Still green with bays each ancient Altar stands,
Above the reach of sacrilegious hands;
Secure from Flames, from Envy's fiercer rage,
Destructive War, and all-involving Age.
See, from each clime the learn'd their incense bring!
Hear, in all tongues consenting Pæans ring!
In praise so just let ev'ry voice be join'd,
And fill the gen'ral chorus of mankind.
Hail, Bards triumphant! born in happier days;
Immortal heirs of universal praise!
Whose honours with increase of ages grow,
As streams roll down, enlarging as they flow;
Nations unborn your mighty names shall sound,
And worlds applaud that must not yet be found!
Oh may some spark of your celestial fire,
The last, the meanest of your sons inspire,
(That on weak wings, from far, pursues your flights;
Glows while he reads, but trembles as he writes)
To teach vain Wits a science little known,
T' admire superior sense, and doubt their own!

Of all the Causes which conspire to blind
Man's erring judgment, and misguide the mind,
What the weak head with strongest bias rules,
Is *Pride*, the never-failing voice of fools.
Whatever nature has in worth denied,

She gives in large recruits* of needful pride;
For as in bodies, thus in souls, we find
What wants in blood and spirits, swell'd with wind:
Pride, where wit fails, steps into our defence,
And fills up all the mighty Void of sense.
If once right reason drives that cloud away,
Truth breaks upon us with resistless day.
Trust not yourself; but your defects to know,
Make use of ev'ry friend—and ev'ry foe.

A *little learning* is a dang'rous thing;
Drink deep, or taste not the Pierian spring.
There shallow draughts intoxicate the brain,
And drinking largely sobers us again.
Fir'd at first sight with what the Muse imparts,
In fearless youth we tempt the heights of Arts,
While from the bounded level of our mind
Short views we take, nor see the lengths behind;
But more advanc'd, behold with strange surprise
New distant scenes of endless science rise!
So pleas'd at first the tow'ring Alps we try,
Mount o'er the vales, and seem to tread the sky,
Th' eternal snows appear already past,
And the first clouds and mountains seem the last;
But, those attain'd, we tremble to survey
The growing labours of the lengthen'd way,
Th' increasing prospects tires our wand'ring eyes,
Hills peep o'er hills, and Alps on Alps arise!

A perfect Judge will read each word of Wit
With the same spirit that its author writ:
Survey the Whole, nor seek slight faults to find
Where nature moves, and rapture warms the mind;
Nor lose, for that malignant dull delight,
The gen'rous pleasure to be charm'd with Wit.
But in such lays as neither ebb, nor flow,

* Supplies.

Correctly cold, and regularly low,
That shunning faults, one quiet tenour keep,
We cannot blame indeed —— but we may sleep.
In wit, as nature, what affects our hearts
Is not th' exactness of peculiar parts;
'T is not a lip, or eye, we beauty call,
But the joint force and full result of all.
Thus when we view some well-proportion'd dome,
(The world's just wonder, and ev'n thine, O Rome!)
No single parts unequally surprize,
All comes united to th' admiring eyes;
No monstrous height, or breadth, or length appear;
The Whole at once is bold, and regular.

Whoever thinks a faultless piece to see,
Thinks what ne'er was, nor is, nor e'er shall be.
In every work regard the writer's End,
Since none can compass more than they intend;
And if the means be just, the conduct true,
Applause, in spight of trivial faults, is due;
As men of breeding, sometimes men of wit,
T' avoid great errors, must the less commit:
Neglect the rules each verbal Critic lays,
For not to know some trifles, is a praise.
Most Critics, fond of some subservient art,
Still make the Whole depend upon a Part:
They talk of principles, but notions prize,
And all to one lov'd Folly sacrifice.

Once on a time, La Mancha's Knight,* they say,
A certain bard encount'ring on the way,
Discours'd in terms as just, with looks as sage,
As e'er could Dennis of the Grecian stage;
Concluding all were desp'rate sots and fools,
Who durst depart from Aristotle's rules.
Our Author, happy in a judge so nice,

* Don Quixote.

Produc'd his Play, and begg'd the Knight's advice;
Made him observe the subject, and the plot,
The manners, passions, unities; what not?
All which, exact to rule, were brought about,
Were but a Combat in the lists left out.
"What! leave the Combat out?" exclaims the Knight;
Yes, or we must renounce the Stagirite.
"Not so by Heav'n" (he answers in a rage),
"Knights, squires, and steeds, must enter on the stage."
So vast a throng the stage can ne'er contain.
"Then build a new, or act it in a plain."

Thus Critics, or less judgment than caprice,
Curious not knowing, not exact but nice,
Form short Ideas; and offend in arts
(As most in manners) by a love to parts.

Some to *Conceit* alone their taste confine,
And glitt'ring thoughts struck out at ev'ry line;
Pleas'd with a work where nothing's just or fit;
One glaring Chaos and wild heap of wit.
Poets like painters, thus, unskill'd to trace
The naked nature and the living grace,
With gold and jewels cover ev'ry part,
And hide with ornaments their want of art.
True Wit is Nature to advantage dress'd,
What oft was thought, but ne'er so well express'd;
Something, whose truth convinc'd at sight we find,
That gives us back the image of our mind.
As shades more sweetly recommend the light,
So modest plainness sets off sprightly wit.
For works may have more wit than does 'em good,
As bodies perish thro' excess of blood.

Others for *Language* all their care express,
And value books, as women men, for Dress:
Their praise is still,—the Style is excellent:
The Sense, they humbly take upon content.

Words are like leaves; and where they most abound,
Much fruit of sense beneath is rarely found,
False Eloquence, like the prismatic glass,
Its gaudy colours spreads on ev'ry place;
The face of Nature we no more survey,
All glares alike, without distinction gay:
But true expression, like th' unchanging Sun,
Clears and improves whate'er it shines upon,
It gilds all objects, but it alters none.
Expression is the dress of thought, and still
Appears more decent, as more suitable;
A vile conceit in pompous words express'd,
Is like a clown in regal purple dress'd:
For diff'rent styles with diff'rent subjects sort,
As several garbs with country, town, and court.
Some by old words to fame have made pretence,
Ancients in phrase, mere moderns in their sense;
Such labour'd nothings, in so strange a style,
Amaze th' unlearn'd, and make the learned smile.
Unlucky, as Fungoso in the play,
These sparks with awkward vanity display
What the fine gentleman wore yesterday;
And but so mimic ancient wits at best,
As apes our grandsires, in their doublets drest.
In words, as fashions, the same rule will hold;
Alike fantastic, if too new, or old:
Be not the first by whom the new are try'd,
Nor yet the last to lay the old aside.
  But most by Numbers judge a Poet's song;
And smooth or rough, with them is right or wrong:
In the bright Muse though thousand charms conspire,
Her voice is all these tuneful fools admire;
Who haunt Parnassus but to please their ear,
Not mend their minds; as some to Church repair,
Not for the doctrine, but the music there.

These equal syllables alone require,
Tho' oft the ear the open vowels tire;
While expletives their feeble aid do join;
And ten low words oft creep in one dull line:
While they ring round the same unvary'd chimes,
With sure returns of still expected rhymes;
Where-e'er you find "the cooling western breeze,"
In the next line, it "whispers through the trees:"
If crystal streams "with pleasing murmurs creep,"
The reader's threaten'd (not in vain) with "sleep:"
Then, at the last and only couplet fraught
With some unmeaning thing they call a thought,
A needless Alexandrine ends the song
That, like a wounded snake, drags its slow length along.
Leave such to tune their own dull rhymes, and know
What 's roundly smooth or languishingly slow;
And praise the easy vigour of a line,
Where Denham's strength, and Waller's sweetness join.
True ease in writing comes from art, not chance,
As those move easiest who have learn'd to dance.
'T is not enough no harshness gives offence,
The sound must seem an Echo to the sense:
Soft is the strain when Zephyr gently blows,
And the smooth stream in smoother numbers flows;
But when loud surges lash the sounding shore,
The hoarse, rough verse should like the torrent roar:
When Ajax strives some rock's vast weight to throw,
The line too labours, and the words move slow;
Not so, when swift Camilla scours the plain,
Flies o'er th' unbending corn, and skims along the main.
Hear how Timotheus' varied lays surprize,
And bid alternate passions fall and rise!
While, at each change, the son of Libyan Jove
Now burns with glory, and then melts with love,
Now his fierce eyes with sparkling fury glow,

Now sighs steal out, and tears begin to flow:
Persians and Greeks like turns of nature found,
And the world's victor stood subdu'd by Sound!
The pow'r of Music all our hearts allow,
And what Timotheus was, is DRYDEN now.

Avoid Extremes; and shun the fault of such,
Who still are pleas'd too little or too much.
At ev'ry trifle scorn to take offence,
That always shows great pride, or little sense;
Those heads, as stomachs, are not sure the best,
Which nauseate all, and nothing can digest.
Yet let not each gay Turn thy rapture move;
For fools admire, but men of sense approve:
As things seem large which we thro' mists descry,
Dulness is ever apt to magnify.

Some foreign writers, some our own despise;
The Ancients only, or the Moderns prize.
Thus Wit, like Faith, by each man is apply'd
To one small sect, and all are damn'd beside.
Meanly they seek the blessing to confine,
And force that sun but on a part to shine,
Which not alone the southern wit sublimes,
But ripens spirits in cold northern climes;
Which from the first has shone on ages past,
Enlights the present, and shall warm the last;
Tho' each may feel increases and decays,
And see now clearer and now darker days.
Regard not then if Wit be old or new,
But blame the false, and value still the true.

Some ne'er advance a Judgment of their own,
But catch the spreading notion of the Town;
They reason and conclude by precedent,
And own stale nonsense which they ne'er invent.
Some judge of author's names, not works, and then
Nor praise nor blame the writings, but the men.

Of all this servile herd the worst is he
That in proud dulness joins with Quality.
A constant Critic at the great man's board,
To fetch and carry nonsense for my Lord.
What woful stuff this madrigal would be,
In some starv'd hackney sonneteer, or me?
But let a Lord once own the happy lines,
How the wit brightens! how the style refines!
Before his sacred name flies ev'ry fault,
And each exalted stanza teems with thought!
    The Vulgar thus through Imitation err;
As oft the Learn'd by being singular;
So much they scorn the crowd, that if the throng
By chance go right, they purposely go wrong;
So Schismatics the plain believers quit,
And are but damn'd for having too much wit.
Some praise at morning what they blame at night;
But always think the last opinion right.
A Muse by these is like a mistress us'd,
This hour she 's idoliz'd, the next abus'd;
While their weak heads like towns unfortify'd,
'Twixt sense and nonsense daily change their side.
Ask them the cause; they 're wiser still, they say;
And still to-morrow 's wiser than to-day.
We think our fathers fools, so wise we grow,
Our wiser sons, no doubt, will think us so.
Once School-divines this zealous isle o'er-spread;
Who knew most Sentences, was deepest read;
Faith, Gospel, all, seem'd made to be disputed,
And none had sense enough to be confuted:
Scotists and Thomists, now, in peace remain,
Amidst their kindred cobwebs in Duck-lane.*
If Faith itself has diff'rent dresses worn,
What wonder modes in Wit should take their turn?

* A second-hand book center.

Oft', leaving what is natural and fit,
The current folly proves the ready wit;
And authors think their reputation safe,
Which lives as long as fools are pleas'd to laugh.
  Some valuing those of their own side or mind,
Still make themselves the measure of mankind:
Fondly we think we honour merit then,
When we but praise ourselves in other men.
Parties in Wit attend on those of State,
And public faction doubles private hate.
Pride, Malice, Folly, against Dryden rose,
In various shapes of Parsons, Critics, Beaus;
But sense surviv'd, when merry jests were past;
For rising merit will buoy up at last.
Might he return, and bless once more our eyes,
New Blackmores and new Milbourns must arise:
Nay should great Homer lift his awful head,
Zoilus again would start up from the dead.
Envy will merit, as its shade, pursue;
But like a shadow, proves the substance true;
For envy'd Wit, like Sol eclips'd, makes known
Th' opposing body 's grossness, not its own,
When first that sun too pow'rful beams displays,
It draws up vapours which obscure its rays;
But ev'n those clouds at last adorn its way.
Reflect new glories, and augment the day.
  Be thou the first true merit to befriend;
His praise is lost, who stays, till all commend.
Short is the date, alas, of modern rhymes,
And 't is but just to let them live betimes.
No longer now that golden age appears,
When Patriarch-wits surviv'd a thousand years:
Now length of Fame (our second life) is lost,
And bare threescore is all ev'n that can boast;
Our sons their fathers' failing language see,

And such as Chaucer is, shall Dryden be.
So when the faithful pencil has design'd
Some bright Idea of the master's mind,
Where a new world leaps out at his command,
And ready Nature waits upon his hand;
When the ripe colours soften and unite,
And sweetly melt into just shade and light;
When mellowing years their full perfection give,
And each bold figure just begins to live,
The treach'rous colours the fair art betray,
And all the bright creation fades away!

Unhappy Wit, like most mistaken things,
Atones not for that envy which it brings.
In youth alone its empty praise we boast,
But soon the short-liv'd vanity is lost:
Like some fair flow'r the early spring supplies,
That gaily blooms, but ev'n in blooming dies.
What is this Wit, which must our cares employ?
The owner's wife, that other men enjoy;
Then most our trouble still when most admir'd,
And still the more we give, the more requir'd;
Whose fame with pains we guard, but lose with ease,
Sure some to vex, but never all to please;
'T is what the vicious fear, the virtuous shun,
By fools 't is hated, and by knaves undone!

If Wit so much from Ign'rance undergo,
Ah let not Learning too commence its foe!
Of old, those met rewards who could excel,
And such were prais'd who but endeavour'd well:
Tho' triumphs were to gen'rals only due,
Crowns were reserv'd to grace the soldiers too.
Now, they who reach Parnassus' lofty crown,
Employ their pains to spurn some others down;
And while self-love each jealous writer rules,
Contending wits become the sport of fools:
But still the worst with most regret commend,

For each ill Author is as bad a Friend.
To what base ends, and by what abject ways,
Are mortals urg'd thro' sacred lust of praise!
Ah ne'er so dire a thirst of glory boast,
Nor in the Critic let the Man be lost.
Good-nature and good-sense must ever join;
To err is human, to forgive, divine.

But if in noble minds some dregs remain
Not yet purg'd off, of spleen and sour disdain;
Discharge that rage on more provoking crimes,
Nor fear a dearth in these flagitious times.
No pardon vile Obscenity should find,
Tho' wit and art conspire to move your mind;
But Dulness with Obscenity must prove
As shameful sure as Impotence in love.
In the fat age of pleasure wealth and ease,
Sprung the rank weed, and thriv'd with large increase:
When love was all an easy Monarch's care;
Seldom at council, never in a war:
Jilts rul'd the state, and statesmen farces writ;
Nay wits had pensions, and young Lords had wit:
The Fair sate panting at a Courtier's play,
And not a Mask went unimprov'd away:*
The modest fan was lifted up no more,
And Virgins smil'd at what they blush'd before.
The following licence of a Foreign reign
Did all the dregs of bold Socinus drain;
Then unbelieving priests reform'd the nation,
And taught more pleasant methods of salvation;
Where Heav'n's free subjects might their rights dispute,
Lest God himself should seem too absolute:
Pulpits their sacred satire learn'd to spare,
And Vice admir'd to find a flatt'rer there!
Encourag'd thus, Wit's Titans brav'd the skies,
And the press groan'd with licens'd blasphemies.

* Ladies wore masks to the playhouse.

These monsters, Critics! with your darts engage,
Here point your thunder, and exhaust your rage!
Yet shun their fault, who, scandalously nice,
Will needs mistake an author into vice;
All seems infected that th' infected spy,
As all looks yellow to the jaundic'd eye.

Learn then what MORALS Critics ought to show,
For 't is but half a Judge's task, to know.
'T is not enough, taste, judgment, learning, join;
In all you speak, let truth and candour shine:
That not alone what to your sense is due
All may allow; but seek your friendship too.
Be silent always when you doubt your sense;
And speak, tho' sure, with seeming diffidence:
Some positive, persisting fops we know,
Who, if once wrong, will needs be always so;
But you, with pleasure own your errors past,
And make each day a Critic on the last.
'T is not enough, your counsel still be true;
Blunt truths more mischief than nice falsehoods do;
Men must be taught as if you taught them not,
And things unknown propos'd as things forgot.
Without Good Breeding, truth is disapprov'd;
That only makes superior sense belov'd
Be niggards of advice on no pretence;
For the worst avarice is that of sense.
With mean complacence ne'er betray your trust,
Nor be so civil as to prove unjust.
Fear not the anger of the wise to raise;
Those best can bear reproof, who merit praise.
'T were well might critics still this freedom take,
But Appius reddens at each word you speak,
And stares, tremendous, with a threat'ning eye,
Like some fierce Tyrant in old tapestry.
Fear most to tax an Honourable fool,

Whose right it is, uncensur'd, to be dull;
Such, without wit, are Poets when they please,
As without learning they can take Degrees.
Leave dang'rous truths to unsuccessful Satires,
And flattery to fulsome Dedicators,
Whom, when they praise, the world believes no more,
Than when they promise to give scribbling o'er.
'T is best sometimes your censure to restrain,
And charitably let the dull be vain:
Your silence there is better than your spite,
For who can rail so long as they can write?
Still humming on, their drowsy course they keep,
And lash'd so long, like tops, are lash'd asleep.
False steps but help them to renew the race,
As, after stumbling, Jades will mend their pace.
What crowds of these, impenitently bold,
In sounds and jingling syllables grown old,
Still run on Poets, in a raging vein,
Ev'n to the dregs and squeezings of the brain,
Strain out the last dull droppings of their sense,
And rhyme with all the rage of Impotence.
Such shameless Bards we have; and yet 't is true,
There are as mad abandon'd Critics too.
The bookful blockhead, ignorantly read,
With loads of learned lumber in his head,
With his own tongue still edifies his ears,
And always list'ning to himself appears.
All books he reads, and all he reads assails,
From Dryden's Fables down to Durfey's Tales.
With him, most authors steal their works, or buy;
Garth did not write his own Dispensary.
Name a new Play, and he 's the Poet's friend,
Nay, show'd his faults—but when would Poets mend?
No place so sacred from such fops is barr'd,
Nor is Paul's church more safe than Paul's churchyard:
Nay, fly to altars; there they 'll talk you dead:

For Fools rush in where Angels fear to tread.
Distrustful sense with modest caution speaks,
It still looks home, and short excursions makes;
But rattling nonsense in full volleys breaks,
And never shock'd, and never turn'd aside,
Bursts out, resistless, with a thund'ring tide.

But where's the man, who counsel can bestow,
Still pleas'd to teach, and yet not proud to know
Unbiass'd, or by favour, or by spite;
Not dully prepossess'd, nor blindly right;
Tho' learn'd, well-bred; and tho' well-bred, sincere,
Modestly bold, and humanly severe:
Who to a friend his faults can freely show,
And gladly praise the merit of a foe?
Blest with a taste exact, yet unconfin'd;
A knowledge both of books and human kind:
Gen'rous converse; a soul exempt from pride;
And love to praise, with reason on his side?

Such once were Critics; such the happy few,
Athens and Rome in better ages knew.
The mighty Stagirite first left the shore,
Spread all his sails, and durst the deeps explore:
He steer'd securely, and discover'd far,
Led by the light of the Mæonian Star.
Poets, a race long unconfin'd, and free,
Still fond and proud of savage liberty,
Receiv'd his laws; and stood convinc'd 't was fit,
Who conquer'd Nature, should preside o'er Wit.

Horace still charms with graceful negligence,
And without method talks us into sense,
Will, like a friend, familiarly convey
The truest notions in the easiest way.
He, who supreme in judgment, as in wit,
Might boldly censure, as he boldly writ,
Yet judg'd with coolness, tho' he sung with fire;
His Precepts teach but what his works inspire.

Our Critics take a contrary extreme,
They judge with fury, but they write with fle'me:
Nor suffers Horace more in wrong Translations
By Wits, than Critics in as wrong Quotations.

See Dionysius Homer's thoughts refine,
And call new beauties forth from ev'ry line!

Fancy and art in gay Petronius please,
The scholar's learning, with the courtier's ease.

In grave Quintilian's copious work, we find
The justest rules, and clearest method join'd:
Thus useful arms in magazines we place,
All rang'd in order, and dispos'd with grace,
But less to please the eye, than arm the hand,
Still fit for use, and ready at command.

Thee, bold Longinus! all the Nine inspire,
And bless their Critic with a Poet's fire.
An ardent Judge, who zealous in his trust,
With warmth gives sentence, yet is always just;
Whose own example strengthens all his laws;
And is himself that great Sublime he draws.

Thus long succeeding Critics justly reign'd,
Licence repress'd, and useful laws ordain'd.
Learning and Rome alike in empire grew;
And Arts still follow'd where her Eagles flew;
From the same foes, at last, both felt their doom,
And the same age saw Learning fall, and Rome.
With Tyranny, then Superstition join'd,
As that the body, this enslav'd the mind;
Much was believ'd, but little understood,
And to be dull was constru'd to be good;
A second deluge Learning thus o'er-run,
And the Monks finish'd what the Goths begun.

At length Erasmus, that great injur'd name,
(The glory of the Priesthood, and the shame!)
Stemm'd the wild torrent of a barb'rous age,
And drove those holy Vandals off the stage.

But see! each Muse, in LEO's golden days,
Starts from her trance, and trims her wither'd bays,
Rome's ancient Genius, o'er its ruins spread,
Shakes off the dust, and rears his rev'rend head
Then Sculpture and her sister-arts revive;
Stones leap'd to form, and rocks began to live;
With sweeter notes each rising Temple rung;
A Raphael painted, and a Vida sung.
Immortal Vida: on whose honour'd brow
The Poet's bays and Critic's ivy grow:
Cremona now shall ever boast thy name,
As next in place to Mantua, next in fame!

But soon by impious arms from Latium chas'd,
Their ancient bounds the banish'd Muses pass'd;
Thence Arts o'er all the northern world advance,
But Critic-learning flourish'd most in France:
The rules a nation, born to serve, obeys;
And Boileau still in right of Horace sways.
But we, brave Britons, foreign laws despis'd,
And kept unconquer'd, and unciviliz'd;
Fierce for the liberties of wit, and bold,
We still defy'd the Romans, as of old.
Yet some there were, among the sounder few
Of those who less presum'd, and better knew,
Who durst assert the juster ancient cause,
And here restor'd Wit's fundamental laws.
Such was the Muse, whose rules and practice tell,
"Nature's chief Master-piece is writing well."
Such was Roscommon, not more learn'd than good,
With manners gen'rous as his noble blood;
To him the wit of Greece and Rome was known,
And ev'ry author's merit, but his own.
Such late was Walsh—the Muse's judge and friend,
Who justly knew to blame or to commend;
To failings mild, but zealous for desert;
The clearest head, and the sincerest heart.

This humble praise, lamented shade! receive,
This praise at least a grateful Muse may give:
The Muse, whose early voice you taught to sing,
Prescrib'd her heights, and prun'd her tender wing,
(Her guide now lost) no more attempts to rise,
But in low numbers short excursions tries:
Content, if hence th' unlearn'd their wants may view,
The learn'd reflect on what before they knew:
Careless of censure, nor too fond of fame;
Still pleas'd to praise, yet not afraid to blame,
Averse alike to flatter, or offend;
Not free from faults, nor yet too vain to mend.

❨ The Rape of the Lock

AN HEROI-COMICAL POEM

Nolueram, Belinda, tuos violare capillos;
. Sed juvat, hoc precibus me tribuisse tuis. MART. [*Epigr*. XII. 84.]

TO MRS. ARABELLA FERMOR

MADAM,

It will be in vain to deny that I have some regard for this piece, since I dedicate it to You. Yet you may bear me witness, it was intended only to divert a few young Ladies, who have good sense and good humour enough to laugh not only at their sex's little unguarded follies, but at their own. But as it was communicated with the air of a Secret, it soon found its way into the world. An imperfect copy having been offer'd to a Bookseller, you had the good-nature for my sake to consent to the publication of one more correct: This I was forc'd to, before I had executed half my design, for the Machinery was entirely wanting to compleat it.

The Machinery, Madam, is a term invented by the Critics, to signify that part which the Deities, Angels, or Dæmons are made to act in a Poem: For the ancient Poets are in one respect like many modern Ladies: let an action be never so trivial in itself, they always make it appear of the utmost importance. These Machines I determined to raise on a very new and odd foundation, the Rosicrucian doctrine of Spirits.

I know how disagreeable it is to make use of hard words before a Lady; but 't is so much the concern of a Poet to have his works understood, and particularly by your Sex, that you must give me leave to explain two or three difficult terms.

The Rosicrucians are a people I must bring you acquainted with. The best account I know of them is in a French book call'd *Le Comte de Gabalis*, which both in its title and size is so like a Novel, that many of the Fair Sex have read it for one by mistake. According to these Gentlemen, the four Elements are inhabited by Spirits, which they call Sylphs, Gnomes, Nymphs, and Salamanders. The Gnomes or Dæmons of Earth delight in mischief; but the Sylphs, whose habitation is in the Air, are the best condition'd creatures imaginable. For they say, any mortals may enjoy the most intimate familiarities with these gentle Spirits, upon a condition very easy to all true Adepts, an inviolate preservation of Chastity.

As to the following Canto's, all the passages of them are as fabulous, as the Vision at the beginning, or the Transformation at the end; (except the loss of your Hair, which I always mention with reverence). The Human persons are as fictitious as the airy ones; and the character of Belinda, as it is now manag'd, resembles you in nothing but in Beauty.

If this Poem had as many Graces as there are in your Person, or in your Mind, yet I could never hope it should pass thro' the world half so Uncensur'd as You have done. But let its fortune be what it will, mine is happy enough, to have given me this occasion of assuring you that I am, with the truest esteem, MADAM,

Your most obedient, Humble Servant,

A. POPE.

CANTO I

WHAT dire offence from am'rous causes springs,
What mighty contests rise from trivial things,
I sing—This verse to CARYL, Muse! is due:
This, ev'n Belinda may vouchsafe to view:
Slight is the subject, but not so the praise,
If She inspire, and He approve my lays.
Say what strange motive, Goddess! could compel
A well-bred Lord t' assault a gentle Belle?

O say what stranger cause, yet unexplor'd,
Could make a gentle Belle reject a Lord?
In tasks so bold, can little men engage,
And in soft bosoms dwells such mighty Rage?
    Sol thro' white curtains shot a tim'rous ray,
And oped those eyes that must eclipse the day:
Now lap-dogs give themselves the rousing shake,
And sleepless lovers, just at twelve, awake:
Thrice rung the bell, the slipper knock'd the ground,
And the press'd watch return'd a silver sound.
Belinda still her downy pillow prest
Her guardian SYLPH prolong'd the balmy rest:
'T was He had summon'd to her silent bed
The morning-dream that hover'd o'er her head;
A Youth more glitt'ring than a Birth-night Beau,
(That ev'n in slumber caus'd her cheek to glow)
Seem'd to her ear his winning lips to lay,
And thus in whispers said, or seem'd to say.
    "Fairest of mortals, thou distinguish'd care
Of thousand bright Inhabitants of Air!
If e'er one vision touch'd thy infant thought,
Of all the Nurse and all the Priest have taught;
Of airy Elves by moonlight shadows seen,
The silver token, and the circled green,
Or virgins visited by Angel-pow'rs,
With golden crowns and wreaths of heav'nly flow'rs;
Hear and believe! thy own importance know,
Nor bound thy narrow views to things below,
Some secret truths, from learned pride conceal'd,
To Maids alone and Children are reveal'd:
What tho' no credit doubting Wits may give?
The Fair and Innocent shall still believe.
Know, then, unnumber'd Spirits round thee fly,
The light Militia of the lower sky:
These, tho' unseen, are ever on the wing,
Hang o'er the Box, and hover round the Ring.

Think what an equipage thou hast in Air,
And view with scorn two Pages and a Chair.
As now your own, our beings were of old,
And once enclos'd in Woman's beauteous mould;
Thence, by a soft transition, we repair
From earthly Vehicles to these of air.
Think not, when Woman's transient breath is fled
That all her vanities at once are dead;
Succeeding vanities she still regards,
And tho' she plays no more, o'erlooks the cards.
Her joy in gilded Chariots, when alive,
And love of Ombre, after death survive.*
For when the Fair in all their pride expire,
To their first Elements their Souls retire:
The Sprites of fiery Termagants in Flame
Mount up, and take a Salamander's name.
Soft yielding minds to Water glide away,
And sip, with Nymphs, their elemental Tea.
The graver Prude sinks downward to a Gnome,
In search of mischief still on Earth to roam.
The light Coquettes in Sylphs aloft repair,
And sport and flutter in the fields of Air.

"Know further yet; whoever fair and chaste
Rejects mankind, is by some Sylph embrac'd:
For Spirits, freed from mortal laws, with ease
Assume what sexes and what shapes they please.
What guards the purity of melting Maids,
In courtly balls, and midnight masquerades,
Safe from the treach'rous friend, the daring spark,
The glance by day, the whisper in the dark,
When kind occasion prompts their warm desires,
When music softens, and when dancing fires?
'T is, but their Sylph, the wise Celestials know,
Tho' Honour is the word with Men below.

* In the reign of Queen Anne Ombre was the favourite game of the ladies, as Piquet of the gentlemen.

"Some nymphs there are, too conscious of their face
For life predestin'd to the Gnomes' embrace.
These swell their prospects and exalt their pride,
When offers are disdain'd, and love deny'd:
Then gay Ideas crowd the vacant brain,
While Peers, and Dukes, and all their sweeping train,
And Garters, Stars, and Coronets appear,
And in soft sounds, Your Grace salutes their ear.
'T is these that early taint the female soul,
Instruct the eyes of young Coquettes to roll,
Teach Infant-cheeks a bidden blush to know,
And little hearts to flutter at a Beau.

"Oft, when the world imagine women stray,
The Sylphs thro' mystic mazes guide their way,
Thro' all the giddy circle they pursue,
And old impertinence expel by new.
What tender maid but must a victim fall
To one man's treat, but for another's ball?
When Florio speaks what virgin could withstand,
If gentle Damon did not squeeze her hand?
With varying vanities, from ev'ry part,
They shift the moving Toyshop of their heart;
Where wigs with wigs, with sword-knots sword-knots strive,
Beaux banish beaux, and coaches coaches drive.
This erring mortals Levity may call;
Oh blind to truth! the Sylphs contrive it all.

"Of these am I, who thy protection claim,
A watchful sprite, and Ariel is my name.
Late, as I rang'd the crystal wilds of air,
In the clear Mirror of thy ruling Star
I saw, alas! some dread event impend,
Ere to the main this morning sun descend,
But heav'n reveals not what, or how, or where:
Warn'd by the Sylph, oh pious maid, beware!
This to disclose is all thy guardian can:
Beware of all, but most beware of Man!"

He said; when Shock, who thought she slept too long,
Leap'd up, and wak'd his mistress with his tongue.
'T was then, Belinda, if report say true,
Thy eyes first open'd on a Billet-doux;
Wounds, Charms, and Ardors were no sooner read,
But all the Vision vanish'd from thy head.
And now, unveil'd, the Toilet stands display'd,
Each silver Vase in mystic order laid.
First, rob'd in white, the Nymph intent adores,
With head uncover'd, the Cosmetic pow'rs.
A heav'nly image in the glass appears,
To that she bends, to that her eyes she rears;
Th' inferior Priestess, at her altar's side,
Trembling begins the sacred rites of Pride.
Unnumber'd treasures ope at once, and here
The various off'rings of the world appear;
From each she nicely culls with curious toil,
And decks the Goddess with the glitt'ring spoil.
This casket India's glowing gems unlocks,
And all Arabia breathes from yonder box.
The Tortoise here and Elephant unite,
Transform'd to combs, the speckled, and the white.
Here files of pins extend their shining rows,
Puffs, Powders, Patches, Bibles, Billet-doux.
Now awful Beauty puts on all its arms;
The fair each moment rises in her charms,
Repairs her smiles, awakens ev'ry grace,
And calls forth all the wonders of her face;
Sees by degrees a purer blush arise,
And keener lightnings quicken in her eyes.
The busy Sylphs surround their darling care,
These set the head, and those divide the hair,
Some fold the sleeve, whilst others plait the gown;
And Betty 's prais'd for labours not her own.

CANTO II

Not with more glories, in th' etherial plain,
The Sun first rises o'er the purpled main,
Than, issuing forth, the rival of his beams
Launch'd on the bosom of the silver Thames.
Fair Nymphs, and well-drest Youths around her shone,
But ev'ry eye was fix'd on her alone.
On her white breast a sparkling Cross she wore,
Which Jews might kiss, and Infidels adore.
Her lively looks a sprightly mind disclose,
Quick as her eyes, and as unfix'd as those:
Favours to none, to all she smiles extends;
Oft she rejects, but never once offends.
Bright as the sun, her eyes the gazers strike,
And, like the sun, they shine on all alike.
Yet graceful ease, and sweetness void of pride,
Might hide her faults, if Belles had faults to hide:
If to her share some female errors fall,
Look on her face, and you 'll forget 'em all.

This Nymph, to the destruction of mankind,
Nourish'd two Locks, which graceful hung behind
In equal curls, and well conspir'd to deck
With shining ringlets the smooth iv'ry neck.
Love in these labyrinths his slaves detains,
And mighty hearts are held in slender chains.
With hairy springes we the birds betray,
Slight lines of hair surprise the finny prey,
Fair tresses man's imperial race ensnare,
And beauty draws us with a single hair.

Th' advent'rous Baron the bright locks admir'd;
He saw, he wish'd, and to the prize aspir'd.
Resolv'd to win, he meditates the way,
By force to ravish, or by fraud betray;

For when success a Lover's toil attends,
Few ask, if fraud or force attain'd his ends.

For this, ere Phœbus rose, he had implor'd
Propitious heav'n, and ev'ry pow'r ador'd,
But chiefly Love—to Love an Altar built,
Of twelve vast French Romances, neatly gilt.
There lay three garters, half a pair of gloves;
And all the trophies of his former loves;
With tender Billet-doux he lights the pyre,
And breathes three am'rous sighs to raise the fire.
Then prostrate falls, and begs with ardent eyes
Soon to obtain, and long possess the prize:
The pow'rs gave ear, and granted half his pray'r,
The rest, the winds dispers'd in empty air.

But now secure the painted vessel glides,
The sun-beams trembling on the floating tides:
While melting music steals upon the sky,
And soften'd sounds along the waters die;
Smooth flow the waves, the Zephyrs gently play,
Belinda smil'd, and all the world was gay.
All but the Sylph—with careful thoughts opprest,
Th' inpending woe sat heavy on his breast.
He summons strait his Denizens of air;
The lucid squadrons round the sails repair:
Soft o'er the shrouds aërial whispers breathe,
That seem'd but Zephyrs to the train beneath.
Some to the sun their insect-wings unfold,
Waft on the breeze, or sink in clouds of gold;
Transparent forms, too fine for mortal sight,
Their fluid bodies half dissolv'd in light,
Loose to the wind their airy garments flew,
Thin glitt'ring textures of the filmy dew,
Dipt in the richest tincture of the skies,
Where light disports in ever-mingling dyes,
While ev'ry beam new transient colours flings,
Colours that change whene'er they wave their wings.

Amid the circle, on the gilded mast,
Superior by the head, was Ariel plac'd;
His purple pinions op'ning to the sun,
He rais'd his azure wand, and thus begun.

"Ye Sylphs and Sylphids, to your chief give ear!
Fays, Fairies, Genii, Elves, and Dæmons, hear!
Ye know the spheres and various tasks assign'd
By laws eternal to th' aërial kind.
Some in the fields of purest Æther play,
And bask and whiten in the blaze of day.
Some guide the course of wand'ring orbs on high,
Or roll the planets thro' the boundless sky.
Some less refin'd, beneath the moon's pale light
Pursue the stars that shoot athwart the night,
Or suck the mists in grosser air below,
Or dip their pinions in the painted bow,
Or brew fierce tempests on the wintry main,
Or o'er the glebe distil the kindly rain.
Others on earth o'er human race preside,
Watch all their ways, and all their actions guide:
Of these the chief the care of Nations own,
And guard with Arms divine the British Throne.

"Our humbler province is to tend the Fair,
Not a less pleasing, tho' less glorious care;
To save the powder from too rude a gale,
Nor let th' imprison'd essences exhale;
To draw fresh colours from the vernal flow'rs;
To steal from rainbows e'er they drop in show'rs
A brighter wash; to curl their waving hairs,
Assist their blushes, and inspire their airs;
Nay oft, in dreams, invention we bestow,
To change a Flounce, or add a Furbelow.

"This day, black Omens threat the brightest Fair,
That e'er deserv'd a watchful spirit's care;
Some dire disaster, or by force, or slight;
But what, or where, the fates have wrapt in night.

Whether the nymph shall break Diana's law,
Or some frail China jar receive a flaw;
Or stain her honour or her new brocade;
Forget her pray'rs, or miss a masquerade;
Or lose her heart, or necklace, at a ball;
Or whether Heav'n has doom'd that Shock must fall.
Haste, then, ye spirits! to your charge repair:
The flutt'ring fan be Zephyretta's care;
The drops to thee, Brillante, we consign;
And, Momentilla, let the watch be thine;
Do thou, Crispissa, tend her fav'rite Lock;
Ariel himself shall be the guard of Shock.

"To fifty chosen Sylphs, of special note,
We trust th' important charge, the Petticoat:
Oft have we known that seven-fold fence to fail,
Tho' stiff with hoops, and arm'd with ribs of whale;
Form a strong line about the silver bound,
And guard the wide circumference around.

"Whatever spirit, careless of his charge,
His post neglects, or leaves the fair at large,
Shall feel sharp vengeance soon o'ertake his sins,
Be stopp'd in vials, or transfix'd with pins;
Or plung'd in lakes of bitter washes lie,
Or wedg'd whole ages in a bodkin's eye:
Gums and Pomatums shall his flight restrain,
While clogg'd he beats his silken wings in vain;
Or Alum styptics with contracting pow'r
Shrink his thin essence like a rivel'd flow'r:
Or, as Ixion fix'd, the wretch shall feel
The giddy motion of the whirling Mill,
In fumes of burning Chocolate shall glow,
And tremble at the sea that froths below!"

He spoke; the spirits from the sails descend;
Some, orb in orb, around the nymph extend;
Some thrid the mazy ringlets of her hair;
Some hang upon the pendants of her ear:

With beating hearts the dire event they wait,
Anxious, and trembling for the birth of Fate.

CANTO III

Close by those meads, for ever crown'd with flow'rs,
Where Thames with pride surveys his rising tow'rs,
There stands a structure of majestic frame,
Which from the neighb'ring Hampton takes its name.
Here Britain's statesmen oft the fall foredoom
Of foreign Tyrants and of Nymphs at home;
Here thou, great Anna! whom three realms obey,
Dost sometimes counsel take—and sometimes Tea.
  Hither the heroes and the nymphs resort,
To taste awhile the pleasures of a Court;
In various talk th' instructive hours they past,
Who gave the ball, or paid the visit last;
One speaks the glory of the British Queen,
And one describes a charming Indian screen;
A third interprets motions, looks, and eyes;
At ev'ry word a reputation dies.
Snuff, or the fan, supply each pause of chat,
With singing, laughing, ogling, *and all that*.
  Mean while, declining from the noon of day,
The sun obliquely shoots his burning ray;
The hungry Judges soon the sentence sign,
And wretches hang that jury-men may dine;
The merchant from th' Exchange returns in peace,
And the long labours of the Toilet cease.
Belinda now, whom thirst of fame invites,
Burns to encounter two advent'rous Knights,
At Ombre singly to decide their doom;
And swells her breast with conquests yet to come.
Straight the three bands prepare in arms to join,
Each band the number of the sacred nine.

Soon as she spreads her hand, th' aërial guard
Descend, and sit on each important card:
First Ariel perch'd upon a Matadore,
Then each, according to the rank they bore;
For Sylphs, yet mindful of their ancient race,
Are, as when women, wondrous fond of place.

Behold, four Kings in majesty rever'd,
With hoary whiskers and a forky beard;
And four fair Queens whose hands sustain a flow'r,
Th' expressive emblem of their softer pow'r;
Four Knaves in garbs succinct, a trusty band,
Caps on their heads, and halberts in their hand;
And particolour'd troops, a shining train,
Draw forth to combat on the velvet plain.

The skilful Nymph reviews her force with care:
Let Spades be trumps! she said, and trumps they were.

Now move to war her sable Matadores,
In show like leaders of the swarthy Moors.
Spadillio* first, unconquerable Lord!
Led off two captive trumps, and swept the board.
As many more Manillio** forc'd to yield,
And march'd a victor from the verdant field.
Him Basto† follow'd, but his fate more hard
Gain'd but one trump and one Plebian card.
With his broad sabre next, a chief in years,
The hoary Majesty of Spades appears,
Puts forth one manly leg, to sight reveal'd,
The rest, his many-colour'd robe conceal'd.
The rebel Knave, who dares his prince engage,
Proves the just victim of his royal rage.
Ev'n mighty Pam,‡ that Kings and Queens o'erthrew

* The ace of spades, the first trump at Ombre.
** The deuce of trumps when trumps are black, the seven when they are red.
† The ace of clubs.
‡ The knave of clubs.

And mow'd down armies in the fights of Lu,*
Sad chance of war! now destitute of aid,
Falls undistinguish'd by the victor spade!
Thus far both armies to Belinda yield;
Now to the Baron fate inclines the field.
His warlike Amazon her host invades,
Th' imperial consort of the crown of Spades.
The Club's black Tyrant first her victim dy'd,
Spite of his haughty mien, and barb'rous pride:
What boots the regal circle on his head,
His giant limbs, in state unwieldy spread;
That long behind he trails his pompous robe,
And, of all monarch's, only grasps the globe?
The Baron now his Diamonds pours apace;
Th' embroider'd King who shows but half his face,
And his refulgent Queen, with pow'rs combin'd
Of broken troops an easy conquest find
Clubs, Diamonds, Hearts, in wild disorder seen,
With throngs promiscuous strow the level green.
Thus when dispers'd a routed army runs,
Of Asia's troops, and Afric's sable sons,
With like confusion different nations fly,
Of various habit, and of various dye,
The pierc'd battalions dis-united fall,
In heaps on heaps; one fate o'erwhelms them all.
The Knave of Diamonds tries his wily arts,
And wins (oh shameful chance!) the Queen of Hearts.
At this, the blood the virgin's cheek forsook,
A livid paleness spreads o'er all her look;
She sees, and trembles at th' approaching ill,
Just in the jaws of ruin, and Codille.**
And now (as oft in some distemper'd State)
On one nice Trick depends the gen'ral fate.
An Ace of Hearts steps forth: The King unseen

* The game of Loo.
** A term used in Ombre.

Lurk'd in her hand, and mourn'd his captive Queen:
He springs to Vengeance with an eager pace,
And falls like thunder on the prostrate Ace.
The nymph exulting fills with shouts the sky;
The walls, the woods, and long canals reply.

Oh thoughtless mortals! ever blind to fate,
Too soon dejected, and too soon elate.
Sudden, these honours shall be snatch'd away,
And curs'd for ever this victorious day.

For lo! the board with cups and spoons is crown'd,
The berries crackle, and the mill turns round;
On shining Altars of Japan they raise
The silver lamp; the fiery spirits blaze:
From silver spouts the grateful liquors glide,
While China's earth receives the smoking tide:
At once they gratify their scent and taste,
And frequent cups prolong the rich repast.
Straight hover round the Fair her airy band;
Some, as she sipp'd the fuming liquor fann'd,
Some o'er her lap their careful plumes display'd,
Trembling, and conscious of the rich brocade.
Coffee, (which makes the politician wise,
And see thro' all things with his half-shut eyes)
Sent up in vapours to the Baron's brain
New Stratagems, the radiant Lock to gain.
Ah cease, rash youth! desist ere 't is too late,
Fear the just Gods, and think of Scylla's Fate!
Chang'd to a bird, and sent to flit in air,
She dearly pays for Nisus' injur'd hair!

But when to mischief mortals bend their will,
How soon they find fit instruments of ill!
Just then, Clarissa drew with tempting grace
A two-edg'd weapon from her shining case:
So Ladies in Romance assist their Knight,
Present the spear, and arm him for the fight.
He takes the gift with rev'rence, and extends

The little engine on his fingers' ends;
This just behind Belinda's neck he spread,
As o'er the fragrant steams she bends her head.
Swift to the Lock a thousand Sprites repair,
A thousand wings, by turns, blow back the hair;
And thrice they twitch'd the diamond in her ear;
Thrice she look'd back, and thrice the foe drew near.
Just in that instant, anxious Ariel sought
The close recesses of the Virgin's thought;
As on the nosegay in her breast reclin'd,
He watch'd th' Ideas rising in her mind,
Sudden he view'd, in spite of all her art,
An earthly Lover lurking at her heart.
Amaz'd, confus'd, he found his pow'r expir'd,
Resign'd to fate, and with a sigh retir'd.

The Peer now spreads the glitt'ring Forfex wide,
T' inclose the Lock; now joins it, to divide.
Ev'n then, before the fatal engine clos'd,
A wretched Sylph too fondly interpos'd;
Fate urg'd the shears, and cut the Sylph in twain,
(But airy substance soon unites again)
The meeting points the sacred hair dissever
From the fair head, for ever, and for ever!

Then flash'd the living lightning from her eyes,
And screams of horror rend th' affrighted skies.
Not louder shrieks to pitying heav'n are cast,
When husbands, or when lap-dogs breathe their last;
Or when rich China vessels fall'n from high,
In glitt'ring dust and painted fragments lie!

"Let wreaths of triumph now my temples twine
(The victor cry'd) the glorious Prize is mine!
While fish in streams, or birds delight in air
Or in a coach and six the British Fair,
As long as Atalantis shall be read,
Or the small pillow grace a Lady's bed,
While visits shall be paid on solemn days,

When num'rous wax-lights in bright order blaze,
While nymphs take treats, or assignations give,
So long my honour, name, and praise shall live!"
    What Time would spare, from Steel receives its date,
And monuments, like men, submit to fate!
Steel could the labour of the Gods destroy,
And strike to dust th' imperial tow'rs of Troy;
Steel could the works of mortal pride confound,
And hew triumphal arches to the ground.
What wonder then, fair nymph! thy hairs should feel,
The conqu'ring force of unresisted steel?

CANTO IV

BUT anxious cares the pensive nymph oppress'd,
And secret passions labour'd in her breast.
Not youthful kings in battle seiz'd alive,
Not scornful virgins who their charms survive,
Not ardent lovers robb'd of all their bliss,
Not ancient ladies when refus'd a kiss,
Not tyrants fierce that unrepenting die,
Not Cynthia when her manteau 's pinn'd awry,
E'er felt such rage, resentment, and despair,
As thou, sad Virgin! for thy ravish'd Hair.
    For, that sad moment, when the Sylphs withdrew
And Ariel weeping from Belinda flew,
Umbriel, a dusky, melancholy sprite,
As ever sully'd the fair face of light,
Down to the central earth, his proper scene,
Repair'd to search the gloomy Cave of Spleen.
    Swift on his sooty pinions flits the Gnome,
And in a vapour reach'd the dismal dome.
No cheerful breeze this sullen region knows,
The dreaded East is all the wind that blows.
Here in a grotto, shelter'd close from air,

And screen'd in shades from day's detested glare,
She sighs for ever on her pensive bed,
Pain at her side, and Megrim at her head.

　Two handmaids wait the throne: alike in place,
But diff'ring far in figure and in face.
Here stood Ill-nature like an ancient maid,
Her wrinkled form in black and white array'd;
With store of pray'rs, for mornings, nights, and noons,
Her hand is fill'd; her bosom with lampoons.

　There Affectation, with a sickly mien,
Shows in her cheek the roses of eighteen,
Practis'd to lisp, and hang the head aside,
Faints into airs, and languishes with pride,
On the rich quilt sinks with becoming woe,
Wrapt in a gown, for sickness, and for show.
The fair ones feel such maladies as these,
When each new night-dress gives a new disease.

　A constant Vapour o'er the palace flies;
Strange phantoms rising as the mists arise;
Dreadful, as hermit's dreams in haunted shades,
Or bright, as visions of expiring maids.
Now glaring fiends, and snakes on rolling spires,
Pale spectres, gaping tombs, and purple fires:
Now lakes of liquid gold, Elysian scenes,
And crystal domes, and angels in machines.

　Unnumber'd throngs on every side are seen,
Of bodies chang'd to various forms by Spleen.
Here living Tea-pots stand, one arm held out,
One bent; the handle this, and that the spout:
A Pipkin there, like Homer's Tripod walks;
Here sighs a Jar, and there a Goose-pie talks;
Men prove with child, as pow'rful fancy works,
And maids turn'd bottles, call aloud for corks:

　Safe past the Gnome thro' this fantastic band,
A branch of healing Spleenwort in his hand.
Then thus address'd the pow'r: "Hail, wayward Queen!

Who rule the sex to fifty from fifteen:
Parent of vapours and of female wit,
Who give th' hysteric, or poetic fit,
On various tempers act by various ways,
Make some take physic, others scribble plays;
Who cause the proud their visits to delay,
And send the godly in a pet to pray.
A nymph there is, that all thy pow'r disdains,
And thousands more in equal mirth maintains.
But oh! if e'er thy Gnome could spoil a grace,
Or raise a pimple on a beauteous face,
Like Citron-waters matrons cheeks inflame,
Or change complexions at a losing game;
If e'er with airy horns I planted heads,
Or rumpled petticoats, or tumbled beds,
Or caus'd suspicion when no soul was' rude,
Or discompos'd the head-dress of a Prude,
Or e'er to costive lap-dog gave disease,
Which not the tears of brightest eyes could ease:
Hear me, and touch Belinda with chagrin,
That single act gives half the world the spleen."

    The Goddess with a discontented air
Seems to reject him, tho' she grants his pray'r.
A wond'rous Bag with both her hands she binds,
Like that where once Ulysses held the winds;
There she collects the force of female lungs,
Sighs, sobs, and passions, and the war of tongues.
A Vial next she fills with fainting fears,
Soft sorrows, melting griefs, and flowing tears.
The Gnome rejoicing bears her gifts away,
Spreads his black wings, and slowly mounts to day.

    Sunk in Thalestris' arms the nymph he found,
Her eyes dejected and her hair unbound.
Full o'er their heads the swelling bag he rent,
And all the Furies issu'd at the vent.
Belinda burns with more than mortal ire,

And fierce Thalestris fans the rising fire.
"O wretched maid!" she spread her hands, and cry'd,
(While Hampton's echoes, "Wretched maid!" reply'd)
"Was it for this you took such constant care
The bodkin, comb, and essence to prepare?
For this your locks in paper durance bound,
For this with tort'ring irons wreath'd around?
For this with fillets strain'd your tender head,
And bravely bore the double loads of lead?
Gods! shall the ravisher display your hair,
While the Fops envy, and the Ladies stare!
Honour forbid! at whose unrivall'd shrine
Ease, pleasure, virtue, all our sex resign.
Methinks already I your tears survey,
Already hear the horrid things they say,
Already see you a degraded toast,
And all your honour in a whisper lost!
How shall I, then, your helpless fame defend?
'T will then be infamy to seem your friend!
And shall this prize, th' inestimable prize,
Expos'd thro' crystal to the gazing eyes,
And heighten'd by the diamond's circling rays,
On that rapacious hand for ever blaze?
Sooner shall grass in Hyde-park Circus grow,
And wits take lodgings in the sound of Bow;
Sooner let earth, air, sea, to Chaos fall,
Men, monkeys, lap-dogs, parrots, perish all!"
    She said; then raging to Sir Plume repairs,
And bids her Beau demand the precious hairs:
(Sir Plume of amber snuff-box justly vain,
And the nice conduct of a clouded cane)
With earnest eyes, and round unthinking face,
He first the snuff-box open'd, then the case,
And thus broke out—"My Lord, why, what the devil?
Z—ds! damn the lock! 'fore Gad, you must be civil!
Plague on 't! 't is past a jest—nay prithee, pox!

Give her the hair"—he spoke, and rapp'd his box.
"It grieves me much" (reply'd the Peer again)
"Who speaks so well should ever speak in vain.
But by this Lock, this sacred Lock I swear,
(Which never more shall join its parted hair;
Which never more its honours shall renew,
Clipp'd from the lovely head where late it grew)
That while my nostrils draw the vital air,
This hand, which won it, shall for ever wear."
He spoke, and speaking, in proud triumph spread
The long-contended honours of her head.

But Umbriel, hateful Gnome! forbears not so;
He breaks the Vial whence the sorrows flow.
Then see! the nymph in beauteous grief appears,
Her eyes half-languishing, half-drown'd in tears;
On her heav'd bosom hung her drooping head,
Which, with a sigh, she rais'd; and thus she said.

"For ever curs'd be this detested day,
Which snatch'd my best, my fav'rite curl away!
Happy! ah ten times happy had I been,
If Hampton-Court these eyes had never seen!
Yet am not I the first mistaken maid,
By love of Courts to num'rous ills betray'd.
Oh had I rather un-admir'd remain'd
In some lone isle, or distant Northern land;
Where the gilt Chariot never marks the way,
Where none learn Ombre, none e'er taste Bohea!
There kept my charms conceal'd from mortal eye,
Like roses, that in deserts bloom and die.
What mov'd my mind with youthful Lords to roam?
Oh had I stay'd, and said my pray'rs at home!
'T was this, the morning omens seem'd to tell,
Thrice from my trembling hand the patch-box fell;
The tott'ring China shook without a wind,
Nay, Poll sat mute, and Shock was most unkind!
A Sylph too warn'd me of the threats of fate,

In mystic visions, now believ'd too late!
See the poor remnants of these slighted hairs!
My hands shall rend what ev'n thy rapine spares:
These in two sable ringlets taught to break,
Once gave new beauties to the snowy neck;
The sister-lock now sits uncouth, alone,
And in its fellow's fate foresees its own;
Uncurl'd it hangs, the fatal shears demands,
And tempts once more thy sacrilegious hands.
Oh hadst thou, cruel! been content to seize
Hairs less in sight, or any hairs but these!"

CANTO V

SHE said: the pitying audience melt in tears.
But Fate and Jove had stopp'd the Baron's ears.
In vain Thalestris with reproach assails,
For who can move when fair Belinda fails?
Not half so fix'd the Trojan could remain,
While Anna begg'd and Dido rag'd in vain.
Then grave Clarissa graceful wav'd her fan;
Silence ensu'd, and thus the nymph began.
　　"Say why are Beauties prais'd and honour'd most,
The wise man's passion, and the vain man's toast?
Why deck'd with all that land and sea afford,
Why Angels call'd, and Angel-like ador'd?
Why round our coaches crowd the white-glov'd Beaux,
Why bows the side-box from its inmost rows;
How vain are all these glories, all our pains,
Unless good sense preserve what beauty gains:
That men may say, when we the front-box grace:
'Behold the first in virtue as in face!'
Oh! if to dance all night, and dress all day,
Charm'd the small-pox, or chas'd old-age away;
Who would not scorn what housewife's cares produce,

Or who would learn one earthly thing of use?
To patch, nay ogle, might become a Saint,
Nor could it sure be such a sin to paint.
But since, alas! frail beauty must decay,
Curl'd or uncurl'd, since Locks will turn to grey;
Since painted, or not painted, all shall fade,
And she who scorns a man, must die a maid;
What then remains but well our pow'r to use,
And keep good-humour still whate'er we lose?
And trust me, dear! good-humour can prevail,
When airs, and flights, and screams, and scolding fail.
Beauties in vain their pretty eyes may roll;
Charms strike the sight, but merit wins the soul."

So spoke the Dame, but no applause ensu'd;
Belinda frown'd, Thalestris call'd her Prude.
"To arms, to arms!" the fierce Virago cries,
And swift as lightning to the combat flies.
All side in parties, and begin th' attack;
Fans clap, silks rustle, and tough whalebones crack;
Heroes' and Heroines' shouts confus'dly rise,
And bass, and treble voices strike the skies.
No common weapons in their hands are found,
Like Gods they fight, nor dread a mortal wound.

So when bold Homer makes the Gods engage,
And heav'nly breasts with human passions rage;
'Gainst Pallas, Mars; Latona, Hermes arms;
And all Olympus rings with loud alarms:
Jove's thunder roars, heav'n trembles all around,
Blue Neptune storms, the bellowing deeps resound:
Earth shakes her nodding tow'rs, the ground gives way,
And the pale ghosts start at the flash of day!

Triumphant Umbriel on a sconce's height
Clapp'd his glad wings, and sate to view the fight:
Propp'd on their bodkin spears, the Sprites survey
The growing combat, or assist the fray.

While thro' the press enrag'd Thalestris flies,

And scatters death around from both her eyes,
A Beau and Witling perish'd in the throng,
One died in metaphor, and one in song.
"O cruel nymph! a living death I bear,"
Cry'd Dapperwit, and sunk beside his chair.
A mournful glance Sir Fopling upwards cast,
"Those eyes are made so killing"—was his last.
Thus on Mæander's flow'ry margin lies
Th' expiring Swan, and as he sings he dies.

When bold Sir Plume had drawn Clarissa down,
Chloe stepp'd in, and kill'd him with a frown;
She smil'd to see the doughty hero slain,
But, at her smile, the Beau reviv'd again.

Now Jove suspends his golden scales in air,
Weighs the Men's wits against the Lady's hair;
The doubtful beam long nods from side to side;
At length the wits mount up, the hairs subside.

See, fierce Belinda on the Baron flies,
With more than usual lightning in her eyes:
Nor fear'd the Chief th' unequal fight to try,
Who sought no more than on his foe to die.
But this bold Lord with manly strength endu'd,
She with one finger and a thumb subdu'd:
Just where the breath of life his nostrils drew,
A charge of Snuff the wily virgin threw;
The Gnomes direct, to ev'ry atom just,
The pungent grains of titillating dust.
Sudden, with starting tears each eye o'erflows,
And the high dome re-echoes to his nose.

"Now meet thy fate," incens'd Belinda cry'd,
And drew a deadly bodkin from her side.
(The same, his ancient personage to deck,
Her great great grandsire wore about his neck,
In three seal-rings; which after, melted down,
Form'd a vast buckle for his widow's gown:
Her infant grandame's whistle next it grew,

The bells she jingled, and the whistle blew;
Then in a bodkin grac'd her mother's hairs,
Which long she wore, and now Belinda wears.)
　"Boast not my fall" (he cry'd) "insulting foe!
Thou by some other shalt be laid as low,
Nor think, to die dejects my lofty mind:
All that I dread is leaving you behind!
Rather than so, ah let me still survive,
And burn in Cupid's flames—but burn alive."
　"Restore the Lock!" she cries; and all around
"Restore the Lock!" the vaulted roofs rebound.
Not fierce Othello in so loud a strain
Roar'd for the handkerchief that caus'd his pain.
But see how oft ambitious aims are cross'd,
And chiefs contend 'till all the prize is lost!
The Lock, obtain'd with guilt, and kept with pain,
In ev'ry place is sought, but sought in vain:
With such a prize no mortal must be blest,
So heav'n decrees! with heav'n who can contest?
　Some thought it mounted to the Lunar sphere,
Since all things lost on earth are treasur'd there.
There Heros' wits are kept in pond'rous vases,
And beaux', in snuff-boxes and tweezer-cases.
There broken vows and death-bed alms are found,
And lovers' hearts with ends of riband bound,
The courtier's promises, and sick man's pray'rs,
The smiles of harlots, and the tears of heirs,
Cages for gnats, and chains to yoke a flea,
Dry'd butterflies, and tomes of casuistry.
　But trust the Muse—she saw it upward rise,
Tho' mark'd by none but quick, poetic eyes:
(So Rome's great founder to the heav'ns withdrew,
To Proculus alone confess'd in view)
A sudden Star, it shot thro' liquid air,
And drew behind a radiant trail of hair.
Not Berenice's Locks first rose so bright,

The heav'ns bespangling with dishevell'd light.
The Sylphs behold it kindling as it flies,
And pleas'd pursue its progress thro' the skies.

This the Beau monde shall from the Mall survey,
And hail with music its propitious ray.
This the blest Lover shall for Venus take,
And send up vows from Rosamonda's lake,
This Partridge soon shall view in cloudless skies,
When next he looks thro' Galileo's eyes;
And hence th' egregious wizard shall foredoom
The fate of Louis, and the fall of Rome.

Then cease, bright Nymph! to mourn thy ravish'd hair,
Which adds new glory to the shining sphere!
Not all the tresses that fair head can boast,
Shall draw such envy as the Lock you lost.
For, after all the murders of your eye,
When after millions slain, yourself shall die:
When those fair suns shall set, as set they must,
And all those tresses shall be laid in dust,
This Lock, the Muse shall consecrate to fame,
And 'midst the stars inscribe Belinda's name.

☾ Elegy

MEMORY OF AN UNFORTUNATE LADY

WHAT beck'ning ghost, along the moon-light shade
Invites my steps, and points to yonder glade?
'T is she!—but why that bleeding bosom gor'd,
Why dimly gleams the visionary sword?
Oh ever beauteous, ever friendly! tell,
Is it, in heav'n, a crime to love too well?
To bear too tender, or too firm a heart,
To act a Lover's, or a Roman's part?
Is there no bright reversion in the sky,
For those who greatly think, or bravely die?

Why bade ye else, ye Pow'rs! her soul aspire
Above the vulgar flight of low desire?
Ambition first sprung from your blest abodes;
The glorious fault of Angels and of Gods;
Thence to their images on earth it flows,
And in the breasts of Kings and Heroes glows.
Most souls, 't is true, but peep out once an age,
Dull sullen pris'ners in the body's cage:
Dim lights of life, that burn a length of years
Useless, unseen, as lamps in sepulchres;
Like Eastern Kings, a lazy state they keep,
And close confin'd to their own palace, sleep.

From these perhaps (ere nature bade her die)
Fate snatch'd her early to the pitying sky.
As into air the purer spirits flow,
And sep'rate from their kindred dregs below;
So flew the soul to its congenial place,
Nor left one virtue to redeem her Race.

But thou, false guardian of a charge too good,
Thou, mean deserter of thy brother's blood!

See on these ruby lips the trembling breath,
These cheeks now fading at the blast of death:
Cold is that breast which warm'd the world before,
And those love-darting eyes must roll no more.
Thus, if Eternal justice rules the ball,
Thus shall your wives, and thus your children fall;
On all the line a sudden vengeance waits,
And frequent herses shall besiege your gates.
There passengers shall stand, and pointing say,
(While the long fun'rals blacken all the way)
"Lo these were they, whose souls the Furies steel'd,
And curs'd with hearts unknowing how to yield."
Thus unlamented pass the proud away,
The gaze of fools, and pageant of a day!
So perish all, whose breast ne'er learn'd to glow
For others good, or melt at others woe.

What can atone (oh ever-injur'd shade!)
Thy fate unpity'd, and thy rites unpaid?
No friend's complaint, no kind domestic tear
Pleas'd thy pale ghost, or grac'd thy mournful bier.
By foreign hands thy dying eyes were clos'd,
By foreign hands thy decent limbs compos'd,
By foreign hands thy humble grave adorn'd,
By strangers honour'd, and by strangers mourn'd!
What tho' no friends in sable weeds appear,
Grieve for an hour, perhaps, then mourn a year,
And bear about the mockery of woe
To midnight dances, and the public show?
What tho' no weeping Loves thy ashes grace,
Nor polish'd marble emulate thy face?
What tho' no sacred earth allow thee room,
Nor hallow'd dirge be mutter'd o'er thy tomb?
Yet shall thy grave with rising flow'rs be drest,
And the green turf lie lightly on thy breast:
There shall the morn her earliest tears bestow,
There the first roses of the year shall blow;

While Angels with their silver wings o'ershade
The ground, now sacred by thy reliques made.
  So peaceful rests, without a stone, a name,
What once had beauty, titles, wealth, and fame.
How lov'd, how honour'd once, avails thee not,
To whom related, or by whom begot;
A heap of dust alone remains of thee,
'T is all thou art, and all the proud shall be!
  Poets themselves must fall, like those they sung,
Deaf the prais'd ear, and mute the tuneful tongue.
Ev'n he, whose soul now melts in mournful lays,
Shall shortly want the gen'rous tear he pays;
Then from his closing eyes thy form shall part,
And the last pang shall tear thee from his heart,
Life's idle business at one gasp be o'er,
The Muse forgot, and thou be lov'd no more!

❡ Prologue

MR. ADDISON'S TRAGEDY OF *CATO*

To WAKE the soul by tender strokes of art,
To raise the genius, and to mend the heart;
To make mankind in conscious virtue bold,
Live o'er each scene, and be what they behold:
For this the Tragic Muse first trod the stage,
Commanding tears to stream thro' ev'ry age;
Tyrants no more their savage nature kept,
And foes to virtue wonder'd how they wept.
Our author shuns by vulgar springs to move
The hero's glory, or the virgin's love;
In pitying Love, we but our weakness show,
And wild Ambition well deserves its woe.
Here tears shall flow from a more gen'rous cause,
Such Tears as Patriots shed for dying Laws:
He bids your breasts with ancient ardour rise,
And calls forth Roman drops from British eyes.
Virtue confess'd in human shape he draws,
What Plato thought, and godlike Cato was:
No common object to your sight displays,
But what with pleasure Heav'n itself surveys,
A brave man struggling in the storms of fate,
And greatly falling, with a falling state.
While Cato gives his little Senate laws,
What bosom beats not in his Country's cause?
Who sees him act, but envies ev'ry deed?
Who hears him groan, and does not wish to bleed?
Ev'n when proud Cæsar 'midst triumphal cars,
The spoils of nations, and the pomp of wars,
Ignobly vain and impotently great,
Show'd Rome her Cato's figure drawn in state;

As her dead Father's rev'rend image past,
The pomp was darken'd, and the day o'ercast;
The Triumph ceas'd, tears gush'd from ev'ry eye;
The World's great Victor pass'd unheeded by;
Her last good man dejected Rome ador'd,
And honour'd Cæsar less than Cato's sword.

   Britons, attend: be worth like this approv'd,
And show, you have the virtue to be mov'd.
With honest scorn the first fam'd Cato view'd
Rome learning arts from Greece, whom she subdu'd;
Your scene precariously subsists too long
On French translation, and Italian song.
Dare to have sense yourselves; assert the stage,
Be justly warm'd with your own native rage:
Such Plays alone should win a British ear,
As Cato's self had not disdain'd to hear.

☾ Eloïsa to Abelard

ARGUMENT

ABELARD and Eloïsa flourished in the twelfth Century; they were two of the most distinguished Persons of their age in learning and beauty, but for nothing more famous than for their unfortunate passion. After a long course of calamities, they retired each to a several Convent, and consecrated the remainder of their days to religion. It was many years after this separation, that a letter of Abelard's to a Friend, which contained the history of his misfortune, fell into the hands of Eloïsa. This awakening all her Tenderness, occasioned those celebrated letters (out of which the following is partly extracted) which gives so lively a picture of the struggles of grace and nature, virtue and passion. [Pope.]

IN THESE deep solitudes and awful cells,
Where heav'nly-pensive contemplation dwells,
And ever-musing melancholy reigns;
What means this tumult in a Vestal's veins?
Why rove my thoughts beyond this last retreat?
Why feels my heart its long-forgotten heat?
Yet, yet I love!—From Abelard it came,
And Eloïsa yet must kiss the name.

Dear fatal name! rest ever unreveal'd,
Nor pass these lips in holy silence seal'd:
Hide it, my heart, within that close disguise,
Where mix'd with God's, his lov'd Idea lies:
O write it not my hand—the name appears
Already written—wash it out, my tears!
In vain lost Eloïsa weeps and prays,
Her heart still dictates, and her hand obeys.

Relentless walls! whose darksome round contains
Repentant sighs, and voluntary pains:
Ye rugged rocks! which holy knees have worn;

Ye grots and caverns shagg'd with horrid thorn!
Shrines! where their vigils pale-ey'd virgins keep,
And pitying saints, whose statues learn to weep!
Tho' cold like you, unmov'd and silent grown,
I have not yet forgot myself to stone.
All is not Heav'n's while Abelard has part,
Still rebel nature holds out half my heart;
Nor pray'rs nor fasts its stubborn pulse restrain,
Nor tears for ages taught to flow in vain.

　　Soon as thy letters trembling I unclose,
That well-known name awakens all my woes.
Oh name for ever sad! for ever dear!
Still breath'd in sighs, still usher'd with a tear.
I tremble too, where'er my own I find,
Some dire misfortune follows close behind.
Line after line my gushing eyes o'erflow,
Led thro' a sad variety of woe:
Now warm in love, now with'ring in my bloom,
Lost in a convent's solitary gloom!
There stern Religion quench'd th' unwilling flame,
There died the best of passions, Love and Fame.

　　Yet write, oh write me all, that I may join
Griefs to thy griefs, and echo sighs to thine.
Nor foes nor fortune take this pow'r away;
And is my Abelard less kind than they?
Tears still are mine, and those I need not spare,
Love but demands what else were shed in pray'r;
No happier task these faded eyes pursue;
To read and weep is all they now can do.

　　Then share thy pain, allow that sad relief;
Ah, more than share it, give me all thy grief.
Heav'n first taught letters for some wretch's aid,
Some banish'd lover, or some captive maid;
They live, they speak, they breathe what love inspires,
Warm from the soul, and faithful to its fires,
The virgin's wish without her fears impart,

Excuse the blush, and pour out all the heart,
Speed the soft intercourse from soul to soul,
And waft a sigh from Indus to the Pole.

　　Thou know'st how guiltless first I met thy flame,
When Love approach'd me under Friendship's name;
My fancy form'd thee of angelic kind,
Some emanation of th' all-beauteous Mind.
Those smiling eyes, attemp'ring ev'ry ray,
Shone sweetly lambent with celestial day.
Guiltless I gaz'd; heav'n listen'd while you sung;
And truths divine came mended from that tongue.
From lips like those what precept fail'd to move?
Too soon they taught me 't was no sin to love:
Back thro' the paths of pleasing sense I ran,
Nor wish'd an Angel whom I lov'd a Man.
Dim and remote the joys of saints I see;
Nor envy them that heav'n I lose for thee.

　　How oft, when press'd to marriage, have I said,
Curse on all laws but those which love has made?
Love, free as air, at sight of human ties,
Spreads his light wings, and in a moment flies.
Let wealth, let honour, wait the wedded dame,
August her deed, and sacred be her fame;
Before true passion all those views remove,
Fame, wealth, and honour! what are you to Love?
The jealous God, when we profane his fires,
Those restless passions in revenge inspires,
And bids them make mistaken mortals groan,
Who seek in love for aught but love alone.
Should at my feet the world's great master fall,
Himself, his throne, his world, I 'd scorn 'em all:
Not Cæsar's empress would I deign to prove;
No, make me mistress to the man I love;
If there be yet another name more free,
More fond than mistress, make me that to thee!
Oh! happy state! when souls each other draw,

When love is liberty, and nature law:
All then is full, possessing, and possess'd,
No craving void left aking in the breast:
Ev'n thought meets thought, ere from the lips it part,
And each warm wish springs mutual from the heart.
This sure is bliss (if bliss on earth there be)
And once the lot of Abelard and me.

Alas, how chang'd! what sudden horrors rise!
A naked Lover bound and bleeding lies!
Where, where was Eloïse? her voice, her hand,
Her poniard, had oppos'd the dire command.
Barbarian, stay! that bloody stroke restrain;
The crime was common, common be the pain.
I can no more; by shame, by rage suppress'd,
Let tears, and burning blushes speak the rest.

Canst thou forget that sad, that solemn day,
When victims at yon altar's foot we lay?
Canst thou forget what tears that moment fell,
When, warm in youth, I bade the world farewell?
As with cold lips I kiss'd the sacred veil,
The shrines all trembled, and the lamps grew pale:
Heav'n scarce believ'd the Conquest it survey'd,
And Saints with wonder heard the vows I made.
Yet then, to those dread altars as I drew,
Not on the Cross my eyes were fix'd, but you:
Not grace, or zeal, love only was my call,
And if I lose thy love, I lose my all.
Come! with thy looks, thy words, relieve my woe;
Those still at least are left thee to bestow.
Still on that breast enamour'd let me lie,
Still drink delicious poison from thy eye,
Pant on thy lip, and to thy heart be press'd;
Give all thou canst—and let me dream the rest.
Ah no! instruct me other joys to prize,
With other beauties charm my partial eyes,
Full in my view set all the bright abode,

And make my soul quit Abelard for God.
    Ah, think at least thy flock deserves thy care,
Plants of thy hand, and children of thy pray'r.
From the false world in early youth they fled,
By thee to mountains, wilds, and deserts led.
You rais'd these hallow'd walls; the desert smil'd,
And Paradise was open'd in the Wild.
No weeping orphan saw his father's stores
Our shrines irradiate, or emblaze the floors;
No silver saints, by dying misers giv'n,
Here brib'd the rage of ill-requited heav'n:
But such plain roofs as Piety could raise,
And only vocal with the Maker's praise.
In these lone walls (their days eternal bound)
These moss-grown domes with spiry turrets crown'd,
Where awful arches make a noon-day night,
And the dim windows shed a solemn light;
Thy eyes diffus'd a reconciling ray,
And gleams of glory brighten'd all the day.
But now no face divine contentment wears,
'T is all blank sadness, or continual tears.
See how the force of others' pray'rs I try,
(O pious fraud of am'rous charity!)
But why should I on others' pray'rs depend?
Come thou, my father, brother, husband, friend!
Ah let thy handmaid, sister, daughter move,
And all those tender names in one, thy love!
The darksome pines that o'er yon rocks reclin'd
Wave high, and murmur to the hollow wind,
The wand'ring streams that shine between the hills,
The grots that echo to the tinkling rills,
The dying gales that pant upon the trees,
The lakes that quiver to the curling breeze;
No more these scenes my meditation aid,
Or lull to rest the visionary maid.
But o'er the twilight groves and dusky caves,

Long-sounding aisles, and intermingled graves,
Black Melancholy sits, and round her throws
A death-like silence, and a dead repose:
Her gloomy presence saddens all the scene,
Shades ev'ry flow'r, and darkens ev'ry green,
Deepens the murmur of the falling floods,
And breathes a browner horror on the woods.

Yet here for ever, ever must I stay;
Sad proof how well a lover can obey!
Death, only death, can break the lasting chain:
And here, ev'n then, shall my cold dust remain,
Here all its frailties, all its flames resign,
And wait till 't is no sin to mix with thine
Ah wretch! believ'd the spouse of God in vain,
Confess'd within the slave of love and man.
Assist me, heav'n! but whence arose that pray'r?
Sprung it from piety, or from despair?
Ev'n here, where frozen chastity retires,
Love finds an altar for forbidden fires.
I ought to grieve, but cannot what I ought;
I mourn the lover, not lament the fault;
I view my crime, but kindle at the view,
Repent old pleasures, and solicit new;
Now turn'd to heav'n, I weep my past offence,
Now think of thee, and curse my innocence.
Of all affliction taught a lover yet,
'T is sure the hardest science to forget!
How shall I lose the sin, yet keep the sense,
And love th' offender, yet detest th' offence?
How the dear object from the crime remove,
Or how distinguish penitence from love?
Unequal task! a passion to resign,
For hearts so touch'd, so pierc'd, so lost as mine.
Ere such a soul regains its peaceful state,
How often must it love, how often hate!
How often hope, despair, resent, regret,

Conceal, disdain,—do all things but forget.
But let heav'n seize it, all at once 't is fir'd:
Not touch'd, but rapt; not waken'd, but inspir'd!
Oh come! oh teach me nature to subdue,
Renounce my love, my life, myself—and you.
Fill my fond heart with God alone, for he
Alone can rival, can succeed to thee.

.How happy is the blameless Vestal's lot!
The world forgetting, by the world forgot:
Eternal sunshine of the spotless mind!
Each pray'r accepted, and each wish resign'd;
Labour and rest, that equal periods keep;
"Obedient slumbers that can wake and weep;"
Desires compos'd, affections ever ev'n;
Tears that delight, and sighs that waft to heav'n.
Grace shines around her with serenest beams,
And whisp'ring Angels prompt her golden dreams.
For her th' unfading rose of Eden blooms,
And wings of Seraphs shed divine perfumes,
For her the Spouse prepares the bridal ring,
For her white virgins Hymenæals sing,
To sounds of heav'nly harps she dies away,
And melts in visions of eternal day.

Far other dreams my erring soul employ,
Far other raptures, of unholy joy:
When at the close of each sad, sorrowing day,
Fancy restores what vengeance snatch'd away,
Then conscience sleeps, and leaving nature free,
All my loose soul unbounded springs to thee.
Oh curst, dear horrors of all-conscious night;
How glowing guilt exalts the keen delight!
Provoking Dæmons all restraint remove,
And stir within me ev'ry source of love.
I hear thee, view thee, gaze o'er all thy charms,
And round thy phantom glue my clasping arms.
I wake:—no more I hear, no more I view,

The phantom flies me, as unkind as you.
I call aloud; it hears not what I say:
I stretch my empty arms; it glides away.
To dream once more I close my willing eyes;
Ye soft illusions, dear deceits, arise!
Alas, no more! methinks we wand'ring go
Thro' dreary wastes, and weep each other's woe,
Where round some mould'ring tow'r pale ivy creeps,
And low-brow'd rocks hang nodding o'er the deeps.
Sudden you mount, you beckon from the skies;
Clouds interpose, waves roar, and winds arise.
I shriek, start up, the same sad prospect find,
And wake to all the griefs I left behind.

For thee the fates, severely kind, ordain
A cool suspense from pleasure and from pain;
Thy life a long dead calm of fix'd repose;
No pulse that riots, and no blood that glows.
Still as the sea, ere winds were taught to blow,
Or moving spirit bade the waters flow;
Soft as the slumbers of a saint forgiv'n,
And mild as op'ning gleams of promis'd heav'n.

Come, Abelard! for what hast thou to dread?
The torch of Venus burns not for the dead.
Nature stands check'd; Religion disapproves;
Ev'n thou art cold—yet Eloïsa loves.
Ah hopeless, lasting flames! like those that burn
To light the dead, and warm th' unfruitful urn.

What scenes appear where'er I turn my view?
The dear Ideas, where I fly, pursue,
Rise in the grove, before the altar rise,
Stain all my soul, and wanton in my eyes.
I waste the Matin lamp in sighs for thee,
Thy image steels between my God and me,
Thy voice I seem in ev'ry hymn to hear,
With ev'ry bead I drop too soft a tear.
When from the censer clouds of fragrance roll,

And swelling organs lift the rising soul,
One thought of thee puts all the pomp to flight,
Priests, tapers, temples, swim before my sight:
In seas of flame my plunging soul is drown'd,
While Altars blaze, and Angels tremble round.

While prostrate here in humble grief I lie,
Kind, virtuous drops just gath'ring in my eye,
While praying, trembling, in the dust I roll,
And dawning grace is op'ning on my soul:
Come, if thou dar'st, all charming as thou art!
Oppose thyself to heav'n; dispute my heart;
Come, with one glance of those deluding eyes
Blot out each bright Idea of the skies;
Take back that grace, those sorrows, and those tears;
Take back my fruitless penitence and pray'rs;
Snatch me, just mounting, from the blest abode;
Assist the fiends, and tear me from my God!

No, fly me, fly me, far as Pole from Pole;
Rise Alps between us! and whole oceans roll!
Ah, come not, write not, think not once of me,
Nor share one pang of all I felt for thee.
Thy oaths I quit, thy memory resign;
Forget, renounce me, hate whate'er was mine.
Fair eyes, and tempting looks (which yet I view!)
Long lov'd, ador'd ideas, all adieu!
Oh Grace serene! oh virtue heav'nly fair!
Divine oblivion of low-thoughted care!
Fresh blooming Hope, gay daughter of the sky!
And Faith, our early immortality!
Enter, each mild, each amicable guest;
Receive, and wrap me in eternal rest!

See in her cell sad Eloïsa spread,
Propt on some tomb, a neighbour of the dead.
In each low wind methinks a Spirit calls,
And more than Echoes talk along the walls.
Here, as I watch'd the dying lamps around,

From yonder shrine I heard a hollow sound.
"Come, sister, come! (it said, or seem'd to say)
"Thy place is here, sad sister, come away!
"Once like thyself, I trembled, wept, and pray'd,
"Love's victim then, tho' now a sainted maid:
"But all is calm in this eternal sleep;
"Here grief forgets to groan, and love to weep,
"Ev'n superstition loses ev'ry fear;
"For God, not man, absolves our frailties here."
    I come, I come! prepare your roseate bow'rs,
Celestial palms, and ever-blooming flow'rs.
Thither, where sinners may have rest, I go,
Where flames refin'd in breasts seraphic glow;
Thou, Abelard! the last sad office pay,
And smooth my passage to the realms of day;
See my lips tremble, and my eye-balls roll,
Suck my last breath, and catch my flying soul!
Ah no—in sacred vestments may'st thou stand,
The hallow'd taper trembling in thy hand,
Present the Cross before my lifted eye,
Teach me at once, and learn of me to die.
Ah then, thy once-loved Eloïsa see!
It will be then no crime to gaze on me.
See from my cheek the transient roses fly!
See the last sparkle languish in my eye!
'Till ev'ry motion, pulse, and breath be o'er
And ev'n my Abelard be lov'd no more.
O Death all-eloquent! you only prove
What dust we dote on, when 't is man we love.
    Then too, when fate shall thy fair frame destroy,
(That cause of all my guilt, and all my joy)
In trance ecstatic may thy pangs be drown'd,
Bright clouds descend, and Angels watch thee round,
From op'ning skies may streaming glories shine,
And saints embrace thee with a love like mine.
    May one kind grave unite each hapless name,

And graft my love immortal on thy fame!
Then, ages hence, when all my woes are o'er,
When this rebellious heart shall beat no more;
If ever chance two wand'ring lovers brings
To Paraclete's white walls and silver springs,
O'er the pale marble shall they join their heads,
And drink the falling tears each other sheds;
Then sadly say, with mutual pity mov'd,
"Oh may we never love as these have lov'd!"
From the full choir when loud Hosannas rise,
And swell the pomp of dreadful sacrifice,
Amid that scene if some relenting eye
Glance on the stone where our cold relics lie,
Devotion's self shall steal a thought from heav'n,
One human tear shall drop and be forgiv'n.
And sure, if fate some future bard shall join
In sad similitude of griefs to mine,
Condemn'd whole years in absence to deplore,
And image charms he must behold no more;
Such if there be, who loves so long, so well;
Let him our sad, our tender story tell;
The well-sung woes will sooth my pensive ghost;
He best can paint 'em who shall feel 'em most.

ℂ The Universal Prayer

FATHER of All! in ev'ry Age,
   In ev'ry Clime ador'd,
By Saint, by Savage, and by Sage,
   Jehovah, Jove, or Lord!

Thou Great First Cause, least understood:
   Who all my Sense confin'd
To know but this, that Thou art Good,
   And that myself am blind;

Yet gave me, in this dark Estate,
   To see the Good from Ill;
And binding Nature fast in Fate,
   Left free the Human Will.

What Conscience dictates to be done,
   Or warns me not to do,
This, teach me more than Hell to shun,
   That, more than Heav'n pursue.

What Blessings thy free Bounty gives,
   Let me not cast away;
For God is pay'd when Man receives,
   T' enjoy is to obey.

Yet not to Earth's contracted Span
   Thy Goodness let me bound,
Or think Thee Lord alone of Man,
   When thousand Worlds are round:

Let not this weak, unknowing hand
   Presume thy bolts to throw,
And deal damnation round the land,
   On each I judge thy Foe.

If I am right, thy grace impart,
   Still in the right to stay;

If I am wrong, oh teach my heart
  To find that better way.

Save me alike from foolish Pride,
  Or impious Discontent,
At aught thy Wisdom has deny'd,
  Or aught thy Goodness lent.

Teach me to feel another's Woe,
  To hide the Fault I see;
That Mercy I to others show,
  That Mercy show to me.

Mean tho' I am, not wholly so,
  Since quick'ned by thy Breath;
Oh lead me wheresoe'er I go,
  Thro' this day's Life or Death.

This day, be Bread and Peace my Lot:
  All else beneath the Sun,
Thou know'st if best bestow'd or not;
  And let Thy Will be done.

To thee, whose Temple is all Space,
  Whose Altar Earth, Sea, Skies,
One Chorus let all Being raise,
  All Nature's Incense rise!

ℭ An Essay on Man

H. ST. JOHN LORD BOLINGBROKE

ARGUMENT OF EPISTLE I

OF THE NATURE AND STATE OF MAN,
WITH RESPECT TO THE UNIVERSE

Of Man in the abstract. I. That we can judge only with regard to our own system, being ignorant of the relations of systems and things, v. 17, &c. II. That Man is not to be deemed imperfect, but a Being suited to his place and rank in the creation, agreeable to the general Order of things, and conformable to Ends and Relations to him unknown, v. 35, &c. III. That it is partly upon his ignorance of future events, and partly upon the hope of a future state, that all his happiness in the present depends, v. 77, &c. IV. The pride of aiming at more knowledge, and pretending to more Perfection, the cause of Man's error and misery. The impiety of putting himself in the place of God, and judging of the fitness or unfitness, perfection or imperfection, justice or injustice of his dispensations, v. 109, &c. V. The absurdity of conceiting himself the final cause of the creation, or expecting that perfection in the moral world, which is not in the natural, v. 131, &c. VI. The unreasonableness of his complaints against Providence, while on the one hand he demands the Perfections of the Angels, and on the other the bodily qualifications of the Brutes; though, to possess any of the sensitive faculties in a higher degree, would render him miserable, v. 173, &c. VII. That throughout the whole visible world, an universal order and gradation in the sensual and mental faculties is observed, which causes a subordination of creature to creature, and of all creatures to Man. The gradations of sense, instinct,

thought, reflection, reason; that Reason alone countervails
all the other faculties, v. 207. VIII. How much further this
order and subordination of living creatures may extend, above
and below us; were any part of which broken, not that part
only, but the whole connected creation must be destroyed,
v. 233. IX. The extravagance, madness, and pride of such a
desire, v. 250. X. The consequence of all, the absolute submission due to Providence, both as to our present and future
state, v. 281, &c. to the end.

EPISTLE I

AWAKE, my ST. JOHN! leave all meaner things
To low ambition, and the pride of Kings.
Let us (since Life can little more supply
Than just to look about us and to die)
Expatiate free o'er all this scene of Man;
A mighty maze! but not without a plan;
A Wild, where weeds and flow'rs promiscuous shoot;
Or Garden, tempting with forbidden fruit.
Together let us beat this ample field,
Try what the open, what the covert yield;
The latent tracts, the giddy heights, explore
Of all who blindly creep, or sightless soar;
Eye Nature's walks, shoot Folly as it flies,
And catch the Manners living as they rise;
Laugh where we must, be candid where we can;
But vindicate the ways of God to Man.

    I. Say first, of God above, or Man below,
What can we reason, but from what we know?
Of Man, what see we but his station here,
From which to reason, or to which refer?
Thro' worlds unnumber'd tho' the God be known,
'T is ours to trace him only in our own.
He, who thro' vast immensity can pierce,

See worlds on worlds compose one universe,
Observe how system into system runs,
What other planets circle other suns,
What vary'd Being peoples ev'ry star,
May tell why Heav'n has made us as we are.
But of this frame the bearings, and the ties,
The strong connexions, nice dependencies,
Gradations just, has thy pervading soul
Look'd thro'? or can a part contain the whole?

Is the great chain, that draws all to agree,
And drawn supports, upheld by God, or thee?
II. Presumptuous Man! the reason wouldst thou find,
Why form'd so weak, so little, and so blind?
First, if thou canst, the harder reason guess,
Why form'd no weaker, blinder, and no less?
Ask of thy mother earth, why oaks are made
Taller or stronger than the weeds they shade?
Or ask of yonder argent fields above,
Why Jove's satellites are less than Jove?

Of Systems possible, if 't is confest
That Wisdom infinite must form the best,
Where all must full or not coherent be,
And all that rises, rise in due degree;
Then, in the scale of reas'ning life, 't is plain,
There must be, somewhere, such a rank as Man:
And all the question (wrangle e'er so long)
Is only this, if God has plac'd him wrong?

Respecting Man, whatever wrong we call,
May, must be right, as relative to all.
In human works, tho' labour'd on with pain,
A thousand movements scarce one purpose gain;
In God's, one single can its end produce;
Yet serves to second too some other use.
So Man, who here seems principal alone,
Perhaps acts second to some sphere unknown,
Touches some wheel, or verges to some goal;

'T is but a part we see, and not a whole.
When the proud steed shall know why Man restrains
His fiery course, or drives him o'er the plains:
When the dull Ox, why now he breaks the clod,
Is now a victim, and now Ægypt's God:
Then shall Man's pride and dulness comprehend
His actions', passions', being's, use and end;
Why doing, suff'ring, check'd, impell'd; and why
This hour a slave, the next a deity.

Then say not Man 's imperfect, Heav'n in fault;
Say rather, Man 's as perfect as he ought:
His knowledge measur'd to his state and place;
His time a moment, and a point his space.
If to be perfect in a certain sphere,
What matter, soon or late, or here or there?
The blest to day is as completely so,
As who began a thousand years ago.

III. Heav'n from all creatures hides the book of Fate,
All but the page prescrib'd, their present state:
From brutes what men, from men what spirits know:
Or who could suffer Being here below?
The lamb thy riot dooms to bleed to-day,
Had he thy Reason, would he skip and play?
Pleas'd to the last, he crops the flow'ry food,
And licks the hand just rais'd to shed his blood.
Oh blindness to the future! kindly giv'n,
That each may fill the circle mark'd by Heav'n:
Who sees with equal eye, as God of all,
A hero perish, or a sparrow fall,
Atoms or systems into ruin hurl'd,
And now a bubble burst, and now a world.

Hope humbly then; with trembling pinions soar;
Wait the great teacher Death; and God adore.
What future bliss, he gives not thee to know,
But gives that Hope to be thy blessing now.
Hope springs eternal in the human breast:

Man never Is, but always To be blest:
The soul, uneasy and confin'd from home,
Rests and expatiates in a life to come.

　Lo, the poor Indian! whose untutor'd mind
Sees God in clouds, or hears him in the wind:
His soul, proud Science never taught to stray
Far as the solar walk, or milky way;
Yet simple Nature to his hope has giv'n,
Behind the cloud-topt hill, an humbler heav'n;
Some safer world in depth of woods embrac'd,
Some happier island in the watry waste,
Where slaves once more their native land behold,
No fiends torment, no Christians thirst for gold.
To Be, contents his natural desire,
He asks no Angel's wing, no Seraph's fire;
But thinks, admitted to that equal sky,
His faithful dog shall bear him company.

　IV. Go, wiser thou! and, in thy scale of sense,
Weigh thy Opinion against Providence;
Call imperfection what thou fancy'st such,
Say, here he gives too little, there too much:
Destroy all Creatures for thy sport or gust,
Yet cry, If Man 's unhappy, God 's unjust;
If Man alone engross not Heav'n's high care,
Alone made perfect here, immortal there:
Snatch from his hand the balance and the rod,
Re-judge his justice, be the GOD of GOD.
In Pride, in reas'ning Pride, our error lies;
All quit their sphere, and rush into the skies.
Pride still is aiming at the blest abodes,
Men would be Angels, Angels would be Gods.
Aspiring to be Gods, if Angels fell,
Aspiring to be Angels, Men rebel:
And who but wishes to invert the laws
Of ORDER, sins against th' Eternal Cause.

　V. Ask for what end the heav'nly bodies shine,

Earth for whose use? Pride answers, " 'T is for mine:
For me kind Nature wakes her genial Pow'r,
Suckles each herb, and spreads out ev'ry flow'r;
Annual for me, the grape, the rose renew
The juice nectareous, and the balmy dew;
For me, the mine a thousand treasures brings;
For me, health gushes from a thousand springs;
Seas roll to waft me, suns to light me rise;
My foot-stool earth, my canopy the skies."
  But errs not Nature from this gracious end,
From burning suns when livid deaths descend,
When earthquakes swallow, or when tempests sweep
Towns to one grave, whole nations to the deep?
"No, ('t is reply'd) the first Almighty Cause
Acts not by partial, but by gen'ral laws;
Th' exceptions few; some change since all began:
And what created perfect?"—Why then Man?
If the great end be human Happiness,
Then Nature deviates; and can Man do less?
As much that end a constant course requires
Of show'rs and sun-shine, as of Man's desires;
As much eternal springs and cloudless skies,
As Men for ever temp'rate, calm, and wise.
If plagues or earthquakes break not Heav'n's design,
Why then a Borgia, or a Catiline?
Who knows but he, whose hand the lightning forms,
Who heaves old Ocean, and who wings the storms;
Pours fierce Ambition in a Cæsar's mind,
Or turns young Ammon loose to scourge mankind?
From pride, from pride, our very reas'ning springs;
Account for moral, as for nat'ral things:
Why charge we Heav'n in those, in these acquit?
In both, to reason right is to submit.
  Better for Us, perhaps, it might appear,
Were there all harmony, all virtue here;
That never air or ocean felt the wind;

That never passion discompos'd the mind.
But ALL subsists by elemental strife;
And Passions are the elements of Life.
The gen'ral ORDER, since the whole began,
Is kept in Nature, and is kept in Man.

VI. What would this Man? Now upward will he soar,
And little less than Angel, would be more;
Now looking downwards, just as griev'd appears
To want the strength of bulls, the fur of bears.
Made for his use all creatures if he call,
Say what their use, had he the pow'rs of all?
Nature to these, without profusion, kind,
The proper organs, proper pow'rs assign'd;
Each seeming want compensated of course,
Here with degrees of swiftness, there of force;
All in exact proportion to the state;
Nothing to add, and nothing to abate.
Each beast, each insect, happy in its own:
Is Heav'n unkind to Man, and Man alone?
Shall he alone, whom rational we call,
Be pleas'd with nothing, if not bless'd with all?

The bliss of Man (could Pride that blessing find)
Is not to act or think beyond mankind;
No pow'rs of body or of soul to share,
But what his nature and his state can bear.
Why has not Man a microscopic eye?
For this plain reason, Man is not a Fly.
Say what the use, were finer optics giv'n,
T' inspect a mite, not comprehend the heav'n?
Or touch, if tremblingly alive all o'er,
To smart and agonize at every pore?
Or quick effluvia darting thro' the brain,
Die of a rose in aromatic pain?
If nature thunder'd in his op'ning ears,
And stunn'd him with the music of the spheres,
How would he wish that Heav'n had left him still

The whisp'ring Zephyr, and the purling rill?
Who finds not Providence all good and wise,
Alike in what it gives, and what denies?

VII. Far as Creation's ample range extends,
The scale of sensual, mental pow'rs ascends:
Mark how it mounts, to Man's imperial race,
From the green myriads in the peopled grass:
What modes of sight betwixt each wide extreme,
The mole's dim curtain, and the lynx's beam:
Of smell, the headlong lioness between,
And hound sagacious on the tainted green:
Of hearing, from the life that fills the Flood,
To that which warbles thro' the vernal wood:
The spider's touch, how exquisitely fine!
Feels at each thread, and lives along the line:
In the nice bee, what sense so subtly true
From pois'nous herbs extracts the healing dew?
How Instinct varies in the grov'ling swine,
Compar'd, half-reas'ning elephant, with thine!
'Twixt that, and Reason, what a nice barrier,
For ever sep'rate, yet for ever near!
Remembrance and Reflection how ally'd;
What thin partitions Sense from Thought divide:
And Middle natures, how they long to join,
Yet never pass th' insuperable line!
Without this just gradation, could they be
Subjected, these to those, or all to thee?
The pow'rs of all subdu'd by thee alone,
Is not thy Reason all these pow'rs in one?

VIII. See, thro' this air, this ocean, and this earth,
All matter quick, and bursting into birth.
Above, how high, progressive life may go!
Around, how wide! how deep extend below!
Vast chain of Being! which from God began,
Natures ethereal, human, angel, man,
Beast, bird, fish, insect, what no eye can see,

No glass can reach; from Infinite to thee,
From thee to Nothing.—On superior pow'rs
Were we to press, inferior might on ours:
Or in the full creation leave a void,
Where, one step broken, the great scale's destroy'd:
From Nature's chain whatever link you strike,
Tenth or ten thousandth, breaks the chain alike.

And, if each system in gradation roll
Alike essential to th' amazing Whole,
The least confusion but in one, not all
That system only, but the Whole must fall.
Let Earth unbalanc'd from her orbit fly,
Planets and Suns run lawless thro' the sky;
Let ruling angels from their spheres be hurl'd,
Being on Being wreck'd, and world on world;
Heav'n's whole foundations to their centre nod,
And Nature tremble to the throne of God.
All this dread ORDER break—for whom? for thee?
Vile worm!—Oh Madness! Pride! Impiety!

IX. What if the foot, ordain'd the dust to tread,
Or hand, to toil, aspir'd to be the head?
What if the head, the eye, or ear repin'd
To serve mere engines to the ruling Mind?
Just as absurd for any part to claim
To be another, in this gen'ral frame:
Just as absurd, to mourn the tasks or pains,
The great directing MIND of ALL ordains.

All are but parts of one stupendous whole,
Whose body Nature is, and God the soul;
That, chang'd thro' all, and yet in all the same;
Great in the earth, as in th' ethereal frame;
Warms in the sun, refreshes in the breeze,
Glows in the stars, and blossoms in the trees,
Lives thro' all life, extends thro' all extent,
Spreads undivided, operates unspent;
Breathes in our soul, informs our mortal part,

As full, as perfect, in a hair, as heart:
As full, as perfect, in vile Man that mourns,
As the rapt Seraph that adores and burns:
To him no high, no low, no great, no small;
He fills, he bounds, connects, and equals all.

    X. Cease then, nor ORDER Imperfection name:
Our proper bliss depends on what we blame.
Know thy own point: This kind, this due degree
Of blindness, weakness, Heav'n bestows on thee.
Submit.—In this, or any other sphere,
Secure to be as blest as thou canst bear:
Safe in the hand of one disposing Pow'r,
Or in the natal, or the mortal hour.
All Nature is but Art, unknown to thee;
All Chance, Direction, which thou canst not see;
All Discord, Harmony not understood;
All partial Evil, universal Good:
And, spite of Pride, in erring Reason's spite,
One truth is clear, WHATEVER IS, IS RIGHT.

ARGUMENT OF EPISTLE II

OF THE NATURE AND STATE OF MAN WITH RESPECT TO HIMSELF, AS AN INDIVIDUAL

    I. The business of Man not to pry into God, but to study himself. His Middle Nature; his Powers and Frailties, v. 1 to 19. The Limits of his Capacity, v. 19, &c. II. The two Principles of Man, Self-love and Reason, both necessary, v. 53, &c. Self-love the stronger, and why, v. 67, &c. Their end the same, v. 81, &c. III. The Passions, and their use, v. 93 to 130. The predominant Passion, and its force, v. 132 to 160. Its Necessity, in directing Men to different purposes, v. 165, &c. Its providential Use, in fixing our Principle, and ascertaining our Virtue, v. 177. IV. Virtue and Vice joined in our mixed Nature; the limits near, yet the things separate and evident: What is the Office of Reason, v. 202 to 216. V. How odious Vice in itself, and how we deceive ourselves into it, v. 217. VI. That, however, the Ends of Providence and general Good are answered in our Passions and Imperfections, v. 238, &c. How usefully these are distributed to all Orders of Men, v. 241. How useful they are to Society, v. 251. And to the Individuals, v. 263. In every state, and every age of life, v. 273, &c.

EPISTLE II

I. Know then thyself, presume not God to scan;
The proper study of Mankind is Man.
Plac'd on this isthmus of a middle state,
A Being darkly wise, and rudely great:
With too much knowledge for the Sceptic side,
With too much weakness for the Stoic's pride,
He hangs between; in doubt to act, or rest;
In doubt to deem himself a God, or Beast;
In doubt his Mind or Body to prefer;
Born but to die, and reas'ning but to err;
Alike in ignorance, his reason such,
Whether he thinks too little, or too much:
Chaos of Thought and Passion, all confus'd;
Still by himself abus'd, or disabus'd;
Created half to rise, and half to fall;
Great lord of all things, yet a prey to all;
Sole judge of Truth, in endless Error hurl'd:
The glory, jest, and riddle of the world!

Go, wond'rous creature! mount where Science guides,
Go, measure earth, weigh air, and state the tides;
Instruct the planets in what orbs to run,
Correct old Time, and regulate the Sun;

Go, soar with Plato to th' empyreal sphere,
To the first good, first perfect, and first fair;
Or tread the mazy round his follow'rs trod,
And quitting sense call imitating God;
As Eastern priests in giddy circles run,
And turn their heads to imitate the Sun.
Go, teach Eternal Wisdom how to rule—
Then drop into thyself, and be a fool!

Superior beings, when of late they saw
A mortal Man unfold all Nature's law,
Admir'd such wisdom in an earthly shape,
And shew'd a NEWTON as we shew an Ape.

Could he, whose rules the rapid Comet bind,
Describe or fix one movement of his Mind?
Who saw its fires here rise, and there descend,
Explain his own beginning, or his end?
Alas what wonder! Man's superior part
Uncheck'd may rise, and climb from art to art:
But when his own great work is but begun,
What Reason weaves, by Passion is undone.

Trace Science then, with Modesty thy guide;
First strip off all her equipage of Pride;
Deduct what is but Vanity, or Dress,
Or Learning's Luxury, or Idleness;
Or tricks to shew the stretch of human brain,
Mere curious pleasure, or ingenious pain;
Expunge the whole, or lop th' excrescent parts
Of all our Vices have created Arts;
Then see how little the remaining sum,
Which serv'd the past, and must the times to come!

II. Two Principles in human nature reign;
Self-love, to urge, and Reason, to restrain;
Nor this a good, nor that a bad we call,
Each works its end, to move or govern all:
And to their proper operation still,
Ascribe all Good; to their improper, Ill.

Self-love, the spring of motion, acts* the soul;
Reason's comparing balance rules the whole.
Man, but for that, no action could attend,
And but for this, were active to no end:
Fix'd like a plant on his peculiar spot,
To draw nutrition, propagate, and rot;
Or, meteor-like, flame lawless thro' the void,
Destroying others, by himself destroy'd.

Most strength the moving principle requires;
Active its task, it prompts, impels, inspires.
Sedate and quiet the comparing lies,
Form'd but to check, delib'rate, and advise.
Self-love still stronger, as its objects nigh;
Reason 's at distance, and in prospect lie:
That sees immediate good by present sense;
Reason, the future and the consequence.
Thicker than arguments, temptations throng,
At best more watchful this, but that more strong.
The action of the stronger to suspend,
Reason still use, to Reason still attend.
Attention, habit and experience gains;
Each strengthens Reason, and Self-love restrains.

Let subtle schoolmen teach these friends to fight,
More studious to divide than to unite;
And Grace and Virtue, Sense and Reason split,
With all the rash dexterity of wit.
Wits, just like Fools, at war about a name,
Have full as oft no meaning, or the same.
Self-love and Reason to one end aspire,
Pain their aversion, Pleasure their desire;
But greedy That, its object would devour,
This taste the honey, and not wound the flow'r;
Pleasure, or wrong or rightly understood,
Our greatest evil, or our greatest good.

III. Modes of Self-love the Passions we may call;

* Actuates.

'T is real good, or seeming, moves them all:
But since not ev'ry good we can divide,
And Reason bids us for our own provide;
Passions, tho' selfish, if their means be fair,
List under Reason, and deserve her care;
Those, that imparted, court a nobler aim,
Exalt their kind, and take some Virtue's name.

In lazy Apathy let Stoics boast
Their Virtue fix'd; 't is fix'd as in a frost;
Contracted all, retiring to the breast;
But strength of mind is Exercise, not Rest:
The rising tempest puts in act the soul,
Parts it may ravage, but preserves the whole.
On life's vast ocean diversely we sail,
Reason the card,* but Passion is the gale;
Nor God alone in the still calm we find,
He mounts the storm, and walks upon the wind.

Passions, like Elements, tho' born to fight,
Yet, mix'd and soften'd, in his work unite:
These 't is enough to temper and employ;
But what composes Man, can Man destroy?
Suffice that Reason keep to Nature's road,
Subject, compound them, follow her and God.
Love, Hope, and Joy, fair Pleasure's smiling train,
Hate, Fear, and Grief, the family of Pain,
These mix'd with art, and to due bounds confin'd,
Make and maintain the balance of the mind:
The lights and shades, whose well accorded strife
Gives all the strength and colour of our life.

Pleasures are ever in our hands or eyes;
And when in act they cease, in prospect rise:
Present to grasp, and future still to find,
The whole employ of body and of mind.
All spread their charms, but charm not all alike;
On diff'rent senses diff'rent objects strike;

* Compass.

Hence diff'rent Passions more or less inflame,
As strong or weak, the organs of the frame;
And hence one MASTER PASSION in the breast,
Like Aaron's serpent, swallows up the rest.

As Man, perhaps, the moment of his breath,
Receives the lurking principle of death;
The young disease, that must subdue at length,
Grows with his growth, and strengthens with his strength:
So, cast and mingled with his very frame,
The Mind's disease, its RULING PASSION came;
Each vital humour which should feed the whole,
Soon flows to this, in body and in soul:
Whatever warms the heart, or fills the head,
As the mind opens, and its functions spread,
Imagination plies her dang'rous art,
And pours it all upon the peccant part.

Nature its mother, Habit is its nurse;
Wit, Spirit, Faculties, but make it worse;
Reason itself but gives it edge and pow'r;
As Heav'n's blest beam turns vinegar more sour.

We, wretched subjects, tho' to lawful sway,
In this weak queen some fav'rite still obey:
Ah! if she lend not arms, as well as rules,
What can she more than tell us we are fools?
Teach us to mourn our Nature, not to mend,
A sharp accuser, but a helpless friend!
Or from a judge turn pleader, to persuade
The choice we make, or justify it made;
Proud of an easy conquest all along,
She but removes weak passions for the strong:
So, when small humours gather to a gout,
The doctor fancies he has driv'n them out.

Yes, Nature's road must ever be preferr'd;
Reason is here no guide, but still a guard:
'T is hers to rectify, not overthrow,
And treat this passion more as friend than foe:

A mightier Pow'r the strong direction sends,
And sev'ral Men impels to sev'ral ends:
Like varying winds, by other passions tost,
This drives them constant to a certain coast.
Let pow'r or knowledge, gold or glory, please,
Or (oft more strong than all) the love of ease;
Thro' life 't is follow'd, ev'n at life's expense;
The merchant's toil, the sage's indolence,
The monk's humility, the hero's pride,
All, all alike, find Reason on their side.

Th' Eternal Art educing good from ill,
Grafts on this Passion our best principle:
'T is thus the Mercury of Man is fix'd,
Strong grows the Virtue with his nature mix'd;
The dross cements what else were too refin'd,
And in one int'rest body acts with mind.

As fruits, ungrateful to the planter's care,
On savage stocks inserted, learn to bear;
The surest Virtues thus from Passions shoot,
Wild Nature's vigour working at the root.
What crops of wit and honesty appear
From spleen, from obstinacy, hate, or fear!
See anger, zeal and fortitude supply;
Ev'n av'rice, prudence; sloth, philosophy;
Lust, thro' some certain strainers well refin'd,
Is gentle love, and charms all womankind;
Envy, to which th' ignoble mind 's a slave,
Is emulation in the learn'd or brave;
Nor Virtue, male or female, can we name,
But what will grow on Pride, or grow on Shame.

Thus Nature gives us (let it check our pride)
The virtue nearest to our vice ally'd:
Reason the bias turns to good from ill,
And Nero reigns a Titus, if he will.
The fiery soul abhorr'd in Catiline,
In Decius charms, in Curtius is divine:

The same ambition can destroy or save,
And makes a patriot as it makes a knave.

    This light and darkness in our chaos join'd,
What shall divide? The God within the mind:

    Extremes in Nature equal ends produce,
In Man they join to some mysterious use;
Tho' each by turns the other's bound invade,
As, in some well-wrought picture, light and shade,
And oft so mix, the diff'rence is too nice
Where ends the Virtue, or begins the Vice.

    Fools! who from hence into the notion fall,
That Vice or Virtue there is none at all.
If white and black blend, soften, and unite
A thousand ways, is there no black or white?
Ask your own heart, and nothing is so plain;
'T is to mistake them costs the time and pain.

    Vice is a monster of so frightful mien,
As, to be hated, needs but to be seen;
Yet seen too oft, familiar with her face,
We first endure, then pity, then embrace.
But where th' Extreme of Vice, was ne'er agreed:
Ask where 's the North? at York, 't is on the Tweed;
In Scotland, at the Orcades; and there,
At Greenland, Zembla, or the Lord knows where.
No creature owns it in the first degree,
But thinks his neighbour further gone than he;
Ev'n those who dwell beneath its very zone,
Or never feel the rage, or never own;
What happier natures shrink at with affright,
The hard inhabitant contends is right.

    Virtuous and vicious ev'ry Man must be,
Few in th' extreme, but all in the degree;
The rogue and fool by fits is fair and wise;
And ev'n the best, by fits, what they despise.
'T is but by parts we follow good or ill;
For, Vice or Virtue, Self directs it still;

Each individual seeks a sev'ral goal;
But HEAV'N's great view is One, and that the Whole.
That counter-works each folly and caprice;
That disappoints th' effect of ev'ry vice;
That, happy frailties to all ranks apply'd,
Shame to the virgin, to the matron pride,
Fear to the statesman, rashness to the chief,
To kings presumption, and to crowds belief:
That, Virtue's ends from Vanity can raise,
Which seeks no int'rest, no reward but praise;
And build on wants, and on defects of mind,
The joy, the peace, the glory of Mankind.

Heav'n forming each on other to depend,
A master, or a servant, or a friend,
Bids each on other for assistance call,
Till one Man's weakness grows the strength of all.
Wants, frailties, passions, closer still ally
The common int'rest, or endear the tie.
To these we owe true friendship, love sincere,
Each home-felt joy that life inherits here;
Yet from the same we learn, in its decline,
Those joys, those loves, those int'rests to resign;
Taught half by Reason, half by mere decay,
To welcome death, and calmly pass away.

Whate'er the Passion, knowledge, fame, or pelf,
Not one will change his neighbour with himself.
The learn'd is happy nature to explore,
The fool is happy that he knows no more;
The rich is happy in the plenty giv'n,
The poor contents him with the care of Heav'n.
See the blind beggar dance, the cripple sing,
The sot a hero, lunatic a king;
The starving chemist in his golden views
Supremely blest, the poet in his Muse.

See some strange comfort ev'ry state attend,
And Pride bestow'd on all, a common friend;

See some fit Passion ev'ry age supply,
Hope travels thro', nor quits us when we die.
   Behold the child, by Nature's kindly law,
Pleas'd with a rattle, tickled with a straw:
Some livelier play-thing gives his youth delight,
A little louder, but as empty quite:
Scarfs, garters, gold, amuse his riper stage,
And beads and pray'r-books are the toys of age:
Pleas'd with this bauble still, as that before;
'Till tir'd he sleeps, and Life's poor play is o'er.
   Mean-while Opinion gilds with varying rays
Those painted clouds that beautify our days;
Each want of happiness by hope supply'd,
And each vacuity of sense by Pride:
These build as fast as knowledge can destroy;
In Folly's cup still laughs the bubble, joy;
One prospect lost, another still we gain;
And not a vanity is giv'n in vain;
Ev'n mean Self-love becomes, by force divine,
The scale to measure others' wants by thine.
See! and confess, one comfort still must rise,
'T is this, Tho' Man's a fool, yet God is WISE.

ARGUMENT OF EPISTLE III

OF THE NATURE AND STATE OF MAN
WITH RESPECT TO SOCIETY

I. The whole Universe one system of Society, v. 7, &c.
Nothing made wholly for itself, nor yet wholly for another,
v. 27. The happiness of Animals mutual, v. 49. II. Reason
or Instinct operate alike to the good of each Individual, v. 79.
Reason or Instinct operate also to Society, in all animals,
v. 109. III. How far Society carried by Instinct, v. 115. How
much farther by Reason, v. 128. IV. Of that which is called

the State of Nature, v. 144. Reason instructed by Instinct in
the invention of Arts, v. 166, and in the Forms of Society,
v. 176. V. Origin of Political Societies, v. 196. Origin of Monarchy, v. 207. Patriarchal government, v. 212. VI. Origin of
true Religion and Government, from the same principle, of
Love, v. 231, &c. Origin of Superstition and Tyranny, from
the same principle, of Fear, v. 237, &c. The Influence of Self-
love operating to the social and public Good, v. 266. Restoration of true Religion and Government on their first principle,
v. 285. Mixt Government, v. 288. Various Forms of each,
and the true end of all, v. 300, &c.

EPISTLE III

   I. HERE then we rest: "The Universal Cause
Acts to one end, but acts by various laws."
In all the madness of superfluous health,
The trim of pride, the impudence of wealth,
Let this great truth be present night and day;
But most be present, if we preach or pray.
   Look round our World; behold the chain of Love
Combining all below and all above.
See plastic Nature working to this end,
The single atoms each to other tend,
Attract, attracted to, the next in place
Form'd and impell'd its neighbour to embrace.
See Matter next, with various life endu'd
Press to one centre still, the gen'ral Good.
See dying vegetables life sustain,
See life dissolving vegetate again:
All forms that perish other forms supply,
(By turns we catch the vital breath, and die,)
Like bubbles on the sea of Matter born,
They rise, they break, and to that sea return.
Nothing is foreign: Parts relate to whole;

One all-extending, all-preserving Soul
Connects each being, greatest with the least;
Made Beast in aid of Man, and Man of Beast;
All serv'd, all serving: nothing stands alone;
The chain holds on, and where it ends, unknown.

   Has God, thou fool! work'd solely for thy good,
Thy joy, thy pastime, thy attire, thy food?
Who for thy table feeds the wanton fawn,
For him as kindly spread the flow'ry lawn:
Is it for thee the lark ascends and sings?
Joy tunes his voice, joy elevates his wings.
Is it for thee the linnet pours his throat?
Loves of his own and raptures swell the note.
The bounding steed you pompously bestride,
Shares with his lord the pleasure and the pride.
Is thine alone the seed that strews the plain?
The birds of heav'n shall vindicate their grain.
Thine the full harvest of the golden year?
Part pays, and justly, the deserving steer:
The hog, that ploughs not nor obeys thy call,
Lives on the labours of this lord of all.

   Know, Nature's children all divide her care;
The fur that warms a monarch, warm'd a bear.
While Man exclaims, "See all things for my use!"
"See man for mine!" replies a pamper'd goose:
And just as short of reason he must fall,
Who thinks all made for one, not one for all.

   Grant that the pow'rful still the weak controul;
Be Man the Wit and Tyrant of the whole:
Nature that Tyrant checks; he only knows,
And helps, another creature's wants and woes.
Say, will the falcon, stooping from above,
Smit with her varying plumage, spare the dove?
Admires the jay the insect's gilded wings?
Or hears the hawk when Philomela sings?
Man cares for all: to birds he gives his woods,

To beasts his pastures, and to fish his floods;
For some his Int'rest prompts him to provide,
For more his pleasure, yet for more his pride:
All feed on one vain Patron, and enjoy
Th' extensive blessing of his luxury.
That very life his learned hunger craves,
He saves from famine, from the savage saves;
Nay, feasts the animal he dooms his feast,
And, 'till he ends the being, makes it blest;
Which sees no more the stroke, or feels the pain,
Than favour'd Man by touch ethereal slain.
The creature had his feast of life before;
Thou too must perish, when thy feast is o'er!

To each unthinking being Heav'n, a friend,
Gives not the useless knowledge of its end:
To Man imparts it; but with such a view
As, while he dreads it, makes him hope it too:
The hour conceal'd, and so remote the fear,
Death still draws nearer, never seeming near.
Great standing miracle! that Heav'n assign'd
Its only thinking thing this turn of mind.

II. Whether with Reason, or with Instinct blest,
Know, all enjoy that pow'r which suits them best;
To bliss alike by that direction tend,
And find the means proportion'd to their end.
Say, where full Instinct is th' unerring guide,
What Pope or Council can they need beside?
Reason, however able, cool at best,
Cares not for service, or but serves when prest,
Stays 'till we call, and then not often near;
But honest Instinct comes a volunteer,
Sure never to o'er-shoot, but just to hit;
While still too wide or short is human Wit;
Sure by quick Nature happiness to gain,
Which heavier Reason labours at in vain,
This too serves always, Reason never long;

One must go right, the other may go wrong.
See then the acting and comparing pow'rs
One in their nature, which are two in ours;
And Reason raise o'er Instinct as you can,
In this 't is God directs, in that 't is Man.

 Who taught the nations of the field and flood
To shun their poison, and to choose their food?
Prescient, the tides or tempests to withstand,
Build on the wave, or arch beneath the sand?
Who made the spider parallels design,
Sure as Demoivre, without rule or line?
Who did the stork, Columbus-like, explore
Heav'ns not his own, and worlds unknown before?
Who calls the council, states the certain day,
Who forms the phalanx, and who points the way?

 III. God in the nature of each being founds
Its proper bliss, and sets its proper bounds:
But as he fram'd a Whole, the Whole to bless,
On mutual Wants built mutual Happiness:
So from the first, eternal ORDER ran,
And creature link'd to creature, man to man.
Whate'er of life all-quick'ning æther keeps,
Or breathes thro' air, or shoots beneath the deeps,
Or pours profuse on earth, one nature feeds
The vital flame, and swells the genial seeds.
Not Man alone, but all that roam the wood,
Or wing the sky, or roll along the flood,
Each loves itself, but not itself alone,
Each sex desires alike, 'till two are one.
Nor ends the pleasure with the fierce embrace;
They love themselves, a third time, in their race.
Thus beast and bird their common charge attend,
The mothers nurse it, and the sires defend;
The young dismiss'd to wander earth or air,
There stops the Instinct, and there ends the care;
The link dissolves, each seeks a fresh embrace,

Another love succeeds, another race.
A longer care Man's helpless kind demands;
That longer care contracts more lasting bands:
Reflection, Reason, still the ties improve,
At once extend the int'rest, and the love;
With choice we fix, with sympathy we burn;
Each Virtue in each Passion takes its turn;
And still new needs, new helps, new habits rise,
That graft benevolence on charities.
Still as one brood, and as another rose,
These nat'ral love maintai..'d, habitual those:
The last, scarce ripen'd into perfect Man,
Saw helpless him from whom their life began:
Mem'ry and fore-cast just returns engage,
That pointed back to youth, this on to age;
While pleasure, gratitude, and hope, combin'd,
Still spread the int'rest, and preserv'd the kind.
  IV. Nor think, in NATURE'S STATE they blindly trod;
The state of Nature was the reign of God:
Self-love and Social at her birth began,
Union the bond of all things, and of Man.
Pride then was not; nor Arts, that Pride to aid;
Man walk'd with beast, joint tenant of the shade;
The same his table, and the same his bed;
No murder cloth'd him, and no murder fed.
In the same temple, the resounding wood,
All vocal beings hymn'd their equal God:
The shrine with gore unstain'd, with gold undrest,
Unbrib'd, unbloody, stood the blameless priest:
Heav'n's attribute was Universal Care,
And Man's prerogative to rule, but spare.
Ah! how unlike the man of times to come!
Of half that live the butcher and the tomb;
Who, foe to Nature, hears the gen'ral groan,
Murders their species, and betrays his own.
But just disease to luxury succeeds,

And ev'ry death its own avenger breeds;
The Fury-passions from that blood began,
And turn'd on Man a fiercer savage, Man.
See him from Nature rising slow to Art!
To copy Instinct then was Reason's part;
Thus then to Man the voice of Nature spake—
"Go, from the Creatures thy instructions take:
Learn from the birds what food the thickets yield;
Learn from the beasts the physic of the field;*
Thy arts of building from the bee receive;
Learn of the mole to plough, the worm to weave;
Learn of the little Nautilus to sail,
Spread the thin oar, and catch the driving gale.
Here too all forms of social union find,
And hence let Reason, late, instruct Mankind:
Here subterranean works and cities see;
There towns aerial on the waving tree.
Learn each small People's genius, policies,
The Ant's republic, and the realm of Bees;
How those in common all their wealth bestow,
And Anarchy without confusion know;
And these for ever, tho' a Monarch reign,
Their sep'rate cells and properties maintain.
Mark what unvary'd laws preserve each state,
Laws wise as Nature, and as fix'd as Fate.
In vain thy Reason finer webs shall draw,
Entangle Justice in her net of Law,
And right, too rigid, harden into wrong;
Still for the strong too weak, the weak too strong.
Yet go! and thus o'er all the creatures sway,
Thus let the wiser make the rest obey;
And, for those Arts mere Instinct could afford,

* See Pliny's *Nat. Hist.* L. VIII. c. 27, where several instances are given of Animals discovering the medicinal efficacy of herbs, by their own use of them; and pointing out to some operations in the art of healing, by their own practice. [Warburton.]

Be crown'd as Monarchs, or as Gods ador'd."
   V. Great Nature spoke; observant Men obey'd;
Cities were built, Societies were made:
Here rose one little state; another near
Grew by like means, and join'd, thro' love or fear.
Did here the trees with ruddier burdens bend,
And there the streams in purer rills descend?
What War could ravish, Commerce could bestow,
And he return'd a friend, who came a foe.
Converse and Love mankind might strongly draw,
When Love was Liberty, and Nature Law.
Thus States were form'd; the name of King unknown,
'Till common int'rest plac'd the sway in one.
'T was Virtue only (or in arts or arms,
Diffusing blessings, or averting harms)
The same which in a Sire the Sons obey'd,
A Prince the Father of a People made.
   VI. 'Till then, by Nature crown'd, each Patriarch state,
King, priest, and parent of his growing state;
On him, their second Providence, they hung,
Their law his eye, their oracle his tongue.
He from the wond'ring furrow call'd the food,
Taught to command the fire, control the flood,
Draw forth the monsters of th' abyss profound,
Or fetch th' aerial eagle to the ground.
'Till drooping, sick'ning, dying they began
Whom they rever'd as God to mourn as Man:
Then, looking up from sire to sire, explor'd
One great first Father, and that first ador'd.
Or plain tradition that this All begun,
Convey'd unbroken faith from sire to son;
The worker from the work distinct was known,
And simple Reason never sought but one:
Ere Wit oblique had broke that steady light,
Man, like his Maker, saw that all was right;
To Virtue, in the paths of Pleasure, trod,

And own'd a Father when he own'd a God.
LOVE all the faith, and all th' allegiance then;
For Nature knew no right divine in Men,
No ill could fear in God; and understood
A sov'reign being but a sov'reign good.
True faith, true policy, united ran,
This was but love of God, and this of Man.

Who first taught souls enslav'd, and realms undone,
Th' enormous faith of many made for one;
That proud exception to all Nature's laws,
T' invert the world, and counter-work its Cause?
Force first made Conquest, and that conquest, Law;
'Till Superstition taught the tyrant awe,
Then shar'd the Tyranny, then lent it aid,
And Gods of Conqu'rors, Slaves of Subjects made:
She 'midst the lightning's blaze, and thunder's sound,
When rock'd the mountains, and when groan'd the ground,
She taught the weak to bend, the proud to pray,
To Pow'r unseen, and mightier far than they:
She, from the rending earth and bursting skies,
Saw Gods descend, and fiends infernal rise:
Here fix'd the dreadful, there the blest abodes;
Fear made her Devils, and weak Hope her Gods;
Gods partial, changeful, passionate, unjust,
Whose attributes were Rage, Revenge, or Lust;
Such as the souls of cowards might conceive,
And, form'd like tyrants, tyrants would believe.
Zeal then, not charity, became the guide;
And hell was built on spite, and heav'n on pride,
Then sacred seem'd th' ethereal vault no more;
Altars grew marble then, and reek'd with gore:
Then first the Flamen tasted living food;
Next his grim idol smear'd with human blood;
With Heav'n's own thunders shook the world below,
And play'd the God an engine on his foe.

So drives Self-love, thro' just and thro' unjust,

To one Man's pow'r, ambition, lucre, lust:
The same Self-love, in all, becomes the cause
Of what restrains him, Government and Laws.
For, what one likes if others like as well,
What serves one will, when many wills rebel?
How shall he keep, what, sleeping or awake,
A weaker may surprise, a stronger take?
His safety must his liberty restrain:
All join to guard what each desires to gain.
Forc'd into virtue thus by Self-defence,
Ev'n Kings learn'd justice and benevolence:
Self-love forsook the path it first pursu'd,
And found the private in the public good.
    'T was then, the studious head or gen'rous mind,
Follow'r of God or friend of human-kind,
Poet or Patriot, rose but to restore
The Faith and Moral Nature gave before;
Re-lum'd her ancient light, not kindled new;
If not God's image, yet his shadow drew:
Taught Pow'r's due use to People and to Kings,
Taught not to slack, nor strain its tender strings,
The less, or greater, set so justly true,
That touching one must strike the other too;
'Till jarring int'rests, of themselves create
Th' according music of a well-mix'd State.
Such is the World's great harmony, that springs
From Order, Union, full Consent of things:
Where small and great, where weak and mighty, made
To serve, not suffer, strengthen, not invade;
More pow'rful each as needful to the rest,
And, in proportion as it blesses, blest;
Draw to one point, and to one centre bring
Beast, Man, or Angel, Servant, Lord, or King.
    For Forms of Government let fools contest;
Whate'er is best administer'd is best:
For Modes of Faith let graceless zealots fight;

His can't be wrong whose life is in the right:
In Faith and Hope the world will disagree,
But all Mankind's concern is Charity:
All must be false that thwart this One great End;
And all of God, that bless Mankind or mend.
    Man, like the gen'rous vine, supported lives;
The strength he gains is from th' embrace he gives.
On their own Axis as the Planets run,
Yet make at once their circle round the Sun;
So two consistent motions act* the Soul;
And one regards Itself, and one the Whole.
    Thus God and Nature link'd the gen'ral frame,
And bade Self-love and Social be the same.

ARGUMENT OF EPISTLE IV

OF THE NATURE AND STATE OF MAN
WITH RESPECT TO HAPPINESS

I. FALSE Notions of Happiness, Philosophical and Popular, answered from v. 19 to 77. II. It is the End of all Men, and attainable by all, v. 30. God intends Happiness to be equal; and to be so, it must be social, since all particular happiness depends on general, and since he governs by general, not particular Laws, v. 37. As it is necessary for Order, and the peace and welfare of Society, that external goods should be unequal, Happiness is not made to consist in these, v. 51. But, notwithstanding that inequality, the balance of Happiness among Mankind is kept even by Providence, by the two Passions of Hope and Fear, v. 70. III. What the Happiness of Individuals is, as far as is consistent with the constitution of this world; and that the good Man has here the advantage, v. 77. The error of imputing to Virtue what

* Actuate.

are only the calamities of Nature, or of Fortune, v. 94.
IV. The folly of expecting that God should alter his general
Laws in favour of particulars, v. 121. V. That we are not
judges who are good; but that, whoever they are, they must
be happiest, v. 133, &c. VI. That external goods are not the
proper rewards, but often inconsistent with, or destructive
of Virtue, v. 165. That even these can make no Man happy
without Virtue: Instanced in Riches, v. 183. Honours, v. 191.
Nobility, v. 203. Greatness, v. 215. Fame, v. 235. Superior
Talents, v. 257, &c. With pictures of human Infelicity in
Men possessed of them all, v. 267, &c. VII. That Virtue only
constitutes a Happiness, whose object is universal, and whose
prospect eternal, v. 307, &c. That the perfection of Virtue
and Happiness consists in a conformity to the ORDER of
PROVIDENCE here, and a Resignation to it here and hereafter,
v. 326, &c.

EPISTLE IV

OH HAPPINESS! our being's end and aim!
Good, Pleasure, Ease, Content! whate'er thy name:
That something still which prompts th' eternal sign,
For which we bear to live, or dare to die,
Which still so near us, yet beyond us lies,
O'er-look'd, seen double, by the fool, and wise.
Plant of celestial seed! if dropt below,
Say, in what mortal soil thou deign'st to grow?
Fair op'ning to some Court's propitious shine,
Or deep with di'monds in the flaming mine?
Twin'd with the wreaths Parnassian laurels yield,
Or reap'd in iron harvests of the field?
Where grows?—where grows it not? If vain our toil,
We ought to blame the culture, not the soil:
Fix'd to no spot is Happiness sincere,*

* Pure, complete.

'T is nowhere to be found, or ev'rywhere;
'T is never to be bought, but always free,
And fled from monarchs, St. John! dwells with thee.

Ask of the Learn'd the way? The Learn'd are blind;
This bids to serve, and that to shun mankind;
Some place the bliss in action, some in ease,
Those call it Pleasure, and Contentment these;
Some sunk to Beasts, find pleasure end in pain;
Some swell'd to Gods, confess ev'n Virtue vain;
Or indolent, to each extreme they fall,
To trust in ev'ry thing, or doubt of all.

Who thus define it, say they more or less
Than this, that Happiness is Happiness?

Take Nature's path, and mad Opinion's leave;
All states can reach it, and all heads conceive;
Obvious her goods, in no extreme they dwell;
There needs but thinking right, and meaning well;
And mourn our various portions as we please,
Equal is Common Sense, and Common Ease.

Remember, Man, "the Universal Cause
Acts not by partial, but by gen'ral laws;"
And makes what Happiness we justly call
Subsist not in the good of one, but all.
There 's not a blessing Individuals find,
But some way leans and hearkens to the kind:
No Bandit fierce, no Tyrant mad with pride,
No cavern'd Hermit, rests self-satisfy'd:
Who most to shun or hate Mankind pretend,
Seek an admirer, or would fix a friend:
Abstract what others feel, what others think,
All pleasures sicken, and all glories sink:
Each has his share; and who would more obtain,
Shall find, the pleasure pays not half the pain.

Order is Heav'n's first law; and this confest,
Some are, and must be, greater than the rest,
More rich, more wise; but who infers from hence

That such are happier, shocks all common sense.
Heav'n to Mankind impartial we confess,
If all are equal in their Happiness:
But mutual wants this Happiness increase;
All Nature's diff'rence keeps all Nature's peace.
Condition, circumstance is not the thing;
Bliss is the same in subject or in king,
In who obtain defence, or who defend,
In him who is, or him who finds a friend:
Heav'n breathes thro' ev'ry member of the whole
One common blessing, as one common soul.
But Fortune's gifts if each alike possest,
And each were equal, must not all contest?
If then to all Men Happiness was meant,
God in Externals could not place Content.

Fortune her gifts may variously dispose,
And these be happy call'd, unhappy those;
But Heav'n's just balance equal will appear,
While those are plac'd in Hope, and these in Fear:
Nor present good or ill, the joy or curse,
But future views of better, or of worse.

Oh sons of earth! attempt ye still to rise,
By mountains pil'd on mountains, to the skies?
Heav'n still with laughter the vain toil surveys,
And buries madmen in the heaps they raise.

Know, all the good that individuals find,
Or God and Nature meant to mere Mankind,
Reason's whole pleasure, all the joys of Sense,
Lie in three words, Health, Peace, and Competence.
But Health consists with Temperance alone;
And Peace, oh Virtue! Peace is all thy own.
The good or bad the gifts of Fortune gain;
But these less taste them, as they worse obtain.
Say, in pursuit of profit or delight,
Who risk the most, that take wrong means, or right?
Of Vice or Virtue, whether blest or curst,

Which meets contempt, or which compassion first?
Count all th' advantage prosp'rous Vice attains,
'T is but what Virtue flies from and disdains:
And grant the bad what happiness they would,
One they must want, which is, to pass for good.
   Oh blind to Truth, and God's whole scheme below,
Who fancy Bliss to Vice, to Virtue Woe!*
Who sees and follows that great scheme the best,
Best knows the blessing, and will most be blest.
But fools the Good alone unhappy call,
For ills or accidents that chance to all.
See FALKLAND dies, the virtuous and the just!
See god-like TURENNE prostrate on the dust!
See SIDNEY bleeds amid the martial strife!
Was this their Virtue, or Contempt of Life?
Say, was it Virtue, more tho' Heav'n ne'er gave,
Lamented DIGBY! sunk thee to the grave?
Tell me, if Virtue made the Son expire,
Why, full of days and honour, lives the Sire?
Why drew Marseille's good bishop purer breath,
When Nature sicken'd, and each gale was death?
Or why so long (in life if long can be)
Lent Heav'n a parent to the poor and me?
   What makes all physical or moral ill?
There deviates Nature, and here wanders Will.
God sends not ill; if rightly understood,
Or partial Ill is universal Good,
Or Change admits, or Nature lets it fall;
Short, and but rare, till Man improv'd it all.
We just as wisely might of Heav'n complain
That righteous Abel was destroy'd by Cain,
As that the virtuous son is ill at ease
When his lewd father gave the dire disease.
Think we, like some weak Prince, th' Eternal Cause
Prone for his fav'rites to reverse his laws?

* i.e., that bliss goes with vice, and woe with virtue.

Shall burning Ætna, if a sage requires,
Forget to thunder, and recall her fires?
On air or sea new motions be imprest,
Oh blameless Bethel! to relieve thy breast?
When the loose mountain trembles from on high,
Shall gravitation cease, if you go by?
Or some old temple, nodding to its fall,
For Chartres' head reserve the hanging wall?
But still this world (so fitted for the knave)
Contents us not. A better shall we have?
A kingdom of the Just then let it be:
But first consider how those Just agree.
The good must merit God's peculiar care;
But who, but God, can tell us who they are?
One thinks on Calvin Heav'n's own spirit fell;
Another deems him instrument of hell;
If Calvin feel Heav'n's blessing, or its rod,
This cries there is, and that, there is no God.
What shocks one part will edify the rest,
Nor with one system can they all be blest.
The very best will variously incline,
And what rewards your Virtue, punish mine.
WHATEVER IS, IS RIGHT.—This world, 't is true,
Was made for Cæsar—but for Titus too:
And which more blest? who chain'd his country, say,
Or he whose Virtue sigh'd to lose a day?
"But sometimes Virtue starves, while Vice is fed."
What then? Is the reward of Virtue bread?
That, Vice may merit, 't is the price of toil;
The knave deserves it, when he tills the soil,
The knave deserves it, when he tempts the main,
Where Folly fights for kings, or dives for gain.
The good man may be weak, be indolent;
Nor is his claim to plenty, but content.
But grant him Riches, your demand is o'er?
"No—shall the good want Health, the good want Pow'r?"

Add Health, and Pow'r, and ev'ry earthly thing,
"Why bounded Pow'r? why private? why no king?"
Nay, why external for internal giv'n?
Why is not Man a God, and Earth a Heav'n?
Who ask and reason thus, will scarce conceive
God gives enough, while he has more to give:
Immense the pow'r, immense were the demand;
Say, at what part of nature will they stand?

What nothing earthly gives, or can destroy,
The soul's calm sunshine, and the heart-felt joy,
Is Virtue's prize: A better would you fix?
Then give humility a coach and six,
Justice a Conq'ror's sword, or Truth a gown,
Or Public Spirit its great cure, a Crown.
Weak, foolish man! will Heav'n reward us there
With the same trash mad mortals wish for here?
The Boy and Man an individual makes,
Yet sigh'st thou now for apples and for cakes?
Go, like the Indian, in another life
Expect thy dog, thy bottle, and thy wife:
As well as dream such trifles are assign'd,
As toys and empires, for a god-like mind.
Rewards, that either would to Virtue bring
No joy, or be destructive of the thing:
How oft by these at sixty are undone
The Virtues of a saint at twenty-one!
To whom can Riches give Repute, or Trust,
Content, or Pleasure, but the Good and Just?
Judges and Senates have been bought for gold,
Esteem and Love were never to be sold.
Oh fool! to think God hates the worthy mind,
The lover and the love of human-kind,
Whose life is healthful, and whose conscience clear,
Because he wants a thousand pounds a year.

Honour and shame from no Condition rise;
Act well your part, there all the honour lies.

Fortune in Men has some small diff'rence made,
One flaunts in rags, one flutters in brocade;
The cobbler apron'd, and the parson gown'd,
The friar hooded, and the monarch crown'd.
"What differ more (you cry) than crown and cowl?"
I 'll tell you, friend! a wise man and a Fool.
You 'll find, if once the monarch acts the monk,
Or, cobbler-like, the parson will be drunk,
Worth makes the man, and want of it, the fellow;
The rest is all but leather or prunella.

    Stuck o'er with titles and hung round with strings,
That thou may'st be by kings, or whores of kings.
Boast the pure blood of an illustrious race,
In quiet flow from Lucrece to Lucrece:
But by your fathers' worth if yours you rate,
Count me those only who were good and great.
Go! if your ancient, but ignoble blood
Has crept thro' scoundrels ever since the flood,
Go! and pretend your family is young;
Nor own, your fathers have been fools so long.
What can ennoble sots, or slaves, or cowards?
Alas! not all the blood of all the HOWARDS.

    Look next on Greatness; say where Greatness lies?
"Where, but among the Heroes and the wise?"
Heroes are much the same, the point 's agreed,
From Macedonia's madman to the Swede;*
The whole strange purpose of their lives, to find
Or make, an enemy of all mankind!
Not one looks backward, onward still he goes,
Yet ne'er looks forward farther than his nose.
No less alike the Politic and Wise;
All sly slow things, with circumspective eyes:
Men in their loose unguarded hours they take,
Not that themselves are wise, but others weak.
But grant that those can conquer, these can cheat;

* i.e., from Alexander the Great to Charles XII.

'T is phrase absurd to call a Villain Great:
Who wickedly is wise, or madly brave,
Is but the more a fool, the more a knave.
Who noble ends by noble means obtains,
Or failing, smiles in exile or in chains,
Like good Aurelius let him reign, or bleed
Like Socrates, that Man is great indeed.

What 's Fame? a fancy'd life in others' breath,
A thing beyond us, ev'n before our death.
Just what you hear, you have, and what's unknown
The same (my Lord) if Tully's, or your own.
All that we feel of it begins and ends
In the small circle of our foes or friends;
To all beside as much an empty shade
An Eugene living, as a Cæsar dead;
Alike or when, or where, they shone, or shine,
Or on the Rubicon, or on the Rhine.
A Wit 's a feather, and a Chief a rod;
An honest Man 's the noblest work of God.
Fame but from death a villain's name can save,
As Justice tears his body from the grave;
When what t' oblivion better were resign'd,
Is hung on high, to poison half mankind.
All fame is foreign, but of true desert;
Plays round the head, but comes not to the heart:
One self-approving hour whole years out-weighs
Of stupid starers, and of loud huzzas;
And more true joy Marcellus exil'd feels,
Than Cæsar with a senate at his heels.

In Parts superior what advantage lies?
Tell (for You can) what is it to be wise?
'T is but to know how little can be known;
To see all others' faults, and feel our own:
Condemn'd in bus'ness or in arts to drudge,
Without a second, or without a judge:
Truths would you teach, or save a sinking land

All fear, none aid you, and few understand.
Painful pre-eminence! yourself to view
Above life's weakness, and its comforts too.

Bring then these blessings to a strict account;
Make fair deductions; see to what they mount:
How much of other each is sure to cost;
How each for other oft is wholly lost;
How inconsistent greater goods with these;
How sometimes life is risk'd, and always ease:
Think, and if still the things thy envy call,*
Say, would'st thou be the Man to whom they fall?
To sigh for ribbands if thou art so silly,
Mark how they grace Lord Umbra, or Sir Billy:
Is yellow dirt the passion of thy life?
Look but on Gripus or on Gripus' wife:
If Parts allure thee, think how Bacon shin'd,
The wisest, brightest, meanest of mankind:
Or ravish'd with the whistling of a Name,
See Cromwell, damn'd to everlasting fame!
If all, united, thy ambition call,
From ancient story learn to scorn them all.
There, in the rich, the honour'd, fam'd, and great,
See the false scale of Happiness complete!
In hearts of Kings, or arms of Queens who lay,
How happy! those to ruin, these betray.
Mark by what wretched steps their glory grows,
From dirt and sea-weed as proud Venice rose;
In each how guilt and greatness equal ran,
And all that rais'd the Hero, sunk the Man:
Now Europe's laurels on their brows behold,
But stain'd with blood, or ill exchang'd for gold:
Then see them broke with toils, or sunk in ease,
Or infamous for plunder'd provinces.
Oh wealth ill-fated! which no act of fame
E'er taught to shine, or sanctify'd from shame!

* Demand.

What greater bliss attends their close of life?
Some greedy minion, or imperious wife.
The trophy'd arches, story'd halls invade
And haunt their slumbers in the pompous shade.
Alas! not dazzled with their noon-tide ray,
Compute the morn and ev'ning to the day;
The whole amount of that enormous fame,
A Tale, that blends their glory with their shame!
    Know then this truth (enough for Man to know)
"Virtue alone is Happiness below."
The only point where human bliss stands still,
And tastes the good without the fall to ill;*
Where only Merit constant pay receives,
Is blest in what it takes, and what it gives;
The joy unequall'd, if its end it gain,
And if it lose, attended with no pain:
Without satiety, tho' e'er so bless'd,
And but more relish'd as the more distress'd:
The broadest mirth unfeeling Folly wears,
Less pleasing far than Virtue's very tears:
Good, from each object, from each place acquir'd,
For ever exercis'd, yet never tir'd;
Never elated, while one man 's oppress'd;
Never dejected, while another 's bless'd;
And where no wants, no wishes can remain,
Since but to wish more Virtue, is to gain.
    See the sole bliss Heav'n could on all bestow!
Which who but feels can taste, but thinks can know:
Yet poor with fortune, and with learning blind,
The bad must miss; the good, untaught, will find;
Slave to no sect, who takes no private road,
But looks thro' Nature up to Nature's God;
Pursues that Chain which links th' immense design,
Joins heav'n and earth, and mortal and divine;
Sees, that no Being any bliss can know,

* Without tending toward ill.

But touches some above, and some below;
Learns, from this union of the rising Whole,
The first, last purpose of the human soul;
And knows, where Faith, Law, Morals, all began,
All end, in LOVE OF GOD, and LOVE OF MAN.

For him alone, Hope leads from goal to goal,
And opens still, and opens on his soul;
'Till lengthen'd on to Faith, and unconfin'd,
It pours the bliss that fills up all the mind.
He sees, why Nature plants in Man alone
Hope of known bliss, and Faith in bliss unknown:
(Nature, whose dictates to no other kind
Are giv'n in vain, but what they seek they find;)
Wise in her present; she connects in this
His greatest Virtue with his greatest Bliss;
At once his own bright prospect to be blest,
And strongest motive to assist the rest.

Self-love thus push'd to social, to divine,
Gives thee to make thy neighbour's blessing thine.
Is this too little for the boundless heart?
Extend it, let thy enemies have part:
Grasp the whole worlds of Reason, Life, and Sense,
In one close system of Benevolence:
Happier as kinder, in whate'er degree,
And height of Bliss but height of Charity.

God loves from Whole to Parts: but human soul
Must rise from Individual to the Whole.
Self-love but serves the virtuous mind to wake,
As the small pebble stirs the peaceful lake;
The centre mov'd, a circle straight succeeds,
Another still, and still another spreads;
Friend, parent, neighbour, first it will embrace;
His country next; and next all human race;
Wide and more wide, th' o'erflowings of the mind
Take ev'ry creature in, of ev'ry kind;
Earth smiles around, with boundless bounty blest,

And Heav'n beholds its image in his breast.
  Come then, my Friend! my Genius! come along;
Oh master of the poet, and the song!
And while the Muse now stoops, or now ascends,
To Man's low passions, or their glorious ends,
Teach me, like thee, in various nature wise,
To fall with dignity, with temper rise;
Form'd by thy converse, happily to steer
From grave to gay, from lively to severe;
Correct with spirit, eloquent with ease,
Intent to reason, or polite to please.
Oh! while along the stream of Time thy name
Expanded flies, and gathers all its fame,
Say, shall my little bark attendant sail,
Pursue the triumph, and partake the gale?
When statesmen, heroes, kings, in dust repose,
Whose sons shall blush their fathers were thy foes,
Shall then this verse to future age pretend
Thou wert my guide, philosopher, and friend?
That urg'd by thee, I turn'd the tuneful art
From sounds to things, from fancy to the heart;
For Wit's false mirror held up Nature's light;
Shew'd erring Pride, WHATEVER IS, IS RIGHT;
That REASON, PASSION, answer one great aim;
That true SELF-LOVE and SOCIAL are the same;
That VIRTUE only makes our Bliss below;
And all our Knowledge is, OURSELVES TO KNOW.

ℭ Moral Essays,

IN FOUR EPISTLES TO SEVERAL PERSONS

Est brevitate opus, ut currat sententia, neu se
Impediat verbis lassis onerantibus aures:
Et sermone opus est modo tristi, sæpe jocoso,
Defendente vicem modo Rhetoris atque Poetæ,
Interdum urbani, parcentis viribus, atque
Extenuantis eas consulto.—Hor. [*Sat.* i. x. 17–22.]

EPISTLE I

To Sir Richard Temple, Lord Cobham

ARGUMENT

OF THE KNOWLEDGE AND CHARACTERS OF MEN

I. THAT it is not sufficient for this knowledge to consider Man in the Abstract: Books will not serve the purpose, nor yet our own Experience singly, v. 1. General maxims, unless they be formed upon both, will be but notional, v. 10. Some Peculiarity in every man, characteristic to himself, yet varying from himself, v. 15. Difficulties arising from our own Passions, Fancies, Faculties, &c. v. 31. The shortness of Life, to observe in, and the uncertainty of the Principles of action in men, to observe by, v. 37, &c. Our own Principle of action often hid from ourselves, v. 41. Some few Characters plain, but in general confounded, dissembled, or inconsistent, v. 51. The same man utterly different in different places and seasons, v. 71. Unimaginable weaknesses in the greatest, v. 70, &c. Nothing constant and certain but God and Nature, v. 95.

No judging of the Motives from the actions; the same actions proceeding from contrary Motives, and the same Motives influencing contrary actions, v. 100. II. Yet to form Characters, we can only take the strongest actions of a man's life, and try to make them agree: The utter uncertainty of this, from Nature itself, and from Policy, v. 120. Characters given according to the rank of men of the world, v. 135. And some reason for it, v. 140. Education alters the Nature, or at least Character of many, v. 149. Actions, Passions, Opinions, Manners, Humours, or Principles all subject to change. No judging by Nature, from v. 158 to 178. III. It only remains to find (if we can) his RULING PASSION: That will certainly influence all the rest, and can reconcile the seeming or real inconsistency of all his actions, v. 175. Instanced in the extraordinary character of Clodio, v. 179. A caution against mistaking second qualities for first, which will destroy all possibility of the knowledge of mankind, v. 210. Examples of the strength of the Ruling Passion, and its continuation to the last breath, v. 222, &c.

YES, you despise the man to Books confin'd,
Who from his study rails at human kind;
Tho' what he learns he speaks, and may advance
Some gen'ral maxims, or be right by chance
The coxcomb bird, so talkative and grave,
That from his cage cries Cuckold, Whore, and Knave,
Tho' many a passenger he rightly call,
You hold him no Philosopher at all.
  And yet the fate of all extremes is such,
Men may be read as well as Books, too much.
To observations which ourselves we make,
We grow more partial for th' Observer's sake;
To written Wisdom, as another's, less:
Maxims are drawn from Notions, these from Guess.
There 's some Peculiar in each leaf and grain,
Some unmark'd fibre, or some varying vein:

Shall only Man be taken in the gross?
Grant but as many sorts of Mind as Moss.
  That each from other differs, first confess;
Next, that he varies from himself no less:
Add Nature's, Custom's, Reason's, Passion's strife,
And all Opinion's colours cast on life.

  Our depths who fathoms, or our shallows finds,
Quick whirls, and shifting eddies, of our minds?
On human actions reason tho' you can,
It may be Reason, but it is not Man:
His Principle of action once explore,
That instant 't is his Principle no more.
Like following life thro' creatures you dissect,
You lose it in the moment you detect.

  Yet more; the diff'rence is as great between
The optics seeing, as the object seen.
All Manners take a tincture from our own;
Or come discolour'd thro' our Passions shown.
Or Fancy's beam enlarges, multiplies,
Contracts, inverts, and gives ten thousand dyes.

  Nor will Life's stream for Observation stay
It hurries all too fast to mark their way:
In vain sedate reflections we would make,
When half our knowledge we must snatch, not take
Oft, in the Passions' wild rotation tost,
Our spring of action to ourselves is lost:
Tir'd, not determin'd, to the last we yield,
And what comes then is master of the field.
As the last image of that troubled heap,
When Sense subsides, and Fancy sports in sleep,
(Tho' past the recollection of the thought,)
Becomes the stuff of which our dream is wrought:
Something as dim to our internal view,
Is thus, perhaps, the cause of most we do.

  True, some are open, and to all men known;
Others so very close, they 're hid from none;

(So Darkness strikes the sense no less than Light)
Thus gracious CHANDOS is belov'd at sight;
And ev'ry child hates Shylock, tho' his soul
Still sits at squat, and peeps not from its hole.
At half mankind when gen'rous Manly raves,
All know 't is Virtue, for he thinks them knaves:
When universal homage Umbra pays,
All see 't is Vice, and itch of vulgar praise.
When Flatt'ry glares, all hate it in a Queen,
While one there is who charms us with his Spleen.

But these plain Characters we rarely find;
Tho' strong the bent, yet quick the turns of mind:
Or puzzling Contraries confound the whole;
Or Affectations quite reverse the soul.
The Dull, flat Falsehood serves for policy;
And in the Cunning, Truth itself's a lie:
Unthought-of Frailties cheat us in the Wise;
The Fool lies hid in inconsistencies.

See the same man, in vigour, in the gout;
Alone, in company; in place, or out;
Early at Bus'ness, and at Hazard late;
Mad at a Fox-chase, wise at a Debate;
Drunk at a Borough, civil at a Ball;
Friendly at Hackney, faithless at Whitehall.

Catius is ever moral, ever grave,
Thinks who endures a knave, is next a knave,
Save just at dinner—then, prefers, no doubt,
A Rogue with Ven'son to a Saint without.

Who would not praise Patritio's high desert,
His hand unstain'd, his uncorrupted heart,
His comprehensive head! all Int'rests weigh'd,
All Europe sav'd, yet Britain not betray'd.
He thanks you not, his pride is in Piquet,
New-market-fame, and judgment at a Bet.

What made (say Montagne, or more sage Charron!)
Otho a warrior, Cromwell a buffoon?

A perjur'd Prince a leaden Saint revere,
A godless Regent tremble at a Star?
The throne a Bigot keep, a Genius quit,
Faithless thro' Piety, and dup'd thro' Wit?
Europe a Woman, Child, or Dotard rule,
And just her wisest monarch made a fool?
    Know, GOD and NATURE only are the same:
In Man, the judgment shoots at flying game,
A bird of passage! gone as soon as found,
Now in the Moon perhaps, now under ground.

    In vain the Sage, with retrospective eye,
Would from th' apparent What conclude the Why,
Infer the Motive from the Deed, and shew,
That what we chanc'd was what we meant to do.
Behold! If Fortune or a Mistress frowns,
Some plunge in bus'ness, others shave their crowns:
To ease the Soul of one oppressive weight,
This quits an Empire, that embroils a State:
The same adust complexion has impell'd
Charles to the Convent, Philip to the Field.
    Not always Actions shew the man: we find
Who does a kindness, is not therefore kind;
Perhaps Prosperity becalm'd his breast,
Perhaps the Wind just shifted from the east:
Not therefore humble he who seeks retreat,
Pride guides his steps, and bids him shun the great:
Who combats bravely is not therefore brave,
He dreads a death-bed like the meanest slave
Who reasons wisely is not therefore wise,
His pride in Reas'ning, not in Acting lies.
    But grant that Actions best discover man;
Take the most strong, and sort them as you can.
The few that glare each character must mark,
You balance not the many in the dark.
What will you do with such as disagree?

Suppress them, or miscall them Policy?
Must then at once (the character to save)
The plain rough Hero turn a crafty Knave?
Alas! in truth the man but chang'd his mind,
Perhaps was sick, in love, or had not din'd.
Ask why from Britain Cæsar would retreat?
Cæsar himself might whisper he was beat.
Why risk the world's great empire for a Punk?*
Cæsar perhaps might answer he was drunk.
But, sage historians! 't is your task to prove
One action Conduct; one, heroic Love.

'T is from high Life high Characters are drawn;
A Saint in Crape is twice a Saint in Lawn;
A Judge is just, a Chanc'llor juster still;
A Gownman, learn'd; a Bishop, what you will;
Wise, if a Minister; but, if a King,
More wise, more learn'd, more just, more ev'rything.
Court-virtues bear, like Gems, the highest rate,
Born where Heav'n's influence scarce can penetrate
In life's low vale, the soil the Virtues like,
They please as beauties, here as wonders strike.
Tho' the same Sun with all-diffusive rays
Blush in the Rose, and in the Di'mond blaze,
We prize the stronger effort of his pow'r,
And justly set the Gem above the Flow'r.

'T is Education forms the common mind,
Just as the Twig is bent, the Tree 's inclin'd.
Boastful and rough, your first Son is a Squire;
The next a Tradesman, meek, and much a liar;
Tom struts a Soldier, open, bold, and brave;
Will sneaks a Scriv'ner, an exceeding knave:
Is he a Churchman? then he 's fond of pow'r:
A Quaker? sly: A Presbyterian? sour:
A smart Free-thinker? all things in an hour. }

Ask men's Opinions: Scoto now shall tell

* Cleopatra.

How Trade increases, and the world goes well;
Strike off his Pension, by the setting sun,
And Britain, if not Europe, is undone.

   That gay Free-thinker, a fine talker once,
What turns him now a stupid silent dunce?
Some God, or Spirit he has lately found:
Or chanc'd to meet a Minister that frown'd.

   Judge we by Nature? Habit can efface,
Int'rest o'ercome, or Policy take place:
By Actions? those Uncertainty divides:
By Passions? these Dissimulation hides:
Opinions? they still take a wider range:
Find, if you can, in what you cannot change.

   Manners with Fortunes, Humours turn with Climes,
Tenets with Books, and Principles with Times.

   Search then the RULING PASSION: there, alone,
The Wild are constant, and the Cunning known;
The Fool consistent, and the False sincere;
Priests, Princes, Women, no dissemblers here.
This clue once found, unravels all the rest,
The prospect clears, and Wharton stands confest.
Wharton, the scorn and wonder of our days,
Whose ruling Passion was the Lust of Praise:
Born with whate'er could win it from the Wise,
Women and Fools must like him or he dies;
Tho' wond'ring Senates hung on all he spoke,
The Club must hail him master of the joke.
Shall parts so various aim at nothing new?
He 'll shine a Tully and a Wilmot* too.
Then turns repentant, and his God adores
With the same spirit that he drinks and whores;
Enough if all around him but admire,
And now the Punk applaud, and now the Friar.
Thus with each gift of nature and of art,

* The Earl of Rochester.

And wanting nothing but an honest heart;
Grown all to all, from no one vice exempt;
And most contemptible, to shun contempt:
His Passion still, to covet gen'ral praise,
His Life, to forfeit it a thousand ways;
A constant Bounty which no friend has made;
An angel Tongue, which no man can persuade;
A Fool with more of Wit than half mankind,
Too rash for Thought, for Action too refin'd:
A Tyrant to the wife his heart approves;
A Rebel to the very king he loves;
He dies, sad outcast of each church and state,
And, harder still! flagitious, yet not great.
Ask you why Wharton broke thro' ev'ry rule?
'T was all for fear the Knaves should call him Fool.

Nature well known, no prodigies remain,
Comets are regular, and Wharton plain.

Yet, in this search, the wisest may mistake,
If second qualities for first they take.
When Catiline by rapine swell'd his store;
When Cæsar made a noble dame a whore;
In this the Lust, in that the Avarice
Were means, not ends; Ambition was the vice.
That very Cæsar, born in Scipio's days,
Had aim'd, like him, by Chastity at praise.
Lucullus, when Frugality could charm,
Had roasted turnips in the Sabine farm.

In vain th' observer eyes the builder's toil,
But quite mistakes the scaffold for the pile.
In this one Passion man can strength enjoy,
As Fits give vigour, just when they destroy.
Time, that on all things lays his lenient hand,
Yet tames not this; it sticks to our last sand.
Consistent in our follies and our sins,
Here honest Nature ends as she begins.

Old Politicians chew on wisdom past,

And totter on in bus'ness to the last;
As weak, as earnest; and as gravely out,
As sober Lanesb'row dancing in the gout.

Behold a rev'rend sire, whom want of grace
Has made the father of a nameless race,
Shov'd from the wall perhaps, or rudely press'd
By his own son, that passes by unbless'd:
Still to his wench he crawls on knocking knees,
And envies ev'ry sparrow that he sees.

A salmon's belly, Helluo, was thy fate;
The doctor call'd, declares all help too late:
"Mercy!" cries Helluo, "mercy on my soul!"
"Is there no hope?—Alas!—then bring the jowl."

The frugal Crone, whom praying priests attend,
Still tries to save the hallow'd taper's end,
Collects her breath, as ebbing life retires,
For one puff more, and in that puff expires.

"Odious! in woollen! 't would a Saint provoke,"
(Were the last words that poor Narcissa spoke)
"No, let a charming Chintz, and Brussels lace
Wrap my cold limbs, and shade my lifeless face:
One would not, sure, be frightful when one 's dead—
And—Betty—give this Cheek a little Red."

The Courtier smooth, who forty years had shin'd
An humble servant to all human kind,
Just brought out this, when scarce his tongue could stir,
"If—where I 'm going—I could serve you, Sir?"

"I give and I devise (old Euclio said,
And sigh'd) my lands and tenements to Ned."
"Your money, Sir;" "My money, Sir, what all?
Why,—if I must—(then wept) I give it Paul."
"The Manor, Sir?"—"The Manor! hold," he cry'd,
"Not that,—I cannot part with that"—and died.

And you! brave COBHAM, to the latest breath
Shall feel your ruling passion strong in death:
Such in those moments as in all the past,
"Oh, save my Country, Heav'n!" shall be your last.

EPISTLE II

To a Lady

OF THE CHARACTERS OF WOMEN

Nothing so true as what you once let fall,
"Most Women have no Characters at all."
Matter too soft a lasting mark to bear,
And best distinguish'd by black, brown, or fair.

How many pictures of one Nymph we view,
All how unlike each other, all how true!
Arcadia's Countess, here, in ermin'd pride,
Is, there, Pastora by a fountain side.
Here Fannia, leering on her own good man,
And there, a naked Leda with a Swan.
Let then the Fair one beautifully cry,
In Magdalen's loose hair, and lifted eye,
Or drest in smiles of sweet Cecilia shine,
With simp'ring Angels, Palms, and Harps divine;
Whether the Charmer sinner it, or saint it,
If Folly grow romantic, I must paint it.

Come then, the colors and the ground prepare!
Dip in the Rainbow, trick her off in Air;
Choose a firm Cloud, before it fall, and in it
Catch, ere she change, the Cynthia of this minute.

Rufa, whose eye quick-glancing o'er the Park,
Attracts each light gay meteor of a Spark,
Agrees as ill with Rufa studying Locke,
As Sappho's di'monds with her dirty smock;
Or Sappho at her toilet's greasy task,
With Sappho fragrant at an ev'ning Masque:
So morning Insects that in muck begun,
Shine, buzz, and fly-blow in the setting-sun.

How soft is Silia! fearful to offend;
The Frail one's advocate, the Weak one's friend:
To her, Calista prov'd her conduct nice;
And good Simplicius asks of her advice.
Sudden, she storms! she raves! You tip the wink,
But spare your censure; Silia does not drink.
All eyes may see from what the change arose,
All eyes may see—a Pimple on her nose.

Papillia, wedded to her am'rous spark,
Sighs for the shades—"How charming is a Park!"
A Park is purchas'd, but the Fair he sees
All bath'd in tears—"Oh odious, odious Trees!"

Ladies, like variegated Tulips, show;
'T is to their Changes half their charms we owe;
Fine by defect, and delicately weak,
Their happy Spots* the nice admirer take,
'T was thus Calypso once each heart alarm'd,
Aw'd without Virtue, without Beauty charm'd;
Her Tongue bewitch'd as oddly as her Eyes,
Less Wit than Mimic, more a Wit than wise;
Strange graces still, and stranger flights she had,
Was just not ugly, and was just not mad;
Yet ne'er so sure our passion to create,
As when she touch'd the brink of all we hate.

Narcissa's nature, tolerably mild,
To make a wash, would hardly stew a child;
Has ev'n been prov'd to grant a Lover's pray'r,
And paid a Tradesman once to make him stare;
Gave alms at Easter, in a Christian trim,
And made a Widow happy, for a whim.
Why then declare Good-nature is her scorn,
When 't is by that alone she can be borne?
Why pique all mortals, yet affect a name?
A fool to Pleasure, yet a slave to Fame:
Now deep in Taylor and the Book of Martyrs,

* Beauty marks.

Now drinking citron with his Grace and Chartres:
Now Conscience chills her, and now Passion burns;
And Atheism and Religion take their turns;
A very Heathen in the carnal part,
Yet still a sad, good Christian at her heart.
　See Sin in State, majestically drunk;
Proud as a Peeress, prouder as a Punk;
Chaste to her Husband, frank to all beside,
A teeming Mistress, but a barren Bride.
What then? let Blood and Body bear the fault,
Her Head 's untouch'd, that noble Seat of Thought:
Such this day's doctrine—in another fit
She sins with Poets thro' pure Love of Wit.
What has not fir'd her bosom or her brain?
Cæsar and Tall-boy, Charles and Charlemagne.
As Helluo, late Dictator of the Feast,
The Nose of Hautgoût, and the Tip of Taste,
Critic'd your wine, and analys'd your meat,
Yet on plain Pudding deign'd at home to eat;
So Philomedé, lect'ring all mankind
On the soft Passion, and the Taste refin'd,
Th' Address, the Delicacy—stoops at once,
And makes her hearty meal upon a Dunce.
　Flavia 's a Wit, has too much sense to Pray;
To Toast our wants and wishes, is her way;
Nor asks of God, but of her Stars, to give
The mighty blessing, "while we live, to live."
Then all for Death, that Opiate of the soul!
Lucretia's dagger, Rosamonda's bowl.
Say, what can cause such impotence of mind?
A Spark too fickle, or a Spouse too kind.
Wise Wretch! with Pleasures too refin'd to please;
With too much Spirit to be e'er at ease;
With too much Quickness ever to be taught;
With too much Thinking to have common Thought:
You purchase Pain with all that Joy can give,

And die of nothing but a Rage to live.
　　Turn then from Wits; and look on Simo's Mate,
No Ass so meek, no Ass so obstinate.
Or her, that owns her Faults, but never mends,
Because she 's honest, and the best of Friends.
Or her, whose life the Church and Scandal share,
For ever in a Passion, or a Pray'r.
Or her, who laughs at Hell, but (like her Grace)
Cries, "Ah! how charming, if there 's no such place!"
Or who in sweet vicissitude appears
Of Mirth and Opium, Ratafie* and Tears,
The daily Anodyne, and nightly Draught,
To kill those foes to Fair ones, Time and Thought.
Woman and Fool are two hard things to hit;
For true No-meaning puzzles more than Wit.
　　But what are these to great Atossa's mind?
Scarce once herself, by turns all Womankind!
Who, with herself, or others, from her birth
Finds all her life one warfare upon earth:
Shines in exposing Knaves, and painting Fools,
Yet is, whate'er she hates and ridicules.
No Thought advances, but her Eddy Brain
Whisks it about, and down it goes again.
Full sixty years the World has been her Trade,
The wisest Fool much Time has ever made.
From loveless youth to unrespected age,
No Passion gratify'd except her Rage.
So much the Fury still out-ran the Wit,
The Pleasure miss'd her, and the Scandal hit.
Who breaks with her, provokes Revenge from Hell,
But he 's a bolder man who dares be well.
Her ev'ry turn with Violence pursu'd,
Nor more a storm her Hate than Gratitude:
To that each Passion turns, or soon or late;
Love, if it makes her yield, must make her hate:

* A kind of liqueur.

Superiors? death! and Equals? what a curse!
But an Inferior not dependant? worse.
Offend her, and she knows not to forgive;
Oblige her, and she 'll hate you while you live:
But die, and she 'll adore you—Then the Bust
And Temple rise—then fall again to dust.
Last night, her Lord was all that 's good and great;
A Knave this morning, and his Will a Cheat.
Strange! by the Means defeated of the Ends,
By Spirit robb'd of Pow'r, by Warmth of Friends,
By Wealth of Follow'rs! without one distress
Sick of herself thro' very selfishness!
Atossa, curs'd with ev'ry granted pray'r,
Childless with all her Children, wants an Heir.
To Heirs unknown descends th' unguarded store,
Or wanders, Heav'n-directed, to the Poor.

Pictures like these, dear Madam, to design,
Asks no firm hand, and no unerring line;
Some wand'ring touches, some reflected light,
Some flying stroke alone can hit 'em right:
For how should equal Colours do the knack?
Chameleons who can paint in white and black?

"Yet Chloe sure was form'd without a spot"—
Nature in her then err'd not, but forgot.
"With ev'ry pleasing, ev'ry prudent part,
Say, what can Chloe want?"—She wants a Heart.
She speaks, behaves, and acts just as she ought;
But never, never, reach'd one gen'rous Thought.
Virtue she finds too painful an endeavour,
Content to dwell in Decencies for ever.
So very reasonable, so unmov'd,
As never yet to love, or to be lov'd.
She, while her Lover pants upon her breast,
Can mark the figures on an Indian chest;
And when she sees her Friend in deep despair,
Observes how much a Chintz exceeds Mohair.

Forbid it Heav'n, a Favour or a Debt
She e'er should cancel—but she may forget.
Safe is your Secret still in Chloe's ear;
But none of Chloe's shall you ever hear.
Of all her Dears she never slander'd one,
But cares not if a thousand are undone.
Would Chloe know if you're alive or dead?
She bids her Footman put it in her head.
Chloe is prudent—Would you too be wise?
Then never break your heart when Chloe dies.

One certain Portrait may (I grant) be seen,
Which Heav'n has varnish'd out, and made a *Queen:*
THE SAME FOR EVER! and describ'd by all
With Truth and Goodness, as with Crown and Ball.
Poets heap Virtues, Painters Gems at will,
And shew their zeal, and hide their want of skill.
'T is well—but, Artists! who can paint or write,
To draw the Naked is your true delight.
That robe of Quality so struts and swells,
None see what Parts of Nature it conceals:
Th' exactest traits of Body or of Mind,
We owe to models of an humble kind.
If QUEENSBURY to strip there's no compelling,
'T is from a Handmaid we must take a Helen,
From Peer or Bishop 't is no easy thing
To draw the man who loves his God, or King:
Alas! I copy (or my draught would fail)
From honest Mah'met, or plain Parson Hale.

But grant, in Public Men sometimes are shown,
A Woman's seen in Private life alone:
Our bolder Talents in full light display'd;
Your virtues open fairest in the shade.
Bred to disguise, in Public 't is you hide;
There, none distinguish 'twixt your Shame or Pride,
Weakness or Delicacy; all so nice,
That each may seem a Virtue, or a Vice.

In Men, we various Ruling Passions find;
In Women, two almost divide the kind;
Those, only fix'd, they first or last obey,
The Love of Pleasure, and the Love of Sway.

That, Nature gives; and where the lesson taught
Is but to please, can Pleasure seem a fault?
Experience, this; by Man's oppression curst,
They seek the second not to loose the first.

Men, some to Bus'ness, some to Pleasure take;
But every Woman is at heart a Rake:
Men, some to Quiet, some to public Strife;
But ev'ry Lady would be Queen for life.

Yet mark the fate of a whole Sex of Queens!
Pow'r all their end, but Beauty all the means:
In Youth they conquer, with so wild a rage,
As leaves them scarce a subject in their Age:
For foreign glory, foreign joy, they roam;
No thought of peace or happiness at home.
But Wisdom's triumph is well-tim'd Retreat,
As hard a science to the Fair as Great!
Beauties, like Tyrants, old and friendless grown,
Yet hate repose, and dread to be alone,
Worn out in public, weary ev'ry eye,
Nor leave one sigh behind them when they die.

Pleasures the sex, as children Birds, pursue,
Still out of reach, yet never out of view;
Sure, if they catch, to spoil the Toy at most,
To covet flying, and regret when lost:
At last, to follies Youth could scarce defend,
It grows their Age's prudence to pretend;
Asham'd to own they gave delight before,
Reduc'd to feign it, when they give no more:
As Hags hold Sabbaths, less for joy than spite,
So these their merry, miserable Night;
Still round and round the Ghosts of Beauty glide,
And haunt the places where their Honour died.

See how the World its Veterans rewards!
A Youth of Frolics, an old Age of Cards;
Fair to no purpose, artful to no end,
Young without Lovers, old without a Friend;
A Fop their Passion, but their Prize a Sot;
Alive, ridiculous, and dead, forgot!
　　Ah! Friend! to dazzle let the Vain design;
To raise the Thought, and touch the Heart be thine!
That Charm shall grow, while what fatigues the Ring,
Flaunts and goes down, an unregarded thing:
So when the Sun's broad beam has tir'd the sight,
All mild ascends the Moon's more sober light,
Serene in Virgin Modesty she shines,
And unobserv'd the glaring Orb declines.
　　Oh! blest with Temper, whose unclouded ray
Can make to-morrow cheerful as to-day;
She, who can love a Sister's charms, or hear
Sighs for a daughter with unwounded ear;
She, who ne'er answers till a Husband cools,
Or if she rules him never shews she rules;
Charms by accepting, by submitting sways,
Yet has her humour most, when she obeys;
Let Fops or Fortune fly which way they will;
Disdains all loss of Tickets, or Codille:
Spleen, Vapours, or Small-pox, above them all,
And Mistress of herself, tho' China fall.
　　And yet, believe me, good as well as ill,
Woman 's at best a Contradiction still.
Heav'n, when it strives to polish all it can
Its last best work, but forms a softer Man;
Picks from each sex, to make the Fav'rite blest,
Your love of Pleasure, or desire of Rest:
Blends, in exception to all gen'ral rules,
Your Taste of Follies, with our Scorn of Fools:
Reserve with Frankness, Art with Truth ally'd,
Courage with Softness, Modesty with Pride;

Fix'd Principles, with Fancy ever new;
Shakes all together, and produces—You.
　Be this a Woman's Fame: with this unblest,
Toasts live a scorn, and Queens may die a jest.
This Phœbus promis'd (I forget the year)
When those blue eyes first open'd on the sphere;
Ascendant Phœbus watch'd that hour with care,
Averted half your Parents' simple Pray'r;
And gave you Beauty, but deny'd the Pelf
That buys your sex a Tyrant o'er itself.
The gen'rous God, who Wit and Gold refines,
And ripens Spirits as he ripens Mines,
Kept Dross for Duchesses, the world shall know it,
To you gave Sense, Good-humour, and a Poet.

EPISTLE III

To Allen, Lord Bathurst

ARGUMENT

OF THE USE OF RICHES

THAT it is known to few, most falling into one of the extremes, Avarice or Profusion, v. 1, &c. The point discuss'd, whether the invention of Money has been more commodious or pernicious to Mankind, v. 21 to 77. That Riches, either to the Avaricious or the Prodigal, cannot afford Happiness, scarcely Necessaries, v. 89 to 160. That Avarice is an absolute Frenzy, without an End or Purpose, v. 113, &c. 152. Conjectures about the Motives of Avaricious men, v. 121 to 153. That the conduct of men, with respect to Riches, can only be accounted for by the ORDER OF PROVIDENCE, which works the general Good out of Extremes, and brings all to its great End by perpetual Revolutions, v. 161 to 178. How a Miser acts upon Principles which appear to him reasonable, v. 179.

How a Prodigal does the same, v. 199. The due Medium, and
true use of Riches, v. 219. The Man of Ross, v. 250. The fate
of the Profuse and the Covetous, in two examples; both miserable in Life and in Death, v. 300, &c. The Story of Sir
Balaam, v. 339 to the end.

P. WHO shall decide, when Doctors disagree,
And soundest Casuists doubt, like you and me?
You hold the word, from Jove to Momus giv'n
That Man was made the standing jest of Heav'n;
And Gold but sent to keep the fools in play,
For some to heap, and some to throw away.
  But I, who think more highly of our kind,
(And surely, Heav'n and I are of a mind)
Opine, that Nature, as in duty bound,
Deep hid the shining mischief under ground:
But when by Man's audacious labour won,
Flam'd forth this rival to its Sire, the Sun,
Then careful Heav'n supply'd two sorts of Men,
To squander These, and Those to hide again.
  Like Doctors thus, when much dispute has past,
We find our tenets just the same at last.
Both fairly owing Riches, in effect,
No grace of Heav'n or token of th' Elect;
Giv'n to the Fool, the Mad, the Vain, the Evil,
To Ward, to Waters, Chartres, and the Devil.
B. What nature wants, commodious* Gold bestows,
'T is thus we eat the bread another sows.
P. But how unequal it bestows, observe,
'T is thus we riot, while, who sow it, starve:
What Nature wants (a phrase I much distrust)
Extends to Luxury, extends to Lust:
Useful, I grant, it serves what life requires,
But, dreadful too, the dark Assassin hires:
B. Trade it may help, Society extend.

* Obliging.

P. But lures the Pirate, and corrupts the Friend.
B. It raises Armies in a Nation's aid.
P. But bribes a Senate, and the Land 's betray'd.
In vain may Heroes fight, and Patriots rave;
If secret Gold sap on from knave to knave.
Once, we confess, beneath the Patriot's cloak,*
From the crack'd bag the dropping Guinea spoke,
And jingling down the back-stairs, told the crew,
"Old Cato is as great a Rogue as you."
Blest paper-credit! last and best supply!
That lends Corruption lighter wings to fly!
Gold imp'd by thee, can compass hardest things,
Can pocket States, can fetch or carry Kings;
A single leaf shall waft an Army o'er,
Or ship off Senates to a distant Shore;
A leaf, like Sibyl's, scatter to and fro
Our fates and fortunes, as the winds shall blow:
Pregnant with thousands flits the Scrap unseen,
And silent sells a King, or buys a Queen.

Oh! that such bulky Bribes as all might see,
Still, as of old, encumber'd Villainy!
Could France or Rome divert our brave designs,
With all their brandies or with all their wines?
What could they more than Knights and Squires confound,
Or water all the Quorum** ten miles round?
A Statesman's slumbers how this speech 'would spoil!
"Sir, Spain has sent a thousand jars of oil;
Huge bales of British cloth blockade the door;
A hundred oxen at your levee roar."

Poor Avarice one torment more would find;
Nor could Profusion squander all in kind.

---

* This is a true story, which happened in the reign of William III. to an unsuspected old Patriot, who coming out at the back-door from having been closeted by the King, where he had receiv'd a large bag of Guineas, the bursting of the bag discovered his business there. P.

** Justices of the Peace.

Astride his cheese Sir Morgan might we meet;
And Worldly crying coals from street to street,
Whom with a wig so wild, and mien so maz'd,
Pity mistakes for some poor tradesman craz'd.
Had Colepepper's whole wealth been hops and hogs,
Could he himself have sent it to the dogs?
His Grace will game: to White's a Bull be led,
With spurning heels and with a butting head.
To White's be carry'd, as to ancient games,
Fair Coursers, Vases, and alluring Dames.
Shall then Uxorio, if the stakes he sweep,
Bear home six Whores, and make his Lady weep?
Or soft Adonis, so perfum'd and fine,
Drive to St. James's a whole herd of swine?
Oh filthy check on all industrious skill,
To spoil the nation's last great trade, Quadrille!*
Since then, my Lord, on such a World we fall,
What say you? B. Say? Why take it, Gold and all.
P. What Riches give us let us then enquire:
Meat, Fire, and Clothes. B. What more? P. Meat,
        Clothes, and Fire.
Is this too little? would you more than live?
Alas! 't is more than Turner finds they give.
Alas! 't is more than (all his Visions past)
Unhappy Wharton, waking, found at last!
What can they give? to dying Hopkins, Heirs;
To Chartres, Vigour; Japhet, Nose and Ears?
Can they, in gems bid pallid Hippia glow,
In Fulvia's buckle ease the throbs below;
Or heal, old Narses, thy obscener ail,
With all th' embroid'ry plaister'd at thy tail?
They might (were Harpax not too wise to spend)
Give Harpax' self the blessing of a friend;
Or find some Doctor that would save the life
Of wretched Shylock, spite of Shylock's Wife:

* A card game.

But thousands die, without or this or that, .
Die, and endow a College, or a Cat.
To some indeed, Heav'n grants the happier fate,
T' enrich a Bastard, or a Son they hate.
   Perhaps you think the Poor might have their part?
Bond damns the Poor, and hates them from his heart:
The grave Sir Gilbert holds it for a rule,
That "ev'ry man in want is knave or fool:
God cannot love (says Blunt, with tearless eyes)
The wretch he starves"—and piously denies:
But the good Bishop, with a meeker air,
Admits, and leaves them, Providence's care.
   Yet, to be just to these poor men of pelf,
Each does but hate his neighbour as himself:
Damn'd to the Mines, an equal fate betides
The Slave that digs it, and the Slave that hides.
B. Who suffer thus, mere Charity should own,
Must act on motives pow'rful, tho' unknown.
P. Some War, some Plague, or Famine they foresee,
Some Revelation hid from you and me.
Why Shylock wants a meal, the cause is found,
He thinks a Loaf will rise to fifty pound.
What made Directors cheat in South-sea year?
To live on Ven'son when it sold so dear.
Ask you why Phryne the whole Auction buys?
Phryne foresees a general Excise.
Why she and Sappho raise that monstrous sum?
Alas! they fear a man will cost a plum.
   Wise Peter sees the World's respect for Gold,
And therefore hopes this Nation may be sold:
Glorious Ambition! Peter, swell thy store,
And be what Rome's great Didius* was before.
   The Crown of Poland, venal twice an age,
To just three millions stinted modest Gage.

---

* A Roman lawyer, so rich as to purchase the Empire when it was
set to sale upon the death of Pertinax.

But nobler scenes Maria's dreams unfold,
Hereditary Realms, and worlds of Gold.
Congenial souls! whose life one Av'rice joins,
And one fate buries in th' Asturian Mines.
    Much injur'd Blunt! why bears he Britain's hate?
A wizard told him in these words our fate:
"At length Corruption, like a gen'ral flood,
(So long by watchful Ministers withstood)
Shall deluge all; and Av'rice, creeping on,
Spread like a low-born mist, and blot the Sun;
Statesman and Patriot ply alike the stocks,
Peeress and Butler share alike the Box,
And Judges job, and Bishops bite the town,
And mighty Dukes pack Cards for half a crown.
See Britain sunk in lucre's sordid charms,
And France reveng'd of ANNE's and EDWARD's arms?"
'T was no Court-badge, great Scriv'ner! fir'd thy brain,
Nor lordly Luxury, nor City Gain:
No, 't was thy righteous end, asham'd to see
Senates degen'rate, Patriots disagree,
And, nobly wishing Party-rage to cease,
To buy both sides, and give thy Country peace.
    "All this is madness," cries a sober sage:
But who, my friend, has reason in his rage?
"The ruling Passion, be it what it will,
The ruling Passion conquers Reason still."
Less mad the wildest whimsey we can frame,
Than ev'n that Passion, if it has no Aim;
For tho' such motives Folly you may call,
The Folly 's greater to have none at all.
    Hear then the truth: " 'T is Heav'n each Passion sends,
And diff'rent men directs to diff'rent ends.
Extremes in Nature equal good produce,
Extremes in Man concur to gen'ral use."
Ask we what makes one keep, and one bestow?
That POW'R who bids the Ocean ebb and flow,

Bids seed-time, harvest, equal course maintain,
Thro' reconcil'd extremes of drought and rain,
Builds life on Death, on Change Duration founds,
And gives th' eternal wheels to know their rounds.

Riches, like insects, when conceal'd they lie,
Wait but for Wings, and in their season fly.
Who see pale Mammon pine amidst his store,
Sees but a backward steward for the Poor;
This year a Reservoir, to keep and spare;
The next, a Fountain, spouting thro' his Heir,
In lavish streams to quench a Country's thirst,
And men and dogs shall drink him till they burst.

Old Cotta sham'd his fortune and his birth,
Yet was not Cotta void of wit or worth:
What tho' (the use of barb'rous spits forgot)
His kitchen vied in coolness with his grot?
His court with nettles, moats with cresses stor'd,
With soups unbought and salads bless'd his board?
If Cotta liv'd on pulse, it was no more
Than Brahmins, Saints, and Sages did before;
To cram the Rich was prodigal expense,
And who would take the Poor from Providence?
Like some lone Chartreux* stands the good old Hall,
Silence without, and Fasts within the wall;
No rafter'd roofs with dance and tabor sound,
No noontide-bell invites the country round;
Tenants with sighs the smokeless tow'rs survey,
And turn th' unwilling steeds another way;
Benighted wanderers, the forest o'er,
Curse the sav'd candle, and unop'ning door;
While the gaunt mastiff growling at the gate,
Affrights the beggar whom he longs to eat.

Not so his Son; he mark'd this oversight,
And then mistook reverse of wrong for right.
(For what to shun will no great knowledge need;

* Carthusian Monastery.

But what to follow, is a task indeed.)
Yet sure, of qualities deserving praise,
More go to ruin Fortunes, than to raise.
What slaughter'd hecatombs, what floods of wine,
Fill the capacious Squire, and deep Divine!
Yet no mean motive this profusion draws,
His oxen perish in his country's cause;
'T is GEORGE and LIBERTY that crowns the cup,
And Zeal for that great House which eats him up.
The woods recede around the naked seat;
The Sylvans groan—no matter—for the Fleet;
Next goes his Wool—to clothe our valiant bands;
Last, for his Country's love, he sells his Lands.
To town he comes, completes the nation's hope,
And heads the bold Train-bands, and burns a Pope.
And shall not Britain now reward his toils,
Britain, that pays her Patriots with her Spoils?
In vain at Court the Bankrupt pleads his cause,
His thankless Country leaves him to her Laws.

The Sense to value Riches, with the Art
T' enjoy them, and the Virtue to impart,
Not meanly, nor ambitiously pursu'd,
Not sunk by sloth, nor rais'd by servitude;
To balance Fortune by a just expense,
Join with Economy, Magnificence;
With Splendour, Charity; with Plenty, Health;
O teach us, BATHURST! yet unspoil'd by wealth!
That secret rare, between th' extremes to move
Of mad Good-nature, and of mean Self-love.

B. To Worth or Want well-weigh'd, be Bounty giv'n,
And ease, or emulate, the care of Heav'n;
(Whose measure full o'erflows on human race)
Mend Fortune's fault, and justify her grace.
Wealth in the gross is death, but life diffus'd;
As Poison heals, in just proportion us'd:
In heaps, like Ambergrise, a stink it lies,

But well-dispers'd, is Incense to the Skies.
    P. Who starves by Nobles, or with Nobles eats?
The Wretch that trusts them, and the Rogue that cheats.
Is there a Lord, who knows a cheerful noon
Without a Fiddler, Flatt'rer, or Buffoon?
Whose table, Wit, or modest Merit share,
Unelbow'd by a Gamester, Pimp, or Play'r?
Who copies Your's or OXFORD's better part,
To ease th' oppress'd, and raise the sinking heart?
Where-e'er he shines, oh Fortune, gild the scene,
And Angels guard him in the golden Mean!
There, English Bounty yet awhile may stand,
And Honour linger ere it leaves the land.
    But all our praises why should Lords engross?
Rise, honest Muse! and sing the MAN of ROSS:
Pleas'd Vaga echoes thro' her winding bounds,
And rapid Severn hoarse applause resounds.
Who hung with woods yon mountain's sultry brow?
From the dry rock who bade the waters flow?
Not to the skies in useless columns tost,
Or in proud falls magnificently lost,
But clear and artless, pouring thro' the plain
Health to the sick, and solace to the swain.
Whose Cause-way parts the vale with shady rows?
Whose Seats the weary Traveller repose?
Who taught that heav'n-directed spire to rise?
"The MAN of ROSS," each lisping babe replies.
Behold the Market-place with poor o'erspread!
The MAN of Ross divides the weekly bread;
He feeds yon Alms-house, neat, but void of state,
Where Age and Want sit smiling at the gate;
Him portion'd maids, apprentic'd orphans blest,
The young who labour, and the old who rest.
Is any sick? the MAN of ROSS relieves,
Prescribes, attends, the med'cine makes, and gives.
Is there a variance; enter but his door,

Balk'd are the Courts, and contest is no more.
Despairing Quacks with curses fled the place,
And vile Attorneys, now an useless race.

   B. Thrice happy man! enabled to pursue
What all so wish, but want the pow'r to do!
Oh say, what sums that gen'rous hand supply?
What mines, to swell that boundless charity?

   P. Of Debts, and Taxes, Wife and Children clear,
This man possest—five hundred pounds a year.
Blush, Grandeur, blush! proud Courts, withdraw your
    blaze!
Ye little Stars! hide your diminish'd rays.

   B. And what? no monument, inscription, stone?
His race, his form, his name almost unknown?

   P. Who builds a Church to God, and not to Fame,
Will never mark the marble with his Name:
Go, search it there,* where to be born and die,
Of rich and poor makes all the history;
Enough, that Virtue fill'd the space between;
Prov'd, by the ends of being, to have been.
When Hopkins dies, a thousand lights attend
The wretch, who living sav'd a candle's end:
Should'ring God's altar a vile image stands,
Belies his features, nay extends his hands;
That live-long wig which Gorgon's self might own,
Eternal buckle takes in Parian stone.
Behold what blessings Wealth to life can lend!
And see, what comfort it affords our end.

   In the worst inn's worst room, with mat half-hung,
The floors of plaister, and the walls of dung,
On once a flock-bed, but repair'd with straw,
With tape-ty'd curtains, never meant to draw,
The George and Garter dangling from that bed
Where tawdry yellow strove with dirty red,
Great Villiers lies—alas! how chang'd from him,

---

* In the parish register.

That life of pleasure, and that soul of whim!
Gallant and gay, in Cliveden's proud alcove,
The bow'r of wanton Shrewsbury and love;
Or just as gay, at Council, in a ring
Of mimic'd Statesmen, and their merry King.
No Wit to flatter left of all his store!
No Fool to laugh at, which he valu'd more.
There, Victor of his health, of fortune, friends,
And fame, this lord of useless thousands ends.

His Grace's fate sage Cutler could foresee,
And well (he thought) advis'd him, "Live like me."
As well his Grace reply'd, "Like you, Sir John?
"That I can do, when all I have is gone."
Resolve me, Reason, which of these is worse,
Want with a full, or with an empty purse?
Thy life more wretched, Cutler, was confess'd,
Arise, and tell me, was thy death more bless'd?
Cutler saw tenants break, and houses fall,
For very want; he could not build a wall.
His only daughter in a stranger's pow'r,
For very want; he could not pay a dow'r.
A few grey hairs his rev'rend temples crown'd,
'T was very want that sold them for two pound.
What ev'n deny'd a cordial at his end,
Banish'd the doctor, and expell'd the friend?
What but a want, which you perhaps think mad,
Yet numbers feel the want of what he had!
Cutler and Brutus, dying both exclaim,
"Virtue! and Wealth! what are ye but a name!"

Say, for such worth are other worlds prepar'd?
Or are they both, in this their own reward?
A knotty point! to which we now proceed.
But you are tir'd—I 'll tell a tale— B. Agreed.

P. Where London's column, pointing at the skies,
Like a tall bully, lifts the head, and lies;
There dwelt a Citizen of sober fame,

A plain good man, and Balaam was his name;
Religious, punctual, frugal, and so forth;
His word would pass for more than he was worth.
One solid dish his week-day meal affords,
An added pudding solemniz'd the Lord's:
Constant at Church, and Change; his gains were sure,
His givings rare, save farthings to the poor.

The Dev'l was piqu'd such saintship to behold,
And long'd to tempt him like good Job of old:
But Satan now is wiser than of yore,
And tempts by making rich, not making poor.

Rous'd by the Prince of Air, the whirlwinds sweep
The surge, and plunge his Father in the deep;
Then full against his Cornish lands they roar,
And two rich ship-wrecks bless the lucky shore.

Sir Balaam now, he lives like other folks,
He takes his chirping pint, and cracks his jokes:
"Live like yourself," was soon my Lady's word;
And lo! two puddings smok'd upon the board.

Asleep and naked as an Indian lay,
An honest factor stole a Gem away:
He pledg'd it to the knight; the knight had wit,
So kept the Di'mond, and the rogue was bit.
Some scruple rose, but thus he eas'd his thought,
"I 'll now give six-pence where I gave a groat;
"Where once I went to Church, I 'll now go twice—
"And am so clear too of all other vice."

The Tempter saw his time; the work he ply'd;
Stocks and Subscriptions pour on ev'ry side,
'Till all the Demon makes his full descent
In one abundant show'r of Cent per Cent,
Sinks deep within him, and possesses whole,
Then dubs Director, and secures his soul.

Behold Sir Balaam, now a man of spirit,
Ascribes his gettings to his parts and merit;
What late he call'd a Blessing, now was Wit,

And God's good Providence, a lucky Hit.
Things change their titles, as our manners turn:
His Counting-house employ'd the Sunday-morn;
Seldom at Church ('t was such a busy life)
But duly sent his family and wife.
There (so the Dev'l ordain'd) one Christmas-tide
My good old Lady catch'd a cold, and died.
A Nymph of Quality admires our Knight;
He marries, bows at Court, and grows polite:
Leaves the dull Cits, and joins (to please the fair)
The well-bred cuckolds in St. James's air:
First, for his Son a gay commission buys,
Who drinks, whores, fights, and in a duel dies:
His daughter flaunts a Viscount's tawdry wife;
She bears a Coronet and P—x for life.
In Britain's Senate he a seat obtains,
And one more Pensioner St. Stephen gains.
My Lady falls to play; so bad her chance,
He must repair it; takes a bribe from France;
The House impeach him; Coningsby harangues;
The Court forsake him, and Sir Balaam hangs:
Wife, son, and daughter, Satan! are thy own,
His wealth, yet dearer, forfeit to the Crown:
The Devil and the King divide the prize,
And sad Sir Balaam curses God and dies.

EPISTLE IV

To Richard Boyle, Earl of Burlington

ARGUMENT

OF THE USE OF RICHES

The Vanity of Expence in People of Wealth and Quality.
The abuse of the word Taste, v. 13. That the first principle

and foundation, in this as in every thing else, is Good Sense,
v. 40. The chief proof of it is to follow Nature even in works
of mere Luxury and Elegance. Instanced in Architecture and
Gardening, where all must be adapted to the Genius and Use
of the Place, and the Beauties not forced into it, but resulting
from it, v. 50. How men are disappointed in their most ex-
pensive undertakings, for want of this true Foundation, without which nothing can please long, if at all; and the best
Examples and Rules will but be perverted into something
burdensome or ridiculous, v. 65, &c. to 92. A description of
the false Taste of Magnificence; the first grand Error of which
is to imagine that Greatness consists in the Size and Dimen-
sion, instead of the Proportion and Harmony of the whole,
v. 97, and the second, either in joining together Parts incoherent, or too minutely resembling, or in the Repetition of
the same too frequently, v. 105, &c. A word or two of false
Taste in Books, in Music, in Painting, even in Preaching and
Prayer, and lastly in Entertainments, v. 133, &c. Yet PROVI-
DENCE is justified in giving Wealth to be squandered in this
manner, since it is dispersed to the Poor and Laborious part
of mankind, v. 169 [recurring to what is laid down in the first
book, Ep. ii. and in the Epistle preceding this, v. 159, &c.].
What are the proper Objects of Magnificence, and a proper
field for the Expence of Great Men, v. 177, &c., and finally,
the Great and Public Works which become a Prince, v. 191,
to the end.

'T is strange, the Miser should his Cares employ
To gain those Riches he can ne'er enjoy:
Is it less strange, the Prodigal should waste
His wealth, to purchase what he ne'er can taste?
Not for himself he sees, or hears, or eats;
Artists must choose his Pictures, Music, Meats:
He buys for Topham, Drawings and Designs,
For Pembroke, Statues, dirty Gods, and Coins;
Rare monkish Manuscripts for Hearne alone,

And Books for Mead, and Butterflies for Sloane.
Think we all these are for himself? no more
Than his fine Wife, alas! or finer Whore.

For what has Virro painted, built, and planted?
Only to show, how many Tastes he wanted.
What brought Sir Visto's ill got wealth to waste?
Some Dæmon whisper'd, "Visto! have a Taste."
Heav'n visits with a Taste the wealthy fool,
And needs no Rod but Ripley with a Rule.
See! sportive fate, to punish awkward pride,
Bids Bubo build, and sends him such a Guide:
A standing sermon, at each year's expense,
That never Coxcomb reach'd Magnificence!

You show us, Rome was glorious, not profuse,
And pompous buildings once were things of Use.
Yet shall, my Lord, your just, your noble rules
Fill half the land with Imitating-Fools;
Who random drawings from your sheets shall take,
And of one beauty many blunders make;
Load some vain Church with old Theatric state,
Turn Arcs of triumph to a Garden-gate;
Reverse your Ornaments, and hang them all
On some patch'd dog-hole ek'd with ends of wall;
Then clap four slices of Pilaster on 't,
That, lac'd with bits of rustic, makes a Front.
Shall call the winds thro' long arcades to roar,
Proud to catch cold at a Venetian door;
Conscious they act a true Palladian part,
And, if they starve, they starve by rules of art.

Oft have you hinted to your brother Peer
A certain truth, which many buy too dear:
Something there is more needful than Expense,
And something previous ev'n to Taste—'t is Sense:
Good Sense, which only is the gift of Heav'n,
And tho' no Science, fairly worth the seven:
A Light, which in yourself you must perceive;

Jones and Le Nôtre have it not to give.
To build, to plant, whatever you intend,
To rear the Column, or the Arch to bend,
To swell the Terrace, or to sink the Grot;
In all, let Nature never be forgot.
But treat the Goddess like a modest fair,
Nor over-dress, nor leave her wholly bare;
Let not each beauty ev'rywhere be spy'd,
Where half the skill is decently to hide.
He gains all points, who pleasingly confounds,
Surprises, varies, and conceals the Bounds.

Consult the Genius of the Place in all;
That tells the Waters or to rise, or fall;
Or helps th' ambitious Hill the heav'ns to scale,
Or scoops in circling theatres the Vale;
Calls in the Country, catches op'ning glades,
Joins willing woods, and varies shades from shades;
Now breaks, or now directs, th' intending Lines;
Paints as you plant, and, as you work, designs.

Still follow Sense, of ev'ry Art the Soul,
Parts answ'ring parts shall slide into a whole,
Spontaneous beauties all around advance,
Start ev'n from Difficulty, strike from Chance;
Nature shall join you; Time shall make it grow
A Work to wonder at—perhaps a Stowe.

Without it, proud Versailles! thy glory falls;
And Nero's Terraces desert their walls:
The vast Parterres a thousand hands shall make,
Lo! Cobham comes, and floats them with a Lake:
Or cut wide views thro' Mountains to the Plain,
You 'll wish your hill or shelter'd seat again.
Ev'n in an ornament its place remark,
Nor in an Hermitage set Dr. Clarke.

Behold Villario's ten years' toil complete;
His Quincunx darkens, his Espaliers meet;
The Wood supports the Plain, the parts unite,

And strength of Shade contends with strength of Light;
A waving Glow the bloomy beds display,
Blushing in bright diversities of day,
With silver-quiv'ring rills mæander'd o'er—
Enjoy them, you! Villario can no more;
Tir'd of the scene Parterres and Fountains yield,
He finds at last he better likes a Field.

 Thro' his young Woods how pleas'd Sabinus stray'd,
Or sat delighted in the thick'ning shade,
With annual joy the redd'ning shoots to greet,
Or see the stretching branches long to meet!
His Son's fine Taste an op'ner Vista loves,
Foe to the Dryads of his Father's groves;
One boundless Green, or flourish'd Carpet views,
With all the mournful family of Yews;
The thriving plants ignoble broomsticks made,
Now sweep those Alleys they were born to shade.

 At Timon's Villa let us pass a day,
Where all cry out, "What sums are thrown away!"
So proud, so grand; of that stupendous air,
Soft and Agreeable come never there.
Greatness, with Timon, dwells in such a draught
As brings all Brobdignag before your thought.
To compass this, his building is a Town,
His pond an Ocean, his parterre a Down:
Who but must laugh, the Master when he sees,
A puny insect, shiv'ring at a breeze!
Lo, what huge heaps of littleness around!
The whole, a labour'd Quarry above ground;
Two Cupids squirt before; a Lake behind
Improves the keenness of the Northern wind.
His Gardens next your admiration call,
On ev'ry side you look, behold the Wall!
No pleasing Intricacies intervene,
No artful wildness to perplex the scene;
Grove nods at grove, each Alley has a brother,

And half the platform just reflects the other.
The suff'ring eye inverted Nature sees,
Trees cut to Statues, Statues thick as trees;
With here a Fountain, never to be play'd;
And there a Summer-house, that knows no shade;
Here Amphitrite sails thro' myrtle bow'rs;
There Gladiators fight, or die in flow'rs;
Un-watered see the drooping sea-horse mourn,
And swallows roost in Nilus' dusty Urn.

My Lord advances with majestic mien,
Smit with the mighty pleasure, to be seen:
But soft,—by regular approach,—not yet,—
First thro' the length of yon hot Terrace sweat;
And when up ten steep slopes you 've dragg'd your thighs,
Just at his Study-door he 'll bless your eyes.

His Study! with what Authors is it stor'd?
In Books, not Authors, curious is my Lord;
To all their dated Backs he turns you round:
These Aldus printed, those Du Sueil has bound.
Lo, some are Vellum, and the rest as good
For all his Lordship knows, but they are Wood.
For Locke or Milton 't is in vain to look,
These shelves admit not any modern book.

And now the Chapel's silver bell you hear,
That summons you to all the Pride of Pray'r:
Light quirks of Music, broken and uneven,
Make the soul dance upon a Jig to Heav'n.
On painted Ceilings you devoutly stare,
Where sprawl the Saints of Verrio or Laguerre,
On gilded clouds in fair expansion lie,
And bring all Paradise before your eye.
To rest, the Cushion and soft Dean invite,
Who never mentions Hell to ears polite.

But hark! the chiming Clocks to dinner call;
A hundred footsteps scrape the marble Hall:
The rich Buffet well-colour'd Serpents grace,

And gaping Tritons spew to wash your face.
Is this a dinner? this a Genial room?
No, 't is a Temple, and a Hecatomb.
A solemn Sacrifice, perform'd in state,
You drink by measure, and to minutes eat.
So quick retires each flying course, you 'd swear
Sancho's dread Doctor and his Wand were there.
Between each Act the trembling salvers ring,
From soup to sweet-wine, and God bless the King.
In plenty starving, tantaliz'd in state,
And complaisantly help'd to all I hate,
Treated, caress'd, and tir'd, I take my leave,
Sick of his civil Pride from Morn to Eve;
I curse such lavish cost, and little skill,
And swear no Day was ever past so ill.

Yet hence the Poor are cloth'd, the Hungry fed;
Health to himself, and to his Infants bread
The Lab'rer bears: What his hard Heart denies,
His charitable Vanity supplies.

Another age shall see the golden Ear
Embrown the Slope, and nod on the Parterre,
Deep Harvests bury all his pride has plann'd,
And laughing Ceres re-assume the land.

Who then shall grace, or who improve the Soil?
Who plants like BATHURST, or who builds like BOYLE.
'T is Use alone that sanctifies Expense,
And Splendour borrows all her rays from Sense.

His Father's Acres who enjoys in peace,
Or makes his Neighbours glad, if he increase:
Whose cheerful Tenants bless their yearly toil,
Yet to their Lord owe more than to the soil;
Whose ample Lawns are not asham'd to feed
The milky heifer and deserving steed;
Whose rising Forests, not for pride or show,
But future Buildings, future Navies, grow:
Let his plantations stretch from down to down,

First shade a Country, and then raise a Town.
   You too proceed! make falling Arts your care,
Erect new wonders, and the old repair;
Jones and Palladio to themselves restore,
And be whate'er Vitruvius was before:
'Till Kings call forth th' Ideas of your mind,
(Proud to accomplish what such hands designed,)
Bid Harbours open, public Ways extend,
Bid Temples, worthier of the God, ascend;
Bid the broad Arch the dang'rous Flood contain,
The Mole projected break the roaring Main;
Back to his bounds their subject Sea command,
And roll obedient Rivers thro' the Land:
These Honours Peace to happy Britain brings,
These are Imperial Works, and worthy Kings.

EPISTLE V

To Mr. Addison

OCCASIONED BY HIS DIALOGUES ON MEDALS

See the wild Waste of all-devouring years!
How Rome her own sad Sepulchre appears,
With nodding arches, broken temples spread!
The very Tombs now vanish'd like their dead!
Imperial wonders rais'd on Nations spoil'd,
Where mix'd with Slaves the groaning Martyr toil'd:
Huge Theatres, that now unpeopled Woods,
Now drain'd a distant country of her Floods:
Fanes, which admiring Gods with pride survey,
Statues of Men, scarce less alive than they!
Some felt the silent stroke of mould'ring age,
Some hostile fury, some religious rage.
Barbarian blindness, Christian zeal conspire,

And Papal piety, and Gothic fire.
Perhaps, by its own ruins sav'd from flame,
Some bury'd marble half preserves a name;
That Name the learn'd with fierce disputes pursue,
And give to Titus old Vespasian's due.

   Ambition sigh'd: She found it vain to trust
The faithless Column and the crumbling Bust:
Huge moles, whose shadow stretch'd from shore to shore,
Their ruins perish'd, and their place no more!
Convinc'd, she now contracts her vast design,
And all her triumphs shrink into a Coin.
A narrow orb each crowded conquest keeps;
Beneath her Palm here sad Judæa weeps;
Now scantier limits the proud Arch confine,
And scarce are seen the prostrate Nile or Rhine;
A small Euphrates thro' the piece is roll'd,
And little Eagles wave their wings in gold.

   The Medal, faithful to its charge of fame,
Thro' climes and ages bears each form and name:
In one short view subjected to our eye
Gods, Emp'rors, Heroes, Sages, Beauties, lie.
With sharpen'd sight pale Antiquaries pore,
Th' inscription value, but the rust adore.
This the blue varnish, that the green endears,
The sacred rust of twice ten hundred years!
To gain Pescennius one employs his schemes,
One grasps a Cecrops in ecstatic dreams.
Poor Vadius, long with learned spleen devour'd,
Can taste no pleasure since his Shield was scour'd;
And Curio, restless by the Fair-one's side,
Sighs for an Otho, and neglects his bride.

   Theirs is the Vanity, the Learning thine:
Touch'd by thy hand, again Rome's glories shine:
Her Gods, and god-like Heroes rise to view,
And all her faded garlands bloom anew.
Nor blush, these studies thy regard engage;

These pleas'd the Fathers of poetic rage;
The verse and sculpture bore an equal part,
And Art reflected images to Art.

Oh when shall Britain, conscious of her claim,
Stand emulous of Greek and Roman fame?
In living medals see her wars enroll'd,
And vanquish'd realms supply recording gold?
Here, rising bold, the Patriot's honest face;
There Warriors frowning in historic brass?
Then future ages with delight shall see
How Plato's, Bacon's, Newton's looks agree;
Or in fair series laurell'd Bards be shown,
A Virgil there, and here an Addison.
Then shall thy CRAGGS (and let me call him mine)
On the cast ore, another Pollio, shine;
With aspect open, shall erect his head,
And round the orb in lasting notes be read,
"Statesman, yet friend to Truth! of soul sincere,
"In action faithful, and in honour clear;
"Who broke no promise, serv'd no private end,
"Who gain'd no title, and who lost no friend;
"Ennobled by himself, by all approv'd,
"And prais'd, unenvy'd, by the Muse he lov'd."

☾ Epistle to Dr. Arbuthnot,

PROLOGUE TO THE SATIRES

P. Shut, shut the door, good John! fatigu'd, I said,
Tie up the knocker, say I 'm sick, I 'm dead.
The Dog-star rages! nay 't is past a doubt,
All Bedlam, or Parnassus, is let out:
Fire in each eye, and papers in each hand,
They rave, recite, and madden round the land.
 What walls can guard me, or what shade can hide?
They pierce my thickets, thro' my Grot they glide;
By land, by water, they renew the charge;
They stop the chariot, and they board the barge.
No place is sacred, not the Church is free;
Ev'n Sunday shines no Sabbath-day to me;
Then from the Mint walks forth the Man of rhyme,
Happy to catch me just at Dinner-time.
 Is there a Parson, much bemus'd in beer,
A maudlin Poetess, a rhyming Peer,
A Clerk, foredoom'd his father's soul to cross,
Who pens a Stanza, when he should *engross?*
Is there, who, lock'd from ink and paper, scrawls
With desp'rate charcoal round his darken'd walls?
All fly to Twit'nam, and in humble strain
Apply to me, to keep them mad or vain.
Arthur, whose giddy son neglects the Laws,
Imputes to me and my damn'd works the cause:
Poor Cornus sees his frantic wife elope,
And curses Wit, and Poetry, and Pope.
 Friend to my Life! (which did not you prolong,
The world had wanted many an idle song)
What *Drop* or *Nostrum* can this plague remove?
Or which must end me, a Fool's wrath or love?

A dire dilemma! either way I 'm sped,
If foes, they write, if friends, they read me dead.
Seiz'd and tied down to judge, how wretched I!
Who can't be silent, and who will not lie.
To laugh, were want of goodness and of grace,
And to be grave, exceeds all Pow'r of face.
I sit with sad civility, I read
With honest anguish, and an aching head;
And drop at last, but in unwilling ears,
This saving counsel, "Keep your piece nine years."

"Nine years!" cries he, who high in Drury-lane,
Lull'd by soft Zephyrs thro' the broken pane,
Rhymes ere he wakes, and prints before *Term* ends,
Oblig'd by hunger, and request of friends:
"The piece, you think, is incorrect? why, take it,
I'm all submission, what you 'd have it, make it."

Three things another's modest wishes bound,
My Friendship, and a Prologue, and ten pound.

Pitholeon sends to me: "You know his Grace,
I want a Patron; ask him for a Place."
'Pitholeon libell'd me,'—"but here 's a letter
Informs you, Sir, 't was when he knew no better.
Dare you refuse him? Curll invites to dine,
He 'll write a *Journal*, or he 'll turn Divine."

Bless me! a packet.—" 'T is a stranger sues,
A Virgin Tragedy, an Orphan Muse."
If I dislike it, "Furies, death and rage!"
If I approve, "Commend it to the Stage."
There (thank my stars) my whole Commission ends,
The Play'rs and I are, luckily, no friends,
Fir'd that the house reject him, " 'Sdeath I 'll print it,
And shame the fools——Your Int'rest, Sir, with Lintot!"
'Lintot, dull rogue! will think your price too much:'
"Not, Sir, if you revise it, and retouch."
All my demurs but double his Attacks;
At last he whispers, "Do; and we go snacks."
Glad of a quarrel, straight I clap the door,

Sir, let me see your works and you no more.
'T is sung, when Midas' Ears began to spring,
(Midas, a sacred person and a king)
His very Minister who spy'd them first,
(Some say his Queen) was forc'd to speak, or burst.
And is not mine, my friend, a sorer case,
When ev'ry coxcomb perks them in my face?
A. Good friend, forbear! you deal in dang'rous things.
I 'd never name Queens, Ministers, or Kings;
Keep close to Ears, and those let asses prick;
'T is nothing— P. Nothing? if they bite and kick?
Out with it, DUNCIAD! let the secret pass,
That secret to each fool, that he 's an Ass:
The truth once told (and wherefore should we lie?)
The Queen of Midas slept, and so may I.
 You think this cruel? take it for a rule,
No creature smarts so little as a fool.
Let peals of laughter, Codrus! round thee break,
Thou unconcern'd canst hear the mighty crack:
Pit, Box, and gall'ry in convulsions hurl'd,
Thou stand'st unshook amidst a bursting world.
Who shames a Scribbler? break one cobweb thro',
He spins the slight, self-pleasing thread anew:
Destroy his fib or sophistry, in vain,
The creature 's at his dirty work again,
Thron'd in the centre of his thin designs,
Proud of a vast extent of flimsy lines!
Whom have I hurt? has Poet yet, or Peer,
Lost the arch'd eye-brow, or Parnassian sneer?
And has not Colley still his Lord, and whore?
His Butchers Henley, his free-masons Moore?
Does not one table Bavius still admit?
Still to one Bishop Philips seem a wit?
Still Sappho— A. Hold! for God's sake—you 'll offend,
No Names!—be calm!—learn prudence of a friend!
I too could write, and I am twice as tall;
But foes like these— P. One Flatt'rer 's worse than all.

Of all mad creatures, if the learn'd are right,
It is the slaver kills, and not the bite.
A fool quite angry is quite innocent:
Alas! 't is ten times worse when they *repent*.
    One dedicates in high heroic prose,
And ridicules beyond a hundred foes:
One from all Grubstreet will my fame defend,
And more abusive, calls himself my friend.
This prints my *Letters*, that expects a bribe,
And others roar aloud, "Subscribe, subscribe."
    There are, who to my person pay their court:
I cough like *Horace*, and, tho' lean, am short,
Ammon's great son one shoulder had too high,
Such *Ovid's* nose, and "Sir! you have an Eye"—
Go on, obliging creatures, make me see
All that disgrac'd my Betters, met in me.
Say for my comfort, languishing in bed,
"Just so immortal *Maro* held his head:"
And when I die, be sure you let me know
Great *Homer* died three thousand years ago.
    Why did I write? what sin to me unknown
Dipt me in ink, my parents', or my own?
As yet a child, nor yet a fool to fame,
I lisp'd in numbers, for the numbers came.
I left no calling for this idle trade,
No duty broke, no father disobey'd.
The Muse but serv'd to ease some friend, not Wife,
To help me thro' this long disease, my Life,
To second, ARBUTHNOT! thy Art and Care,
And teach the Being you preserv'd, to bear.
    But why then publish? *Granville* the polite,
And knowing *Walsh*, would tell me I could write;
Well-natur'd *Garth* inflam'd with early praise;
And *Congreve* lov'd, and *Swift* endur'd my lays;
The courtly *Talbot, Somers, Sheffield*, read;
Ev'n mitred *Rochester* would nod the head,
And *St. John's* self (great *Dryden's* friends before)

With open arms receiv'd one Poet more.
Happy my studies, when by these approv'd!
Happier their author, when by these belov'd!
From these the world will judge of men and books,
Not from the *Burnets*, *Oldmixons*, and *Cookes*.

Soft were my numbers; who could take offence,
While pure Description held the place of Sense?
Like gentle *Fanny's* was my flow'ry theme,
A painted mistress, or a purling stream.
Yet then did *Gildon* draw his venal quill;—
I wish'd the man a dinner, and sat still.
Yet then did *Dennis* rave in furious fret;
I never answer'd,—I was not in debt.
If want provok'd, or madness made them print,
I wag'd no war with *Bedlam* or the *Mint*.

Did some more sober Critic come abroad;
If wrong, I smil'd; if right, I kiss'd the rod.
Pains, reading, study, are their just pretence,
And all they want is spirit, taste, and sense.
Commas and points they set exactly right,
And 't were a sin to rob them of their mite.
Yet ne'er one sprig of laurel grac'd these ribalds,
From slashing *Bentley* down to pidling *Tibalds*:
Each wight, who reads not, and but scans and spells,
Each Word-catcher, that lives on syllables,
Ev'n such small Critics some regard may claim,
Preserv'd in *Milton's* or in *Shakespeare's* name.
Pretty! in amber to observe the forms
Of hairs, or straws, or dirt, or grubs, or worms!
The things, we know, are neither rich nor rare,
But wonder how the devil they got there.

Were others angry: I excus'd them too;
Well might they rage, I gave them but their due.
A man's true merit 't is not hard to find;
But each man's secret standard in his mind,
That Casting-weight pride adds to emptiness,
This, who can gratify? for who can *guess*?

The Bard whom pilfer'd Pastorals renown,
Who turns a Persian tale for half a Crown,
Just writes to make his barrenness appear,
And strains, from hard-bound brains, eight lines a year;
He, who still wanting, tho' he lives on theft,
Steals much, spends little, yet has nothing left:
And He, who now to sense, now nonsense leaning,
Means not, but blunders round about a meaning:
And He, whose fustian 's so sublimely bad,
It is not Poetry, but prose run mad:
All these, my modest Satire bade *translate*,
And own'd that nine such Poets made a *Tate*.
How did they fume, and stamp, and roar, and chafe!
And swear, not ADDISON himself was safe.

Peace to all such! but were there One whose fires
True Genius kindles, and fair Fame inspires;
Blest with each talent and each art to please,
And born to write, converse, and live with ease:
Should such a man, too fond to rule alone,
Bear, like the Turk, no brother near the throne.
View him with scornful, yet with jealous eyes,
And hate for arts that caus'd himself to rise;
Damn with faint praise, assent with civil leer,
And without sneering, teach the rest to sneer;
Willing to wound, and yet afraid to strike,
Just hint a fault, and hesitate dislike;
Alike reserv'd to blame, or to commend,
A tim'rous foe, and a suspicious friend;
Dreading ev'n fools, by Flatterers besieg'd,
And so obliging, that he ne'er oblige'd;
Like *Cato*, give his little Senate laws,
And sit attentive to his own applause;
While Wits and Templars ev'ry sentence raise,
And wonder with a foolish face of praise:——
Who but must laugh, if such a man there be?
Who would not weep, if ATTICUS were he?

What tho' my Name stood rubric on the walls

Or plaister'd posts, with claps, in capitals?
Or smoking forth, a hundred hawkers' load,
On wings of winds came flying all abroad?
I sought no homage from the Race that write;
I kept, like *Asian* Monarchs, from their sight:
Poems I heeded (now be-rhym'd so long)
No more than thou, great GEORGE! a birth-day song.
I ne'er with wits or witlings pass'd my days,
To spread about the itch of verse and praise;
Nor like a puppy, daggled* thro' the town,
To fetch and carry sing-song up and down;
Nor at Rehearsals sweat, and mouth'd, and cry'd,
With handkerchief and orange at my side;
But sick of fops, and poetry, and prate,
To *Bufo* left the whole *Castalian* state.

   Proud as *Apollo* on his forked hill,
Sat full-blown *Bufo*, puff'd by ev'ry quill;
Fed with soft Dedication all day long,
Horace and he went hand in hand in song.
His Library (where busts of Poets dead
And a true *Pindar* stood without a head,)
Receiv'd of wits an undistinguish'd race,
Who first his judgment ask'd, and then a place:
Much they extoll'd his pictures, much his seat,
And flatter'd ev'ry day, and some days eat:
Till grown more frugal in his riper days,
He paid some bards with port, and some with praise;
To some a dry rehearsal was assign'd,
And others (harder still) he paid in kind.
Dryden alone (what wonder?) came not nigh,
Dryden alone escap'd this judging eye:
But still the *Great* have kindness in reserve,
He help'd to bury whom he help'd to starve.

   May some choice patron bless each gray goose quill!
May ev'ry *Bavius* have his *Bufo* still! ·
So, when a Statesman wants a day's defence,

   * Dragged through the mire.

Or Envy holds a whole week's war with Sense,
Or simple pride for flatt'ry makes demands,
May dunce by dunce be whistled off my hands!
Blest be the *Great!* for those they take away,
And those they left me; for they left me GAY;
Left me to see neglected Genius bloom,
Neglected die, and tell it on his tomb:
Of all thy blameless life the sole return
My Verse, and QUEENSB'RY weeping o'er thy urn.
   Oh let me live my own, and die so too!
(To live and die is all I have to do:)
Maintain a Poet's dignity and ease,
And see what friends, and read what books I please;
Above a Patron, tho' I condescend
Sometimes to call a minister my friend.
I was not born for Courts or great affairs;
I pay my debts, believe, and say my pray'rs;
Can sleep without a Poem in my head;
Nor know, if *Dennis* be alive or dead.
   Why am I ask'd what next shall see the light?
Heav'ns! was I born for nothing but to write?
Has Life no joys for me? or, (to be grave)
Have I no friend to serve, no soul to save?
"I found him close with *Swift*"—'Indeed? no doubt,
(Cries prating *Balbus*) 'something will come out.'
'T is all in vain, deny it as I will.
'No, such a Genius never can lie still;'
And then for mine obligingly mistakes
The first Lampoon Sir *Will.* or *Bubo* makes.
Poor guiltless I! and can I choose but smile,
When ev'ry Coxcomb knows me by my *Style?*
   Curst be the verse, how well soe'er it flow,
That tends to make one worthy man my foe,
Give Virtue scandal, Innocence a fear,
Or from the soft-eyed Virgin steal a tear.
But he who hurts a harmless neighbour's peace,
Insults fall'n worth, or Beauty in distress,

Who loves a Lie, lame Slander helps about,
Who writes a Libel, or who copies out:
That Fop, whose pride affects a patron's name,
Yet absent, wounds an author's honest fame:
Who can *your* merit *selfishly* approve,
And show the *sense* of it without the *love*;
Who has the vanity to call you friend,
Yet wants the honour, injur'd, to defend;
Who tells whate'er you think, whate'er you say,
And, if he lie not, must at least betray:
Who to the *Dean*, and *silver bell* can swear,
And sees at *Canons* what was never there;
Who reads, but with a lust to misapply,
Make Satire a Lampoon, and Fiction, Lie.
A lash like mine no honest man shall dread,
But all such babbling blockheads in his stead.

    Let *Sporus* tremble— A. What? that thing of silk,
Sporus, that mere white curd of Ass's milk?
Satire or sense, alas! can *Sporus* feel?
Who breaks a butterfly upon a wheel?
P. Yet let me flap this bug with gilded wings,
This painted child of dirt, that stinks and stings;
Whose buzz the witty and the fair annoys,
Yet wit ne'er tastes, and beauty ne'er enjoys:
So well-bred spaniels civilly delight
In mumbling of the game they dare not bite.
Eternal smiles his emptiness betray,
As shallow streams run dimpling all the way.
Whether in florid impotence he speaks,
And, as the prompter breathes, the puppet squeaks;
Or at the ear of *Eve*, familiar Toad,
Half froth, half venom, spits himself abroad,
In puns, or politics, or tales, or lies,
Or spite, or smut, or rhymes, or blasphemies.
His wit all see-saw, between *that* and *this*,
Now high, now low, now master up, now miss,
And he himself one vile Antithesis.

Amphibious thing! that acting either part.
The trifling head or the corrupted heart,
Fop at the toilet, flatt'rer at the board,
Now trips a Lady, and now struts a Lord.
Eve's tempter thus the Rabbins have exprest,
A Cherub's face, a reptile all the rest;
Beauty that shocks you, parts that none will trust;
Wit that can creep, and pride that licks the dust.

Not Fortune's worshipper, nor fashion's fool,
Not Lucre's madman, nor Ambition's tool,
Not proud, or servile;—be one Poet's praise,
That, if he pleas'd, he pleas'd by manly ways:
That Flatt'ry, ev'n to Kings, he held a shame,
And thought a Lie in verse or prose the same.
That not in Fancy's maze he wander'd long,
But stoop'd to Truth, and moraliz'd his song:
That not for Fame, but Virtue's better end,
He stood the furious foe, the timid friend,
The damning critic, half approving wit,
The coxcomb hit, or fearing to be hit;
Laugh'd at the loss of friends he never had,
The dull, the proud, the wicked, and the mad;
The distant threats of vengeance on his head,
The blow unfelt, the tear he never shed;
The tale reviv'd, the lie so oft o'erthrown,
Th' imputed trash, and dulness not his own;
The morals blacken'd when the writings scape,
The libell'd person, and the pictur'd shape;
Abuse, on all he lov'd, or lov'd him, spread,
A friend in exile, or a father, dead;
The whisper, that to greatness still too near,
Perhaps, yet vibrates on his Sov'reign's ear:
Welcome for thee, fair *Virtue!* all the past;
For thee, fair Virtue! welcome ev'n the *last!*

A. But why insult the poor, affront the great?
P. A knave 's a knave, to me, in ev'ry state:
Alike my scorn, if he succeed or fail,

Sporus at court, or *Japhet* in a jail,
A hireling scribbler, or a hireling peer,
Knight of the post corrupt, or of the shire;
If on a Pillory, or near a Throne,
He gain his Prince's ear, or lose his own.
    Yet soft by nature, more a dupe than wit,
Sappho can tell you how this man was bit;
This dreaded Sat'rist *Dennis* will confess
Foe to his pride, but friend to his distress:
So humble, he has knock'd at *Tibbald's* door,
Has drunk with *Cibber*, nay has rhym'd for *Moore*.
Full ten years slander'd, did he once reply?
Three thousand suns went down on *Welsted's* lie.
To please a Mistress one aspers'd his life;
He lash'd him not, but let her be his wife.
Let *Budgel* charge low *Grubstreet* on his quill,
And write whate'er he pleas'd, except his Will;
Let the two *Curlls* of Town and Court, abuse
His father, mother, body, soul, and muse.
Yet why? that Father held it for a rule,
It was a sin to call our neighbour fool:
That harmless Mother thought no wife a whore:
Hear this, and spare his family, *James Moore!*
Unspotted names, and memorable long!
If there be force in Virtue, or in Song.
    Of gentle blood (part shed in Honour's cause,
While yet in *Britain* Honour had applause)
Each parent sprung—A. What fortune, pray?—P. Their own,
And better got, than *Bestia's* from the throne.
Born to no Pride, inheriting no Strife,
Nor marrying Discord in a noble wife,
Stranger to civil and religious rage,
The good man walk'd innoxious thro' his age.
Nor Courts he saw, no suits would ever try,
Nor dar'd an Oath, nor hazarded a Lie.
Un-learn'd, he knew no schoolman's subtle art,

No language, but the language of the heart.
By Nature honest, by Experience wise,
Healthy by temp'rance, and by exercise;
His life, tho' long, to sickness past unknown,
His death was instant, and without a groan.
O grant me, thus to live, and thus to die!
Who sprung from Kings shall know less joy than I.
   O Friend! may each domestic bliss be thine!
Be no unpleasing Melancholy mine:
Me, let the tender office long engage,
To rock the cradle of reposing Age,
With lenient arts extend a Mother's breath,
Make Languor smile, and smooth the bed of Death,
Explore the thought, explain the asking eye,
And keep a while one parent from the sky!
On cares like these if length of days attend,
May Heav'n, to bless those days, preserve my friend,
Preserve him social, cheerful, and serene,
And just as rich as when he serv'd a QUEEN.
A. Whether that blessing be deny'd or giv'n,
Thus far was right, the rest belongs to Heav'n.

ℭ Satires and Epistles of Horace Imitated

THE Occasion of publishing these Imitations was the clamour raised on some of my Epistles. An Answer from Horace was both more full, and of more Dignity, than any I could have made in my own person; and the Example of much greater Freedom in so eminent a Divine as Dr. Donne, seem'd a proof with what indignation and contempt a Christian may treat Vice or Folly, in ever so low, or ever so high a Station. Both these Authors were acceptable to the Princes and Ministers under whom they lived. The Satires of Dr. Donne I versified, at the desire of the Earl of Oxford while he was Lord Treasurer, and of the Duke of Shrewsbury who had been Secretary of State; neither of whom look'd upon a Satire on Vicious Courts as any Reflection on those they serv'd in. And indeed there is not in the world a greater error, than that which Fools are so apt to fall into, and Knaves with good reason to encourage, the mistaking a Satirist for a Libeller; whereas to a true Satirist nothing is so odious as a Libeller, for the same reason as to a man truly virtuous nothing is so hateful as a Hypocrite.

Uni æquus Virtuti atque ejus Amicis. [Pope.]

They are not Translations; neither of the close nor of the loose kind, and are therefore at once removed from comparison even with Dryden's magnificent versions, splendid in their very faults, of Juvenal. Nor do they properly bear the name of Imitations; for an Imitation of an earlier author is an attempt to produce a poem in his style and manner, though not necessarily on the same subject. Thomson's *Castle of Indolence* is an Imitation of Spenser; Johnson's *London* is an Imitation of Boileau, or, indeed, of Oldham and of Pope himself. But Pope differs quite sufficiently in manner and style from Horace to place his so-called 'Imitations' out of the category to which they assume to belong. They are rather Adaptations, or as Warburton has correctly suggested, Parodies; in other words, they take as much of the ancient form as suits the purposes of the modern poet, they occasionally cling closely to its outlines, occasionally desert them altogether. It was the form which came most readily, and originally almost accidentally, to Pope's hands; and which he justly thought himself free to use in his own way. The example of the First Epistle of the Second Book will best illustrate these remarks. In Pope's 'Imitation' the original is here turned upside down, and what in Horace is a panegyric, in the English poem becomes a covert satire. As Pope meant to suggest that George II, was a parody on Augustus, so his Epistle is a parody on, and not an imitation of, the Latin poem.

It is therefore obvious that any comparison or contrast between the Latin and English poets, interesting and suggestive as it doubtless is from other points of view, is idle with reference to the relation between these 'Imitations' and their 'originals.' Warburton is true to his self-imposed task of vindicating the Christian orthodoxy of Pope, in pointing out, ever and anon, passages where the latter has substituted for the Epicurean heresies of the genial Roman turns of thought more becoming the friend of an embryo bishop. Horace designed his Satires and Epistles as humorous sketches of society, seasoned with such personal allusions as appeared necessary to enliven his pictures, or as suggested themselves to a ready wit which can never teach a lesson without applying it. What with him was ornament, with Pope was purpose. Whatever may have been the philosophical system with which Warburton laboured so hard to credit him, the centre of that system was Pope; nor were his friends and foes so much introduced into these Imitations to point morals, as the morals preached to introduce his friends and foes, and himself.

The ease with which Pope moved in a form which imposed no restraint on his wit, makes these 'Imitations' the most enjoyable of all his productions. He closed the last Dialogue of the 'Epilogue' with an announcement of his resolution never to publish any more poems of the kind. Yet it was at the time (1741) when he was meditating a new Dunciad that he informed Lord Marchmont that 'uneasy desire of fame' and 'keen resentment of injuries' were 'both asleep together'; and even if we regard as spurious the fragment of an unpublished Satire entitled '1740,' found among his papers by Bolingbroke, and full of personal allusions to 'Bub,' and 'Hervey' and others, we may remain in doubt, whether had he lived he would or could have adhered to his determination. But he had done enough to establish himself as the unapproached master of personal satire in a poetic form; and to damn a multitude of victims, helpless against the strokes of genius, to everlasting fame.

THE FIRST SATIRE

OF THE

SECOND BOOK OF HORACE

SATIRE I

To Mr. Fortescue

P. There are, (I scarce can think it, but am told,)
There are, to whom my Satire seems too bold:
Scarce to wise Peter complaisant enough,
And something said of Chartres much too rough.
The lines are weak, another 's pleas'd to say,
Lord Fanny spins a thousand such a day.
Tim'rous by nature, of the Rich in awe,
I come to Counsel learned in the Law:
You 'll give me, like a friend both sage and free,
Advice; and (as you use) without a Fee.

    F. I 'd write no more.

                    P. Not write? but then I think,
And for my soul I cannot sleep a wink.
I nod in company, I wake at night,
Fools rush into my head, and so I write.

    F. You could not do a worse thing for your life.
Why, if the nights seem tedious,—take a Wife:
Or rather truly, if your point be rest,
Lettuce and cowslip-wine; *Probatum est.*
But talk with Celsus, Celsus will advise
Hartshorn, or something that shall close your eyes.
Or, if you needs must write, write Cæsar's Praise,
You 'll gain at least a *Knighthood*, or the *Bays.*

    P. What? like Sir Richard, rumbling, rough, and fierce.
With Arms, and George, and Brunswick crowd the verse,
Rend with tremendous sound your ears asunder,

With Gun, Drum, Trumpet, Blunderbuss, and Thunder?
Or nobly wild, with Budgel's fire and force,
Paint Angels trembling round his falling Horse?

    F. Then all your Muse's softer art display,
Let CAROLINA smooth the tuneful lay,
Lull with AMELIA's liquid name the Nine,
And sweetly flow thro' all the Royal Line.

    P. Alas! few verses touch their nicer ear;
They scarce can bear their *Laureate* twice a year;
And justly CÆSAR scorns the Poet's lays:
It is to *History* he trusts for Praise.

    F. Better be Cibber, I 'll maintain it still,
Than ridicule all Taste, blaspheme Quadrille,
Abuse the City's best good men in metre,
And laugh at Peers that put their trust in Peter.
Ev'n those you touch not, hate you.

                    P. What should ail them?

    F. A hundred smart in Timon and in Balaam:
The fewer still you name, you wound the more;
Bond is but one, but Harpax is a score.

    P. Each mortal has his pleasure: none deny
Scarsdale his bottle, Darty his Ham-pie;
Ridotta sips and dances, till she see
The doubling Lustres dance as fast as she;
F— loves the Senate, Hockley-hole his brother,
Like in all else, as one Egg to another.
I love to pour out all my self, as plain
As downright SHIPPEN, or as old Montaigne:
In them, as certain to be lov'd as seen,
The Soul stood forth, nor kept a thought within;
In me what spots (for spots I have) appear,
Will prove at least the medium must be clear.
In this impartial glass, my Muse intends
Fair to expose myself, my foes, my friends;
Publish the present age; but where my text
Is Vice too high, reserve it for the next:

My foes shall wish my Life a longer date,
And ev'ry friend the less lament my fate.
My head and heart thus flowing thro' my quill,
Verse-man or Prose-man, term me which you will,
Papist or Protestant, or both between,
Like good Erasmus in an honest Mean,
In moderation placing all my glory,
While Tories call me Whig, and Whigs a Tory.

Satire 's my weapon, but I 'm too discreet
To run a muck, and tilt at all I meet;
I only wear it in a land of Hectors,
Thieves, Supercargoes, Sharpers, and Directors.
Save but our *Army!* and let Jove encrust
Swords, pikes, and guns, with everlasting rust!
Peace is my dear delight—not FLEURY'S more:
But touch me, and no Minister so sore.
Whoe'er offends, at some unlucky time
Slides into verse, and hitches in a rhyme,
Sacred to Ridicule his whole life long,
And the sad burthen of some merry song.

Slander or Poison dread from Delia's rage,
Hard words or hanging, if your Judge be Page.
From furious Sappho scarce a milder fate,
P-x'd by her love, or libell'd by her hate.
Its proper pow'r to hurt, each creature feels;
Bulls aim their horns, and Asses lift their heels;
'T is a Bear's talent not to kick, but hug;
And no man wonders he 's not stung by Pug.
So drink with Walters, or with Chartres eat,
They 'll never poison you, they 'll only cheat.

Then, learned Sir! (to cut the matter short)
Whate'er my fate,—or well or ill at Court,
Whether Old age, with faint but cheerful ray,
Attends to gild the Ev'ning of my day,
Or Death's black wing already be display'd,
To wrap me in the universal shade;

Whether the darken'd room to muse invite,
Or whiten'd wall provoke the skew'r to write:
In durance, exile, Bedlam or the Mint,—
Like Lee or Budgel, I will rhyme and print.

    F. Alas young man! your days can ne'er be long,
In flow'r of age you perish for a song!
Plums and Directors, Shylock and his Wife,
Will club their Testers,* now, to take your life!

    P. What? arm'd for Virtue when I point the pen,
Brand the bold front of shameless guilty men;
Dash the proud Gamester in his gilded Car;
Bare the mean Heart that lurks beneath a *Star;*
Can there be wanting, to defend Her cause,
Lights of the Church, or Guardians of the Laws?
Could pension'd Boileau lash in honest strain
Flatt'rers and Bigots ev'n in Louis' reign?
Could Laureate Dryden Pimp and Friar engage,
Yet neither Charles nor James be in a rage?
And I not strip the gilding off a knave,
Unplac'd, unpension'd, no man's heir, or slave?
I will, or perish in the gen'rous cause:
Hear this, and tremble! you, who 'scape the Laws.
Yes, while I live, no rich or noble knave
Shall walk the World, in credit, to his grave.
To VIRTUE ONLY and HER FRIENDS A FRIEND,
The World beside may murmur, or commend.
Know, all the distant din that world can keep,
Rolls o'er my Grotto, and but soothes my sleep.
There, my retreat the best Companions grace,
Chiefs out of war, and Statesmen out of place.
There ST. JOHN mingles with my friendly bowl
The Feast of Reason and the Flow of Soul:
And HE, whose lightning pierc'd th' Iberian Lines,
Now forms my Quincunx, and now ranks my Vines,

---

* "Shylock and his wife" are the Wortley Montagus; "testers" = six-pences.

Or tames the Genius of the stubborn plain,
Almost as quickly as he conquer'd Spain.

   Envy must own, I live among the Great,
No Pimp of Pleasure, and no Spy of State.
With eyes that pry not, tongue that ne'er repeats,
Fond to spread friendships, but to cover heats;
To help who want, to forward who excel;
This, all who know me, know; who love me, tell;
And who unknown defame me, let them be
Scribblers or Peers, alike are *Mob* to me.
This is my plea, on this I rest my cause—
What saith my Counsel, learned in the laws?

   F. Your Plea is good; but still I say, beware!
Laws are explain'd by Men—so have a care.
It stands on record, that in Richard's times
A man was hang'd for very honest rhymes.
Consult the Statute: *quart*. I think, it is,
Edwardi sext. or *prim. et quint. Eliz*.
See *Libels*, *Satires*—here you have it—read.

   P. *Libels* and *Satires!* lawless things indeed!
But grave *Epistles*, bringing Vice to light,
Such as a King might read, a Bishop write;
Such as Sir ROBERT would approve——

                                  F. Indeed?
The Case is alter'd—you may then proceed;
In such a cause the Plaintiff will be hiss'd;
My Lords the Judges laugh, and you 're dismiss'd.

THE SECOND SATIRE

OF THE

SECOND BOOK OF HORACE

SATIRE II

To Mr. Bethel

What, and how great, the Virtue and the Art
To live on little with a cheerful heart,
(A doctrine sage, but truly none of mine,)
Let 's talk, my friends, but talk before we dine.
Not when a gilt Buffet's reflected pride
Turns you from sound Philosophy aside;
Not when from plate to plate your eyeballs roll,
And the brain dances to the mantling bowl.

Hear Bethel's Sermon, one not vers'd in schools,
But strong in sense, and wise without the rules.

Go work, hunt, exercise! (he thus began)
Then scorn a homely dinner, if you can.
Your wine lock'd up, your Butler stroll'd abroad,
Or fish deny'd (the river yet unthaw'd),
If then plain bread and milk will do the feat,
The pleasure lies in you, and not the meat.

Preach as I please, I doubt our curious men
Will choose a pheasant still before a hen;
Yet hens of Guinea full as good I hold,
Except you eat the feathers green and gold.
Of carps and mullets why prefer the great,
(Tho' cut in pieces ere my Lord can eat)
Yet for small Turbots such esteem profess?
Because God made these large, the other less.

Oldfield with more than Harpy throat endued,
Cries "Send me, Gods! a whole Hog barbecued!

Oh blast it, South-winds! till a stench exhale
Rank as the ripeness of a rabbit's tail.
By what Criterion do ye eat, d' ye think,
If this is priz'd for sweetness, that for stink?
When the tir'd glutton labours thro' a treat,
He finds no relish in the sweetest meat,
He calls for something bitter, something sour,
And the rich feast concludes extremely poor:
Cheap eggs, and herbs, and olives still we see;
Thus much is left of old Simplicity!
The Robin-red-breast till of late had rest,
And children sacred held a Martin's nest,
Till Becca-ficos sold so dev'lish dear
To one that was, or would have been a Peer.
Let me extol a Cat, on oysters fed,
I 'll have a party at the Bedford-head;
Or ev'n to crack live Crawfish recommend;
I 'd never doubt at Court to make a friend.

 'T is yet in vain, I own, to make a pother
About one vice, and fall into the other:
Between Excess and Famine lies a mean;
Plain, but not sordid; tho' not splendid, clean.

 Avidien, or his Wife (no matter which,
For him you 'll call a dog, and her a bitch)
Sell their presented partridges, and fruits,
And humbly live on rabbits and on roots:
One half-pint bottle serves them both to dine,
And is at once their vinegar and wine.
But on some lucky day (as when they found
A lost Bank-bill, or heard their Son was drown'd)
At such a feast, old vinegar to spare,
Is what two souls so gen'rous cannot bear:
Oil, tho' it stink, they drop by drop impart,
But souse the cabbage with a bounteous heart.

 He knows to live, who keeps the middle state,
And neither leans on this side, nor on that;

Nor stops, for one bad cork, his butler's pay,
Swears, like Albutius, a good cook away;
Nor lets, like Nævius, ev'ry error pass,
The musty wine, foul cloth, or greasy glass.

Now hear what blessings Temperance can bring:
(Thus said our friend, and what he said I sing,)
First Health: The stomach (cramm'd from ev'ry dish,
A tomb of boil'd and roast, and flesh and fish,
Where bile, and wind, and phlegm, and acid jar,
And all the man is one intestine war)
Remembers oft the School-boy's simple fare,
The temp'rate sleeps, and spirits light as air.

How pale, each Worshipful and Rev'rend guest
Rise from a Clergy, or a City feast!
What life in all that ample body, say?
What heav'nly particle inspires the clay?
The Soul subsides, and wickedly inclines
To seem but mortal, ev'n in sound Divines.

On morning wings how active springs the Mind
That leaves the load of yesterday behind!
How easy ev'ry labour it pursues!
How coming to the Poet ev'ry Muse!
Not but we may exceed, some holy time,
Or tir'd in search of Truth, or search of Rhyme;
Ill health some just indulgence may engage,
And more the sickness of long life, Old age;
For fainting Age what cordial drop remains,
If our intemp'rate Youth the vessel drains?

Our fathers prais'd rank ven'son. You suppose
Perhaps, young men! our fathers had no nose.
Not so: a Buck was then a week's repast,
And 't was their point, I ween, to make it last;
More pleas'd to keep it till their friends could come,
Than eat the sweetest by themselves at home.
Why had I not in those good times my birth,
Ere coxcomb-pies or coxcombs were on earth?

Unworthy he, the voice of Fame to hear,
That sweetest music to an honest ear;
(For 'faith, Lord Fanny! you are in the wrong,
The world's good word is better than a song)
Who has not learned, fresh sturgeon and ham-pie
Are no rewards for want, and infamy!
When Luxury has lick'd up all thy pelf,
Curs'd by thy neighbours, thy trustees, thyself,
To friends, to fortune, to mankind a shame,
Think how posterity will treat thy name;
And buy a rope, that future times may tell
Thou hast at least bestow'd one penny well.

"Right," cries his Lordship, "for a rogue in need
"To have a Taste is insolence indeed:
"In me 't is noble, suits my birth and state,
"My wealth unwieldy, and my heap too great."
Then, like the Sun, let Bounty spread her ray,
And shine that superfluity away.
Oh Impudence of wealth! with all thy store,
How dar'st thou let one worthy man be poor?
Shall half the new-built churches round thee fall?
Make Quays, build Bridges, or repair White-hall:
Or to thy country let that heap be lent,
As M * * o's* was, but not at five per cent.

Who thinks that Fortune cannot change her mind,
Prepares a dreadful jest for all mankind.
And who stands safest? tell me, is it he
That spreads and swells in puff'd prosperity,
Or blest with little, whose preventing care
In peace provides fit arms against a war?

Thus BETHEL spoke, who always speaks his thought,
And always thinks the very thing he ought:
His equal mind I copy what I can,
And, as I love, would imitate the Man
In South-sea days not happier, when surmis'd

* The Duchess of Marlborough's.

The Lord of Thousands, than if now *Excis'd;*
In forest planted by a Father's hand,
Than in five acres now of rented land.
Content with little, I can piddle here
On brocoli and mutton, round the year;
But ancient friends (tho' poor, or out of play)
That touch my bell, I cannot turn away.
'T is true, no Turbots dignify my boards,
But gudgeons, flounders, what my Thames affords:
To Hounslow-heath I point and Bansted-down,
Thence comes your mutton, and these chicks my own:
From yon old walnut-tree a show'r shall fall;
And grapes, long ling'ring on my only wall,
And figs from standard and espalier join;
The dev'l is in you if you cannot dine:
Then cheerful healths (your Mistress shall have place),
And, what 's more rare, a Poet shall say Grace.
	Fortune not much of humbling me can boast;
Tho' double tax'd, how little have I lost?
My Life's amusements have been just the same,
Before, and after, Standing Armies came.
My lands are sold, my father's house is gone;
I 'll hire another's; is not that my own,
And yours, my friends? thro' whose free-opening gate
None comes too early, none departs too late;
(For I, who hold sage Homer's rule the best,
Welcome the coming, speed the going guest).
"Pray heav'n it last!" (cries SWIFT!) "as you go on;
"I wish to God this house had been your own:
"Pity! to build, without a son or wife:
"Why, you'll enjoy it only all your life."
Well, if the use be mine, can it concern one,
Whether the name belong to Pope or Vernon?
What 's *Property?* dear Swift! you see it alter
From you to me, from me to Peter Walter;
Or, in a mortgage, prove a Lawyer's share;

Or, in a jointure, vanish from the heir;
Or in pure equity (the case not clear)
The Chanc'ry takes your rents for twenty year:
At best, it falls to some ungracious son,
Who cries, "My father's damn'd and all 's my own."
Shades, that to BACON could retreat afford,
Become the portion of a booby Lord;
And Hemsley, once proud Buckingham's delight,
Slides to a Scriv'ner or a city Knight.
Let lands and houses have what Lords they will,
Let Us be fix'd, and our own masters still.

THE FIRST EPISTLE

OF THE

FIRST BOOK OF HORACE

EPISTLE I

To Lord Bolingbroke

St. John, whose love indulg'd my labours past,
Matures my present, and shall bound my last!
Why will you break the Sabbath of my days?
Now sick alike of Envy and of Praise,
Public too long, ah let me hide my Age!
See, Modest Cibber now has left the Stage:
Our Gen'rals now, retir'd to their Estates,
Hang their old Trophies o'er the Garden gates,
In Life's cool Ev'ning satiate of Applause,
Nor fond of bleeding, ev'n in BRUNSWICK'S cause.

A Voice there is, that whispers in my ear,
('T is Reason's voice, which sometimes one can hear)
"Friend Pope! be prudent, let your Muse take breath,
"And never gallop Pegasus to death;

"Lest stiff, and stately, void of fire or force,
"You limp, like Blackmore on a Lord Mayor's horse."
   Farewell then Verse, and Love, and ev'ry Toy,
The Rhymes and Rattles of the Man or Boy;
What right, what true, what fit we justly call,
Let this be all my care—for this is All:
To lay this harvest up, and hoard with haste
What ev'ry day will want, and most, the last.
   But ask not, to what Doctors I apply?
Sworn to no Master, of no Sect am I:
As drives the storm, at any door I knock:
And house with Montaigne now, or now with Locke.
Sometimes a Patriot, active in debate,
Mix with the World, and battle for the State,
Free as young Lyttelton, her Cause pursue,
Still true to Virtue, and as warm as true:
Sometimes with Aristippus, or St. Paul,
Indulge my candor, and grow all to all;
Back to my native Moderation slide,
And win my way by yielding to the tide.
   Long, as to him who works for debt, the day,
Long as the Night to her whose Love 's away,
Long as the Year's dull circle seems to run,
When the brisk Minor pants for twenty-one:
So slow th' unprofitable moments roll,
That lock up all the Functions of my soul;
That keep me from myself; and still delay
Life's instant business to a future day:
That task, which as we follow, or despise,
The eldest is a fool, the youngest wise;
Which done, the poorest can no wants endure;*
And which not done, the richest must be poor.
   Late as it is, I put myself to school,
And feel some comfort, not to be a fool.
Weak tho' I am of limb, and short of sight,

* i.e., can want nothing.

Far from a Lynx, and not a Giant quite;
I 'll do what Mead and Cheselden advise,
To keep these limbs, and to preserve these eyes.
Not to go back, is somewhat to advance,
And men must walk at least before they dance.

Say, does thy blood rebel, thy bosom move
With wretched Av'rice, or as wretched Love?
Know, there are Words, and Spells, which can control
Between the Fits this Fever of the soul:
Know, there are Rhymes, which fresh and fresh apply'd
Will cure the arrant'st Puppy of his Pride.
Be furious, envious, slothful, mad, or drunk,
Slave to a Wife, or Vassal to a Punk,
A Switz, a High-dutch, or a Low-dutch Bear;
All that we ask is but a patient Ear.

'T is the first Virtue, Vices to abhor;
And the first Wisdom, to be Fool no more.
But to the world no bugbear is so great,
As want of figure, and a small Estate.
To either India see the Merchant fly,
Scar'd at the spectre of pale Poverty!
See him, with pains of body, pangs of soul,
Burn through the Tropic, freeze beneath the Pole!
Wilt thou do nothing for a nobler end,
Nothing, to make Philosophy thy friend?
To stop thy foolish views, thy long desires,
And ease thy heart of all that it admires?

Here, Wisdom calls: "Seek Virtue first, be bold!
"As Gold to Silver, Virtue is to Gold."
There, London's voice: "Get Money, Money still!
"And then let Virtue follow, if she will."
This, this the saving doctrine, preach'd to all,
From low St. James's up to high St. Paul;
From him whose quills stand quiver'd at his ear,
To him who notches sticks at Westminster.

Barnard in spirit, sense, and truth abounds;

"Pray then, what wants he?" Fourscore thousand pounds;
A Pension, or such Harness for a slave
As Bug now has, and Dorimant would have.
Barnard, thou art a Cit, with all thy worth;
But Bug and D*l, their *Honours*, and so forth.

　Yet ev'ry child another song will sing:
"Virtue, brave boys! 't is Virtue makes a King."
True, conscious Honour is to feel no sin,
He 's arm'd without that 's innocent within;
Be this thy Screen, and this thy wall of Brass;
Compar'd to this, a Minister 's an Ass.

　And say, to which shall our applause belong,
This new Court jargon, or the good old song?
The modern language of corrupted Peers,
Or what was spoke at Cressy and Poitiers?
Who counsels best? who whispers, "Be but great,
"With Praise or Infamy leave that to fate;
"Get Place and Wealth, if possible, with grace;
"If not, by any means get Wealth and Place—"
For what? to have a Box where Eunuchs sing,*
And foremost in the Circle eye a King.
Or he, who bids thee face with steady view
Proud Fortune, and look shallow Greatness thro':
And, while he bids thee, sets th' Example too?
If such a doctrine, in St. James's air,
Shou'd chance to make the well-drest Rabble stare;
If honest S*z take scandal at a Spark,
That less admires the Palace than the Park:
Faith I shall give the answer Reynard gave:
"I cannot like, dread Sir, your Royal Cave:
"Because I see, by all the tracks about,
"Full many a Beast goes in, but none come out."
Adieu to Virtue, if you 're once a Slave:
Send her to Court, you send her to her grave.

　Well, if a King 's a Lion, at the least

　　* The Italian *castrati* were great drawing-cards.

The People are a many-headed Beast:
Can they direct what measures to pursue,
Who know themselves so little what to do?
Alike in nothing but one Lust of Gold,
Just half the land would buy, and half be sold:
Their Country's wealth our mightier Misers drain,
Or cross, to plunder Provinces, the Main;
The rest, some farm the Poor-box, some the Pews;
Some keep Assemblies, and would keep the Stews;
Some with fat Bucks on childless dotards fawn;
Some win rich Widows by their Chine and Brawn;
While with the silent growth of ten per cent,
In dirt and darkness, hundreds stink content.

Of all these ways, if each pursues his own,
Satire be kind, and let the wretch alone:
But shew me one who has it in his pow'r
To act consistent with himself an hour.
Sir Job sail'd forth, the ev'ning bright and still,
"No place on earth (he cry'd) like Greenwich hill!"
Up starts a Palace; lo, th' obedient base
Slopes at its foot, the woods its sides embrace,
The silver Thames reflects its marble face.
Now let some whimsy, or that dev'l within
Which guides all those who know not what they mean,
But give the Knight (or give his Lady) spleen;
"Away, away! take all your scaffolds down,
"For Snug 's the word: My dear! we 'll live in Town."

At am'rous Flavio is the stocking thrown?
That very night he longs to lie alone.
The Fool, whose Wife elopes some thrice a quarter,
For matrimonial solace dies a martyr.
Did ever Proteus, Merlin, any witch,
Transform themselves so strangely as the Rich?
Well, but the Poor—The Poor have the same itch;
They change their weekly Barber, weekly News,
Prefer a new Japanner to their shoes,

Discharge their Garrets, move their beds, and run
(They know not whither) in a Chaise and one;
They hire their sculler, and when once aboard,
Grow sick, and damn the climate—like a Lord.
 You laugh, half Beau, half Sloven if I stand,
My wig all powder, and all snuff my band;
You laugh, if coat and breeches strangely vary,
White gloves, and linen worthy Lady Mary!
But when no Prelate's Lawn with hair-shirt lin'd,
Is half so incoherent as my Mind,
When (each opinion with the next at strife,
One ebb and flow of follies all my life)
I plant, root up; I build, and then confound,
Turn round to square, and square again to round;
You never change one muscle of your face,
You think this Madness but a common case,
Nor once to Chanc'ry, nor to Hale apply;
Yet hang your lip, to see a Seam awry!
Careless how ill I with myself agree,
Kind to my dress, my figure, not to Me.
Is this my Guide, Philosopher, and Friend?
This, he who loves me, and who ought to mend?
Who ought to make me (what he can, or none,)
That Man divine whom Wisdom calls her own;
Great without Title, without Fortune bless'd;
Rich ev'n when plunder'd, honour'd while oppress'd;
Lov'd without youth, and follow'd without pow'r;
At home, tho' excil'd; free, tho' in the Tower;
In short, that reas'ning, high, immortal Thing,
Just less than Jove, and much above a King,
Nay, half in heav'n—except (what 's mighty odd)
A Fit of Vapours clouds this Demi-God.

THE SIXTH EPISTLE

OF THE

FIRST BOOK OF HORACE

EPISTLE VI

To Mr. Murray

"Not to admire, is all the Art I know,
"To make men happy, and to keep them so."
(Plain truth, dear Murray, needs no flow'rs of speech,
So take it in the very words of Creech.)
  This Vault of Air, this congregated Ball,
Self-center'd Sun, and Stars that rise and fall,
There are, my Friend! whose philosophic eyes
Look thro', and trust the Ruler with his skies,
To him commit the hour, the day, the year,
And view this dreadful All without a fear.
Admire we then what Earth's low entrails hold,
Arabian shores, or Indian seas infold;
All the mad trade of Fools and Slaves for Gold?
Or Popularity? or Stars and Strings?
The Mob's applauses, or the gifts of Kings?
Say with what eyes we ought at Courts to gaze,
And pay the Great our homage of Amaze?
  If weak the pleasure that from these can spring,
The fear to want them is as weak a thing:
Whether we dread, or whether we desire,
In either case, believe me, we admire;
Whether we joy or grieve, the same the curse,
Surpris'd at better, or surpris'd at worse.
Thus good or bad, to one extreme betray
Th' unbalanc'd Mind, and snatch the Man away;
For Virtue's self may too much zeal be had;

The worst of Madmen is a Saint run mad.
  Go then, and if you can, admire the state
Of beaming diamonds, and reflected plate;
Procure a TASTE to double the surprise,
And gaze on Parian Charms with learned eyes:
Be struck with bright Brocade, or Tyrian Dye,
Our Birth-day Nobles' splendid Livery.
If not so pleas'd, at Council-board rejoice,
To see their Judgments hang upon thy Voice;
From morn to night, at Senate, Rolls, and Hall,
Plead much, read more, dine late, or not at all.
But wherefore all this labour, all this strife?
For Fame, for Riches, for a noble Wife?
Shall One whom Nature, Learning, Birth, conspir'd
To form, not to admire but be admir'd,
Sigh, while his Chloe blind to Wit and Worth
Weds the rich Dulness of some Son of earth?
Yet Time ennobles, or degrades each Line;
It brighten'd *Craggs's*, and may darken thine:
And what is Fame? the Meanest have their Day,
The Greatest can but blaze, and pass away.
Grac'd as thou art, with all the Pow'r of Words,
So known, so honour'd, at the House of Lords:
Conspicuous Scene! another yet is nigh,
(More silent far) where Kings and Poets lie;
Where MURRAY (long enough his Country's pride)
Shall be no more than TULLY, or than HYDE!
  Rack'd with Sciatics, martyr'd with the Stone,
Will any mortal let himself alone?
See Ward by batter'd Beaux invited over,
And desp'rate Misery lays hold on Dover.
The case is easier in the Mind's disease;
There all Men may be cur'd, whene'er they please.
Would ye be blest? despise low Joys, low Gains;
Disdain whatever CORNBURY disdains;
Be virtuous, and be happy for your pains.

But art thou one, whom new opinions sway,
One who believes as Tindal leads the way,
Who Virtue and a Church alike disowns,
Thinks that but words, and this but brick and stones?
Fly then, on all the wings of wild desire,
Admire whate'er the maddest can admire.
Is Wealth thy passion? Hence! from Pole to Pole,
Where winds can carry, or where waves can roll,
For Indian spices, for Peruvian Gold,
Prevent the greedy, and out-bid the bold:
Advance thy golden Mountain to the skies;
On the broad base of fifty thousand rise,
Add one round hundred, and (if that 's not fair)
Add fifty more, and bring it to a square.
For, mark th' advantage; just so many score
Will gain a Wife with half as many more,
Procure her Beauty, make that beauty chaste,
And then such Friends—as cannot fail to last.
A Man of wealth is dubb'd a Man of worth,
Venus shall give him Form, and Anstis Birth.
(Believe me, many a German Prince is worse,
Who proud of Pedigree, is poor of Purse.)
His wealth brave Timon gloriously confounds;
Ask'd for a groat, he gives a hundred pounds;
Or if three Ladies like a luckless Play,
Takes the whole House upon the Poet's Day.
Now, in such exigencies not to need,
Upon my word, you must be rich indeed;
A noble superfluity it craves,
Not for yourself, but for your Fools and Knaves;
Something, which for your Honour they may cheat,
And which it much becomes you to forget.
If Wealth alone then make and keep us blest,
Still, still be getting, never, never rest.

But if to Pow'r and Place your passion lie,
If in the Pomp of Life consist the joy;

Then hire a Slave, or (if you will) a Lord
To do the Honours, and to give the Word;
Tell at your Levee, as the Crowds approach,
To whom to nod, whom take into your Coach,
Whom honour with your hand: to make remarks,
Who rules in Cornwall, or who rules in Berks:
"This may be troublesome, is near the Chair;
"That makes three members, this can choose a May'r."
Instructed thus, you bow, embrace, protest,
Adopt him Son, or Cousin at the least,
Then turn about, and laugh at your own Jest.

   Or if your life be one continu'd Treat,
If to live well means nothing but to eat;
Up, up! cries Gluttony, 't is break of day,
Go drive the Deer, and drag the finny prey;
With hounds and horns go hunt an Appetite—
So Russel did, but could not eat at night,
Call'd happy Dog! the Beggar at his door,
And envy'd Thirst and Hunger to the Poor.

   Or shall we ev'ry Decency confound,
Thro' Taverns, Stews, and Bagnio's take our round,
Go dine with Chartres, in each Vice out-do
K—l's lewd Cargo, or Ty—y's Crew,
From Latian Syrens, French Circean Feasts,
Return well travell'd, and transform'd to Beasts,
Or for a Titled Punk, or foreign Flame,
Renounce our Country, and degrade our Name?

   If, after all, we must with Wilmot own,
The Cordial Drop of Life is Love alone,
And Swift cry wisely, "Vive la Bagatelle!"
The Man that loves and laughs, must sure do well.
Adieu—if this advice appear the worst,
E'en take the Counsel which I gave you first:
Or better Precepts if you can impart,
Why do, I 'll follow them with all my heart.

THE FIRST EPISTLE

OF THE

SECOND BOOK OF HORACE

EPISTLE I

To Augustus*

While you, great Patron of Mankind! sustain
The balanc'd World, and open all the Main;
Your Country, chief, in Arms abroad defend,
At home, with Morals, Arts, and Laws amend;
How shall the Muse, from such a Monarch, steal
An hour, and not defraud the Public Weal?
 Edward and Henry, now the Boast of Fame,
And virtuous Alfred, a more sacred Name,
After a Life of gen'rous Toils endur'd,
The Gaul subdu'd, or Property secur'd,
Ambition humbled, mighty Cities storm'd,
Or Laws establish'd, and the world reform'd;
Clos'd their Long Glories, with a sigh, to find
Th' unwilling Gratitude of base mankind!
All human Virtue, to its latest breath,
Finds Envy never conquer'd but by Death.
The great Alcides, ev'ry Labour past,
Had still this Monster to subdue at last.
Sure fate of all, beneath whose rising ray,
Each star of meaner merit fades away!
Oppress'd we feel the beam directly beat,
Those Suns of Glory please not till they set.
 To thee, the World its present homage pays,
The Harvest early, but mature the praise:

* George II.

Great Friend of LIBERTY! in *Kings* a Name
Above all Greek, above all Roman fame:
Whose Word is Truth, as sacred and rever'd,
As Heav'n's own Oracles from Altars heard.
Wonder of Kings! like whom, to mortal eyes
None e'er has risen, and none e'er shall rise.

Just in one instance, be it yet confest
Your People, Sir, are partial in the rest:
Foes to all living worth except your own,
And Advocates for folly dead and gone.
Authors, like coins, grow dear as they grow old;
It is the rust we value, not the gold.
Chaucer's worst ribaldry is learn'd by rote,
And beastly Skelton Heads of Houses quote:
One likes no language but the Faery Queen;
A Scot will fight for Christ's Kirk o' the Green;*
And each true Briton is to Ben so civil,
He swears the Muses met him at the Devil.**

Tho' justly Greece her eldest sons admires,
Why should not We be wiser than our sires?
In ev'ry Public virtue we excel;
We build, we paint, we sing, we dance as well,
And learned Athens to our art must stoop,
Could she behold us tumbling thro' a hoop.

If Time improve our Wit as well as Wine,
Say at what age a Poet grows divine?
Shall we, or shall we not, account him so,
Who died, perhaps, an hundred years ago?
End all dispute; and fix the year precise
When British bards begin t' immortalize?

"Who lasts a century can have no flaw,
"I hold that Wit a Classic, good in law."

Suppose he wants a year, will you compound?
And shall we deem him Ancient, right and sound,

* Because a Scottish King (James I) composed it.
** A tavern frequented by Ben Jonson.

Or damn to all eternity at once,
At ninety-nine, a Modern and a Dunce?
   "We shall not quarrel for a year or two;
"By courtesy of England, he may do."
   Then by the rule that made the Horse-tail bear,
I pluck out year by year, as hair by hair,
And melt down Ancients like a heap of snow:
While you to measure merits, look in Stowe,
And estimating authors by the year,
Bestow a Garland only on a Bier.

   Shakespear (whom you and ev'ry Play-house bill
Style the divine, the matchless, what you will)
For gain, not glory, wing'd his roving flight,
And grew Immortal in his own despite.
Ben, old and poor, as little seem'd to heed
The Life to come, in ev'ry Poet's Creed.
Who now reads Cowley? if he pleases yet,
His Moral pleases, not his pointed wit;
Forget his Epic, nay Pindaric Art;
But still I love the language of his heart.

   "Yet surely, surely, these were famous men!
"What boy but hears the sayings of old Ben?
"In all debates where Critics bear a part,
"Not one but nods, and talks of Jonson's Art,
"Of Shakespear's Nature, and of Cowley's Wit;
"How Beaumont's judgment check'd what Fletcher writ;
"How Shadwell hasty, Wycherley was slow;
"But for the Passions, Southern sure and Rowe.
"These, only these, support the crowded stage,
"From eldest Heywood down to Cibber's age."

   All this may be; the People's Voice is odd,
It is, and it is not, the voice of God.
To Gammer Gurton* if it give the bays,
And yet deny the Careless Husband** praise,

* *Gammer Gurton's Needle* an early Elizabethan play.
** A play by Cibber.

Or say our Fathers never broke a rule;
Why then, I say, the Public is a fool.
But let them own, that greater Faults than we
They had, and greater Virtues, I 'll agree.
Spenser himself affects the Obsolete,
And Sidney's verse halts ill on Roman feet:
Milton's strong pinion now not Heav'n can bound,
Now Serpent-like, in prose he sweeps the ground,
In Quibbles Angel and Archangel join,
And God the Father turns a School-divine.
Not that I 'd lop the Beauties from his book,
Like slashing Bentley with his desp'rate hook,
Or damn all Shakespear, like th' affected Fool
At court, who hates whate'er he read at school.

But for the Wits of either Charles's days,
The Mob of Gentlemen who wrote with Ease;
Sprat, Carew, Sedley, and a hundred more,
(Like twinkling stars the Miscellanies o'er)
One Simile, that solitary shines
In the dry desert of a thousand lines,
Or lengthen'd Thought that gleams through many a page,
Has sanctify'd whole poems for an age.
I lose my patience, and I own it too,
When works are censur'd, not as bad but new;
While if our Elders break all reason's laws,
These fools demand not pardon, but Applause.

On Avon's bank, where flow'rs eternal blow,
If I but ask, if any weed can grow;
One Tragic sentence if I dare deride
Which Betterton's grave action dignify'd,
Or well-mouth'd Booth with emphasis proclaims,
(Tho' but, perhaps, a muster-roll of Names)
How will our Fathers rise up in a rage,
And swear, all shame is lost in George's Age!
You 'd think no Fools disgrac'd the former reign,
Did not some grave Examples yet remain,

Who scorn a Lad should teach his father skill,
And, having once been wrong, will be so still.
He, who to seem more deep than you or I,
Extols old Bards, or Merlin's Prophecy,
Mistake him not; he envies, not admires,
And to debase the Sons, exalts the Sires.
Had ancient times conspir'd to disallow
What then was new, what had been ancient now?
Or what remain'd, so worthy to be read
By learned Critics, of the mighty Dead?

In Days of Ease, when now the weary Sword
Was sheath'd, and *Luxury* with *Charles* restor'd;
In ev'ry taste of foreign Courts improv'd,
"All, by the King's Example, liv'd and lov'd."
Then Peers grew proud in Horsemanship t' excel,
Newmarket's Glory rose, as Britain's fell;
The Soldier breath'd the Gallantries of France,
And ev'ry flow'ry Courtier writ Romance.
Then Marble, soften'd into life, grew warm:
And yielding Metal flow'd to human form:
Lely on animated Canvas stole
The Sleepy Eye, that spoke the melting soul.
No wonder then, when all was Love and sport,
The willing Muses were debauch'd at Court:
On each enervate string they taught the note
To pant, or tremble thro' an Eunuch's throat.

But Britain, changeful as a Child at play,
Now calls in Princes, and now turns away.
Now Whig, now Tory, what we lov'd we hate;
Now all for Pleasure, now for Church and State;
Now for Prerogative, and now for Laws;
Effects unhappy from a Noble Cause.

Time was, a sober Englishman would knock
His servants up, and rise by five o'clock,
Instruct his Family in ev'ry rule,
And send his Wife to church, his Son to school.

To worship like his Fathers, was his care;
To teach their frugal Virtues to his Heir;
To prove, that Luxury could never hold;
And place, on good Security, his Gold.
Now times are chang'd, and one Poetic Itch
Has seiz'd the Court and City, poor and rich:
Sons, Sires, and Grandsires, all will wear the bays,
Our Wives read Milton, and our Daughters Plays,
To Theatres, and to Rehearsals throng,
And all our Grace at table is a Song.
I, who so oft renounce the Muses, lie,
Not—'s self e'er tells more *Fibs* than I;
When sick of Muse, our follies we deplore,
And promise our best Friends to rhyme no more;
We wake next morning in a raging fit,
And call for pen and ink to show our Wit.

He serv'd a 'Prenticeship, who sets up shop;
Ward try'd on Puppies, and the Poor, his Drop;
Ev'n Radcliff's Doctors travel first to France,
Nor dare to practise till they 've learn'd to dance.
Who builds a Bridge that never drove a pile?
(Should Ripley venture, all the world would smile)
But those who cannot write, and those who can,
All rhyme, and scrawl, and scribble, to a man.

Yet, Sir, reflect, the mischief is not great;
These Madmen never hurt the Church or State:
Sometimes the Folly benefits Mankind;
And rarely Av'rice taints the tuneful mind.
Allow him but his plaything of a Pen,
He ne'er rebels, or plots, like other men:
Flight of Cashiers, or Mobs, he 'll never mind;
And knows no losses while the Muse is kind.
To cheat a Friend, or Ward, he leaves to Peter;
The good man heaps up nothing but mere metre,
Enjoys his Garden and his book in quiet;
And then—a perfect Hermit in his diet.

Of little use the Man you may suppose,
Who says in verse what others say in prose;
Yet let me show, a Poet 's of some weight,
And (tho' no Soldier) useful to the State.
What will a Child learn sooner than a Song?
What better teach a Foreigner the tongue?
What 's long or short, each accent where to place,
And speak in public with some sort of grace?
I scarce can think him such a worthless thing,
Unless he praise some Monster of a King;
Or Virtue, or Religion turn to sport,
To please a lewd or unbelieving Court.
Unhappy Dryden!—In all Charles's days,
Roscommon only boasts unspotted bays;
And in our own (excuse some Courtly stains)
No whiter page than Addison remains.
He, from the taste obscene reclaims our youth,
And sets the Passions on the side of Truth,
Forms the soft bosom with the gentlest art,
And pours each human Virtue in the heart.
Let Ireland tell how Wit upheld her cause,
Her Trade supported, and supplied her Laws;
And leave on SWIFT this grateful verse engrav'd:
'The Rights a Court attack'd, a Poet sav'd.'
Behold the hand that wrought a Nation's cure,
Stretch'd to relieve the Idiot and the Poor,
Proud Vice to brand, or injur'd Worth adorn,
And stretch the Ray to Ages yet unborn.
Not but there are, who merit other palms;
Hopkins and Sternhold glad the heart with Psalms:
The Boys and Girls whom charity maintains,
Implore your help in these pathetic strains:
How could Devotion touch the country pews,
Unless the Gods bestow'd a proper Muse?
Verse cheers their leisure, Verse assists their work,
Verse prays for Peace, or sings down Pope and Turk.

The silenc'd Preacher yields to potent strain,
And feels that grace his pray'r besought in vain;
The blessing thrills thro' all the lab'ring throng,
And Heav'n is won by Violence of Song,
  Our rural Ancestors, with little blest,
Patient of labour when the end was rest,
Indulg'd the day that hous'd their annual grain,
With feasts, and off'rings, and a thankful strain:
The joy their wives, their sons, and servants share,
Ease of their toil, and part'ners of their care:
The laugh, the jest, attendants on the bowl,
Smooth'd ev'ry brow, and open'd ev'ry soul:
With growing years the pleasing Licence grew,
And Taunts alternate innocently flew.
But Times corrupt, and Nature, ill-inclin'd,
Produc'd the point that left a sting behind;
Till friend with friend, and families at strife,
Triumphant Malice rag'd thro' private life.
Who felt the wrong, or fear'd it, took th' alarm,
Appeal'd to Law, and Justice lent her arm.
At length, by wholesome dread of statutes bound,
The Poets learn'd to please, and not to wound:
Most warp'd to Flatt'ry's side; but some, more nice,
Preserv'd the freedom, and forbore the vice.
Hence Satire rose, that just the medium hit,
And heals with Morals what it hurts with Wit.

  We conquer'd France, but felt our Captive's charms;
Her Arts victorious triumph'd o'er our Arms;
Britain to soft refinements less a foe,
Wit grew polite, and Numbers learn'd to flow.
Waller was smooth; but Dryden taught to join
The varying verse, the full-resounding line,
The long majestic March, and Energy divine.
Tho' still some traces of our rustic vein
And splay-foot verse, remain'd, and will remain.
Late, very late, correctness grew our care,

When the tir'd Nation breath'd from civil war.
Exact Racine, and Corneille's noble fire,
Show'd us that France had something to admire.
Not but the Tragic spirit was our own,
And full in Shakespear, fair in Otway shone:
But Otway fail'd to polish or refine,
And fluent Shakespear scarce effac'd a line.
Ev'n copious Dryden wanted, or forgot,
The last and greatest Art, the Art to blot.
Some doubt, if equal pains, or equal fire
The humbler Muse of Comedy require.
But in known Images of life, I guess
The labour greater, as th' indulgence less.
Observe how seldom ev'n the best succeed:
Tell me if Congreve's Fools are Fools indeed?
What pert, low Dialogue has Farquhar writ!
How Van* wants grace, who never wanted wit!
The stage how loosely does Astræa tread,
Who fairly puts all Characters to bed!
And idle Cibber, how he breaks the laws,
To make poor Pinky eat with vast applause!
But fill their purse, our Poet's work is done,
Alike to them, by Pathos or by Pun.

O you! whom Vanity's light bark conveys
On Fame's mad voyage by the wind of praise,
With what a shifting gale your course you ply,
For ever sunk too low, or borne too high!
Who pants for glory finds but short repose,
A breath revives him, or a breath o'erthrows.
Farewell the stage! if just as thrives the play,
The silly bard grows fat, or falls away.

There still remains, to mortify a Wit,
The many-headed Monster of the Pit:
A senseless, worthless, and unhonour'd crowd;
Who, to disturb their betters mighty proud,

* i.e., Vanbrugh.

Clatt'ring their sticks before ten lines are spoke,
Call for the Farce, the Bear, or the Black-joke.
What dear delight to Britons Farce affords!
Ever the taste of Mobs, but now of Lords;
(Taste, that eternal wanderer, which flies
From heads to ears, and now from ears to eyes.)*
The play stands still; damn action and discourse,
Back fly the scenes, and enter foot and horse;
Pageants on Pageants, in long order drawn,
Peers, Heralds, Bishops, Ermine, Gold and Lawn;
The Champion too! and, to complete the jest,
Old Edward's Armour beams on Cibber's breast.
With laughter sure Democritus had died,
Had he beheld an Audience gape so wide.
Let Bear or Elephant be e'er so white,
The people, sure, the people are the sight!
Ah luckless Poet! stretch thy lungs and roar,
That Bear or Elephant shall heed thee more;
While all its throats the Gallery extends,
And all the Thunder of the Pit ascends!
Loud as the Wolves, on Orcas' stormy steep,
Howl to the roarings of the Northern deep.
Such is the shout, the long-applauding note,
At Quin's high plume, or Oldfield's petticoat;
Or when from Court a birth-day suit bestow'd,
Sinks the lost Actor in the tawdry load.
Booth enters—hark! the Universal peal!
"But has he spoken?" Not a syllable.
What shook the stage, and made the People stare?
Cato's long Wig, flow'r'd gown, and lacquer'd chair.

　　Yet lest you think I rally more than teach,
Or praise malignly Arts I cannot reach,
Let me for once presume t' instruct the times,
To know the Poet from the Man of rhymes:
'T is he, who gives my breast a thousand pains,

* That is to say, from plays to operas, and from operas to pantomimes.

Can make me feel each Passion that he feigns;
Enrage, compose, with more than magic Art,
With Pity, and with Terror, tear my heart;
And snatch me, o'er the earth, or thro' the air,
To Thebes, to Athens, when he will, and where.

But not this part of the Poetic state
Alone, deserves the favour of the Great;
Think of those Authors, Sir, who would rely
More on a Reader's sense, than Gazer's eye.
Or who shall wander where the Muses sing?
Who climb their mountain, or who taste their spring?
How shall we fill a Library with Wit,
When Merlin's Cave is half unfurnish'd yet?

My Liege! why Writers little claim your thought,
I guess; and, with their leave, will tell the fault:
We Poets are (upon a Poet's word)
Of all mankind, the creatures most absurd:
The season, when to come, and when to go,
To sing, or cease to sing, we never know;
And if we will recite nine hours in ten,
You lose your patience, just like other men.
Then too we hurt ourselves, when to defend
A single verse, we quarrel with a friend;
Repeat unask'd; lament, the Wit's too fine
For vulgar eyes, and point out ev'ry line.
But most, when straining with too weak a wing,
We needs will write Epistles to the King;
And from the moment we oblige the town,
Expect a place, or pension from the Crown;
Or dubb'd Historians, by express command,
T' enroll your Triumphs o'er the seas and land,
Be call'd to Court to plan some work divine,
As once for LOUIS, Boileau and Racine.

Yet think, great Sir! (so many Virtues shown)
Ah think, what Poet best may make them known?
Or choose at least some Minister of Grace,

Fit to bestow the Laureate's weighty place.
   Charles, to late times to be transmitted fair,
Assign'd his figure to Bernini's care;
And great Nassau* to Kneller's hand decreed
To fix him graceful on the bounding Steed;
So well in paint and stone they judg'd of merit:
But Kings in Wit may want discerning Spirit.
The Hero William, and the Martyr Charles,
One knighted Blackmore, and one pension'd Quarles;
Which made old Ben, and surly Dennis swear,
"No Lord 's anointed, but a Russian Bear."
   Not with such majesty, such bold relief,
The Forms august, of King, or conqu'ring Chief,
E'er swell'd on marble; as in verse have shin'd
(In polish'd verse) the Manners and the Mind.
Oh! could I mount on the Mæonian wing,
Your Arms, your Actions, your repose to sing!
What seas you travers'd, and what fields you fought!
Your Country's Peace, how oft, how deeply bought!
How barb'rous rage subsided at your word,
And Nations wonder'd while they dropp'd the sword!
How, when you nodded, o'er the land and deep,
Peace stole her wing, and wrapt the world in sleep;
'Till earth's extremes your mediation own,
And Asia's Tyrants tremble at your Throne—
But Verse, alas! your Majesty disdains;
And I 'm not us'd to Panegyric strains:
The Zeal of Fools offends at any time,
But most of all, the Zeal of Fools in rhyme.
Besides, a fate attends on all I write,
That when I am at praise, they say I bite.
A vile Encomium doubly ridicules:
There 's nothing blackens like the ink of fools
If true, a woeful likeness; and if lies,
"Praise undeserv'd is scandal in disguise:"

* William III.

Well may he blush, who gives it, or receives;
And when I flatter, let my dirty leaves
(Like Journals, Odes, and such forgotten things
As Eusden, Philips, Settle, writ of Kings)
Clothe spice, line trunks, or, flutt'ring in a row,
Befringe the rails of Bedlam and Soho.

THE SECOND EPISTLE

OF

THE SECOND BOOK OF HORACE

Dear Col'nel, Cobham's and your country's Friend!
You love a Verse, take such as I can send.
A Frenchman comes, presents you with his Boy,
Bows and begins—"This Lad, Sir, is of Blois:
"Observe his shape how clean! his locks how curl'd!
"My only son, I'd have him see the world:
"His French is pure; his Voice too—you shall hear.
"Sir, he 's your slave, for twenty pound a year.
"Mere wax as yet, you fashion him with ease,
"Your Barber, Cook, Upholst'rer, what you please:
"A perfect genius at an Opera-song—
"To say too much, might do my honour wrong.
"Take him with all his virtues, on my word;
"His whole ambition was to serve a Lord:
"But, Sir, to you, with what would I not part?
"Tho' faith, I fear, 't will break his Mother's heart.
"Once (and but once) I caught him in a lie,
"And then, unwhipp'd, he had the grace to cry:
"The fault he has I fairly shall reveal,
"(Could you o'erlook but that) it is to steal."
   If, after this, you took the graceless lad,
Could you complain, my Friend, he prov'd so bad?

Faith, in such case, if you should prosecute,
I think Sir Godfrey should decide the suit;
Who sent the Thief that stole the Cash away,
And punish'd him that put it in his way.

Consider then, and judge me in this light;
I told you when I went, I could not write;
You said the same, and are you discontent
With Laws, to which you gave your own assent?
Nay worse, to ask for Verse at such a time!
D' ye think me good for nothing but to rhyme?

In ANNA's Wars, a Soldier poor and old
Had dearly earn'd a little purse of gold;
Tir'd with a tedious march, one luckless night,
He slept, poor dog! and lost it, to a doit.
This put the man in such a desp'rate mind,
Between revenge, and grief, and hunger join'd
Against the foe, himself, and all mankind,
He leap'd the trenches, scal'd a Castle-wall,
Tore down a Standard, took the Fort and all.
"Prodigious well;" his great Commander cry'd,
Gave him much praise, and some reward beside.
Next pleas'd his Excellence a town to batter:
(Its name I know not, and it 's no great matter)
"Go on, my Friend (he cry'd), see yonder walls!
"Advance and conquer! go where glory calls!
"More honours, more rewards, attend the brave."
Don't you remember what reply he gave?
"D' ye think me, noble Gen'ral, such a Sot?
"Let him take Castles who has ne'er a groat."

Bred up at home, full early I begun
To read in Greek the wrath of Peleus' son.
Besides, my Father taught me from a lad,
The better art to know the good from bad:
(And little sure imported to remove,
To hunt for Truth in Maudlin's learned grove.)
But knottier points we knew not half so well,

Depriv'd us soon of our paternal Cell,
And certain Laws, by suff'rers thought unjust,
Deny'd all posts of profit or of trust:
Hopes after hopes of pious Papists fail'd,
While mighty WILLIAM's thund'ring arm prevail'd,
For Right Hereditary tax'd and fin'd,
He stuck to poverty with peace of mind;
And me, the Muses help'd to undergo it;
Convict a Papist he, and I a Poet.
But (thanks to Homer) since I live and thrive,
Indebted to no Prince or Peer alive,
Sure I should want the care of ten Monroes,
If I would scribble, rather than repose.
Years follow'ng years, steal something ev'ry day,
At last they steal us from ourselves away;
In one our Frolics, one Amusements end,
In one a Mistress drops, in one a Friend:
This subtle Thief of life, this paltry Time,
What will it leave me, if it snatch my rhyme?
If ev'ry wheel of that unweary'd Mill,
That turn'd ten thousand verses, now stands still?
　　But after all, what would you have me do?
When out of twenty I can please not two;
When this Heroics only deigns to praise,
Sharp Satire that, and that Pindaric lays?
One likes the Pheasant's wing, and one the leg
The vulgar boil, the learned roast an egg;
Hard task! to hit the palate of such guests,
When Oldfield loves, what Dartineuf detests.
　　But grant I may relapse, for want of grace,
Again to rhyme, can London be the place?
Who there his Muse, or self, or soul attends,
In crowds, and courts, law, business, feasts, and friends?
My counsel sends to execute a deed;
A Poet begs me, I will hear him read;
'In Palace-yard at nine you 'll find me there—'

'At ten for certain, Sir, in Bloomsb'ry square—'
'Before the Lords at twelve my Cause comes on—
'There 's a Rehearsal, Sir, exact at one.—'
"Oh but a Wit can study in the streets,
"And raise his mind above the mob he meets."
Not quite so well however as one ought;
A hackney coach may chance to spoil a thought;
And then a nodding beam, or pig of lead,
God knows, may hurt the very ablest head.
Have you not seen, at Guild-hall's narrow pass,
Two Aldermen dispute it with an Ass?
And Peers give way, exalted as they are,
Ev'n to their own S-r-v—nce in a Car?

Go, lofty Poet! and in such a crowd,
Sing thy sonorous verse—but not aloud.
Alas! to Grottos and to Groves we run,
To ease and silence, ev'ry Muse's son:
Blackmore himself, for any grand effort,
Would drink and doze at Tooting or Earl's-Court
How shall I rhyme in this eternal roar?
How match the bards whom none e'er match'd before?
The Man, who, stretch'd in Isis' calm retreat,
To books and study gives sev'n years complete,
See! strew'd with learned dust, his night-cap on,
He walks, an object new beneath the sun!
The boys flock round him, and the people stare:
So stiff, so mute! some statue you would swear,
Stept from its pedestal to take the air!
And here, while town, and court, and city roars,
With mobs, and duns, and soldiers, at their doors;
Shall I, in London, act this idle part?
Composing songs, for Fools to get by heart?

The Temple late two brother Sergeants saw,
Who deem'd each other Oracles of Law;
With equal talents, these congenial souls,
One lull'd th' Exchequer, and one stunn'd the Rolls;

Each had a gravity would make you split,
And shook his head at Murray, as a Wit.
" 'T was, Sir, your law"—and "Sir, your eloquence—"
"Yours, Cowper's manner"—and "yours, Talbot's sense."
Thus we dispose of all poetic merit,
Yours Milton's genius, and mine Homer's spirit.
Call Tibbald Shakespear, and he 'll swear the Nine,
Dear Cibber! never match'd one Ode of thine.
Lord! how we strut thro' Merlin's Cave, to see
No Poets there, but Stephen, you, and me.
Walk with respect behind, while we at ease
Weave laurel Crowns, and take what names we please.
"My dear Tibullus!" if that will not do,
"Let me be Horace, and be Ovid you:
"Or, I 'm content, allow me Dryden's strains,
"And you shall rise up Otway for your pains."
Much do I suffer, much, to keep in peace
This jealous, waspish, wrong-head, rhyming race;
And much must flatter, if the whim should bite
To court applause by printing what I write:
But let the Fit pass o'er, I 'm wise enough,
To stop my ears to their confounded stuff.
   In vain bad Rhymers all mankind reject,
They treat themselves with most profound respect;
'T is to small purpose that you hold your tongue:
Each prais'd within, is happy all day long;
But how severely with themselves proceed
The men, who write such Verse as we can read?
Their own strict Judges, not a word they spare
That wants or force, or light, or weight, or care,
Howe'er unwillingly it quits its place,
Nay tho' at Court (perhaps) it may find grace:
Such they 'll degrade; and sometimes, in its stead,
In downright charity revive the dead;
Mark where a bold expressive phrase appears,
Bright thro' the rubbish of some hundred years;

Command old words that long have slept, to wake,
Words, that wise Bacon, or brave Raleigh spake;
Or bid the new be English, ages hence,
(For Use will farther what 's begot by Sense)
Pour the full tide of eloquence along,
Serenely pure, and yet divinely strong,
Rich with the treasures of each foreign tongue;
Prune the luxuriant, the uncouth refine,
But show no mercy to an empty line:
Then polish all, with so much life and ease,
You think 't is Nature, and a knack to please:
"But ease in writing flows from Art, not chance;
"As those move easiest who have learn'd to dance."

If such the plague and pains to write by rule,
Better (say I) be pleas'd, and play the fool;
Call, if you will, bad rhyming a disease,
It gives men happiness, or leaves them ease.
There liv'd *in Primo Georgii* (they record)
A worthy member, no small fool, a Lord;
Who, tho' the House was up, delighted sate,
Heard, noted, answer'd, as in full debate:
In all but this, a man of sober life,
Fond of his Friend, and civil to his Wife;
Not quite a mad-man, tho' a pasty fell,
And much too wise to walk into a well.
Him, the damn'd Doctors and his Friends immur'd,
They bled, they cupp'd, they purg'd; in short, they cur'd.
Whereat the gentleman began to stare—
"My Friends?" he cry'd, "pox take you for your care!
That from a Patriot of distinguish'd note,
Have bled and purg'd me to a simple Vote."
Well, on the whole, plain Prose must be my fate:
Wisdom (curse on it) will come soon or late.
There is a time when Poets will grow dull:
I 'll e'en leave verses to the boys at school:
To rules of Poetry no more confin'd,

I learn to smooth and harmonize my Mind,
Teach ev'ry thought within its bounds to roll,
And keep the equal measure of the Soul.

Soon as I enter at my country door,
My mind resumes the thread it dropt before;
Thoughts which at Hyde-park-corner I forgot,
Meet and rejoin me, in the pensive Grot.
There all alone, and compliments apart,
I ask these sober questions of my heart.

If, when the more you drink, the more you crave,
You tell the Doctor; when the more you have,
The more you want; why not with equal ease
Confess as well your Folly, as Disease?
The heart resolves this matter in a trice,
"Men only feel the Smart, but not the Vice."

When golden Angels cease to cure the Evil,
You give all royal Witchcraft to the Devil;
When servile Chaplains cry, that birth and place
Endue a Peer with honour, truth, and grace,
Look in that breast, most dirty D—! be fair,
Say, can you find out one such lodger there?
Yet still, not heeding what your heart can teach,
You go to church to hear these Flatt'rers preach.

Indeed, could wealth bestow or wit or merit,
A grain of courage, or a spark of spirit,
The wisest man might blush, I must agree,
If D* * * lov'd sixpence more than he.

If there be truth in Law, and Use can give
A Property, that 's yours on which you live.
Delightful Abs-court, if its fields afford
Their fruits to you, confesses you its lord:
All Worldly's hens, nay partridge, sold to town:
His Ven'son too, a guinea makes your own:
He bought at thousands, what with better wit
You purchase as you want, and bit by bit;
Now, or long since, what diff'rence will be found?

You pay a penny, and he paid a pound.
 Heathcote himself, and such large-acred men,
Lords of fat E'sham, or of Lincoln fen,
Buy every stick of wood that lends them heat,
Buy every Pullet they afford to eat.
Yet these are Wights, who fondly call their own
Half that the Dev'l o'erlooks from Lincoln town.
The Laws of God, as well as of the land,
Abhor, a Perpetuity should stand:
Estates have wings, and hang in Fortune's pow'r
Loose on the point of ev'ry wav'ring hour,
Ready, by force, or of your own accord,
By sale, at least by death, to change their lord.
Man? and *for ever?* wretch! what wouldst thou **have?**
Heir urges heir, like wave impelling wave.
All vast possessions (just the same the case
Whether you call them Villa, Park, or Chase)
Alas, my BATHURST! what will they avail?
Join Cotswood hills to Saperton's fair dale,
Let rising Granaries and Temples here,
There mingled farms and pyramids appear,
Link towns to towns with avenues of oak,
Enclose whole downs in walls, 't is all a joke!
Inexorable Death shall level all,
And trees, and stones, and farms, and farmer fall.
 Gold, Silver, Iv'ry, Vases sculptur'd high,
Paint, Marble, Gems, and robes of Persian dye,
There are who have not—and thank heav'n there are,
Who, if they have not, think not worth their care.
 Talk what you will of Taste, my friend, you 'll find,
Two of a face, as soon as of a mind.
Why, of two brothers, rich and restless one
Ploughs, burns, manures, and toils from sun to sun;
The other slights, for women, sports, and wines,
All Townshend's Turnips, and all Grosvenor's mines:
Why one like Bu— with pay and scorn content,

Bows and votes on, in Court and Parliament;
One, driv'n by strong Benevolence of soul,
Shall fly, like Oglethorpe, from pole to pole:
Is known alone to that Directing Pow'r,
Who forms the Genius in the natal hour;
That God of Nature, who, within us still,
Inclines our action, not constrains our will;
Various of temper, as of face or frame,
Each individual: His great End the same.

Yes, Sir, how small soever be my heap,
A part I will enjoy, as well as keep.
My heir may sigh, and think it want of grace
A man so poor would live without a place;
But sure no statute in his favour says,
How free, or frugal, I shall pass my days:
I, who at some times spend, at others spare,
Divided between carelessness and care.
'T is one thing madly to disperse my store;
Another, not to heed to treasure more;
Glad, like a Boy, to snatch the first good day,
And pleas'd, if sordid want be far away.

What is 't to me (a passenger, God wot!)
Whether my vessel be first-rate or not?
The Ship itself may make a better figure,
But I that sail, am neither less nor bigger.
I neither strut with ev'ry fav'ring breath,
Nor strive with all the tempest in my teeth.
In pow'r, wit, figure, virtue, fortune, plac'd
Behind the foremost, and before the last.

"But why all this of Av'rice? I have none."
I wish you joy, Sir, of a Tyrant gone;
But does no other lord it at this hour,
As wild and mad: the Avarice of pow'r?
Does neither Rage inflame, nor Fear appal?
Not the black fear of death, that saddens all?
With terrors round, can Reason hold her throne,

Despise the known, nor tremble at th' unknown?
Survey both worlds, intrepid and entire,
In spite of witches, devils, dreams, and fire?
Pleas'd to look forward, pleas'd to look behind,
And count each birth-day with a grateful mind?
Has life no sourness, drawn so near its end?
Canst thou endure a foe, forgive a friend?
Has age but melted the rough parts away,
As winter-fruits grow mild ere they decay?
Or will you think, my friend, your business done,
When, of a hundred thorns, you pull out one?

  Learn to live well, or fairly make your will;
You 've play'd, and lov'd, and eat, and drank your fill:
Walk sober off; before a sprightlier age
Comes titt'ring on, and shoves you from the stage:
Leave such to trifle with more grace and ease,
Whom Folly pleases, and whose Follies please.

☾ Sober Advice from Horace

IMITATED FROM HIS
SECOND SERMON

The Tribe of Templars, Play'rs, Apothecaries,
Pimps, Poets, Wits, Lord *Fanny*'s, Lady *Mary*'s,
And all the Court in Tears, and half the Town,
Lament dear charming *Oldfield*, dead and gone!
Engaging *Oldfield!* who, with Grace and Ease,
Could joyn the Arts, to ruin, and to please.

  Not so, who of Ten Thousand gull'd her Knight,
Then ask'd Ten Thousand for a second Night:
The Gallant too, to whom she pay'd it down,
Liv'd to refuse that Mistress half a Crown.

  Con. Philips cries, "A sneaking Dog I hate."
That's all three Lovers have for their Estate!
"Treat on, treat on," is her eternal Note,
And Lands and Tenements go down her Throat.

Some damn the Jade, and some the Cullies blame,
But not Sir *H—t*, for he does the same.

   With all a Women's Virtues but the P—x,
Fufidia, thrives in Money, Land, and Stocks:
For Int'rest, ten *per Cent.* her constant Rate is;
Her Body? hopeful Heirs may have it *gratis*.
She turns her very Sister to a Job,
And, in the Happy Minute, picks your Fob:
Yet starves herself, so little her own Friend,
And thirsts and hungers only at one End:
A Self-Tormentor, worse than (in the Play)
The Wretch, whose Av'rice drove his *Son* away.

   But why all this? I'll tell ye, 'tis my Theme:
"Women and Fools are always in Extreme.
Rufa's at either end a Common-Shoar,
Sweet *Moll* and *Jack* are Civet-Cat and Boar;
Nothing in Nature is so lewd as *Peg*,
Yet, for the World, she would not shew her Leg!
While bashful *Jenny*, ev'n at Morning-Prayer,
Spreads her Fore-Buttocks to the Navel bare.
But diff'rent Taste in diff'rent Men prevails,
And one is fired by Heads, and one by Tails;
Some feel no Flames but at the *Court* or *Ball*,
And others hunt white Aprons in the *Mall*.
   My Lord of *L—n*, chancing to remark
A *noted Dean* much busy'd in the Park,
"Proceed (he cry'd) proceed, my Reverend Brother,
" 'Tis *Fornicatio simplex*, and no other:
"Better than lust for Boys, with *Pope* and *Turk*,
"Or others Spouses, like my Lord of—[York].
   May no such Praise (cries *J—s*) e'er be mine!
J—s, who bows at *Hi—sb—w*'s *hoary Shrine*.
   All you, who think the *City* ne'er can thrive,
Till ev'ry Cuckold-maker's flea'd alive;
Attend, while I their Miseries explain,

And pity Men of Pleasure still in Pain!
Survey the Pangs they bear, the Risques they run,
Where the most lucky are but last undone.
See wretched *Monsieur* flies to save his Throat,
And quits his Mistress, Money, Ring, and Note!
See good Sir *George* of ragged Livery stript,
By worthier Footmen pist upon and whipt!
Plunder'd by Thieves, or Lawyers which is worse,
One bleeds in Person, and one bleeds in Purse;
This meets a Blanket, and that meets a Cudgel—
And all applaud the Justice—All, but *Budgel*.

How much more safe, dear Countrymen! his State,
Who trades in Frigates of the second Rate?
And yet some Care of *S—st* should be had,
Nothing so mean for which he can't run mad;
His Wit confirms him but a Slave the more,
And makes a Princess whom he found a Whore.
The Youth might save much Trouble and Expence,
Were he a Dupe of only common Sense.
But here's his point; A Wench (he cries) for me!
"I never touch a Dame of Quality.

To *Palmer's* Bed no Actress comes amiss,
He courts the whole *Personæ Dramatis:*
He too can say, "With Wives I never sin."
But Singing-Girls and Mimicks draw him in.
Sure, worthy Sir, the Diff'rence is not great,
With *whom* you lose your Credit and Estate?
This, or that Person, what avails to shun?
What's wrong is wrong, wherever it be done:
The Ease, Support, and Lustre of your Life,
Destroy'd alike with Strumpet, Maid, or Wife.

What push'd poor *Ellis* on th' Imperial Whore?
'Twas but to be where CHARLES had been before.
The fatal Steel unjustly was apply'd,
When not his Lust offended, but his Pride:
Too hard a Penance for defeated Sin,

Himself shut out, and *Jacob Hall* let in.

Suppose that honest Part that rules us all,
Should rise, and say—"Sir *Robert!* or Sir *Paul!*
"Did I demand, in my most vig'rous hour,
"A Thing descended from the Conqueror?
"Or when my pulse beat highest, ask for any
"Such Nicety, as Lady or Lord *Fanny?*—
What would you answer? Could you have the Face,
When the poor Suff'rer humbly mourn'd his Case,
To cry "You weep the Favours of her GRACE?

Hath not indulgent Nature spread a Feast,
And giv'n enough for Man, enough for Beast?
But Man corrupt, perverse in all his ways,
In search of Vanities from Nature strays:
Yea, tho' the Blessing's more than he can use,
Shuns the permitted, the forbid pursues!
Weigh well the Cause from whence these Evils spring,
'Tis in thyself, and not in God's good Thing:
Then, lest Repentance punish such a Life,
Never, ah, never! kiss thy Neighbour's Wife.

First, Silks and Diamonds veil no finer Shape,
Or plumper Thigh, than lurk in humble Crape:
And *secondly*, how innocent a *Belle*
Is she who shows what Ware she has to sell;
Not Lady-like, displays a milk-white Breast,
And hides in sacred Sluttishness the rest.

Our ancient Kings (and sure those Kings were wise,
Who judg'd themselves, and saw with their own Eyes)
A War-horse never for the Service chose,
But ey'd him round, and stript off all the Cloaths;
For well they knew, proud Trappings serve to hide
A heavy Chest, thick Neck, or heaving Side.
But Fools are ready Chaps, agog to buy,
Let but a comely Fore-hand strike the Eye:
No Eagle sharper, every Charm to find,
To all defects, *Ty—y* not so blind:

Goose-rump'd, Hawk-nos'd, Swan-footed, is my Dear?
They'll praise her *Elbow*, *Heel*, or *Tip o'th' Ear*.
   A Lady's Face is all you see undress'd;
(For none but Lady M— shows the Rest)
But if to Charms more latent you pretend,
What Lines encompass, and what Works defend!
Dangers on Dangers! obstacles by dozens!
Spies, Guardians, Guests, old Women, Aunts, and
     Cozens!
Could you directly to her Person go,
Stays will obstruct above, and Hoops below,
And if the Dame says yes, the Dress says no.
Not thus at *N—dh—m*'s; your judicious Eye
May measure there the Breast, the Hip, the Thigh!
And will you run to Perils, Sword, and Law,
All for a Thing you ne're so much as *saw?*
   "The Hare once seiz'd the Hunter heeds no more
"The little Scut he so pursu'd before,
"Love follows flying Game (as *Sucklyn* sings)
"And 'tis for that the wanton Boy has Wings."
Why let him Sing—but when you're in the Wrong,
Think ye to cure the Mischief with a Song?
Has Nature set no bounds to wild Desire?
No Sense to guide, no Reason to enquire,
What solid Happiness, what empty Pride?
And what is best indulg'd, or best deny'd?
If neither Gems adorn, nor Silver tip
The flowing Bowl, will you not wet your Lip?
When sharp with Hunger, scorn you to be fed,
Except on *Pea-Chicks*, at the *Bedford-head?*
Or, when a tight, neat Girl, will serve the Turn,
In errant Pride continue stiff, and burn?
I'm a plain Man, whose Maxim is profest,
"The Thing at hand is of all Things the *best*.
But Her who will, and then will not comply,
Whose Word is *If*, *Perhaps*, and *By-and-By*,

Z—ds! let some Eunuch or Platonic take—
So *B*—*t* cries, Philosopher and Rake!
Who asks no more (right reasonable Peer)
Than not to wait too long, nor pay too dear.
Give me a willing Nymph! 'tis all I care,
Extremely clean, and tolerably fair,
Her Shape her own, whatever Shape she have,
And just that White and Red which Nature gave.
Her I transported touch, transported view,
And call her *Angel! Goddess! Montague!*
No furious Husband thunders at the Door;
No barking Dog, no Household in a Roar;
From gleaming Swords no shrieking Women run;
No wretched Wife cries out, *Undone! Undone!*
Seiz'd in the Fact, and in her Cuckold's Pow'r,
She kneels, she weeps, and worse! resigns her Dow'r.
Me, naked me, to Posts, to Pumps they draw,
To Shame eternal, or eternal Law.
Oh Love! be deep Tranquility my Luck!
No Mistress *H*—*ysh*—*m* near, no Lady *B*—*ck!*
For, to be taken, is the Dev'll in Hell;
This Truth, let *L*—*l, J*—*ys, O*—*w* tell.

FINIS

ℂ The Satires of Dr. John Donne,

SATIRE II

YES; thank my stars! as early as I knew
This Town, I had the sense to hate it too;
Yet here; as ev'n in Hell, there must be still
One Giant-Vice, so excellently ill,
That all beside, one pities, not abhors;
As who knows Sappho, smiles at other whores.

    I grant that Poetry 's a crying sin;
It brought (no doubt) th' *Excise* and *Army* in:
Catch'd like the Plague, or Love, the Lord knows how,
But that the cure is starving, all allow.
Yet like the Papist's, is the Poet's state,
Poor and disarm'd, and hardly worth your hate!

    Here a lean Bard, whose wit could never give
Himself a dinner, makes an Actor live:
The Thief condemn'd, in law already dead,
So prompts, and saves a rogue who cannot read.
Thus, as the pipes of some carv'd Organ move,
The gilded puppets dance and mount above.
Heav'd by the breath th' inspiring bellows blow:
Th' inspiring bellows lie and pant below.

    One sings the Fair; but songs no longer move;
No rat is rhym'd to death, nor maid to love:
In love's, in nature's spite, the siege they hold,
And scorn the flesh, the dev'l, and all but gold.

    These write to Lords, some mean reward to get,
As needy beggars sing at doors for meat.
Those write because all write, and so have still
Excuse for writing, and for writing ill.

    Wretched indeed! but fár more wretched yet
Is he who makes his meal on others' wit:

'T is chang'd, no doubt, from what it was before;
His rank digestion makes it wit no more:
Sense, past thro' him, no longer is the same;
For food digested takes another name.
    I pass o'er all those Confessors and Martyrs,
Who live like S—tt—n, or who die like Chartres,
Out-cant old Esdras, or out-drink his heir,
Out-usure Jews, or Irishmen out-swear;
Wicked as Pages, who in early years
Act sins which Prisca's Confessor scarce hears.
Ev'n those I pardon, for whose sinful sake
Schoolmen new tenements in hell must make;
Of whose strange crimes no Canonist can tell
In what Commandment's large contents they dwell.
    One, one man only breeds my just offence;
Whom crimes gave wealth, and wealth gave Impudence:
Time, that at last matures a clap to pox,
Whose gentle progress makes a calf an ox,
And brings all natural events to pass,
Hath made him an Attorney of an Ass.
No young divine, new-benefic'd, can be
More pert, more proud, more positive than he
What further could I wish the fop to do,
But turn a wit, and scribble verses too;
Pierce the soft lab'rinth of a Lady's ear
With rhymes of this *per cent.* and that *per year?*
Or court a Wife, spread out his wily parts,
Like nets or lime-twigs, for rich Widows' hearts;
Call himself Barrister to ev'ry wench,
And woo in language of the Pleas and Bench?
Language, which Boreas might to Auster hold
More rough than forty Germans when they scold.
    Curs'd be the wretch, so venal and so vain:
Paltry and proud, as drabs in Drury Lane.
'T is such a bounty as was never known,
If PETER deigns to help you to your *own:*

What thanks, what praise, if *Peter* but supplies,
And what a solemn face if he denies!
Grave, as when pris'ners shake the head and swear
'T was only Suretyship that brought 'em there.
His *Office* keeps your Parchment fates entire,
He starves with cold to save them from the fire;
For you he walks the streets thro' rain or dust,
For not in Chariots *Peter* puts his trust;
For you he sweats and labours at the laws,
Takes God to witness he affects your cause,
And lies to ev'ry Lord in ev'ry thing,
Like a King's Favourite—or like a King.
These are the talents that adorn them all,
From wicked Waters ev'n to godly * *
Not more of Simony beneath black gowns,
Not more of bastardy in heirs to Crowns,
In shillings and in pence at first they deal;
And steal so little, few perceive they steal;
Till, like the Sea, they compass all the land,
From *Scots* to *Wight*, from *Mount* to *Dover* strand:
And when rank Widows purchase luscious nights,
Or when a Duke to *Jansen* punts at White's,
Or City-heir in mortgage melts away;
Satan himself feels far less joy than they.
Piecemeal they win this acre first, then that,
Glean on, and gather up the whole estate.
Then strongly fencing ill-got wealth by law,
Indentures, Cov'nants, Articles they draw,
Large as the fields themselves, and larger far
Than Civil Codes, with all their Glosses, are;
So vast, our new Divines, we must confess,
Are Fathers of the Church for writing less.
But let them write for you, each rogue impairs
The deeds, and dext'rously omits, *ses heirs*:
No Commentator can more slily pass
O'er a learn'd, unintelligible place;

Or, in quotation, shrewd Divines leave out
Those words, that would against them clear the doubt.
So Luther thought the Pater-noster long,
When doom'd to say his beads and Even-song;
But having cast his cowl, and left those laws,
Adds to Christ's pray'r, the *Pow'r and Glory* clause.
The lands are bought; but where are to be found
Those ancient woods, that shaded all the ground?
We see no new-built palaces aspire,
No kitchens emulate the vestal fire.
Where are those troops of Poor, that throng'd of yore
The good old landlord's hospitable door?
Well, I could wish, that still in lordly domes
Some beasts were kill'd, tho' not whole hecatombs;
That both extremes were banish'd from their walls,
Carthusian fasts, and fulsome Bacchanals;
And all mankind might that just Mean observe,
In which none e'er could surfeit, none could starve.
These as good works, 't is true, we all allow;
But oh! these works are not in fashion now:
Like rich old wardrobes, things extremely rare,
Extremely fine, but what no man will wear.
Thus much I 've said, I trust, without offence;
Let no Court Sycophant pervert my sense,
Nor sly informer watch these words to draw
Within the reach of Treason, or the Law.

SATIRE IV

WELL, if it be my time to quit the stage,
Adieu to all the follies of the age!
I die in charity with fool and knave,
Secure of peace at least beyond the grave.
I 've had my Purgatory here betimes,
And paid for all my satires, all my rhymes.
The Poet's hell, its tortures, fiends, and flames,

To this were trifles, toys and empty names.
    With foolish pride my heart was never fir'd,
Nor the vain itch t' admire, or be admir'd;
I hop'd for no commission from his Grace;
I bought no benefice, I begg'd no place;
Had no new verses, nor new suit to show;
Yet went to Court!—the Dev'l would have it so.
But, as the Fool that in reforming days
Would go to Mass in jest (as story says)
Could not but think, to pay his fine was odd,
Since 't was no form'd design of serving God;
So was I punish'd, as if full as proud
As prone to ill, as negligent of good,
As deep in debt, without a thought to pay,
As vain, as idle, and as false, as they
Who live at Court, for going once that way!
Scarce was I enter'd, when, behold! there came
A thing which Adam had been pos'd to name;
Noah had refus'd it lodging in his Ark,
Where all the Race of Reptiles might embark:
A verier monster, that on Afric's shore
The sun e'er got, or slimy Nilus bore,
Or Sloane or Woodward's wondrous shelves contain,
Nay, all that lying Travellers can feign.
The watch would hardly let him pass at noon,
At night, would swear him dropt out of the Moon.
One whom the mob, when next we find or make
A popish plot, shall for a Jesuit take,
And the wise Justice starting from his chair
Cry: "By your Priesthood tell me what you are?"
    Such was the wight; th' apparel on his back
Tho' coarse, was rev'rend, and tho' bare, was black:
The suit, if by the fashion one might guess,
Was velvet in the youth of good Queen *Bess*,
But mere tuff-taffety what now remain'd;
So Time, that changes all things, had ordain'd!

Our sons shall see it leisurely decay,
First turn plain rash, then vanish quite away.

    This thing has travell'd, speaks each language too,
And knows what 's fit for every state to do;
Of whose best phrase and courtly accent join'd,
He forms one tongue, exotic and refin'd,
Talkers I 've learn'd to bear; Motteux I knew,
Henley himself I 've heard, and Budgel too.
The Doctor's Wormwood style, the Hash of tongues
A Pedant makes, the storm of Gonson's lungs,
The whole Artill'ry of the terms of War,
And (all those plagues in one) the bawling Bar;
These I could bear; but not a rogue so civil,
Whose tongue will compliment you to the Devil.
A tongue, that can cheat widows, cancel scores,
Make Scots speak treason, cozen subtlest whores,
With royal Favourites in flatt'ry vie,
And Oldmixon and Burnet both out-lie.

    He spies me out, I whisper: 'Gracious God!
What sin of mine could merit such a rod?
That all the shot of dulness now must be
From this thy blunderbuss discharg'd on me!'
"Permit," (he cries) "no stranger to your fame
"To crave your sentiment, if— 's your name.
"What *Speech* esteem you most?" 'The *King's*,' said I.
"But the best *words?*"—'O Sir, the *Dictionary*.'
"You miss my aim: I mean the most acute
"And perfect *Speaker?*"—'Onslow, past dispute.'
"But, Sir, of writers?" 'Swift, for closer style,
'But Ho * * y for a period of a mile.'
"Why yes, 't is granted, these indeed may pass:
"Good common linguists, and so Panurge was;
"Nay troth th' Apostles (tho' perhaps too rough)
"Had once a pretty gift of Tongues enough:
"Yet these were all poor Gentlemen! I dare
"Affirm, 't was Travel made them what they were."

Thus others' talents having nicely shown,
He came by sure transition to his own:
Till I cry'd out: 'You prove yourself so able,
'Pity! you was not Druggerman* at Babel;
'For had they found a linguist half so good,
'I make no question but the Tow'r had stood.'
"Obliging Sir! for Courts you sure were made:
"Why then for ever bury'd in the shade?
"Spirits like you, should see and should be seen,
"The King would smile on you—at least the Queen."
'Ah gentle Sir! your Courtiers so cajole us—
'But Tully has it, *Nunquam minus solus:*
'And as for Courts, forgive me, if I say
'No lessons now are taught the Spartan way:
'Tho' in his pictures Lust be full display'd,
'Few are the Converts Aretine has made;
'And tho' the Court show Vice exceeding clear,
'None should, by my advice, learn Virtue there.'
At this entranc'd, he lifts his hands and eyes,
Squeaks like a high-stretch'd lutestring, and replies:
"Oh 't is the sweetest of all earthly things
"To gaze on Princes, and to talk of Kings!"
'Then, happy Man who shows the Tombs!' said I,
'He dwells amidst the royal Family:
'He ev'ry day, from King to King can walk,
'Of all our Harries, all our Edwards talk,
'And get by speaking truth of monarchs dead,
'What few can of the living, Ease and Bread.'
"Lord, Sir, a mere Mechanic! strangely low,
"And coarse of phrase,—your English all are so.
"How elegant your Frenchmen?" 'Mine, d'ye mean?
'I have but one, I hope the fellow 's clean.'
"Oh! Sir, politely so! nay, let me die,
"Your only wearing is your Padua-soy."
'Not, Sir, my only, I have better still,

* Dragoman, interpreter.

'And this you see is but my dishabille—'
Wild to get loose, his Patience I provoke,
Mistake, confound, object at all he spoke.
But as coarse iron, sharpen'd, mangles more,
And itch most hurts when anger'd to a sore;
So when you plague a fool, 't is still the curse,
You only make the matter worse and worse.

 He past it o'er; affects an easy smile
At all my peevishness, and turns his style.
He asks, "What News?" I tell him of new Plays,
New Eunuchs, Harlequins, and Operas.
He hears, and as a Still with simples in it
Between each drop it gives, stays half a minute,
Loth to enrich me with too quick replies,
By little and by little, drops his lies.
Mere household trash! of birth-nights, balls, and shows,
More than ten Holinsheds, or Halls, or Stowes.
When the *Queen* frown'd, or smil'd, he knows; and what
A subtle Minister may make of that;
Who sins with whom: who got his Pension rug,
Or quicken'd a Reversion by a drug;
Whose place is quarter'd out, three parts in four,
And whether to a Bishop, or a Whore;
Who having lost his credit, pawn'd his rent,
Is therefore fit to have a Government;
Who in the secret, deals in Stocks secure,
And cheats th' unknowing Widow and the Poor;
Who makes a Trust or Charity a Job.
And gets an Act of Parliament to rob;
Why Turnpikes rise, and now no Cit nor clown
Can gratis see the country, or the town;
Shortly no lad shall chuck, or lady vole,
But some excising Courtier will have toll.
He tells what strumpet places sells for life,
What 'Squire his lands, what citizen his Wife:
And last (which proves him wiser still than all)

What Lady's face is not a whited wall.
  As one of Woodward's patients, sick, and sore,
I puke, I nauseate,—yet he thrusts in more:
Trims Europe's balance, tops the statesman's part,
And talks Gazettes and Post-boys o'er by heart.
Like a big wife at sight of loathsome meat
Ready to cast, I yawn, I sigh, and sweat.
Then as a licens'd spy, whom nothing can
Silence or hurt, he libels the great Man;
Swears ev'ry place entail'd for years to come,
In sure succession to the day of doom;
He names the price for ev'ry office paid,
And says our wars thrive ill, because delay'd;
Nay hints, 't is by connivance of the Court,
That Spain robs on, and Dunkirk 's still a Port.
Not more amazement seiz'd on Circe's guests
To see themselves fall endlong into beasts,
Than mine, to find a subject staid and wise
Already half turn'd traitor by surprise.
I felt th' infection slide from him to me,
As in the pox, some give it to get free;
And quick to swallow me, methought I saw
One of our Giant Statutes ope its jaw.
  In that nice moment, as another Lie
Stood just a-tilt, the Minister came by.
To him he flies, and bows, and bows again,
Then, close as Umbra, joins the dirty train,
Not Fannius' self more impudently near,
When half his nose is in his Prince's ear.
I quak'd at heart; and still afraid, to see
All the Court fill'd with stranger things than he,
Ran out as fast, as one that pays his bail
And dreads more actions, hurries from a jail.
  Bear me, some God! oh quickly bear me hence
To wholesome Solitude, the nurse of sense;
Where Contemplation prunes her ruffled wings,

And the free soul looks down to pity Kings!
There sober thought pursu'd th' amusing theme,
Till Fancy colour'd it, and form'd a Dream.
A Vision hermits can to Hell transport,
And forc'd ev'n me to see the damn'd at Court.
Not Dante dreaming all th' infernal state,
Beheld such scenes of envy, sin, and hate.
Base Fear becomes the guilty, not the free;
Suits Tyrants, Plunderers, but suits not me:
Shall I, the Terror of this sinful town,
Care, if a liv'ry'd Lord or smile or frown?
Who cannot flatter, and detest who can,
Tremble before a noble Serving-man?
O my fair mistress, Truth! shall I quit thee
For huffing, braggart, puff'd Nobility?
Thou, who since yesterday hast roll'd o'er all
The busy, idle blockheads of the ball,
Hast thou, oh Sun! beheld an emptier fort,
Than such as swell this bladder of a court?
Now pox on those who show a *Court in wax!*
It ought to bring all courtiers on their backs:
Such painted puppets! such a varnish'd race
Of hollow gew-gaws, only dress and face!
Such waxen noses, stately staring things—
No wonder some folks bow, and think them Kings.

See! where the British youth, engag'd no more
At Fig's, at White's, with felons, or a whore,
Pay their last duty to the Court, and come
All fresh and fragrant, to the drawing-room;
In hues as gay, and odours as divine,
As the fair fields they sold to look so fine.
"That 's velvet for a King!" the flatt'rer swears;
'T is true, for ten days hence 't will be King Lear's.
Our Court may justly to our stage give rules,
That helps it both to fools-coats and to fools.
And why not players strut in courtiers' clothes?

For these are actors too, as well as those:
Wants reach all states; they beg but better drest,
And all is splended poverty at best.
    Painted for sight, and essenc'd for the smell,
Like frigates fraught with spice and cochinel,
Sail in the Ladies: how each pirate eyes
So weak a vessel, and so rich a prize!
Top-gallant he, and she in all her trim,
He boarding her, she striking sail to him:
"Dear Countess! you have charms all hearts to hit!"
And "Sweet Sir Fopling! you have so much wit!"
Such wits and beauties are not prais'd for nought,
For both the beauty and the wit are bought.
'T wou'd burst ev'n Heraclitus with the spleen,
To see those antics, Fopling and Courtine:
The Presence seems, with things so richly odd,
The mosque of Mahound, or some queer Pagod.
See them survey their limbs by Durer's rules,
Of all beau-kind the best-proportion'd fools!
Adjust their clothes, and to confession draw
Those venial sins, an atom, or a straw;
But oh! what terrors must distract the soul
Convicted of that mortal crime, a hole;
Or should one pound of powder less bespread
Those monkey tails that wag behind their head.
Thus finish'd, and corrected to a hair,
They march, to prate their hour before the Fair.
So first to preach a white-glov'd Chaplain goes,
With band of Lily, and with cheek of Rose,
Sweeter than Sharon, in immac'late trim,
Neatness itself impertinent in him.
Let but the Ladies smile, and they are blest:
Prodigious! how the things *protest, protest:*
Peace, fools, or Gonson will for Papists seize you,
If once he catch you at your *Jesu! Jesu!*
    Nature made ev'ry Fop to plague his brother,

Just as one Beauty mortifies another.
But here 's the Captain that will plague them both,
Whose air cries Arm! whose very look 's an oath:
The Captain 's honest, Sirs, and that 's enough,
Tho' his soul 's bullet, and his body buff.
He spits fore-right; his haughty chest before,
Like batt'ring-rams, beats open ev'ry door:
And with a face as red, and as awry,
As Herod's hang-dogs in old Tapestry,
Scarecrow to boys, the breeding woman's curse,
Has yet a strange ambition to look worse;
Confounds the civil, keeps the rude in awe,
Jests like a licens'd fool, commands like law.

Frighted, I quit the room, but leave it so
As men from Jails to execution go;
For hung with deadly sins I see the wall,
And lin'd with Giants deadlier than 'em all:
Each man an *Askapart*,* of strength to toss
For Quoits, both Temple-bar and Charing-cross.
Scar'd at the grizly forms, I sweat, I fly,
And shake all o'er, like a discover'd spy.

Courts are too much for wits so weak as mine:
Charge them with Heav'n's Artill'ry, bold Divine!
From such alone the Great rebukes endure,
Whose Satire 's sacred, and whose rage secure:

'T is mine to wash a few light stains, but theirs
To deluge sin, and drown a Court in tears.
Howe'er what 's now *Apocrypha*, my Wit,
In time to come, may pass for holy writ.

* A giant.

ℂ Epilogue to the Satires

IN TWO DIALOGUES

DIALOGUE I

Fr.* Not twice a twelve-month you appear in Print,
And when it comes, the Court see nothing in't
You grow correct, that once with Rapture writ,
And are, besides, too *moral* for a Writ.
Decay of Parts, alas! we all must feel—
Why now, this moment, don't I see you steal?
'T is all from Horace; Horace long before ye
Said, "Tories call'd him Whig, and Whigs a Tory;"
And taught his Romans, in much better metre,
"To laugh at Fools who put their trust in Peter."
    But Horace, Sir, was delicate, was nice;
Bubo observes, he lash'd no sort of *Vice:*
Horace would say, Sir Billy *serv'd the Crown,*
Blunt could *do Bus'ness,* H—ggins *knew the Town;*
In Sappho touch the *Failings of the Sex,*
In rev'rend Bishops note some *small Neglects,*
And own, the Spaniard did a *waggish thing,*
Who cropt our Ears, and sent them to the King.
His sly, polite, insinuating style
Could please at Court, and make Augustus smile:
An artful Manager, that crept between
His Friend and Shame, and was a kind of *Screen.*
But 'faith your very Friends will soon be sore;
Patriots there are, who wish you'd jest no more—
And where 's the Glory? 't will be only thought
The Great man** never offer'd you a groat.

* Friend; no one in particular.
** Walpole.

Go see Sir ROBERT—
                P. See Sir ROBERT!—hum—
And never laugh—for all my life to come?
Seen him I have, but in his happier hour
Of Social Pleasure, ill-exchang'd for Pow'r;
Seen him, uncumber'd with the Venal tribe,
Smile without Art, and win without a Bribe.
Would he oblige me? let me only find,
He does not think me what he thinks mankind.
Come, come, at all I laugh he laughs, no doubt;
The only diff'rence is I dare laugh out.
    F. Why yes: with *Scripture* still you may be free;
A Horse-laugh, if you please, at *Honesty;*
A Joke on JEKYL, or some odd *Old Whig*
Who never chang'd his Principle, or Wig:
A Patriot is a Fool in ev'ry age,
Whom all Lord Chamberlains allow the Stage:
These nothing hurts; they keep their Fashion still,
And wear their strange old Virtue, as they will.
If any ask you, "Who 's the Man, so near
"His Prince, that writes in Verse, and has his ear?"
Why, answer, LYTTLETON, and I 'll engage
The worthy Youth shall ne'er be in a rage;
But were his Verses vile, his Whisper base,
You 'd quickly find him in Lord *Fanny's* case.
Sejanus, Wolsey, hurt not honest FLEURY,
But well may put some Statesmen in a fury.
    Laugh then at any, but at Fools or Foes;
These you but anger, and you mend not those.
Laugh at your friends, and, if your Friends are sore,
So much the better, you may laugh the more.
To Vice and Folly to confine the jest,
Sets half the world, God knows, against the rest;
Did not the Sneer of more impartial men
At Sense and Virtue, balance all again.
Judicious Wits spread wide the Ridicule,

And charitably comfort Knave and Fool.
   P. Dear Sir, forgive the Prejudice of Youth:
Adieu Distinction, Satire, Warmth, and Truth!
Come, harmless Characters, that no one hit;
Come, Henley's Oratory, Osborne's Wit!
The Honey dropping from Favonio's tongue,
The Flow'rs of Bubo, and the Flow of Y—ng!
The gracious Dew of Pulpit Eloquence,
And all the well-whipt Cream of Courtly Sense,
That First was H—vy's, F—'s next, and then
The S—te's, and then H—vy's once again.
O come, that easy Ciceronian style,
So Latin, yet so English all the while,
As, tho' the Pride of Middleton and Bland,
All Boys may read, and Girls may understand!
Then might I sing, without the least offence,
And all I sung should be the *Nation's Sense;*
Or teach the melancholy Muse to mourn,
Hang the sad Verse on Carolina's Urn,
And hail her passage to the Realms of Rest,
All Parts perform'd, and *all* her Children blest!
So—Satire is no more—I feel it die—
No *Gazetteer* more innocent than I—
And let, a' God's name, ev'ry Fool and Knave
Be grac'd thro' Life, and flatter'd in his Grave.
   F. Why so? if Satire knows its Time and Place,
You still may lash the greatest—in Disgrace:
For Merit will by turns forsake them all:
Would you know when? exactly when they fall.
But let all Satire in all Changes spare
Immortal S—k, and grave De—re.
Silent and soft, as Saints remove to Heav'n,
All Ties dissolv'd and ev'ry Sin forgiv'n,
These may some gentle ministerial Wing
Receive, and place for ever near a King!
There, where no Passion, Pride, or Shame transport,

Lull'd with the sweet Nepenthe of a Court;
There, where no Father's, Brother's, Friend's disgrace
Once break their rest, or stir them from their Place:
But past the Sense of human Miseries,
All Tears are wip'd for ever from all eyes;
No cheek is known to blush, no heart to throb,
Save when they lose a Question, or a Job.
  P. Good Heav'n forbid, that I should blast their glory,
Who know how like Whig Ministers to Tory,
And, when three Sov'reigns died, could scarce be vext,
Consid'ring what a *gracious Prince* was next.
Have I, in silent wonder, seen such things
As Pride in Slaves, and Avarice in Kings;
And at a Peer, or Peeress, shall I fret,
Who starves a Sister, or forswears a debt?
Virtue, I grant you, is an empty boast;
But shall the Dignity of *Vice* be lost?
Ye Gods! shall Cibber's Son, without rebuke,
Swear like a Lord, or Rich out-whore a Duke?
A Fav'rite's Porter with his Master vie,
Be brib'd as often, and as often lie?
Shall Ward draw Contracts with a Statesman's skill?
Or Japhet pocket, like his Grace, a Will?
Is it for Bond, or Peter, (paltry things)
To pay their Debts, or keep their Faith, like Kings?
If Blount despatch'd himself, he play'd the man,
And so may'st thou, illustrious Passeran!
But shall a Printer, weary of his life,
Learn, from their Books, to hang himself and Wife?
This, this, my friend, I cannot, must not bear;
Vice thus abus'd, demands a Nation's care;
This calls the Church to deprecate our Sin,
And hurls the Thunder of the Laws on *Gin*.
  Let modest FOSTER, if he will, excel
Ten Metropolitans in preaching well:
A simple Quaker, or a Quaker's Wife,

Out-do Llandaff in Doctrine,—yea in Life:
Let humble ALLEN, with an awkward Shame,
Do good by stealth, and blush to find it Fame.
Virtue may choose the high or low Degree,
'T is just alike to Virtue, and to me;
Dwell in a Monk, or light upon a King,
She 's still the same, belov'd, contented thing.
Vice is undone, if she forgets her Birth,
And stoops from Angels to the Dregs of Earth:
But 't is the *Fall* degrades her to a Whore;
Let *Greatness* own her, and she 's mean no more;
Her Birth, her Beauty, Crowds and Courts confess;
Chaste Matrons praise her, and grave Bishops bless;
In golden Chains the willing World she draws,
And hers the Gospel is, and hers the Laws,
Mounts the Tribunal, lifts her scarlet head,
And sees pale Virtue carted in her stead.
Lo! at the wheels of her Triumphal Car,
Old England's Genius, rough with many a Scar,
Dragg'd in the dust! his arms hang idly round,
His Flag inverted trails along the ground!
Our Youth, all livery'd o'er with foreign Gold,
Before her dance: behind her crawl the Old!
See thronging Millions to the Pagod run,
And offer Country, Parent, Wife, or Son!
Hear her black Trumpet thro' the Land proclaim,
That NOT TO BE CORRUPTED IS THE SHAME.
In Soldier, Churchman, Patriot, Man in Pow'r,
'T is Av'rice all, Ambition is no more!
See, all our Nobles begging to be Slaves!
See, all our Fools aspiring to be Knaves!
The Wit of Cheats, the Courage of a Whore,
Are what ten thousand envy and adore;
All, all look up, with reverential Awe,
At Crimes that 'scape, or triumph o'er the Law;
While Truth, Worth, Wisdom, daily they decry—

"Nothing is Sacred now but Villainy."
   Yet may this Verse (if such a Verse remain)
Shew, there was one who held it in disdain.

DIALOGUE II

Fr. 'T is all a Libel—Paxton (Sir) will say.
   P. Not yet, my Friend! to-morrow 'faith it may;
And for that very cause I print to-day.
How should I fret to mangle ev'ry line,
In rev'rence to the Sins of *Thirty nine!*
Vice with such Giant strides comes on amain,
Invention strives to be before in vain;
Feign what I will, and paint it e'er so strong,
Some rising Genius sins up to my Song.
   F. Yet none but you by Name the guilty lash;
Ev'n Guthry saves half Newgate by a Dash.
Spare then the Person, and expose the Vice.
   P. How, Sir? not damn the Sharper, but the Dice?
Come on then, Satire! gen'ral, unconfin'd,
Spread thy broad wing, and souse on all the kind.
Ye Statesmen, Priests, of one religion all!
Ye Tradesmen vile, in Army, Court, or Hall,
Ye Rev'rend Atheists— F. Scandal! name them! Who?
   P. Why, that 's the thing you bid me not to do.
Who starv'd a Sister, who forswore a Debt,
I never nam'd; the Town 's enquiring yet.
The pois'ning Dame— F. You mean— P. I don't.—
     F. You do!
   P. See, now I keep the Secret, and not you!
The bribing Statesman— F. Hold, too high you go.
   P. The brib'd Elector— F. There you stoop too low.
   P. I fain would please you, if I knew with what;
Tell me, which Knave is lawful Game, which not?
Must great Offenders, once escap'd the Crown,

Like royal Harts, be never more run down?
Admit your Law to spare the Knight requires,
As Beasts of Nature may we hunt the Squires?
Suppose I censure—you know what I mean—
To save a Bishop, may I name a Dean?

F. A Dean, Sir? no: his Fortune is not made;
You hurt a man that 's rising in the Trade.

P. If not the Tradesman who set up to-day,
Much less the 'Prentice who to-morrow may.
Down, down, proud Satire! tho' a Realm be spoil'd,
Arraign no mightier Thief than wretched *Wild;*
Or, if a Court or Country 's made a job,
Go drench a Pick-pocket, and join the Mob.

But, Sir, I beg you (for the Love of Vice!)
The matter 's weighty, pray consider twice;
Have you less pity for the needy Cheat,
The poor and friendless Villain, than the Great?
Alas! the small Discredit of a Bribe
Scarce hurts the Lawyer, but undoes the Scribe.
Then better sure it Charity becomes
To tax Directors, who (thank God) have Plums;
Still better, Ministers; or, if the thing
May pinch ev'n there—why lay it on a King.

F. Stop! stop!

               P. Must Satire, then, nor rise nor fall?
Speak out, and bid me blame no Rogues at all.

F. Yes, strike that *Wild*, I 'll justify the blow.

P. Strike? why the man was hang'd ten years ago:
Who now that obsolete Example fears?
Ev'n Peter trembles only for his Ears.

F. What? always Peter? Peter thinks you mad;
You make men desp'rate if they once are bad:
Else might he take to Virtue some years hence—

P. As S—k, if he lives, will love the Prince.

F. Strange spleen to S—k!

               P. Do I wrong the Man?

God knows, I praise a Courtier where I can.
When I confess, there is who feels for Fame,
And melts to Goodness, need I SCARB'ROW name?
Pleas'd let me own, in *Esher's* peaceful Grove
(Where *Kent* and Nature vie for PELHAM'S Love)
The Scene, the Master, opening to my view,
I sit and dream I see my CRAGGS anew!
   Ev'n in a Bishop I can spy Desert;
Secker is decent, *Rundel* has a Heart,
Manners with Candour are to *Benson* giv'n,
To *Berkeley*, ev'ry Virtue under Heav'n.
   But does the Court a worthy Man remove?
That instant, I declare, he has my Love:
I shun his Zenith, court his mild Decline;
Thus SOMERS once and HALIFAX, were mine.
Oft, in the clear, still Mirror of Retreat,
I study'd SHREWSBURY, the wise and great:
CARLETON'S calm Sense, and STANHOPE'S noble Flame,
Compar'd, and knew their gen'rous End the same;
How pleasing ATTERBURY'S softer hour!
How shin'd the Soul, unconquer'd in the Tow'r!
How can I PULT'NEY, CHESTERFIELD forget,
While Roman Spirit charms, and Attic Wit:
ARGYLL, the State's whole Thunder born to wield,
And shake alike the Senate and the Field:
Or WYNDHAM, just to Freedom and the Throne,
The Master of our Passions, and his own?
Names, which I long have lov'd, nor lov'd in vain,
Rank'd with their Friends, not number'd with their Train;
And if yet higher the proud List should end,
Still let me say: No Follower, but a Friend.
   Yet think not, Friendship only prompts my lays;
I follow *Virtue;* where she shines, I praise:
Point she to Priest or Elder, Whig or Tory,
Or round a Quaker's Beaver cast a Glory.
I never (to my sorrow I declare)

Din'd with the MAN of Ross, or my LORD MAY'R.
Some, in their choice of Friends (nay, look not grave)
Have still a secret Bias to a Knave:
To find an honest man I beat about,
And love him, court him, praise him, in or out.
    F. Then why so few commended?

                              P. Not so fierce!
Find you the Virtue, and I 'll find the Verse.
But random Praise—the task can ne'er be done;
Each Mother asks it for her booby Son,
Each Widow asks it for *the Best of Men*,
For him she weeps, and him she weds again.
Praise cannot stoop, like Satire, to the ground;
The Number may be hang'd, but not be crown'd.
Enough for half the Greatest of these days,
To 'scape my Censure, not expect my Praise.
And they not Rich? what more can they pretend?
Dare they to hope a Poet for their Friend?
What RICH'LIEU wanted, LOUIS scarce could gain,
And what young AMMON wish'd, but wish'd in vain.
No Pow'r the Muse's Friendship can command;
No Pow'r, when Virtue claims it, can withstand:
To *Cato*, *Virgil* pay'd one honest line;
O let my Country's Friends illumine mine!
—What are you thinking? F. 'Faith the thought 's no sin:
I think your Friends are out, and would be in.
    P. If merely to come in, Sir, they go out,
The way they take is strangely round about.
    F. They too may be corrupted, you 'll allow?
    P. I only call those Knaves who are so now.
    Is that too little? Come then, I 'll comply—
Spirit of *Arnall!* aid me while I lie.
COBHAM 's a Coward, POLWARTH is a Slave,
And LYTTLETON a dark, designing Knave,
ST. JOHN has ever been a wealthy Fool—
But let me add, Sir ROBERT 's mighty dull,

Has never made a Friend in private life,
And was, besides, a Tyrant to his Wife.
  But pray, when others praise him, do I blame?
Call Verres, Wolsey, any odious name?
Why rail they then, if but a Wreath of mine,
Oh All-accomplish'd St. John! deck thy shrine?
  What? shall each spur-gall'd Hackney of the day,
When Paxton gives him double Pots and Pay,
Or each new-pension'd Sycophant, pretend
To break my Windows, if I treat a Friend?
Then wisely plead, to me they meant no hurt,
But 't was my Guest at whom they threw the dirt?
Sure, if I spare the Minister, no rules
Of Honour bind me, not to maul his Tools;
Sure, if they cannot cut, it may be said
His Saws are toothless, and his Hatchet 's Lead.
  It anger'd TURENNE, once upon a day,
To see a Footman kick'd that took his pay:
But when he heard th' Affront the Fellow gave,
Knew one a Man of Honour, one a Knave;
The prudent Gen'ral turn'd it to a jest,
And begg'd, he 'd take the pains to kick the rest:
Which not at present having time to do—
F. Hold, Sir! for God's sake where 's th' Affront to you?
Against your worship when had S—k writ?
Or P—ge pour'd forth the Torrent of his Wit?
Or grant the Bard whose distich all commend
[*In Pow'r a Servant, out of Pow'r a friend*]
To W—le guilty of some venial sin;
What 's that to you who ne'er was out nor in?
  The Priest whose Flattery be-dropt the Crown,
How hurt he you? he only stain'd the Gown
And how did, pray, the florid Youth offend,
Whose Speech you took, and gave it to a Friend?
P. 'Faith, it imports not much from whom it came;
Whoever borrow'd, could not be to blame,

Since the whole House did afterwards the same.
Let Courtly Wits to Wits afford supply,
As Hog to Hog in huts of Westphaly;
If one, thro' Nature's Bounty or his Lord's,
Has what the frugal, dirty soil affords,
From him the next receives it, thick or thin,
As pure a mess almost as it came in;
The blessed benefit, not there confin'd,
Drops to the third, who nuzzles close behind;
From tail to mouth, they feed and they carouse:
The last full fairly gives it to the *House*.
   F. This filthy simile, this beastly line
Quite turns my stomach—
                          P. So does Flatt'ry mine;
And all your courtly Civet-cats can vent,
Perfume to you, to me is Excrement.
But hear me further—Japhet, 't is agreed,
Writ not, and Chartres scarce could write or read,
In all the Courts of Pindus guiltless quite;
But Pens can forge, my Friend, that cannot write;
And must no Egg in Japhet's face be thrown,
Because the Deed he forg'd was not my own?
Must never Patriot then declaim at Gin,
Unless, good man! he has been fairly in?
No zealous Pastor blame a failing Spouse,
Without a staring Reason on his brows?
And each Blasphemer quite escape the rod,
Because the insult 's not on Man, but God?
   Ask you what Provocation I have had?
The strong Antipathy of Good to Bad.
When Truth or Virtue an Affront endures,
Th' Affront is mine, my friend, and should be yours.
Mine as a Foe profess'd to false Pretence,
Who think a Coxcomb's Honour like his Sense;
Mine, as a Friend to ev'ry worthy mind;
And mine as Man, who feel for all mankind.

F. You 're strangely proud.

          P. So proud, I am no Slave:
So impudent, I own myself no Knave:
So odd, my Country's Ruin makes me grave.
Yes, I am proud; I must be proud to see
Men not afraid of God, afraid of me:
Safe from the Bar, the Pulpit, and the Throne,
Yet touch'd and sham'd by Ridicule alone.

  O sacred weapon! left for Truth's defence,
Sole Dread of Folly, Vice, and Insolence!
To all but Heav'n-directed hands deny'd,
The Muse may give thee, but the Gods must guide:
Rev'rent I touch thee! but with honest zeal,
To rouse the Watchmen of the public Weal;
To Virtue's work provoke the tardy Hall,
And goad the Prelate slumb'ring in his Stall.
Ye tinsel Insects! whom a Court maintains,
That counts your Beauties only by your Stains,
Spin all your Cobwebs o'er the Eye of Day!
The Muse's wing shall brush you all away:
All his Grace preaches, all his Lordship sings,
All that makes Saints of Queens, and Gods of Kings.
All, all but Truth, drops dead-born from the Press,
Like the last Gazette, or the last Address.

  When black Ambition stains a public Cause,
A Monarch's sword when mad Vain-glory draws,
Not Waller's Wreath can hide the Nation's Scar,
Nor Boileau turn the Feather to a Star.

  Not so, when diadem'd with rays divine,
Touch'd with the Flame that breaks from *Virtue's* Shrine,
Her Priestless Muse forbids the Good to die,
And opes the Temple of *Eternity*.
There, other Trophies deck the truly brave,
Than such as Anstis casts into the Grave;
Far other Stars than * and * * wear,
And may descend to Mordington from STAIR:

(Such as on HOUGH's unsully'd Mitre shine,
Or beam, good DIGBY, from a heart like thine)
Let *Envy* howl, while Heav'n's whole Chorus sings,
And bark at Honour not conferr'd by Kings;
Let *Flatt'ry* sickening see the Incense rise,
Sweet to the World, and grateful to the Skies:
Truth guards the Poet, sanctifies the line,
And makes immortal, Verse as mean as mine.

Yes, the last Pen for Freedom let me draw,
When Truth stands trembling on the edge of Law;
Here, Last of Britons! let your Names be read;
Are none, none living? let me praise the Dead,
And for that Cause which made your Fathers shine,
Fall by the Votes of their degen'rate Line.

FR. Alas! alas! pray end what you began,
And write next winter more *Essays on Man.*

ℭ Imitations of Horace

BOOK I. EPISTLE VII

IMITATED IN THE MANNER OF DR. SWIFT

'T is true, my Lord, I gave my word,
I would be with you, June the third;
Chang'd it to August, and (in short)
Have kept it—as you do at Court.
You humour me when I am sick,
Why not when I am splenetic?
In town, what Objects could I meet?
The shops shut up in ev'ry street,
And Fun'rals black'ning all the Doors,
And yet more melancholy Whores:
And what a dust in every place!
And a thin Court that wants your Face,
And Fevers raging up and down,
And W * and H * * both in town!
  "The Dog-days are no more the case"
'T is true; but Winter comes apace:
Then southward let your Bard retire,
Hold out some months 'twixt Sun and Fire,
And you shall see the first warm Weather,
Me and the Butterflies together.
  My Lord, your Favours well I know;
'T is with Distinction you bestow;
And not to ev'ry one that comes,
Just as a Scotsman does his Plums.
"Pray take them, Sir,—Enough 's a Feast:
"Eat some, and pocket up the rest"—
What? rob your Boys? those pretty rogues!
"No, Sir, you 'll leave them to the Hogs."
Thus Fools with Compliments besiege ye,

Contriving never to oblige ye.
Scatter your Favours on a Fop,
Ingratitude 's the certain crop;
And 't is but just, I 'll tell ye wherefore,
You give the things you never care for.
A wise man always is or should
Be mighty ready to do good;
But makes a diff'rence in his thought
Betwixt a Guinea and a Groat.

Now this I 'll say: you 'll find in me
A safe Companion, and a free;
But if you 'd have me always near—
A word, pray, in your Honour's ear.
I hope it is your Resolution
To give me back my Constitution!
The sprightly Wit, the lively Eye,
Th' engaging Smile, the Gaiety,
That laugh'd down many a Summer Sun,
And kept you up so oft till one:
And all that voluntary Vein,
As when Belinda rais'd my Strain.

A Weasel once made shift to slink
In at a Corn-loft thro' a Chink;
But having amply stuff'd his skin,
Could not get out as he got in:
Which one belonging to the House
('T was not a Man, it was a Mouse)
Observing, cry'd, "You 'scape not so,
"Lean as you came, Sir, you must go."

Sir, you may spare your Application,
I 'm no such Beast, nor his Relation;
Nor one that Temperance advance,
Cramm'd to the throat with Ortolans:
Extremely ready to resign
All that may make me none of mine.
South-sea Subscriptions take who please,

Leave me but Liberty and Ease.
'T was what I said to Craggs and Child,
Who prais'd my Modesty, and smil'd.
Give me, I cry'd, (enough for me)
My Bread, and Independency!
So bought an Annual Rent or two,
And liv'd—just as you see I do;
Near fifty, and without a Wife,
I trust that sinking Fund, my Life.
Can I retrench? Yes, mighty well,
Shrink back to my Paternal Cell,
A little House, with Trees a-row,
And, like its Master, very low.
There died my Father, no man's Debtor,
And there I 'll die, nor worse nor better.

To set this matter full before ye,
Our old Friend Swift will tell his Story.

"Harley, the Nation's great Support,"—
But you may read it; I stop short.

BOOK II. SATIRE VI

THE FIRST PART IMITATED IN THE YEAR 1714, BY
DR. SWIFT; THE LATTER PART ADDED AFTERWARDS

I 'VE often wish'd that I had clear
For life, six hundred pounds a year,
A handsome House to lodge a Friend,
A River at my garden's end,
A Terrace-walk, and half a Rood
Of Land, set out to plant a Wood,
Well, now I have all this and more,
I ask not to increase my store;
But here a Grievance seems to lie,
All this is mine but till I die;
I can't but think 't would sound more clever,
To me and to my Heirs for ever.

If I ne'er got or lost a groat,
By any Trick, or any Fault;
And if I pray by Reason's rules,
And not like forty other Fools:
As thus, "Vouchsafe, oh gracious Maker!
"To grant me this and t' other Acre:
"Or, if it be thy Will and Pleasure,
"Direct my Plough to find a Treasure:"
But only what my Station fits,
And to be kept in my right wits.
Preserve, Almighty Providence,
Just what you gave me, Competence:
And let me in these shades compose
Something in Verse as true as Prose;
Remov'd from all th' Ambitious Scene,
Nor puff'd by Pride, nor sunk by Spleen.

In short, I 'm perfectly content,
Let me but live on this side Trent;
Nor cross the Channel twice a year,
To spend six months with Statesmen here.

I must by all means come to town,
'T is for the service of the Crown.
"Lewis, the Dean will be of use,
"Send for him up, take no excuse."
The toil, the danger of the Seas;
Great Ministers ne'er think of these;
Or let it cost five hundred pound,
No matter where the money 's found,
It is but so much more in debt,
And that they ne'er consider'd yet.

"Good Mr. Dean, go change your gown,
"Let my Lord know you 're come to town."
I hurry me in haste away,
Not thinking it is Levee-day;
And find his Honour in a Pound,
Hemm'd by a triple Circle round,

Chequer'd with Ribbons blue and green:
How should I thrust myself between?
Some Wag observes me thus perplext,
And, smiling, whispers to the next,
"I thought the Dean had been too proud,
"To jostle here among a crowd."
Another in a surly fit,
Tells me I have more Zeal than Wit,
"So eager to express your love,
"You ne'er consider whom you shove,
"But rudely press before a Duke."
I own I 'm pleas'd with this rebuke,
And take it kindly meant to show
What I desire the World should know.

    I get a whisper, and withdraw;
When twenty Fools I never saw
Come with Petitions fairly penn'd,
Desiring I would stand their friend.

    This, humbly offers me his Case—
That, begs my int'rest for a Place—
A hundred other Men's affairs,
Like bees, are humming in my ears.
"To-morrow my Appeal comes on,
"Without your help the Cause is gone"—
"The Duke expects my Lord and you,
"About some great Affair, at Two—"
"Put my Lord Bolingbroke in mind,
"To get my Warrant quickly sign'd:
"Consider, 't is my first request."—
'Be satisfied, I 'll do my best:'—
Then presently he falls to tease,
"You may for certain, if you please;
"I doubt not, if his Lordship knew—
"And, Mr. Dean, one word from you"—

    'T is (let me see) three years and more,
(October next it will be four)

Since HARLEY bid me first attend,
And chose me for an humble friend;
Would take me in his Coach to chat,
And question me of this and that;
As, "What 's o'clock?" And, "How 's the Wind?"
"Whose Chariot 's that we left behind?"
Or gravely try to read the lines
Writ underneath the Country Signs;
Or, "Have you nothing new to-day
"From Pope, from Parnell, or from Gay?"
Such tattle often entertains
My Lord and me as far as Staines,
As once a week we travel down
To Windsor, and again to Town,
Where all that passes, *inter nos*,
Might be proclaim'd at Charing-Cross.

   Yet some I know with envy swell,
Because they see me us'd so well:
"How think you of our Friend the Dean?
"I wonder what some people mean;
"My Lord and he are grown so great,
"Always together, *tête à tête;*
"What, they admire him for his jokes—
"See but the fortune of some Folks!"
There flies about a strange report
Of some Express arriv'd at Court;
I 'm stopp'd by all the Fools I meet,
And catechis'd in ev'ry street.
"You, Mr. Dean, frequent the Great;
"Inform us, will the Emp'ror treat?
"Or do the Prints and Papers lie?"
'Faith, Sir, you know as much as I.'
"Ah Doctor, how you love to jest?
" 'T is now no secret"—'I protest
' 'T is one to me'—"Then tell us, pray,
"When are the Troops to have their pay?"

And, tho' I solemnly declare
I know no more than my Lord Mayor,
They stand amaz'd, and think me grown
The closest mortal ever known.

Thus in a sea of folly toss'd,
My choicest Hours of life are lost;
Yet always wishing to retreat,
Oh, could I see my Country Seat!
There, leaning near a gentle Brook,
Sleep, or peruse some ancient Book,
And there in sweet oblivion drown
Those Cares that haunt the Court and Town.
O charming Noons! and Nights divine!
Or when I sup, or when I dine.
My Friends above, my Folks below,
Chatting and laughing all-a-row,
The Beans and Bacon set before 'em,
The Grace-cup serv'd with all decorum:
Each willing to be pleas'd, and please,
And ev'n the very Dogs at ease!
Here no man prates of idle things,
How this or that Italian sings,
A Neighbour's Madness, or his Spouse's,
Or what 's in either of the Houses:
But something much more our concern,
And quite a scandal not to learn:
Which is the happier, or the wiser,
A man of Merit, or a Miser?
Whether we ought to choose our Friends,
For their own Worth, or our own Ends?
What good, or better, we may call,
And what, the very best of all?
Our Friend Dan Prior, told, (you know)
A Tale extremely *à propos:*
Name a Town Life, and in a trice,

He had a Story of two Mice.
Once on a time (so runs the Fable)
A Country Mouse, right hospitable,
Receiv'd a Town Mouse at his Board,
Just as a Farmer might a Lord.
A frugal Mouse upon the whole,
Yet lov'd his Friend, and had a Soul,
Knew what was handsome, and would do't,
On just occasion, *coute qui coute.*
He brought him Bacon (nothing lean),
Pudding, that might have pleas'd a Dean;
Cheese, such as men in Suffolk make,
But wish'd it Stilton for his sake;
Yet, to his Guest tho' no way sparing,
He ate himself the rind and paring.
Our Courtier scarce could touch a bit,
But show'd his Breeding and his Wit;
He did his best to seem to eat,
And cry'd, "I vow you 're mighty neat.
"But Lord, my Friend, this savage Scene!
"For God's sake, come, and live with Men:
"Consider, Mice, like Men, must die,
"Both small and great, both you and I:
"Then spend your life in Joy and Sport,
"(This doctrine, Friend, I learnt at Court)."
　　The veriest Hermit in the Nation
May yield, God knows, to strong temptation.
Away they come, thro' thick and thin,
To a tall house near Lincoln's-Inn;
('T was on the night of a Debate,
When all their Lordships had sat late.)
　　Behold the place, where if a Poet
Shin'd in Description, he might show it;
Tell how the Moon-beam trembling falls,
And tips with Silver all the walls;
Palladian walls, Venetian doors,

Grotesco roofs, and Stucco floors:
But let it (in a word) be said,
The Moon was up, and Men a-bed,
The Napkins white, the Carpet red:
The Guests withdrawn had left the Treat,
And down the Mice sate, *tête-à-tête*.

Our Courtier walks from dish to dish,
Tastes for his Friend of Fowl and Fish;
Tells all their names, lays down the law,
"*Que ça est bon! Ah goûtez ça!*
"That Jelly 's rich, this Malmsey healing,
"Pray, dip your Whiskers and your Tail in."
Was ever such a happy Swain?
He stuffs and swills, and stuffs again.
"I 'm quite asham'd—'t is mighty rude
"To eat so much—but all 's so good.
"I have a thousand thanks to give—
"My Lord alone knows how to live."
No sooner said, but from the Hall
Rush Chaplain, Butler, Dogs and all:
"A Rat, a Rat! clap to the door"—
The Cat comes bouncing on the floor,
O for the heart of Homer's Mice,
Or Gods to save them in a trice!
(It was by Providence they think,
For your damn'd Stucco has no chink.)
"An 't please your Honour, quoth the Peasant,
"This same Dessert is not so pleasant:
"Give me again my hollow Tree,
"A crust of Bread, and Liberty!"

BOOK IV. ODE I

To Venus

AGAIN? new Tumults in my breast?
   Ah spare me, Venus! let me, let me rest?

I am not now, alas! the man
   As in the gentle Reign of My Queen Anne.
Ah sound no more thy soft alarms,
   Nor circle sober fifty with thy Charms.
Mother too fierce of dear Desires!
   Turn, turn to willing hearts your wanton fires.
To *Number five* direct your Doves,
   There spread round MURRAY all your blooming Loves;
Noble and young, who strikes the heart
   With ev'ry sprightly, ev'ry decent part;
Equal, the injur'd to defend,
   To charm the Mistress, or to fix the Friend.
He, with a hundred Arts refin'd,
   Shall stretch thy conquests over half the kind:
To him each Rival shall submit,
   Make but his Riches equal to his Wit.
Then shall thy Form the Marble grace,
   (Thy Grecian Form) and Chloe lend the Face:
His House, embosom'd in the Grove,
   Sacred to social life and social love,
Shall glitter o'er the pendant green,
   Where Thames reflects the visionary scene:
Thither, the silver-sounding lyres
   Shall call the smiling Loves, and young Desires;
There, ev'ry Grace and Muse shall throng,
   Exalt the dance, or animate the song;
There Youths and Nymphs, in concert gay,
   Shall hail the rising, close the parting day.
With me, alas! those joys are o'er;
   For me, the vernal garlands bloom no more.
Adieu, fond hope of mutual fire,
   The still-believing, still-renew'd desire;
Adieu, the heart-expanding bowl,
   And all the kind Deceivers of the soul!
But why? ah tell me, ah too dear!
   Steals down my cheek th' involuntary Tear?

Why words so flowing, thoughts so free,
  Stop, or turn nonsense, at one glance of thee?
Thee, drest in Fancy's airy beam,
  Absent I follow thro' th' extended Dream;
Now, now I seize, I clasp thy charms,
  And now you burst (ah cruel!) from my arms;
And swiftly shoot along the Mall,
  Or softly glide by the Canal,
Now, shown by Cynthia's silver ray,
  And now, on rolling waters snatch'd away.

PART OF THE NINTH ODE
OF THE FOURTH BOOK

Lest you should think that verse should die,
  Which sounds the Silver Thames along,
Taught, on the wings of Truth to fly
  Above the reach of vulgar song;

Tho' daring Milton sits sublime,
  In Spenser native Muses play;
Nor yet shall Waller yield to time,
  Nor pensive Cowley's moral lay.

Sages and Chiefs long since had birth
  Ere Cæsar was, or Newton nam'd;
These rais'd new Empires o'er the Earth,
  And Those, new Heav'ns and Systems fram'd.

Vain was the Chief's, the Sage's pride!
  They had no Poet, and they died.
In vain they schem'd, in vain they bled!
  They had no Poet, and are dead.

ℂ The Dunciad:

To Dr. Jonathan Swift

BOOK THE FIRST

ARGUMENT

THE Proposition, the Invocation, and the Inscription. Then the Original of the great Empire of Dulness, and cause of the continuance thereof. The College of the Goddess in the City, with her private Academy for Poets in particular; the Governors of it, and the four Cardinal Virtues. Then the Poem hastes into the midst of things, presenting her, on the evening of a Lord Mayor's day, revolving the long succession of her Sons, and the glories past and to come. She fixes her eye on Bays to be the Instrument of that great Event which is the Subject of the Poem. He is described pensive among his Books, giving up the Cause, and apprehending the Period of her Empire: After debating whether to betake himself to the Church, or to Gaming, or to Party-writing, he raises an Altar of proper books, and (making first his solemn prayer and declaration) purposes thereon to sacrifice all his unsuccessful writings. As the pile is kindled, the Goddess, beholding the flame from her seat, flies and puts it out, by casting upon it the poem of Thule. She forthwith reveals herself to him, transports him to her Temple, unfolds her Arts, and initiates him into her Mysteries; then denouncing the death of Eusden the Poet Laureate, anoints him, carries him to Court, and proclaims him Successor.

BOOK I

THE Mighty Mother, and her Son, who brings
The Smithfield Muses to the ear of Kings,
I sing. Say you, her instruments the Great!
Call'd to this work by Dulness, Jove, and Fate:
You by whose care, in vain decry'd and curst,
Still Dunce the second reigns like Dunce the first;
Say, how the Goddess bade Britannia sleep,
And pour'd her Spirit o'er the land and deep.

In eldest time, ere mortals writ or read,
Ere Pallas issu'd from the Thund'rer's head,
Dulness o'er all possess'd her ancient right,
Daughter of Chaos and eternal Night:
Fate in their dotage this fair Idiot gave,
Gross as her sire, and as her mother grave,
Laborious, heavy, busy, bold, and blind,
She rul'd, in native Anarchy, the mind.

Still her old Empire to restore she tries,
For, born a Goddess, Dulness never dies.

O Thou! whatever title please thine ear,
Dean, Drapier, Bickerstaff, or Gulliver!
Whether thou choose Cervantes' serious air,
Or laugh and shake in Rab'lais' easy chair,
Or praise the Court, or magnify Mankind,
Or thy griev'd Country's copper chains unbind;
From thy Bœotia tho' her Pow'r retires,
Mourn not, my SWIFT, at aught our Realm acquires.
Here pleas'd behold her mighty wings outspread
To hatch a new Saturnian age of Lead.

Close to those walls where Folly holds her throne,
And laughs to think Monroe would take her down,
Where o'er the gates, by his fam'd father's hand,
Great Cibber's brazen, brainless brothers stand;
One Cell there is, conceal'd from vulgar eye,

The Cave of Poverty and Poetry.
Keen, hollow winds howl thro' the bleak recess,
Emblem of Music caus'd by Emptiness.
Hence Bards, like Proteus long in vain tied down,
Escape in Monsters, and amaze the town.
Hence Miscellanies spring, the weekly boast
Of Curl's chaste press, and Lintot's rubric post:
Hence hymning Tyburn's elegiac lines,
Hence Journals, Medleys, Merc'ries, MAGAZINES;
Sepulchral Lies, our holy walls to grace,
And New-year Odes, and all the Grub-street race.

In clouded Majesty here Dulness shone;
Four guardian Virtues, round, support her throne:
Fierce champion Fortitude, that knows no fears
Of hisses, blows, or want, or loss of ears:
Calm Temperance, whose blessings those partake
Who hunger, and who thirst for scribbling sake:
Prudence, whose glass presents th' approaching jail:
Poetic Justice, with her lifted scale,
Where, in nice balance, truth with gold she weighs,
And solid pudding against empty praise.

Here she beholds the Chaos dark and deep,
Where nameless Somethings in their causes sleep,
'Till genial Jacob, or a warm Third day,
Call forth each mass, a Poem, or a Play:
How hints, like spawn, scarce quick in embryo lie,
How new-born nonsense first is taught to cry,
Maggots half-form'd in rhyme exactly meet,
And learn to crawl upon poetic feet.
Here one poor word an hundred clenches makes,
And ductile Dulness new mæanders takes;
There motley images her fancy strike,
Figures ill pair'd, and Similes unlike.
She sees a Mob of Metaphors advance,
Pleas'd with the madness of the mazy dance;
How Tragedy and Comedy embrace;

How Farce and Epic get a jumbled race;
How Time himself stands still at her command,
Realms shift their place, and Ocean turns to land.
Here gay Description Egypt glads with show'rs,
Or gives to Zembla fruits, to Barca flow'rs:
Glitt'ring with ice here hoary hills are seen,
There painted valleys of eternal green;
In cold December fragrant chaplets blow,
And heavy harvests nod beneath the snow.

All these and more the cloud-compelling Queen
Beholds thro' fogs, that magnify the scene.
She, tinsell'd o'er in robes of varying hues,
With self-applause her wild creation views;
Sees momentary monsters rise and fall, .
And with her own fools-colours gilds them all,
'T was on the day when * * rich and grave,
Like Cimon, triumph'd both on land and wave:
(Pomps without guilt, of bloodless swords and maces,
Glad chains, warm furs, broad banners, and broad faces)
Now Night descending, the proud scene was o'er,
But liv'd in Settle's numbers one day more.
Now May'rs and Shrieves all hush'd and satiate lay,
Yet ate, in dreams, the custard of the day;
While pensive Poets painful vigils keep,
Sleepless themselves, to give their readers sleep.
Much to the mindful Queen the feast recalls
What City Swans once sung within the walls;
Much she revolves their arts, their ancient praise,
And sure succession down from Heywood's days.
She saw, with joy, the line immortal run,
Each sire imprest, and glaring in his son:
So watchful Bruin forms, with plastic care,
Each growing lump, and brings it to a Bear.
She saw old Prynne in restless Daniel shine,
And Eusden eke out Blackmore's endless line;
She saw slow Philips creep like Tate's poor page,

And all the mighty Mad in Dennis rage.
   In each she marks her Image full exprest,
But chief in BAYS's monster-breeding breast:
Bays, form'd by nature Stage and Town to bless,
And act, and be, a Coxcomb with success.
Dulness, with transport eyes the lively Dunce,
Remembering she herself was Pertness once.
Now (shame to Fortune!) an ill Run at Play
Blank'd his bold visage, and a thin Third day:
Swearing and supperless the Hero sate,
Blasphem'd his Gods, the Dice, and damn'd his Fate;
Then gnaw'd his pen, then dash'd it on the ground,
Sinking from thought to thought, a vast profound!
Plung'd for his sense, but found no bottom there;
Yet wrote and flounder'd on in mere despair.
Round him much Embryo, much Abortion lay,
Much future Ode, and abdicated Play;
Nonsense precipitate, like running Lead,
That slipp'd thro' Cracks and Zig-zags of the Head;
All that on Folly Frenzy could beget,
Fruits of dull Heat, and Sooterkins* of Wit,
Next, o'er his Books his eyes began to roll,
In pleasing memory of all he stole,
How here he sipp'd, how there he plunder'd snug,
And suck'd all o'er, like an industrious Bug.
Here lay poor Fletcher's half-eat scenes, and here
The Frippery of crucify'd Moliere;
There hapless Shakespear, yet of Tibbald sore,
Wish'd he had blotted for himself before.
The rest on Out-side merit but presume,
Or serve (like other Fools) to fill a room;
Such with their shelves as due proportion hold,
Or their fond parents drest in red and gold;
Or where the pictures for the page atone,
And Quarles is sav'd by Beauties not his own.

* False births.

Here swells the shelf with Ogilby the great;
There, stamp'd with arms, Newcastle shines complete:
Here all his suff'ring brotherhood retire,
And 'scape the martyrdom of jakes and fire:
A Gothic Library! of Greece and Rome
Well purg'd, and worthy Settle, Banks, and Broome.

But, high above, more solid Learning shone,
The Classics of an Age that heard of none;
There Caxton slept, with Wynkyn at his side,
One clasp'd in wood, and one in strong cow-hide;
There sav'd by spice, like mummies, many a year,
Dry Bodies of Divinity appear;
De Lyra there a dreadful front extends,
And here the groaning shelves Philemon bends.

Of these twelve volumes, twelve of amplest size,
Redeem'd from tapers and defrauded pies,
Inspir'd he seizes; these an altar raise;
An hecatomb of pure unsully'd lays
That altar crowns; A folio Common-place
Founds the whole pile, of all his works the base;
Quartos, octavos, shape the less'ning pyre;
A twisted Birth-day Ode completes the spire.

Then he: "Great Tamer of all human art!
First in my care, and ever at my heart;
Dulness! whose good old cause I yet defend,
With whom my Muse began, with whom shall end.
E'er since Sir Fopling's Periwig was Praise,
To the last honours of the Butt and Bays:
O thou! of Bus'ness the directing soul!
To this our head like bias to the bowl,
Which, as more pond'rous, made its aim more true,
Obliquely waddling to the mark in view:
O! ever gracious to perplex'd mankind,
Still spread a healing mist before the mind;
And, lest we err by Wit's wild dancing light,
Secure us kindly in our native night.

Or, if to Wit a coxcomb make pretence,
Guard the sure barrier between that and Sense;
Or quite unravel all the reas'ning thread,
And hang some curious cobweb in its stead!
As, forc'd from wind-guns, lead itself can fly,
And pond'rous slugs cut swiftly thro' the sky;
As clocks to weight their nimble motion owe,
The wheels above urg'd by the load below:
Me Emptiness, and Dulness could inspire,
And were my Elasticity and Fire.
Some Dæmon stole my pen (forgive th' offence)
And once betray'd me into common sense:
Else all my Prose and Verse were much the same;
This prose on stilts, that poetry fall'n lame.
Did on the stage my Fops appear confin'd?
My life gave ampler lessons to mankind.
Did the dead letter unsuccessful prove?
The brisk Example never fail'd to move.
Yet sure had Heav'n decreed to save the State,
Heav'n had decreed these works a longer date.
Could Troy be sav'd by any single hand,
This grey-goose weapon must have made her stand.
What can I now? my Fletcher cast aside,
Take up the Bible, once my better guide?
Or tread the path by vent'rous Heroes trod,
This Box my Thunder, this right hand my God?
Or chair'd at White's amidst the Doctors sit,
Teach Oaths to Gamesters, and to Nobles Wit?
Or bidst thou rather Party to embrace?
(A friend to Party thou, and all her race;
'T is the same rope at diff'rent ends they twist;
To Dulness Ridpath is as dear as Mist.)
Shall I, like Curtius, desp'rate in my zeal,
O'er head and ears plunge for the Commonweal?
Or rob Rome's ancient geese of all their glories,
And cackling save the Monarchy of Tories?

Hold—to the Minister I more incline;
To serve his cause, O Queen! is serving thine.
And see! thy very Gazetteers give o'er,
Ev'n Ralph repents, and Henley writes no more.
What then remains? Ourself. Still, still remain
Cibberian forehead, and Cibberian brain.
This brazen Brightness, to the 'Squire so dear;
This polish'd Hardness, that reflects the Peer:
This arch Absurd, that wit and fool delights;
This Mess, toss'd up of Hockley-hole and Whites;
Where Dukes and Butchers join to wreathe my crown,
At once the Bear and Fiddle of the town.
    "O born in sin, and forth in folly brought!
Works damn'd, or to be damn'd! (your father's fault)
Go, purify'd by flames ascend the sky,
My better and more christian progeny!
Unstain'd, untouch'd, and yet in maiden sheets;
While all your smutty sisters walk the streets.
Ye shall not beg, like gratis-given Bland,
Sent with a Pass, and vagrant thro' the land;
Not sail with Ward, to Ape-and-monkey climes,
Where vile Mundungus trucks for viler rhymes:
Not sulphur-tipt, emblaze an Ale-house fire;
Not wrap up Oranges, to pelt your sire!
O! pass more innocent, in infant state,
To the mild Limbo of our Father Tate:
Or peaceably forgot, at once be blest
In Shadwell's bosom with eternal Rest!
Soon to that mass of Nonsense to return,
Where things destroy'd are swept to things unborn."
    With that, a Tear (portentous sign of Grace!)
Stole from the Master of the sev'nfold Face;
And thrice he lifted high the Birth-day brand,
And thrice he dropt it from his quiv'ring hand;
Then lights the structure, with averted eyes:
The rolling smoke involves the sacrifice.

The op'ning clouds disclose each work by turns:
Now flames the Cid, and now Perolla burns;
Great Cæsar roars, and hisses in the fires;
King John in silence modestly expires;
No merit now the dear Nonjuror claims,
Moliere's old stubble in a moment flames.
Tears gush'd again, as from pale Priam's eyes
When the last blaze sent Ilion to the skies.

 Rous'd by the light, old Dulness heav'd the head,
Then snatch'd a sheet of Thule from her bed;
Sudden she flies, and whelms it o'er the pyre;
Down sink the flames, and with a hiss expire.

 Her ample presence fills up all the place;
A veil of fogs dilates her awful face:
Great in her charms! as when on Shrieves and May'rs
She looks, and breathes herself into their airs.
She bids him wait her to her sacred Dome:
Well pleas'd he enter'd, and confess'd his home.
So Spirits ending their terrestrial race
Ascend, and recognize their Native Place.
This the Great Mother* dearer held than all
The clubs of Quidnuncs, or her own Guildhall:
Here stood her Opium, here she nurs'd her Owls,
And here she plann'd th' Imperial seat of Fools.

 Here to her Chosen all her works she shews;
Prose swell'd to verse, verse loit'ring into prose:
How random thoughts now meaning chance to find,
Now leave all memory of sense behind;
How Prologues into Prefaces decay,
And these to Notes are fritter'd quite away.
How Index-learning turns no student pale,
Yet holds the eel of science by the tail:
How, with less reading than makes felons scape,
Less human genius than God gives an ape,
 Small thanks to France, and none to Rome or Greece,

---

* Dullness.

A vast, vamp'd, future, old, reviv'd, new piece,
'Twixt Plautus, Fletcher, Shakespear, and Corneille,
Can make a Cibber, Tibbald, or Ozell.

The Goddess then, o'er his anointed head,
With mystic words, the sacred Opium shed.
And lo! her bird (a monster of a fowl,
Something betwixt a Heideggre and Owl)
Perch'd on his crown. "All hail! and hail again,
My son: the promis'd land expects thy reign.
Know, Eusden thirsts no more for sack or praise;
He sleeps among the dull of ancient days;
Safe, where no Critics damn, no duns molest,
Where wretched Withers, Ward, and Gildon rest,
And high-born Howard, more majestic sire,
With Fool of Quality completes the quire.
Thou, Cibber! thou, his Laurel shalt support,
Folly, my son, has still a Friend at Court.
Lift up your Gates, ye Princes, see him come!
Sound, sound, ye Viols; be the Cat-call dumb!
Bring, bring the madding Bay, the drunken Vine;
The creeping, dirty, courtly Ivy join.
And thou! his Aid-de-camp, lead on my sons,
Light-arm'd with Points, Antitheses, and Puns.
Let Bawdry, Billingsgate, my daughters dear,
Support his front, and Oaths bring up the rear:
And under his, and under Archer's wing,
Gaming and Grub-street skulk behind the King.

"O! when shall rise a Monarch all our own,
And I, a Nursing-mother, rock the throne;
'Twixt Prince and People close the Curtain draw,
Shade him from Light, and cover him from Law;
Fatten the Courtier, starve the learned band,
And suckle Armies, and dry-nurse the land:
Till Senates nod to Lullabies divine,
And all be sleep, as at an Ode of thine."

She ceas'd. Then swells the Chapel-royal throat:

"God save King Cibber!" mounts in ev'ry note.
Familiar White's, "God save King Colley!" cries;
"God save King Colley!" Drury-lane replies:
To Needham's quick the voice triumphal rode,
But pious Needham dropt the name of God;
Back to the Devil* the last echoes roll,
And "Coll!" each Butcher roars at Hockley-hole.
   So when Jove's block descended from on high
(As sings thy great forefather Ogilby)
Loud thunder to its bottom shook the bog,
And the hoarse nation croak'd, "God save King Log!"

ℭ The Dunciad

BOOK THE SECOND

ARGUMENT

   The King being proclaimed, the solemnity is graced with public Games, and sports of various kinds; not instituted by the Hero, as by Æneas in Virgil, but for greater honour by the Goddess in person (in like manner as the games Pythia, Isthmia, &c. were anciently said to be ordained by the Gods, and as Thetis herself appearing, according to Homer, Odyss. xxiv. proposed the prizes in honour of her son Achilles). Hither flock the Poets and Critics, attended, as is but just, with their Patrons and Booksellers. The Goddess is first pleased, for her disport, to propose games to the Booksellers, and setteth up the Phantom of a Poet, which they contend to overtake. The Races described, with their divers accidents. Next, the game for a Poetess. Then follow the Exercises for the Poets, of tickling, vociferating, diving: The first holds forth the arts and practices of Dedicators, the second of Dis-

* The Devil Tavern.

putants and fustian Poets, the third of profound, dark, and dirty Party-writers. Lastly, for the Critics, the Goddess proposes (with great propriety) an Exercise, not of their parts, but their patience, in hearing the works of two voluminous Authors, one in verse, and the other in prose, deliberately read without sleeping: The various effects of which, with the several degrees and manners of their operation, are here set forth; till the whole number, not of Critics only, but of spectators, actors, and all present, fall asleep; which naturally and necessarily ends the games.

BOOK II

HIGH on a gorgeous seat, that far out-shone
Henley's gilt tub, or Fleckno's Irish throne,
Or that where on her Curls the Public pours,
All-bounteous, fragrant Grains and Golden show'rs,
Great Cibber sate: The proud Parnassian sneer,
The conscious simper, and the jealous leer,
Mix on his look: All eyes direct their rays
On him, and crowds turn Coxcombs as they gaze:
His Peers shine round him with reflected grace,
New edge their dulness, and new bronze their face.
So from the Sun's broad beam in shallow urns
Heav'n's twinkling Sparks draw light, and point their horns.
    Not with more glee, by hands pontific crown'd,
With scarlet hats wide-waving circled round,
Rome in her Capitol saw Querno sit,
Thron'd on seven hills, the Antichrist of wit.
    And now the Queen, to glad her sons, proclaims,
By herald Hawkers, high heroic Games.
They summon all her Race: an endless band
Pours forth, and leaves unpeopled half the land.
A motley mixture! in long wigs, in bags,
In silks, in crapes, in Garters, and in Rags,
From drawing-rooms, from colleges, from garrets,

On horse, on foot, in hacks, and gilded chariots:
All who true Dunces in her cause appear'd,
And all who knew those Dunces to reward.
Amid that area wide they took their stand,
Where the tall may-pole once o'er-look'd the Strand.
But now (so ANNE and Piety ordain)
A Church collects the saints of Drury-lane.
With Authors, Stationers* obey'd the call,
(The field of glory is a field for all).
Glory, and gain, th' industrious tribe provoke;
And gentle Dulness ever loves a joke.
A Poet's form she plac'd before their eyes,
And bade the nimblest racer seize the prize;
No meagre, muse-rid mope, adust and thin,
In a dun night-gown of his own loose skin;
But such a bulk as no twelve bards could raise,
Twelve starv'ling bards of these degen'rate days.
All as a partridge plump, full-fed, and fair,
She form'd this image of well-body'd air;
With pert flat eyes she window'd well its head:
A brain of feathers, and a heart of lead;
And empty words she gave, and sounding strain,
But senseless, lifeless! idol void and vain!
Never was dash'd out, at one lucky hit,
A fool, so just a copy of a wit;
So like, that critics said, and courtiers swore,
A Wit it was, and call'd the phantom Moore.
All gaze with ardour: some a poet's name,
Others a sword-knot and lac'd suit inflame.
But lofty Lintot in the circle rose:
"This prize is mine; who tempt it are my foes;
"With me began this genius, and shall end."
He spoke: and who with Lintot shall contend?
Fear held them mute. Alone, untaught to fear,
Stood dauntless Curl; "Behold that rival here!

* Booksellers.

"The race by vigour, not by vaunts is won;
"So take the hindmost, Hell," (he said) "and run."
Swift as a bard the bailiff leaves behind,
He left huge Lintot, and out-stripp'd the wind.
As when a dab-chick waddles thro' the copse
On feet and wings, and flies, and wades, and hops:
So lab'ring on, with shoulders, hands, and head,
Wide as a wind-mill all his figure spread,
With arms expanded Bernard rows his state,
And left-legg'd Jacob seems to emulate.
Full in the middle way there stood a lake,
Which Curl's Corinna chanc'd that morn to make:
(Such was her wont, at early dawn to drop
Her evening cates before his neighbour's shop,)
Here fortun'd Curl to slide; loud shout the band,
And "Bernard! Bernard!" rings thro' all the Strand.
Obscene with filth the miscreant lies bewray'd,
Fall'n in the plash his wickedness had laid:
Then first (if Poets aught of truth declare)
The caitiff Vaticide conceiv'd a pray'r.

"Hear, Jove! whose name my bards and I adore,
As much at least as any God's, or more;
And him and his if more devotion warms,
Down with the Bible, up with the Pope's Arms."*

A place there is, betwixt earth, air, and seas,
Where, from Ambrosia, Jove retires for ease.
There in his seat two spacious vents appear,
On this he sits, to that he leans his ear,
And hears the various vows of fond mankind;
Some beg an eastern, some a western wind:
All vain petitions, mounting to the sky,
With reams abundant this abode supply;
Amus'd he reads, and then returns the bills
Sign'd with that Ichor which from Gods distils.
In office here fair Cloacina** stands,

* The Bible, Curl's sign; the Crosskey's, Lintot's.
** The Roman goddess of the sewers.

And ministers to Jove with purest hands.
Forth from the heap she pick'd her Vot'ry's pray'r,
And plac'd it next him, a distinction rare!
Oft had the Goddess heard her servants call,
From her black grottos near the Temple-wall,
List'ning delighted to the jest unclean
Of link-boys vile, and watermen obscene;
Where as he fish'd her nether realms for Wit,
She oft had favour'd him, and favours yet.
Renew'd by ordure's sympathetic force,
As oil'd with magic juices for the course,
Vig'rous he rises; from th' effluvia strong
Imbibes new life, and scours and stinks along;
Re-passes Lintot, vindicates the race,
Nor heeds the brown dishonours of his face.

And now the victor stretch'd his eager hand,
Where the tall Nothing stood, or seem'd to stand;
A shapeless shade, it melted from his sight,
Like forms in clouds, or visions of the night.
To seize his papers, Curl, was next thy care;
His papers light fly diverse, tost in air;
Songs, sonnets, epigrams the winds uplift,
And whisk 'em back to Evans, Young, and Swift.
Th' embroider'd suit at least he deem'd his prey;
That suit an unpaid tailor snatch'd away.
No rag, no scrap, of all the beau, or wit,
That once so flutter'd, and that once so writ.

Heav'n rings with laughter. Of the laughter vain,
Dulness, good Queen, repeats the jest again.
Three wicked imps of her own Grubstreet choir,
She deck'd like Congreve, Addison, and Prior;
Mears, Warner, Wilkins run: delusive thought!
Breval, Bond, Besaleel, the varlets caught.
Curl stretches after Gay, but Gay is gone:
He grasps an empty Joseph for a John;
So Proteus, hunted in a nobler shape,

Became, when seiz'd, a puppy or an ape.
   To him the Goddess: "Son! thy grief lay down,
And turn this whole illusion on the town:
As the sage dame, experienc'd in her trade,
By names of Toasts retails each batter'd jade;
(Whence hapless Monsieur much complains at Paris
Of wrongs from Duchesses and Lady Maries;)
Be thine, my stationer! this magic gift;
Cook shall be Prior, and Concanen, Swift:
So shall each hostile name become our own,
And we too boast our Garth and Addison."
   With that she gave him (piteous of his case,
Yet smiling at his rueful length of face)
A shaggy Tap'stry, worthy to be spread
On Codrus' old, or Dunton's modern bed;
Instructive work! whose wry-mouth'd portraiture
Display'd the fates her confessors endure.
Earless on high, stood unabash'd De Foe,*
And Tutchin flagrant from the scourge below.
There Ridpath, Roper, cudgell'd might ye view;
The very worsted still look black and blue.
Himself among the story'd chiefs he spies,
As, from the blanket, high in air he flies;
And "Oh!" (he cry'd) "what street, what lane but knows
Our purgings, pumpings, blanketings, and blows?
In ev'ry loom our labours shall be seen,
And the fresh vomit run for ever green!"
   See in the circle next, Eliza plac'd,
Two babes of love close clinging to her waist;
Fair as before her works she stands confess'd,
In flow'rs and pearls by bounteous Kirkall dress'd.
The Goddess then: "Who best can send on high
"The salient spout, far-streaming to the sky;
"His be yon Juno of majestic size,
"With cow-like udders, and with ox-like eyes.

---

* Defoe, though put in the pillory, did not lose his ears.

"This China Jordan let the chief o'ercome
"Replenish, not ingloriously, at home."
    Osborne and Curl accept the glorious strife,
(Tho' this his Son dissuades, and that his Wife).
One on his manly confidence relies;
One on his vigour and superior size.
First Osborne lean'd against his letter'd post;
It rose, and labour'd to a curve at most.
So Jove's bright bow displays its wat'ry round,
(Sure sign that no spectator shall be drown'd).
A second effort brought but new disgrace:
The wild Mæander wash'd the Artist's face;
Thus the small jet, which hasty hands unlock,
Spirts in the gard'ner's eyes who turns the cock.
Not so from shameless Curl; impetuous spread
The stream, and smoking flourish'd o'er his head.
So (fam'd like thee for turbulence and horns)
Eridanus his humble fountain scorns;
Thro' half the heav'ns he pours th' exalted urn;
His rapid waters in their passage burn.
    Swift as it mounts, all follow with their eyes:
Still happy Impudence obtains the prize.
Thou triumph'st, Victor of the high-wrought day,
And the pleas'd dame, soft smiling, lead'st away.
Osborne, thro' perfect modesty o'ercome,
Crown'd with the Jordan, walks contented home.
    But now for Authors nobler palms remain;
"Room for my Lord!" three jockeys in his train;
Six huntsmen with a shout precede his chair:
He grins, and looks broad nonsense with a stare.
His Honour's meaning Dulness thus exprest,
"He wins this Patron, who can tickle best."
    He chinks his purse, and takes his seat of state:
With ready quills the Dedicators wait;
Now at his head the dext'rous task commence,
And, instant, fancy feels th' imputed sense;

Now gentle touches wanton o'er his face,
He struts Adonis, and affects grimace;
Rolli the feather to his ear conveys,
Then his nice taste directs our Operas:
Bentley* his mouth with classic flatt'ry opes,
And the puff'd orator bursts out in tropes.
But Welsted most the Poet's healing balm
Strives to extract from his soft, giving palm;
Unlucky Welsted! thy unfeeling master,
The more thou ticklest, gripes his fist the faster.
   While thus each hand promotes the pleasing pain,
And quick sensations skip from vein to vein;
A youth unknown to Phœbus, in despair,
Puts his last refuge all in heav'n and pray'r.
What force have pious vows! The Queen of Love
His sister sends, her vot'ress, from above.
As, taught by Venus, Paris learnt the art
To touch Achilles' only tender part;
Secure, thro' her, the noble prize to carry,
He marches off his Grace's Secretary.
   "Now turn to diff'rent sports," (the Goddess cries)
"And learn, my sons, the wond'rous pow'r of Noise.
To move, to raise, to ravish ev'ry heart,
With Shakespear's nature, or with Jonson's art,
Let others aim: 't is yours to shake the soul
With Thunder rumbling from the mustard-bowl,
With horns and trumpets now to madness swell,
Now sink in sorrows with a tolling bell;
Such happy arts attention can command,
When fancy flags, and sense is at a stand.
Improve we these. Three Cat-calls be the bribe
Of him, whose chatt'ring shames the monkey-tribe;
And his this Drum, whose hoarse heroic bass
Drowns the loud clarion of the braying Ass."
   Now thousand tongues are heard in one loud din;

* Not the famous Dr. Bentley but his nephew.

The monkey-mimics rush discordant in;
'T was chatt'ring, grinning, mouthing, jabb'ring all,
And Noise and Norton, Brangling and Breval,
Dennis and Dissonance, and captious Art,
And Snip-snap short, and Interruption smart,
And Demonstration thin, and Theses thick,
And Major, Minor, and Conclusion quick.
"Hold!" (cry'd the Queen), "a Cat-call each shall win
Equal your merits! equal is your din!
But that this well-disputed game may end,
Sound forth, my Brayers, and the welkin rend."

As, when the long-ear'd milky mothers wait
At some sick miser's triple bolted gate,
For their defrauded, absent foals they make
A moan so loud, that all the guild awake;
Sore sighs sir Gilbert, starting at the bray,
From dreams of millions, and three groats to pay.
So swells each wind-pipe; Ass intones to Ass;
Harmonic twang! of leather, horn, and brass;
Such as from lab'ring lungs th' Enthusiast blows,
High Sound, attemper'd to the vocal nose;
Or such as bellow from the deep Divine;
There, Webster! peal'd thy voice, and Whitfield! thine.
But far o'er all, sonorous Blackmore's strain;
Walls, steeples, skies, bray back to him again.
In Tot'nham fields, the brethren, with amaze,
Prick all their ears up, and forget to graze;
Long Chanc'ry-lane retentive rolls the sound,
And courts to courts return it round and round;
Thames wafts it thence to Rufus' roaring hall,*
And Hungerford re-echoes bawl for bawl.
All hail him victor in both gifts of song,
Who sings so loudly, and who sings so long,

This labour past, by Bridewell all descend,
(As morning pray'r and flagellation end)

* Westminster Hall.

To where Fleet-ditch with disemboguing streams
Rolls the large tribute of dead dogs to Thames,
The king of dykes! than whom no sluice of mud
With deeper sable blots the silver flood.
"Here strip, my children! here at once leap in,
"Here prove who best can dash thro' thick and thin,
"And who the most in love of dirt excel,
"Or dark dexterity of groping well.
"Who flings most filth, and wide pollutes around
"The stream, be his the Weekly Journals bound;
"A pig of lead to him who dives the best;
"A peck of coals a-piece shall glad the rest."
  In naked majesty Oldmixon stands,
And Milo-like surveys his arms and hands;
Then, sighing, thus, "And am I now three-score?
"Ah why, ye Gods, should two and two make four?"
He said, and climb'd a stranded lighter's height,
Shot to the black abyss, and plung'd downright.
The Senior's judgment all the crowd admire,
Who but to sink the deeper, rose the higher.
  Next Smedley div'd; slow circles dimpled o'er
The quaking mud, that clos'd, and op'd no more,
All look, all sigh, and call on Smedley lost;
"Smedley" in vain resounds thro' all the coast.
  Then * essay'd; scarce vanish'd out of sight,
He buoys up instant, and returns to light:
He bears no token of the sabler streams,
And mounts far off among the Swans of Thames.
  True to the bottom see Concanen creep,
A cold, long-winded native of the deep;
If perseverance gain the Diver's prize,
Not everlasting Blackmore this denies;
No noise, no stir, no motion canst thou make,
Th' unconscious stream sleeps o'er thee like a lake.
  Next plung'd a feeble, but a desp'rate pack,
With each a sickly brother at his back:

Sons of a Day! just buoyant on the flood,
Then number'd with the puppies in the mud.
Ask ye their names? I could as soon disclose
The names of these blind puppies as of those.
Fast by, like Niobe (her children gone)
Sits Mother Osborne, stupefy'd to stone!
And Monumental brass this record bears,
"These are,—ah no! these were, the Gazetteers!"

Not so bold Arnall; with a weight of skull,
Furious he dives, precipitately dull.
Whirlpools and storms his circling arm invest,
With all the might of gravitation blest.
No crab more active in the dirty dance,
Downward to climb, and backward to advance.
He brings up half the bottom on his head,
And loudly claims the Journals and the Lead.

The plunging Prelate, and his pond'rous Grace,
With holy envy gave one Layman place.
When lo! a burst of thunder shook the flood;
Slow rose a form, in majesty of Mud;
Shaking the horrors of his sable brows,
And each ferocious feature grim with ooze.
Greater he looks, and more than mortal stares;
Then thus the wonders of the deep declares.

First he relates, how sinking to the chin,
Smit with his mien the Mud-nymphs suck'd him in:
How young Lutetia, softer than the down,
Nigrina black, and Merdamante brown,
Vied for his love in jetty bow'rs below,
As Hylas fair was ravished long ago.
Then sung, how shown him by the Nut-brown maids
A branch of Styx here rises from the Shades,
That tinctur'd as it runs with Lethe's streams,
And wafting Vapours from the Land of dreams,
(As under seas Alpheus' secret sluice
Bears Pisa's off'rings to his Arethuse)

Pours into Thames: and hence the mingled wave
Intoxicates the pert, and lulls the grave:
Here brisker vapours o'er the TEMPLE creep,
There, all from Paul's to Aldgate drink and sleep.

    Thence to the banks where rev'rend Bards repose,
They led him soft; each rev'rend Bard arose;
And Milbourn chief, deputed by the rest,
Gave him the cassock, surcingle, and vest.
"Receive" (he said) "these robes which once were mine,
"Dulness is sacred in a sound divine."

    He ceas'd, and spread the robe; the crowd confess
The rev'rend Flamen in his lengthen'd dress.
Around him wide a sable Army stand,
A low-born, cell-bred, selfish, servile band,
Prompt or to guard or stab, to saint or damn,
Heav'n's Swiss, who fight for any God or Man.

    Thro' Lud's fam'd gates, along the well-known Fleet,
Rolls the black troop, and overshades the street;
'Till show'rs of Sermons, Characters, Essays,
In circling fleeces whiten all the ways:
So clouds, replenish'd from some bog below,
Mount in dark volumes, and descend in snow.
Here stopt the Goddess; and in pomp proclaims
A gentler exercise to close the games.

    "Ye Critics! in whose heads, as equal scales,
"I weigh what author's heaviness prevails;
"Which most conduce to soothe the soul in slumbers,
"My H—ley's periods, or my Blackmore's numbers;
"Attend the trial we propose to make:
"If there be man, who o'er such works can wake,
"Sleep's all-subduing charms who dares defy,
"And boasts Ulysses' ear with Argus' eye;
"To him we grant our amplest pow'rs to sit
"Judge of all present, past, and future wit;
"To cavil, censure, dictate, right or wrong;
"Full and eternal privilege of tongue."

  Three College Sophs, and three pert Templars came,
The same their talents, and their tastes the same;
Each prompt to query, answer, and debate,
And smit with love of Poesy and Prate,
The pond'rous books two gentle readers bring;
The heroes sit, the vulgar form a ring.
The clam'rous crowd is hush'd with mugs of Mum,*
'Till all, tun'd equal, send a gen'ral hum.
Then mount the Clerks, and in one lazy tone
Thro' the long, heavy, painful page drawl on;
Soft creeping, words on words, the sense compose;
At ev'ry line they stretch, they yawn, they doze.
As to soft gales top-heavy pines bow low
Their heads, and lift them as they cease to blow:
Thus oft they rear, and of the head decline,
As breathe, or pause, by fits, the airs divine;
And now to this side, now to that they nod,
As verse, or prose, infuse the drowsy God.
Thrice Budgel aim'd to speak, but thrice supprest
By potent Arthur, knock'd his chin and breast.
Toland and Tindal, prompt at priests to jeer,
Yet silent bow'd to *Christ's No kingdom here.*
Who sate the nearest, by the words o'ercome,
Slept first; the distant nodded to the hum.
Then down are roll'd the books; stretch'd o'er 'em lies
Each gentle clerk, and mutt'ring seals his eyes,
As what a Dutchman plumps into the lakes,
One circle first, and then a second makes;
What Dulness dropt among her sons imprest
Like motion, from one circle to the rest;
So from the mid-most the mutation spreads
Round and more round, o'er all the *sea of heads.*
At last Centlivre felt her voice to fail;
Motteux himself unfinish'd left his tale;
Boyer the State, and Law the Stage gave o'er;

   * Strong ale.

Morgan and Mandevil could prate no more;
Norton, from Daniel and Ostrœa sprung,
Bless'd with his father's front, and mother's tongue,
Hung silent down his never-blushing head;
And all was hush'd, as Folly's self lay dead.

Thus the soft gifts of Sleep conclude the day,
And stretch'd on bulks, as usual, Poets lay.
Why should I sing, what bards the nightly Muse
Did slumb'ring visit, and convey to stews;
Who prouder march'd, with magistrates in state,
To some fam'd round-house, ever open gate!
How Henley lay inspir'd beside a sink,
And to mere mortals seem'd a Priest in drink:
While others, timely, to the neighb'ring Fleet*
(Haunt of the Muses) made their safe retreat.

☾ The Dunciad

BOOK THE THIRD

ARGUMENT

After the other persons are disposed in their proper places
of rest, the Goddess transports the King to her Temple, and
there lays him to slumber with his head on her lap; a position
of marvellous virtue, which causes all the visions of wild en-
thusiasts, projectors, politicians, inamoratos, castle-builders,
chemists, and poets. He is immediately carried on the wings
of Fancy, and led by a mad Poetical Sibyl to the Elysian
shade; where, on the banks of Lethe, the souls of the dull are
dipped by Bavius, before their entrance into this world. There
he is met by the ghost of Settle, and by him made acquainted
with the wonders of the place, and with those which he him-

---

* A debtors' prison.

self is destined to perform. He takes him to a Mount of Vision, from whence he shews him the past triumphs of the Empire of Dulness, then the present, and lastly the future: how small a part of the world was ever conquered by Science, how soon those conquests were stopped, and those very nations again reduced to her dominion. Then distinguishing the Island of Great-Britain, shews by what aids, by what persons, and by what degrees it shall be brought to her Empire. Some of the persons he causes to pass in review before his eyes, describing each by his proper figure, character, and qualifications. On a sudden the Scene shifts, and a vast number of miracles and prodigies appear, utterly surprising and unknown to the King himself, till they are explained to be the wonders of his own reign now commencing. On this subject Settle breaks into a congratulation, yet not unmixed with concern, that his own times were but types of these. He prophesies how first the nation shall be over-run with Farces, Operas, and Shows; how the throne of Dulness shall be advanced over the Theatres, and set up even at Court; then how her Sons shall preside in the seats of Arts and Sciences: giving a glimpse or Pisgah-sight of the future Fulness of her Glory, the accomplishment whereof is the subject of the fourth and last book.

BOOK III

But in her Temple's last recess enclos'd,
On Dulness' lap th' Anointed head repos'd.
Him close she curtains round with Vapours blue,
And soft besprinkles with Cimmerian dew.
Then raptures high the seat of Sense o'erflow,
Which only heads refin'd from Reason know.
Hence, from the straw where Bedlam's Prophet nods,
He hears loud Oracles, and talks with Gods:
Hence the Fool's Paradise, the Statesman's Scheme,
The air-built Castle, and the golden Dream,
The Maid's romantic wish, the Chemist's flame,

And Poet's vision of eternal Fame.

And now, on Fancy's easy wing convey'd,
The King descending views th' Elysian Shade.
A slip-shod Sibyl led his steps along,
In lofty madness meditating song;
Her tresses staring from Poetic dreams,
And never wash'd, but in Castalia's streams.
Taylor, their better Charon, lends an oar,
(Once swan of Thames, tho' now he sings no more.)
Benlowes, propitious still to blockheads, bows;
And Shadwell nods the Poppy on his brows.
Here, in a dusky vale were Lethe rolls,
Old Bavius sits, to dip poetic souls,
And blunt the sense, and fit it for a skull
Of solid proof, impenetrably dull:
Instant, when dipt, away they wing their flight,
Where Brown and Mears unbar the gates of Light,
Demand new bodies, and in Calf's array
Rush to the world, impatient for the day.
Millions and millions on these banks he views,
Thick as the stars of night, or morning dews,
As thick as bees o'er vernal blossoms fly,
As thick as eggs at Ward in pillory.

Wond'ring he gaz'd: When lo! a Sage* appears,
By his broad shoulders known, and length of ears,
Known by the band and suit which Settle wore
(His only suit) for twice three years before:
All as the vest, appear'd the wearer's frame,
Old in new state; another, yet the same.
Bland and familiar as in life, begun
Thus the great Father to the greater Son.

"Oh born to see what none can see awake!
Behold the wonders of th' oblivious Lake.
Thou, yet unborn, hast touch'd this sacred shore;
The hand of Bavius drench'd thee o'er and o'er.

* Dante.

But blind to former, as to future fate,
What mortal knows his pre-existent state?
Who knows how long thy transmigrating soul
Might from Bœotian to Bœotian roll?
How many Dutchmen she vouchsaf'd to thrid?
How many stages thro' old Monks she rid?
And all who since, in mild benighted days,
Mix'd the Owl's ivy with the Poet's bays?
As man's Mæanders to the vital spring
Roll all their tides; then back their circles bring;
Or whirligigs twirl'd round by skilful swain,
Suck the thread in, then yield it out again:
All nonsense thus, of old or modern date,
Shall in thee centre, from thee circulate.
For this our Queen unfolds to vision true
Thy mental eye, for thou hast much to view:
Old scenes of glory, times long cast behind
Shall, first recall'd, rush forward to thy mind:
Then stretch thy sight o'er all her rising reign,
And let the past and future fire thy brain.

"Ascend this hill, whose cloudy point commands
Her boundless empire over seas and lands.
See, round the Poles where keener spangles shine,
Where spices smoke beneath the burning Line,
(Earth's wide extremes) her sable flag display'd,
And all the nations cover'd in her shade.

"Far eastward cast thine eye, from whence the Sun
And orient Science their bright course begun:
One god-like Monarch* all that pride confounds,
He, whose long wall the wand'ring Tartar bounds;
Heav'ns! what a pile! whole ages perish there,
And one bright blaze turns Learning into air.

"Thence to the south extend thy gladden'd eyes;
There rival flames with equal glory rise,

---

* Chi Ho-am-ti Emperor of China, who built the great wall and destroyed all the books. [Pope.]

From shelves to shelves see greedy Vulcan roll,
And lick up all the Physic of the Soul.
How little, mark! that portion of the ball,
Where, faint at best, the beams of Science fall:
Soon as they dawn, from Hyperborean skies
Embody'd dark, what clouds of Vandals rise!
Lo! where Mæotis sleeps, and hardly flows
The freezing Tanais thro' a waste of snows,
The North by myriads pours her mighty sons,
Great nurse of Goths, of Alans, and of Huns!
See Alaric's stern port! the martial frame
Of Genseric! and Attila's dread name!
See the bold Ostrogoths on Latium fall;
See the fierce Visigoths on Spain and Gaul!
See, where the morning gilds the palmy shore
(The soil that arts and infant letters bore)
His conqu'ring tribes th' Arabian prophet draws,
And saving Ignorance enthrones by Laws.
See Christians, Jews, one heavy sabbath keep,
And all the western world believe and sleep.

 "Lo! Rome herself, proud mistress now no more
Of arts, but thund'ring against heathen lore;
Her grey-hair'd Synods damning books unread,
And Bacon* trembling for his brazen head.
Padua, with sighs, beholds her Livy burn,
And ev'n th' Antipodes Virgilius mourn.
See the Cirque falls, th' unpillar'd Temple nods,
Streets pav'd with Heroes, Tiber chok'd with Gods:
'Till Peter's keys some christ'ned Jove adorn,
And Pan to Moses lends his pagan horn;
See, graceless Venus to a Virgin turn'd,
Or Phidias broken, and Apelles burn'd.

 "Behold yon' Isle, by Palmers, Pilgrims trod,
Men bearded, bald, cowl'd, uncowl'd, shod, unshod,
Peel'd, patch'd, and pyebald, linsey-wolsey brothers,

 * Roger Bacon.

Grave Mummers! sleeveless some, and shirtless others.
That once was Britain—Happy! had she seen
No fiercer sons, had Easter never been.
In peace, great Goddess, ever be ador'd;
How keen the war, if Dulness draw the sword!
Thus visit not thy own! on this blest age
Oh spread thy Influence, but restrain thy Rage!

   "And see, my son! the hour is on its way,
That lifts our Goddess to imperial sway:
This fav'rite Isle, long sever'd from her reign,
Dove-like, she gathers to her wings again.
Now look thro' Fate! behold the scene she draws!
What aids, what armies to assert her cause!
See all her progeny, illustrious sight!
Behold, and count them, as they rise to light.
As Berecynthia, while her offspring vie
In homage to the mother of the sky,
Surveys around her, in the blest abode,
An hundred sons, and ev'ry son a God:
Not with less glory mighty Dulness crown'd
Shall take thro' Grubstreet her triumphant round;
And her Parnassus glancing o'er at once,
Behold an hundred sons, and each a Dunce.

   "Mark first that youth who takes the foremost place,
And thrust his person full into your face.
With all thy Father's virtues blest, be born!
And a new Cibber shall the stage adorn.

   "A second see, by meeker manners known,
And modest as the maid that sips alone;
From the strong fate of drams if thou get free,
Another Durfey, Ward! shall sing in thee.
Thee shall each ale-house, thee each gill-house mourn,
And answ'ring gin-shops sourer sights return.

   "Jacob, the scourge of Grammar, mark with awe,
Nor less revere him, blunderbuss of Law.
Lo P—p—le's brow, tremendous to the town,

Horneck's fierce eye, and Roome's funereal frown.
Lo sneering Goode, half malice and half whim,
A friend in glee, ridiculously grim.
Each Cygnet sweet, of Bath and Tunbridge race,
Whose tuneful whistling makes the waters pass;
Each Songster, Riddler, ev'ry nameless name,
All crowd, who foremost shall be damn'd to Fame.
Some strain in rhyme; the Muses, on their racks,
Scream like the winding of ten thousand jacks;
Some free from rhyme or reason, rule or check,
Break Priscian's head, and Pegasus's neck;
Down, down they larum, with impetuous whirl,
The Pindars, and the Miltons of a Curl.

"Silence, ye Wolves! while Ralph to Cynthia howls,
And makes night hideous—Answer him, ye Owls!

"Sense, speech, and measure, living tongues and dead,
Let all give way, and Morris may be read.
Flow, Welsted, flow! like thine inspirer, Beer,
Tho' stale, not ripe; tho' thin, yet never clear;
So sweetly mawkish, and so smoothly dull;
Heady, not strong; o'erflowing, tho' not full.

"Ah Dennis! Gildon ah! what ill-starr'd rage
Divides a friendship long confirm'd by age?
Blockheads with reason wicked wits abhor;
But fool with fool is barb'rous civil war.
Embrace, embrace, my sons! be foes no more!
Nor glad vile Poets with true Critics' gore.

"Behold yon Pair, in strict embraces join'd;
How like in manners, and how like in mind!
Equal in wit, and equally polite,
Shall this a *Pasquin*, that a *Grumbler* write;
Like are their merits, like rewards they share,
That shines a Consul, this Commissioner.

"But who is he, in closet close y-pent,
Of sober face, with learned dust besprent?

Right well mine eyes arede* the myster wight,**
On parchment scraps y-fed, and Wormius hight.
To future ages may thy dulness last,
As thou preserv'st the dulness of the past!

  "There, dim in clouds, the poring Scholiasts mark,
Wits, who, like owls, see only in the dark,
A Lumber-house of books in ev'ry head,
For ever reading, never to be read!

  "But, where each Science lifts its modern type,
Hist'ry her Pot, Divinity her Pipe,
While proud Philosophy repines to show,
Dishonest sight! his breeches rent below;
Embrown'd with native bronze, lo! Henley stands,
Turning his voice, and balancing his hands.
How fluent nonsense trickles from his tongue!
How sweet the periods, neither said, nor sung!
Still break the benches, Henley! with thy strain,
While Sherlock, Hare, and Gibson preach in vain.
Oh great Restorer of the good old Stage,
Preacher at once, and Zany of thy age!
Oh worthy thou of Ægypt's wise abodes,
A decent priest, where monkeys were the gods!
But fate with butchers placed thy priestly stall,
Meek modern faith to murder, hack, and maul;
And bade thee live, to crown Britannia's praise,
In Toland's, Tindal's, and in Woolston's days.

  "Yet oh, my sons, a father's words attend:
(So may the fates preserve the ears you lend)
'Tis yours a Bacon or a Locke to blame,
A Newton's genius, or a Milton's flame:
But oh! with One, immortal One dispense;
The source of Newton's Light, of Bacon's Sense.
Content, each Emanation of his fires

  * Read, peruse.
  ** Uncouth mortal.

That beams on earth, each Virtue he inspires,
Each Art he prompts, each Charm he can create,
Whate'er he gives, are giv'n for you to hate.
Persist, by all divine in Man unaw'd,
But 'Learn, ye Dunces! not to scorn your God.' "

 Thus he, for then a ray of Reason stole
Half thro' the solid darkness of his soul;
But soon the cloud return'd—and thus the Sire:
"See now, what Dulness and her sons admire!
See what the charms, that smite the simple heart
Not touch'd by Nature, and not reach'd by Art."

 His never-blushing head he turn'd aside,
(Not half so pleas'd when Goodman prophesy'd)
And look'd, and saw a sable Sorc'rer rise,
Swift to whose hand a winged volume flies:
All sudden, Gorgons hiss, and Dragons glare,
And ten-horn'd fiends and Giants rush to war.
Hell rises, Heav'n descends, and dance on Earth:
Gods, imps, and monsters, music, rage, and mirth,
A fire, a jig, a battle, and a ball,
'Till one wide conflagration swallows all.

 Thence a new world to Nature's laws unknown,
Breaks out refulgent, with a heav'n its own:
Another Cynthià her new journey runs,
And other planets circle other suns.
The forests dance, the rivers upward rise,
Whales sport in woods, and dolphins in the skies;
And last, to give the whole creation grace,
Lo! one vast Egg produces human race.

 Joy fills his soul, joy innocent of thought;
'What pow'r,' he cries, 'what pow'r these wonders wrought?'
"Son, what thou seek'st is in thee! Look, and find
Each monster meets his likeness in thy mind.
Yet would'st thou more? in yonder cloud behold,
Whose sars'net skirts are edg'd with flamy gold,
A matchless youth! his nod these worlds controls,

Wings the red lightning, and the thunder rolls.
Angel of Dulness, sent to scatter round
Her magic charms o'er all unclassic ground:
Yon stars, yon suns, he rears at pleasure higher,
Illumes their light, and sets their flames on fire.
Immortal Rich! how calm he sits at ease
'Mid snows of paper, and fierce hail of pease;
And proud his Mistress' orders to perform,
Rides in the whirlwind, and directs the storm.

  "But lo! to dark encounter in mid air
New wizards rise; I see my Cibber there!
Booth in his cloudy tabernacle shrin'd,
On grinning dragons thou shalt mount the wind.
Dire is the conflict, dismal is the din,
Here shouts all Drury, there all Lincoln's-inn;
Contending Theatres our empire raise,
Alike their labours, and alike their praise.

  "And are these wonders, Son, to thee unknown?
Unknown to thee? these wonders are thy own.
These Fate reserv'd to grace thy reign divine,
Foreseen by me, but ah! withheld from mine.
In Lud's old walls tho' long I rul'd, renown'd
Far as loud Bow's stupendous bells resound;
Tho' my own Aldermen conferr'd the bays,
To me committing their eternal praise,
Their full-fed Heroes, their pacific May'rs
Their annual trophies, and their monthly wars;
Tho' long my Party built on me their hopes,
For writing Pamphlets, and for roasting Popes;
Yet lo! in me what authors have to brag on!
Reduc'd at last to hiss in my own dragon.
Avert it, Heav'n! that thou, my Cibber, e'er
Should'st wag a serpent-tail in Smithfield fair!
Like the vile straw that's blown about the streets,
The needy Poet sticks to all he meets,
Coach'd, carted, trod upon, now loose, now fast,

And carry'd off in some Dog's tail at last.
Happier thy fortunes! like a rolling stone,
Thy giddy dulness still shall lumber on,
Safe in its heaviness, shall never stray,
But lick up ev'ry blockhead in the way.
Thee shall the Patriot, thee the Courtier taste,
And ev'ry year be duller than the last.
Till rais'd from booths, to Theatre, to Court,
Her seat imperial Dulness shall transport.
Already Opera prepares the way,
The sure fore-runner of her gentle sway:
Let her thy heart, next Drabs and Dice, engage,
The third mad passion of thy doting age.
Teach thou the warbling Polypheme to roar,
And scream thyself as none e'er scream'd before!
To aid our cause, if Heav'n thou can'st not bend,
Hell thou shalt move; for Faustus is our friend:
Pluto with Cato thou for this shalt join,
And link the Mourning Bride to Proserpine.
Grubstreet! thy fall should men and Gods conspire,
Thy stage shall stand, ensure it but from Fire.
Another Æschylus appears! prepare
For new abortions, all ye pregnant fair!
In flames, like Semele's, be brought to bed,
While op'ning Hell spouts wild-fire at your head.

  "Now, Bavius, take the poppy from thy brow,
And place it here! here all ye Heroes bow!
This, this is he, foretold by ancient rhymes:
Th' Augustus born to bring Saturnian times.
Signs following signs lead on the mighty year!
See! the dull stars roll round and re-appear.
See, see, our own true Phœbus wears the bays!
Our Midas sits Lord Chancellor of Plays!
On Poets' Tombs see Benson's titles writ!
Lo! Ambrose Philips is preferr'd for Wit!
See under Ripley rise a new White-hall,

While Jones' and Boyle's united Labours fall;
While Wren with sorrow to the grave descends;
Gay dies unpension'd with a hundred friends;
Hibernian Politics, O Swift! thy fate;
And Pope's, ten years to comment and translate.
    "Proceed, great days! till Learning fly the shore,
Till Birch shall blush with noble blood no more,
Till Thames see Eton's sons for ever play,
Till Westminster's whole year be holiday,
Till Isis' Elders reel, their pupils' sport,
Till Alma Mater lie dissolv'd in Port!"
    'Enough! enough!' the raptur'd Monarch cries;
And thro' the Iv'ry Gate the Vision flies.

☾ The Dunciad

BOOK THE FOURTH

ARGUMENT

The Poet being, in this Book, to declare the Completion of the Prophecies mentioned at the end of the former, makes a new Invocation; as the greater Poets are wont, when some high and worthy matter is to be sung. He shews the Goddess coming in her Majesty, to destroy Order and Science, and to substitute the Kingdom of the Dull upon earth. How she leads captive the Sciences, and silenceth the Muses, and what they be who succeed in their stead. All her Children, by a wonderful attraction, are drawn about her; and bear along with them divers others, who promote her Empire by connivance, weak resistance, or discouragement of Arts; such as Half-wits, tasteless Admirers, vain Pretenders, the Flatterers of Dunces, or the Patrons of them. All these crowd round her; one of them offering to approach her is driven back by a Rival; but she commends and encourages both. The first who speak in form are the Geniuses of the Schools, who assure her of their care to advance her Cause, by confining Youth to Words, and keeping them out of the way of real Knowledge. Their Address, and her gracious Answer; with her Charge to them and the Universities. The Universities appear by their proper Deputies, and assure her that the same method is observed in the progress of Education. The speech of Aristarchus on this subject. They are drawn off by a band of young Gentlemen returned from Travel with their Tutors; one of whom delivers to the Goddess, in a polite oration, an account of the whole Conduct and Fruits of their Travels: presenting to her at the same time a young Nobleman perfectly accomplished. She receives him graciously, and endues him with the happy quality of Want of Shame. She sees loitering about her a number of Indolent Persons abandoning all business and duty, and dying with laziness: To these approaches the Antiquary Annius, intreating her to make them Virtuoso's, and assign them over to him. But Mummius, another Antiquary, complaining of his fraudulent proceeding, she finds a method to reconcile their difference. Then enter a troop of people fantastically adorned, offering her strange and exotic presents: Amongst them one stands forth and demands justice on another, who had deprived him of one of the greatest Curiosities in nature; but he justifies himself so well, that the Goddess gives them both her approbation. She recommends to them to find proper employment for the Indolents beforementioned, in the study of Butterflies, Shells, Birds-nests, Moss, &c. but with particular caution, not to proceed beyond Trifles, to any useful or extensive views of Nature, or of the Author of Nature. Against the last of these apprehensions, she is secured by a hearty address from the Minute Philosophers and Freethinkers, one of whom speaks in the name of the rest. The Youth, thus instructed and principled, are delivered to her in a body, by the hands of Silenus, and then admitted to taste the cup of the Magus her High Priest, which causes a total oblivion of all Obligations, divine, civil, moral, or rational. To these her Adepts she sends Priests, Attendants, and Comforters of various kinds; confers on them Orders and Degrees; and then dismissing them with a speech, confirming to each his Privileges, and telling what she expects from each, concludes with a Yawn of extraordinary virtue: The Progress and Effects whereof on all Orders of men, and the Consummation of all, in the restoration of Night and Chaos, conclude the Poem.

BOOK IV

YET, yet a moment, one dim Ray of Light
Indulge, dread Chaos, and eternal Night!
Of darkness visible so much be lent,
As half to shew, half veil, the deep Intent.
Ye Pow'rs! whose Mysteries restor'd I sing,
To whom Time bears me on his rapid wing,
Suspend awhile your Force inertly strong,
Then take at once the Poet and the Song.

Now flam'd the Dog-star's unpropitious ray,
Smote ev'ry Brain, and wither'd ev'ry Bay;
Sick was the Sun, the Owl forsook his bow'r,
The moon-struck Prophet felt the madding hour:
Then rose the Seed of Chaos, and of Night,
To blot out Order, and extinguish Light,
Of dull and venal a new World to mould,
And bring Saturnian days of Lead and Gold.

She mounts the Throne: her head a Cloud conceal'd,
In broad Effulgence all below reveal'd;
('T is thus aspiring Dulness ever shines)
Soft on her lap her Laureate son reclines.

Beneath her footstool, *Science* groans in Chains,
And *Wit* dreads Exile, Penalties, and Pains.
There foam'd rebellious *Logic*, gagg'd and bound,
There, stript, fair *Rhet'ric* languish'd on the ground;
His blunted Arms by *Sophistry* are borne,

And shameless *Billingsgate* her Robes adorn.
Morality, by her false guardians drawn,
Chicane in Furs, and *Casuistry* in Lawn,
Gasps, as they straiten at each end the cord,
And dies, when Dulness gives her Page the word.
Mad *Máthesis* alone was unconfin'd,
Too mad for mere material chains to bind,
Now to pure Space lifts her ecstatic stare,
Now running round the Circle finds it square.
But held in ten-fold bonds the *Muses* lie,
Watch'd both by Envy's and by Flatt'ry's eye:
There to her heart sad Tragedy addrest
The dagger wont to pierce the Tyrant's breast;
But sober History restrain'd her rage,
And promis'd Vengeance on a barb'rous age.
There sunk Thalia, nerveless, cold, and dead,
Had not her Sister Satire held her head:
Nor could'st thou, CHESTERFIELD! a tear refuse,
Thou wept'st, and with thee wept each gentle Muse.
  When lo! a Harlot form soft sliding by,
With mincing step, small voice, and languid eye:
Foreign her air, her robe's discordant pride
In patch-work flutt'ring, and her head aside:
By singing Peers up-held on either hand,
She tripp'd and laugh'd, too pretty much to stand;
Cast on the prostrate Nine a scornful look,
Then thus in quaint Recitativo spoke.
  "O *Cara! Cara!* silence all that train:
Joy to great Chaos! let Division reign:
Chromatic tortures soon shall drive them hence,
Break all their nerves, and fritter all their sense:
One Trill shall harmonize joy, grief, and rage,
Wake the dull Church, and lull the ranting Stage;
To the same notes thy sons shall hum, or snore,
And all thy yawning daughters cry, *encore.*
Another Phœbus, thy own Phœbus, reigns,

Joys in my jigs, and dances in my chains.
But soon, ah soon, Rebellion will commence,
If Music meanly borrows aid from Sense.
Strong in new Arms, lo! Giant HANDEL stands,
Like bold Briareus, with a hundred hands;
To stir, to rouse, to shake the soul he comes,
And Jove's own Thunders follow Mars's Drums.
Arrest him, Empress; or you sleep no more—"
She heard, and drove him to th' Hibernian shore.

And now had Fame's posterior Trumpet blown,
And all the Nations summon'd to the Throne.
The young, the old, who feel her inward sway,
One instinct seizes, and transports away.
None need a guide, by sure attraction led,
And strong impulsive gravity of Head;
None want a place, for all their Centre found,
Hung to the Goddess, and coher'd around.
Not closer, orb in orb, conglob'd are seen
The buzzing Bees about their dusky Queen.

The gath'ring number, as it moves along,
Involves a vast involuntary throng,
Who gently drawn, and struggling less and less,
Roll in her Vortex, and her pow'r confess.
Not those alone who passive own her laws,
But who, weak rebels, more advance her cause.
Whate'er of dunce in College or in Town
Sneers at another, in toupee or gown;
Whate'er of mongrel no one class admits,
A wit with dunces, and a dunce with wits.

Nor absent they, no members of her state,
Who pay her homage in her sons, the Great;
Who, false to Phœbus, bow the knee to Baal;
Or, impious, preach his word without a call.
Patrons, who sneak from living worth to dead,
Withhold the pension, and set up the head;
Or vest dull Flatt'ry in the sacred Gown;

Or give from fool to fool the Laurel crown.
And (last and worst) with all the cant of wit,
Without the soul, the Muse's Hypocrite.
　There march'd the bard and blockhead, side by side,
Who rhym'd for hire, and patroniz'd for pride.
Narcissus, prais'd with all a Parson's pow'r,
Look'd a white lily sunk beneath a show'r
There mov'd Montalto with superior air;
His stretch'd-out arm display'd a volume fair;
Courtiers and Patriots in two ranks divide,
Thro' both he pass'd, and bow'd from side to side:
But as in graceful act, with awful eye
Compos'd he stood, bold Benson thrust him by:
On two unequal crutches propt he came,
Milton's on this, on that one Johnston's name.
The decent Knight retir'd with sober rage,
Withdrew his hand, and clos'd the pompous page.
But (happy for him as the times went then)
Appear'd Apollo's May'r and Aldermen,
On whom three hundred gold-capt youths await,
To lug the pond'rous volume off in state.
　When Dulness, smiling—"Thus revive the Wits!
But murder first, and mince them all to bits;
As erst Medea (cruel, so to save!)
A new Edition of old Æson gave;
Let standard-authors, thus, like trophies borne,
Appear more glorious as more hack'd and torn
And you, my Critics! in the chequer'd shade,
Admire new light thro' holes yourselves have made.
　Leave not a foot of verse, a foot of stone,
A Page, a Grave, that they can call their own;
But spread, my sons, your glory thin or thick,
On passive paper, or on solid brick.
So by each Bard an Alderman shall sit,
A heavy Lord shall hang at ev'ry Wit,
And while on Fame's triumphal Car they ride,

Some Slave of mine be pinion'd to their side."
   Now crowds on crowds around the Goddess press,
Each eager to present their first Address.
Dunce scorning Dunce beholds the next advance,
But Fop shews Fop superior complaisance.
When lo! a Spectre rose, whose index-hand
Held forth the virtue of the dreadful wand;
His beaver'd brow a birchen garland wears,
Dropping with Infant's blood, and Mother's tears.
O'er ev'ry vein a shudd'ring horror runs;
Eton and Winton* shake thro' all their Sons.
All Flesh is humbled, Westminster's bold race
Shrink, and confess the genius of the place:
The pale Boy-Senator yet tingling stands,
And holds his breeches close with both his hands.
Then thus. 'Since Man from beast by Words is known,
Words are Man's province, Words we teach alone.
When Reason doubtful, like the Samian letter,**
Points him two ways, the narrower is the better.
Plac'd at the door of Learning, youth to guide,
We never suffer it to stand too wide.
To ask, to guess, to know, as they commence,
As Fancy opens the quick springs of Sense,
We ply the Memory, we load the brain,
Bind rebel Wit and double chain on chain;
Confine the thought, to exercise the breath;
And keep them in the pale of Words till death.
Whate'er the talents, or howe'er design'd,
We hang one jingling padlock on the mind:
A Poet the first day he dips his quill;
And what the last? A very Poet still.
Pity! the charm works only in our wall,
Lost, lost too soon in yonder House or Hall.†

* Winchester.
** The letter Y.
† The House of Commons and Westminster Hall.

There truant WYNDHAM ev'ry Muse gave o'er,
There TALBOT sunk, and was a Wit no more!
How sweet an Ovid, MURRAY was our boast!
How many Martials were in PULT'NEY lost!
Else sure some Bard, to our eternal praise,
In twice ten thousand rhyming nights and days,
Had reach'd the Work, the all that mortal can;
And South beheld that Master-piece of Man.'
  "Oh" (cry'd the Goddess) "for some pedant Reign!
Some gentle JAMES, to bless the land again;
To stick the Doctor's Chair into the Throne,
Give law to Words, or war with Words alone,
Senates and Courts with Greek and Latin rule,
And turn the Council to a Grammar School!
For sure, if Dulness sees a grateful Day,
'T is in the shade of Arbitrary Sway.
O! if my sons may learn one earthly thing,
Teach but that one, sufficient for a king;
That which my Priests, and mine alone, maintain,
Which as it dies, or lives, we fall, or reign:
May you, may Cam and Isis, preach it long!
'The RIGHT DIVINE of Kings to govern wrong.' "
  Prompt at the call, around the Goddess roll
Broad hats, and hoods, and caps, a sable shoal:
Thick and more thick the black blockade extends,
A hundred head of Aristotle's friends.
Nor wert thou, Isis! wanting to the day,
[Tho' Christ-church long kept prudishly away.]
Each staunch Polemic, stubborn as a rock,
Each fierce Logician, still expelling Locke,
Came whip and spur, and dash'd thro' thin and thick
On German Crouzaz, and Dutch Burgersdyck.
As many quit the streams that murm'ring fall
To lull the sons of Marg'ret and Clare-hall,
Where Bentley late tempestuous wont to sport
In troubled waters, but now sleeps in Port.

Before them march'd that awful Aristarch;
Plough'd was his front with many a deep Remark:
His Hat, which never vail'd to human pride,
Walker with rev'rence took, and laid aside.
Low bow'd the rest: He, kingly, did but nod;
So upright Quakers please both Man and God.
"Mistress! dismiss that rabble from your throne:
Avaunt —— is Aristarchus yet unknown?
Thy mighty Scholiast, whose unweary'd pains
Made Horace dull, and humbled Milton's strains.
Turn what they will to Verse, their toil is vain,
Critics like me shall make it Prose again.
Roman and Greek Grammarians! know your Better:
Author of something yet more great than Letter;
While tow'ring o'er your Alphabet, like Saul,
Stands our Digamma, and o'er-tops them all.
'T is true, on Words is still our whole debate,
Disputes of *Me* or *Te*, of *aut* or *at*,
To sound or sink in *cano*, O or A,
Or give up Cicero to C or K.
Let Freind affect to speak as Terence spoke,
And Alsop never but like Horace joke:
For me, what Virgil, Pliny may deny,
Manilius or Solinus shall supply:
For Attic Phrase in Plato let them seek,
I poach in Suidas for unlicens'd Greek.
In ancient Sense if any needs will deal,
Be sure I give them Fragments, not a Meal;
What Gellius or Stobæus hash'd before,
Or chew'd by blind old Scholiasts o'er and o'er.
The critic Eye, that microscope of Wit,
Sees hairs and pores, examines bit by bit:
How parts relate to parts, or they to whole,
The body's harmony, the beaming soul,
Are things which Kuster, Burman, Wasse shall see,
When Man's whole frame is obvious to a *Flea*.

"Ah, think not, Mistress! more true Dulness lies
In Folly's Cap, than Wisdom's grave disguise.
Like buoys that never sink into the flood,
On Learning's surface we but lie and nod.
Thine is the genuine head of many a house,
And much Divinity, without a Noῦς.
Nor could a BARROW work on ev'ry block,
Nor has one ATTERBURY spoil'd the flock.
See! still thy own, the heavy Canon roll,
And Metaphysic smokes involve the Pole.
For thee we dim the eyes, and stuff the head
With all such reading as was never read:
For thee explain a thing till all men doubt it,
And write about it, Goddess, and about it:
So spins the silk-worm small its slender store,
And labours till it clouds itself all o'er.

"What tho' we let some better sort of fool
Thrid ev'ry science, run thro' ev'ry school?
Never by tumbler thro' the hoops was shown
Such skill in passing all, and touching none;
He may indeed (if sober all this time)
Plague with Dispute, or persecute with Rhyme.
We only furnish what he cannot use,
Or wed to what he must divorce, a Muse:
Full in the midst of Euclid dip at once,
And petrify a Genius to a Dunce:
Or set on Metaphysic ground to prance,
Show all his paces, not a step advance.
With the same CEMENT, ever sure to bind,
We bring to one dead level ev'ry mind.
Then take him to develop, if you can,
And hew the Block off* and get out the Man.
But wherefore waste I words? I see advance

---

* A notion of Aristotle, that there was originally in every block of
marble a Statue, which would appear on the removal of the superfluous
parts. [Pope.]

Whore, Pupil, and lac'd Governor from France.
Walker! our hat"—— nor more he deign'd to say,
But, stern as Ajax' spectre, strode away.
  In flow'd at once a gay embroider'd race,
And titt'ring push'd the Pedants off the place:
Some would have spoken, but the voice was drown'd
By the French horn, or by the op'ning hound.
The first came forwards, with as easy mien,
As if he saw St. James's and the Queen.
When thus th' attendant Orator begun,
"Receive, great Empress! thy accomplish'd Son:
Thine from the birth, and sacred from the rod,
A dauntless infant! never scar'd with God.
The Sire saw, one by one, his Virtues wake:
The mother begg'd the blessing of a Rake.
Thou gav'st that Ripeness, which so soon began,
And ceas'd so soon, he ne'er was Boy, nor Man,
Thro' School and College, thy kind cloud o'ercast,
Safe and unseen the young Æneas past:
Thence bursting glorious, all at once let down,
Stunn'd with his giddy Larum half the town.
Intrepid then, o'er seas and lands he flew:
Europe he saw, and Europe saw him too.
There all thy gifts and graces we display,
Thou, only thou, directing all our way!
To where the Seine, obsequious as she runs,
Pours at great Bourbon's feet her silken sons;
Or Tiber, now no longer Roman, rolls,
Vain of Italian Arts, Italian Souls:
To happy Convents, bosom'd deep in vines,
Where slumber Abbots, purple as their wines:
To Isles of fragrance, lily-silver'd vales,
Diffusing languor in the panting gales:
To lands of singing, or of dancing slaves,
Love-whisp'ring woods, and lute-resounding waves.
But chief her shrine where naked Venus keeps,

And Cupids ride the Lion of the Deeps;
Where, eas'd of Fleets, the Adriatic main
Wafts the smooth Eunuch and enamour'd swain.
Led by my hand, he saunter'd Europe round,
And gather'd ev'ry Vice on Christian ground;
Saw ev'ry Court, heard ev'ry King declare
His royal Sense of Op'ras or the Fair;
The Stews and Palace equally explor'd,
Intrigu'd with glory, and with spirit whor'd;
Try'd all *hors-d'œuvres*, all *liqueurs* defin'd,
Judicious drank, and greatly-daring din'd;
Dropt the dull lumber of the Latin store,
Spoil'd his own language, and acquir'd no more;
All Classic learning lost on Classic ground;
And last turn'd *Air*, the Echo of a Sound!
See now, half-cur'd, and perfectly well-bred,
With nothing but a Solo in his head;
As much Estate, and Principle, and Wit,
As Jansen, Fleetwood, Cibber shall think fit;
Stol'n from a Duel, follow'd by a Nun,
And, if a Borough choose him not, undone;
See, to my country happy I restore
This glorious Youth, and add one Venus more.
Her too receive (for her my soul adores)
So may the sons of sons of sons of whores,
Prop thine, O Empress! like each neighbour Throne,
And make a long Posterity thy own."
Pleas'd, she accepts the Hero, and the Dame
Wraps in her Veil, and frees from sense of Shame.

  Then look'd, and saw a lazy, lolling sort,
Unseen at Church, at Senate, or at Court,
Of ever-listless Loit'rers, that attend
No Cause, no Trust, no Duty, and no Friend.
Thee too, my Paridel! she mark'd thee there,
Stretch'd on the rack of a too easy chair,
And heard thy everlasting yawn confess

The Pains and Penalties of Idleness.
She pity'd! but her Pity only shed
Benigner influence on thy nodding head.

But Annius, crafty Seer, with ebon wand,
And well dissembled em'rald on his hand,
False as his Gems, and canker'd as his Coins,
Came, cramm'd with capon, from where Pollio dines.
Soft, as the wily Fox is seen to creep,
Where bask on sunny banks the simple sheep,
Walk round and round, now prying here, now there,
So he; but pious, whisper'd first his pray'r.

"Grant, gracious Goddess! grant me still to cheat,
O may thy cloud still cover the deceit!
Thy choicer mists on this assembly shed,
But pour them thickest on the noble head.
So shall each youth, assisted by our eyes,
See other Cæsars, other Homers rise;
Thro' twilight ages hunt th' Athenian fowl,
Which Chalcis Gods, and mortals call an Owl,
Now see an Attys, now a Cecrops clear,
Nay, Mahomet! the Pigeon at thine ear;
Be rich in ancient brass, tho' not in gold,
And keep his Lares, tho' his house be sold;
To headless Phœbe his fair bride postpone,
Honour a Syrian Prince above his own;
Lord of an Otho, if I vouch it true;
Blest in one Niger, till he knows of two."

Mummius o'erheard him; Mummius, Fool-renown'd,
Who like his Cheops stinks above the ground,
Fierce as a startled Adder, swell'd, and said,
Rattling an ancient Sistrum at his head:

'Speak'st thou of Syrian Princes? Traitor base!
Mine, Goddess! mine is all the horned race.
True, he had wit, to make their value rise;
From foolish Greeks to steal them, was as wise;
More glorious yet, from barb'rous hands to keep,

When Sallee Rovers chas'd him on the deep.
Then taught by Hermes, and divinely bold,
Down his own throat he risk'd the Grecian gold,
Receiv'd each Demi-God, with pious care,
Deep in his Entrails—I rever'd them there,
I bought them, shrouded in that living shrine,
And, at their second birth, they issue mine.'
   "Witness, great Ammon! by whose horns I swore,"
(Reply'd soft Annius) "this our paunch before
Still bears them, faithful; and that thus I eat,
Is to refund the Medals with the meat.
To prove me, Goddess! clear of all design,
Bid me with Pollio sup, as well as dine:
There all the Learn'd shall at the labour stand,
And Douglas lend his soft, obstetric hand."
   The Goddess smiling seem'd to give consent;
So back to Pollio, hand in hand, they went.
   Then thick as Locusts black'ning all the ground,
A tribe, with weeds and shells fantastic crown'd.
Each with some wond'rous gift approach'd the Pow'r,
A Nest, a Toad, a Fungus, or a Flow'r.
But far the foremost, two, with earnest zeal,
And aspect ardent to the Throne appeal.
   The first thus open'd: "Hear thy suppliant's call,
Great Queen, and common Mother of us all!
Fair from its humble bed I rear'd this Flow'r,
Suckled, and cheer'd, with air, and sun, and show'r,
Soft on the paper ruff its leaves I spread,
Bright with the gilded button tipt its head;
Then thron'd in glass, and named it CAROLINE;
Each maid cry'd, Charming! and each youth, Divine!
Did Nature's pencil ever blend such rays,
Such vary'd light in one promiscuous blaze?
Now prostrate! dead! behold that Caroline:
No maid cries, Charming! and no youth, Divine!
And lo the wretch! whose vile, whose insect lust

Laid this gay daughter of the Spring in dust.
Oh punish him, or to the Elysian shades
Dismiss my soul, where no Carnation fades!"
He ceas'd, and wept. With innocence of mien,
Th' Accus'd stood forth, and thus address'd the Queen.

"Of all th' enamell'd race, whose silv'ry wing
Waves to the tepid Zephyrs of the spring,
Or swims along the fluid atmosphere,
Once brightest shin'd this child of Heat and Air.
I saw, and started from its vernal bow'r,
The rising game, and chas'd from flow'r to flow'r.
It fled, I follow'd; now in hope, now pain;
It stopt, I stopt; it mov'd, I mov'd again.
At last it fix'd, 't was on what plant it pleas'd,
And where it fix'd, the beauteous bird I seiz'd:
Rose or Carnation was below my care;
I meddle, Goddess! only in my sphere.
I tell the naked fact without disguise,
And, to excuse it, need but shew the prize;
Whose spoils this paper offers to your eye,
Fair ev'n in death! this peerless *Butterfly*."

"My sons!" (she answer'd) "both have done your parts:
Live happy both, and long promote our arts!
But hear a Mother, when she recommends
To your fraternal care our sleeping friends.
The common Soul, of Heav'n's more frugal make,
Serves but to keep fools pert, and knaves awake:
A drowsy Watchman, that just gives a knock,
And breaks our rest, to tell us what's a-clock.
Yet by some object ev'ry brain is stirr'd;
The dull may waken to a humming-bird;
The most recluse, discreetly open'd, find
Congenial matter in the Cockle-kind;
The mind, in Metaphysics at a loss,
May wander in a wilderness of Moss;
The head that turns at super-lunar things,

Pois'd with a tail, may steer on Wilkins' wings.

"O! would the Sons of Men once think their Eyes
And Reason giv'n them but to study *Flies!*
See Nature in some partial narrow shape,
And let the Author of the Whole escape:
Learn but to trifle; or, who most observe,
To wonder at their Maker, not to serve!"

"Be that my task" (replies a gloomy Clerk,
Sworn foe to Myst'ry, yet divinely dark;
Whose pious hope aspires to see the day
When Moral Evidence shall quite decay,
And damns implicit faith, and holy lies,
Prompt to impose, and fond to dogmatize:)
"Let others creep by timid steps, and slow,
On plain Experience lay foundations low,
By common sense to common knowledge bred,
And last, to Nature's Cause thro' Nature led.
All-seeing in thy mists, we want no guide,
Mother of Arrogance, and Source of Pride!
We nobly take the high Priori Road,
And reason downward, till we doubt of God;
Make Nature still encroach upon his plan;
And shove him off as far as e'er we can:
Thrust some Mechanic Cause into his place;
Or bind in Matter, or diffuse in Space.
Or, at one bound o'er-leaping all his laws,
Make God Man's Image, Man the final Cause,
Find Virtue local, all Relation scorn,
See all in *Self*, and but for self be born:
Of naught so certain as our *Reason* still,
Of naught so doubtful as of *Soul* and *Will*,
Oh hide the God still more! and make us see
Such as Lucretius drew, a God like Thee:
Wrapt up in Self, a God without a Thought,
Regardless of our merit or default.
Or that bright Image to our fancy draw,

Which Theocles in raptur'd vision saw,
While thro' Poetic scenes the GENIUS roves,
Or wanders wild in Academic Groves;
That NATURE our Society adores,
Where Tindal dictates, and Silenus snores."
    Rous'd at his name, up rose the bousy Sire,
And shook from out his Pipe the seeds of fire;
Then snapt his box, and strok'd his belly down:
Rosy and rev'rend, tho' without a Gown.
Bland and familiar to the throne he came,
Led up the Youth, and call'd the Goddess *Dame:*
Then thus: "From Priest-craft happily set free,
Lo! ev'ry finish'd Son returns to thee:
First slave to Words, then vassal to a Name,
Then dupe to Party; child and man the same;
Bounded by Nature, narrow'd still by Art,
A trifling head, and a contracted heart.
Thus bred, thus taught, how many have I seen,
Smiling on all, and smil'd on by a Queen?
Mark'd out for Honours, honour'd for their Birth,
To thee the most rebellious things on earth:
Now to thy gentle shadow all are shrunk,
All melted down, in Pension, or in Punk!
So K * so B * * sneak'd into the grave,
A Monarch's half, and half a Harlot's slave.
Poor W * * nipt in Folly's broadest bloom,
Who praises now? his Chaplain on his Tomb.
Then take them all, oh take them to thy breast!
Thy *Magus,* Goddess! shall perform the rest."
    With that, a WIZARD OLD his *Cup* extends;
Which whoso tastes, forgets his former friends,
Sire, Ancestors, Himself. One casts his eyes
Up to a *Star,* and like Endymion dies.
A *Feather,* shooting from another's head,
Extracts his brain; and Principle is fled;
Lost is his God, his Country, ev'ry thing;

And nothing left but Homage to a King!
The vulgar herd turn off to roll with Hogs,
To run with Horses, or to hunt with Dogs;
But, sad example! never to escape
Their Infamy, still keep the human shape.
But she, good Goddess, sent to ev'ry child
Firm Impudence, or Stupefaction mild;
And straight succeeded, leaving shame no room,
Cibberian forehead, or Cimmerian gloom.

Kind Self-conceit to some her glass applies,
Which no one looks in with another's eyes:
But as the Flatt'rer or Dependant paint,
Beholds himself a Patriot, Chief, or Saint.

On others' Int'rest her gay liv'ry flings,
Int'rest that waves on Party-colour'd wings:
Turn'd to the Sun, she casts a thousand dyes,
And, as she turns, the colours fall or rise.

Others the Syren Sisters warble round,
And empty heads console with empty sound.
No more, alas! the voice of Fame they hear,
The balm of Dulness trickling in their ear.
Great C * *, H * *, P * *, R * *, K *,
Why all your Toils? your Sons have learn'd to sing.
How quick Ambition hastes to ridicule!
The Sire is made a Peer, the Son a Fool.

On some, a Priest succinct in amice* white
Attends; all flesh is nothing in his sight!
Beeves, at his touch, at once to jelly turn,
And the huge Boar is shrunk into an Urn:
The board with specious miracles he loads,
Turns Hares to Larks, and Pigeons into Toads.
Another (for in all what one can shine?)
Explains the *Sève* and *Verdeur*** of the Vine.

---

* A coat.
** French Terms relating to Wines, which signify their flavour and
poignancy. [Pope.]

What cannot copious Sacrifice atone?
Thy Truffles, Perigord! thy Hams, Bayonne!
With French Libation, and Italian Strain,
Wash Bladen white, and expiate Hays's stain.
KNIGHT lifts the head, for what are crowds undone,
To three essential Partridges in one?
Gone ev'ry blush, and silent all reproach,
Contending Princes mount them in their Coach.

Next, bidding all draw near on bended knees,
The Queen confers her *Titles* and *Degrees*.
Her children first of more distinguish'd sort,
Who study Shakespeare at the Inns of Court,
Impale a Glow-worm, or Vertú profess,
Shine in the dignity of F.R.S.
Some, deep Free-Masons, join the silent race
Worthy to fill Pythagoras's place:
Some Botanists, or Florists at the least,
Or issue Members of an Annual feast.
Nor past the meanest unregarded, one
Rose a Gregorian, one a Gormogon.
The last, not least in honour or applause,
Isis and Cam made DOCTORS of her LAWS.

Then, blessing all, "Go, Children of my care!
To Practice now from Theory repair.
All my commands are easy, short, and full:
My Sons! be proud, be selfish, and be dull.
Guard my Prerogative, assert my Throne:
This Nod confirms each Privilege your own.
The Cap and Switch be sacred to his Grace;
With Staff and Pumps the Marquis lead the Race;
From Stage to Stage the licens'd Earl may run,
Pair'd with his Fellow-Charioteer the Sun;
The learned Baron Butterflies design,
Or draw to silk Arachne's subtile line;
The Judge to dance his brother Sergeant call;
The Senator at Cricket urge the Ball;

The Bishop stow (Pontific Luxury!)
An hundred Souls of Turkeys in a pie;
The sturdy Squire to Gallic masters stoop,
And drown his Lands and Manors in a Soupe.
Others import yet nobler arts from France,
Teach Kings to fiddle, and make Senates dance.
Perhaps more high some daring son may soar,
Proud to my list to add one Monarch more!
And nobly conscious, Princes are but things
Born for First Ministers, as Slaves for Kings,
Tyrant supreme! shall three Estates command,
And MAKE ONE MIGHTY DUNCIAD OF THE LAND!"
    More she had spoke, but yawn'd—All Nature nods:
What Mortal can resist the Yawn of Gods?
Churches and Chapels instantly it reach'd;
(St. James's first, for leaden G—— preach'd)
Then catch'd the Schools; the Hall scarce kept awake;
The Convocation gap'd, but could not speak:
Lost was the Nation's Sense, nor could be found,
While the long solemn Unison went round:
Wide, and more wide, it spread o'er all the realm;
Ev'n Palinurus nodded at the Helm:
The Vapour mild o'er each Committee crept;
Unfinish'd Treaties in each Office slept;
And Chiefless Armies doz'd out the Campaign;
And Navies yawn'd for Orders on the Main.
    O Muse! relate (for you can tell alone,
Wits have short Memories, and Dunces none),
Relate, who first, who last resign'd to rest;
Whose Heads she partly, whose completely, blest;
What Charms could Faction, what Ambition lull,
The Venal quiet, and entrance the Dull;
'Till drown'd was Sense, and Shame, and Right, and Wrong—
O sing, and hush the Nations with thy Song!

*   *   *   *   *   *

In vain, in vain—the all-composing Hour
Resistless falls: the Muse obeys the Pow'r.
She comes! she comes! the sable Throne behold
Of *Night* primæval and of *Chaos* old!
Before her, *Fancy's* gilded clouds decay,
And all its varying Rain-bows die away.
Wit shoots in vain its momentary fires,
The meteor drops, and in a flash expires.
As one by one, at dread Medea's strain,
The sick'ning stars fade off th' ethereal plain;
As Argus' eyes by Hermes' wand opprest,
Clos'd one by one to everlasting rest;
Thus at her felt approach, and secret might,
Art after *Art* goes out, and all is Night.
See skulking *Truth* to her old cavern fled,
Mountains of Casuistry heap'd o'er her head!
Philosophy, that lean'd on Heav'n before,
Shrinks to her second cause, and is no more.
Physic of *Metaphysic* begs defence,
And *Metaphysic* calls for aid on *Sense!*
See *Mystery* to *Mathematics* fly!
In vain! they gaze, turn giddy, rave, and die.
Religion blushing veils her sacred fires,
And unawares *Morality* expires.
For *public* Flame, nor *private*, dares to shine;
Nor *human* Spark is left, nor Glimpse *divine!*
Lo! thy dread Empire, CHAOS! is restor'd;
Light dies before thy uncreating word;
Thy hand, great Anarch! lets the curtain fall,
And universal Darkness buries All.

TO ROBERT EARL OF OXFORD, AND
EARL MORTIMER

TO ROBERT EARL OF OXFORD, AND EARL MORTIMER

SUCH were the notes thy once-loved poet* sung,
Till death untimely stopp'd his tuneful tongue.
Oh, just beheld and lost! admired and mourn'd!
With softest manners, gentlest arts adorn'd!
Bless'd in each science, bless'd in every strain!
Dear to the Muse!—to Harley dear—in vain!
For him, thou oft hast bid the world attend,
Fond to forget the statesman in the friend;
For Swift and him, despised the farce of state,
The sober follies of the wise and great;
Dext'rous, the craving, fawning crowd to quit,
And pleased to 'scape from flattery to wit.

Absent or dead, still let a friend be dear,
(A sigh the absent claims, the dead a tear,)
Recall those nights that closed thy toilsome days,
Still hear thy Parnell in his living lays,
Who, careless now, of int'rest, fame, or fate,
Perhaps forgets that Oxford e'er was great;
Or, deeming meanest what we greatest call,
Beholds thee glorious only in thy fall.

And sure, if aught below the seats divine
Can touch immortals, 'tis a soul like thine:
A soul supreme, in each hard instance tried,
Above all pain, all passion, and all pride,
The rage of power, the blast of public breath,
The lust of lucre, and the dread of death.

In vain to deserts thy retreat is made;

* Parnell

329

The Muse attends thee to thy silent shade:
'Tis hers the brave man's latest steps to trace,
Rejudge his acts, and dignify disgrace.
When Int'rest calls off all her sneaking train,
And all th' obliged desert, and all the vain;
She waits, or to the scaffold, or the cell,
When the last lingering friend has bid farewell.
Ev'n now she shades thy ev'ning walk with bays,
(No hireling she, no prostitute to praise;)
Ev'n now, observant of the parting ray,
Eyes the calm sunset of thy various day,
Through fortune's cloud one truly great can see,
Nor fears to tell that Mortimer is he.

ON MR. GAY,

IN WESTMINSTER ABBEY, 1732

OF Manners gentle, of Affections mild;
In Wit, a Man; Simplicity, a Child:
With native Humour temp'ring virtuous Rage,
Form'd to delight at once and lash the age:
Above Temptation, in a Low Estate,
And uncorrupted, ev'n among the Great:
A safe Companion, and an easy Friend,
Unblam'd thro' Life, lamented in thy End.
These are Thy Honours! not that here thy Bust
Is mix'd with Heroes, or with Kings thy dust;
But that the Worthy and the Good shall say,
Striking their pensive bosoms—*Here* lies GAY.

INTENDED FOR SIR ISAAC NEWTON,

IN WESTMINSTER ABBEY

Nature and Nature's Laws lay hid in Night:
GOD said, *Let Newton be!* and all was Light.

ON MRS. TOFTS,

A CELEBRATED OPERA-SINGER

So bright is thy Beauty, so charming thy Song,
As had drawn both the Beasts and their Orpheus along;
But such is thy Av'rice, and such is thy Pride,
That the Beasts must have starv'd, and the Poet have died.

EPIGRAM

You beat your Pate, and fancy Wit will come:
Knock as you please, there 's nobody at home.

EPITAPH

Well then, poor G—— lies under Ground!
   So there 's an End of honest Jack.
So little Justice here he found,
   'T is ten to one he 'll ne'er come back.

EPITAPH

Here Francis C——* lies. Be civil;
The rest God knows—perhaps the Devil!

THE BALANCE OF EUROPE

Now Europe 's balanc'd, neither Side prevails;
For nothing 's left in either of the Scales.

A DIALOGUE, 1717

Pope.—Since my old friend is grown so great
   As to be Minister of State,

* Chartres.

  I 'm told, but 't is not true, I hope,
  That Craggs will be ashamed of Pope.
CRAGGS.—Alas! if I am such a creature
   To grow the worse for growing greater;
   Why, faith, in spite of all my brags,
   'T is Pope must be ashamed of Craggs.

THE THREE GENTLE SHEPHERDS

OF gentle Philips will I ever sing,
With gentle Philips shall the valleys ring.
My numbers too for ever will I vary,
With gentle Budgell and with gentle Carey.
Or if in ranging of the names I judge ill,
With gentle Carey and with gentle Budgell:
Oh! may all gentle bards together place ye,
Men of good hearts, and men of delicacy
May satire ne'er befool ye, or beknave ye,
And from all wits that have a knack, God save ye.

LINES

WRITTEN IN WINDSOR FOREST

ALL hail, once pleasing, once inspiring shade!
 Scene of my youthful loves and happier hours!
Where the kind Muses met me as I stray'd.
 And gently press'd my hand, and said "Be ours!—
Take all thou e'er shalt have, a constant Muse:
 At Court thou may'st be liked, but nothing gain:
Stock thou may'st buy and sell, but always lose,
 And love the brightest eyes, but love in vain."

THE CHALLENGE

A COURT BALLAD

I.

To one fair lady out of Court,
    And two fair ladies in,
Who think the Turk and Pope a sport,
    And wit and love no sin!
Come, these soft lines, with nothing stiff in,
To Bellenden, Lepell, and Griffin.
        With a fa, la, la.

II.

What passes in the dark third row,
    And what behind the scene,
Couches and crippled chairs I know,
    And garrets hung with green;
I know the swing of sinful hack,
Where many damsels cry alack.
        With a fa, la, la.

III.

Then why to Courts should I repair,
    Where 's such ado with Townshend?
To hear each mortal stamp and swear,
    And every speech with "Zounds" end;
To hear them rail at honest Sunderland,
And rashly blame the realm of Blunderland.
        With a fa, la, la.

IV.

Alas! like Schutz I cannot pun,
    Like Grafton court the Germans;
Tell Pickenbourg how slim she 's grown,
    Like Meadows run to sermons;
To court ambitious men may roam,

But I and Marlbro' stay at home.
With a fa, la, la.

V.

In truth, by what I can discern,
Of courtiers, 'twixt you three,
Some wit you have, and more may learn
From Court, than Gay or Me:
Perhaps, in time, you 'll leave high diet,
To sup with us on milk and quiet.
With a fa, la, la.

VI.

At Leicester Fields, a house full high,
With door all painted green,
Where ribbons wave upon the tie,
(A Milliner, I mean;)
There may you meet us three to three,
For Gay can well make two of Me.
With a fa, la, la.

VII.

But should you catch the prudish itch,
And each become a coward,
Bring sometimes with you lady Rich.
And sometimes mistress Howard;
For virgins, to keep chaste, must go
Abroad with such as are not so.
With a fa, la, la.

VIII.

And thus, fair maids, my ballad ends;
God send the king safe landing;
And make all honest ladies friends
To armies that are standing;
Preserve the limits of those nations,
And take off ladies' limitations.
With a fa, la, la.

SONG, BY A PERSON OF QUALITY

WRITTEN IN THE YEAR 1733

I.

FLUTT'RING spread thy purple Pinions,
    Gentle *Cupid*, o'er my Heart;
I a Slave in thy Dominions;
    Nature must give Way to Art.

II.

Mild *Arcadians*, ever blooming,
    Nightly nodding o'er your Flocks,
See my weary Days consuming,
    All beneath yon flow'ry Rocks.

III.

Thus the *Cyprian* Goddess weeping,
    Mourn'd *Adonis*, darling Youth:
Him the Boar in Silence creeping,
    Gor'd with unrelenting Tooth.

IV.

Cynthia, tune harmonious Numbers;
    Fair *Discretion*, string the Lyre;
Sooth my ever-waking Slumbers:
    Bright *Apollo*, lend thy Choir.

V.

Gloomy *Pluto*, King of Terrors,
    Arm'd in adamantine Chains,
Lead me to the Crystal Mirrors,
    Wat'ring soft Elysian Plains.

VI.

Mournful Cypress, verdant Willow,
    Gilding my *Aurelia's* Brows,

Morpheus hov'ring o'er my Pillow,
　　Hear me pay my dying Vows.

VII.

Melancholy smooth *Mæander*,
　　Swiftly purling in a Round,
On thy Margin Lovers wander,
　　With thy flow'ry Chaplets crown'd.

VIII.

Thus when *Philomela* drooping,
　　Softly seeks her silent Mate,
See the Bird of *Juno* stooping;
　　Melody resigns to Fate.

ON A CERTAIN LADY AT COURT

I KNOW the thing that 's most uncommon;
　　(Envy, be silent, and attend!)
I know a reasonable Woman,
　　Handsome and witty, yet a Friend.

Not warp'd by Passion, aw'd by Rumour,
　　Not grave thro' Pride, or gay through Folly,
An equal Mixture of good Humour,
　　And sensible soft Melancholy.

"Has she no faults then (Envy says), Sir?"
　　Yes, she has one, I must aver;
When all the World conspires to praise her,
　　The Woman 's deaf, and does not hear.

A FAREWELL TO LONDON

IN THE YEAR 1715

DEAR, damn'd distracting town, farewell!
　　Thy fools no more I 'll tease:

This year in peace, ye critics, dwell,
   Ye harlots, sleep at ease!

Soft B—— and rough C——s adieu,
   Earl Warwick make your moan,
The lively H——k and you
   May knock up whores alone.

To drink and droll be Rowe allow'd
   Till the third watchman's toll;
Let Jervas gratis paint, and Frowde
   Save three-pence and his soul.

Farewell, Arbuthnot's raillery
   On every learned sot;
And Garth, the best good Christian he,
   Although he knows it not.

Lintot, farewell! thy bard must go;
   Farewell, unhappy Tonson!
Heaven gives thee for thy loss of Rowe,
   Lean Philips, and fat Johnson.

Why should I stay? Both parties rage;
   My vixen mistress squalls;
The wits in envious feuds engage:
   And Homer (damn him!) calls.

The love of arts lies cold and dead
   In Halifax's urn:
And not one Muse of all he fed
   Has yet the grace to mourn.

My friends, by turns, my friends confound,
   Betray, and are betrayed:
Poor Y——r 's sold for fifty pound,
   And B——ll is a jade.

Why make I friendships with the great
   When I no favour seek?

Or follow girls, seven hours in eight?
   I us'd but once a week.

Still idle, with a busy air,
   Deep whimsies to contrive;
The gayest valetudinaire,
   Most thinking rake, alive.

Solicitous for others' ends,
   Though fond of dear repose;
Careless or drowsy with my friends,
   And frolic with my foes.

Luxurious lobster-nights, farewell,
   For sober, studious days!
And Burlington's delicious meal,
   For salads, tarts, and pease!

Adieu to all, but Gay alone,
   Whose soul, sincere and free,
Loves all mankind, but flatters none,
   And so may starve with me.

EPIGRAM

ENGRAVED ON THE COLLAR OF A DOG WHICH I GAVE TO HIS ROYAL HIGHNESS

I AM his Highness' dog at Kew;
   Pray tell me, sir, whose dog are you?

VERSES TO MR. C.

ST. JAMES'S PALACE. LONDON, OCT. 22

FEW words are best; I wish you well;
   BETHEL, I 'm told, will soon be here;
Some morning walks along the Mall,
   And ev'ning friends, will end the year.

If, in this interval, between
  The falling leaf and coming frost,
You please to see, on Twit'nam green,
  Your friend, your poet, and your host:

For three whole days you here may rest
  From Office bus'ness, news and strife;
And (what most folks would think a jest)
  Want nothing else, except your wife.

EPIGRAM

A GOLD watch found on cinder whore,
Or a good verse on J——y M——e,
Proves but what either should conceal,
Not that they 're rich, but that they steal.

ℭ From a Letter to a Noble Lord*

ON OCCASION OF SOME LIBELS WRITTEN AND
PROPAGATED AT COURT IN THE YEAR 1732–3

Nov. 30, 1733.

MY LORD,—Your Lordship's Epistle has been published some days, but I had not the pleasure and pain of seeing it till yesterday: pain, to think your Lordship should attack me at all; pleasure, to find that you can attack me so weakly. As I want not the humility, to think myself in every way but *one* your inferior, it seems but reasonable that I should take the only method either of self-defence or retaliation, that is left me against a person of your quality and power. And as by your choice of this weapon, your pen, you generously (and modestly too, no doubt) meant to put yourself upon a level with me, I will as soon believe that your Lordship would give a wound to a man unarmed, as that you would deny me the use of it in my own defence.

I presume you will allow me to take the same liberty in my answer to so candid, polite, and ingenious a nobleman, which your Lordship took in yours, to so *grave, religious*, and *respectable* a clergyman. As you answered his Latin in English, permit me to answer your verse in prose. And though your Lordship's reasons for not writing in Latin, might be stronger than mine for not writing in verse, yet I may plead two good ones, for this conduct:—the one, that I want the talent of spinning *a thousand lines in a* day, (which, I think is as much time as this subject deserves,) and the other, that I take your Lordship's verse to be as much prose as this letter. But no doubt it was your choice, in writing to a friend, to renounce all the pomp of poetry, and give us this excellent model of the familiar.

When I consider the great difference betwixt the rank your

* Lord Hervey ("Sporus").

Lordship holds in the *world*, and the rank which your writings are like to hold in the learned world, I presume that distinction of style is but necessary, which you will see observed through this letter. When I speak of *you*, my Lord, it will be with all the deference due to the inequality which Fortune has made between you and myself: but when I speak of your *writings*, my Lord, I must, I can, do nothing but trifle.

I should be obliged indeed to lessen this respect, if all the nobility (and especially the elder brothers) are but so many hereditary fools, if the privilege of lords be to want brains, if noblemen can hardly write or read, if all their business is but to dress and vote, and all their employment in court, to tell lies, flatter in public, slander in private, be false to each other, and follow nothing but self-interest. Bless me, my Lord, what an account is this you give of them? and what would have been said of me, had I immolated, in this manner, the whole body of the nobility, at the stall of a well-fed prebendary?

Were it the mere excess of your Lordship's wit, that carried you thus triumphantly over all the bounds of decency, I might consider your Lordship on your Pegasus, as a sprightly hunter on a mettled horse; and while you were trampling down all our works, patiently suffer the injury, in pure admiration of the noble sport. But should the case be quite otherwise; should your Lordship be only like a boy that is run away with; and run away with by a very foal; really common charity, as well as respect for a noble family, would oblige me to stop your career, and to help you down from this Pegasus.

Surely the little praise of a *writer* should be a thing below your ambition: you, who were no sooner born, but in the lap of the Graces; no sooner at school, but in the arms of the Muses; no sooner in the world, but you practised all the skill of it; no sooner in the court, but you possessed all the art of it! Unrivalled as you are, in making a figure, and in making a speech, methinks, my Lord, you may well give up the poor talent of turning a distich. And why this fondness for poetry? Prose admits of the two excellences you most admire, diction and fiction; it admits of the talents you chiefly possess, a most fertile invention, and most florid expression; it is with prose, nay the plainest prose, that you best could teach our nobility to vote, which you justly observe, is half at least of their business: and give me leave to prophesy, it is to your talent in prose, and not in verse, to your speaking, not your writing, to your art at court, not your art of poetry, that your Lordship must owe your future figure in the world.

My Lord, whatever you imagine, this is the advice of a friend, and one who remembers he formerly had the honour of some profession of friendship from you: whatever was his real share in it, whether small or great, yet as your Lordship could never have had the least *loss* by continuing it, or the least interest by withdrawing it, the misfortune of losing it, I fear, must have been owing to his own deficiency or neglect. But as to any actual fault which deserved to forfeit it in such a degree, he protests he is to this day guiltless and ignorant. It could at most be but a fault of omission; but indeed by omission, men of your Lordship's uncommon merit may sometimes think themselves so injured, as to be capable of an inclination to injure another; who, though very much below their quality, may be above the injury.

I never heard of the least displeasure you had conceived against me, till I was told that an imitation I had made of Horace had offended some persons, and among them your Lordship. I could not have apprehended that a few *general strokes* about a *Lord scribbling carelessly*, a *pimp*, or a *spy* at court, a *sharper* in a gilded chariot, &c.—that these, I say, should be ever applied as they have been, by any malice but that which is the greatest in the world, the malice of ill people to themselves.

Your Lordship so well knows, (and the whole court and town through your means so well know,) how far the resentment was carried upon that imagination, not only in the nature of the libel you propagated against me, but in the extraordinary manner, place, and presence, in which it was propagated, that I shall only say, it seemed to me to exceed the bounds of justice, common sense, and decency.

I wonder yet more, how a lady, of great wit, beauty, and fame for her poetry, (between whom and your Lordship there is a natural, a just, and a well-grounded esteem,) could be prevailed upon to take a part in that proceeding. Your resentments against me indeed might be equal, as my offence to you both was the same; for neither had I the least misunderstanding with that lady, till after I was the author of my own misfortune in discontinuing her acquaintance. I may venture to own a truth, which cannot be unpleasing to either of you; I assure you my reason for so doing, was merely that you had both *too much wit* for me; and that I could not do with *mine*, many things which you could with *yours*. The injury done you in withdrawing myself could be but small, if the value you had for me was no greater than you have been pleased since to profess. But surely, my Lord, one may say, neither the revenge, nor the language you held, bore any proportion to the pretended offence: the appellations of *foe* to *human kind*, an *enemy* like the *devil* to all that have *being; ungrateful, unjust*, deserving to be *whipped, blanketed, kicked*, nay *killed:* a *monster*, an *assassin*, whose conversation every man ought to *shun*, and against whom all doors should be shut; I beseech you, my Lord, had you the least right to give, or to encourage or justify any other in giving such language as this to me? Could I be treated in terms more strong or more atrocious, if during my acquaintance with you I had been a betrayer, a backbiter, a whisperer, an eaves-dropper, or an informer? Did I in all that time ever throw a false die, or palm a foul card upon you? Did I ever borrow, steal, or accept either money, wit, or advice from you? Had I ever the honour to join with either of you in one ballad, satire, pamphlet, or epigram on any person living or dead? Did I ever do you so great an injury as to put off my own verses for yours, especially on those persons whom they might most offend? I am confident you cannot answer in the affirmative; and I can truly affirm, that ever since I lost the happiness of your conversation, I have not published or written one syllable of or to either of you; never hitched your names in a verse, or trifled with your good names in company. Can I be honestly charged with any other crime but an omission (for the word *neglect*, which I used before, slipped from my pen unguardedly) to continue my admiration of you all my life, and still to contemplate, face to face, your many excellences and perfections? I am persuaded you can reproach me truly with no great faults, except my natural ones, which I am as ready to own, as to do all justice to the contrary beauties in you. It is true, my Lord, I am short, not well shaped, generally ill-dressed, if not sometimes dirty. Your Lordship and Ladyship are still in bloom; your figures such, as rival the Apollo of Belvidere, and the Venus of Medicis; and your faces so finished, that neither sickness nor passion can deprive them of *colour*. I will allow your own in particular to be the finest that ever *man* was blest with. Preserve it, my Lord, and reflect that to be a critic would cost it too many frowns, and to be a statesman too many wrinkles! I further confess, I am now somewhat old; but so your Lordship and this excellent Lady, with all your beauty, will, I hope, one day be. I know your genius and hers so perfectly tally, that you cannot but join in admiring each other, and by consequence in the contempt of all such as myself. You have both, in my regard, been like—(your Lordship, I know, loves a *simile*, and it will be one suitable to your quality)— you have been like two princes, and I like a *poor animal* sacrificed between them to cement a lasting league; I hope I have not bled in vain; but that such an amity may endure for ever! For though it be what common understandings would hardly conceive, two *wits* however may be persuaded that it is in friendship as in enmity, the more *danger* the more honour.

Give me the liberty, my Lord, to tell you, why I never replied to those *verses on the imitator of Horace*. They regarded nothing but my *figure*, which I set no value upon; and my *morals*, which, I knew, needed no defence. Any honest man has the pleasure to be conscious, that it is out of the power of the wittiest, nay the greatest person in the kingdom, to lessen him *that way*, but at the expense of his own truth, honour, or justice. . . .

There was another reason why I was silent as to that paper —I took it for a *lady's* (on the printer's word in the title-page,) and thought it too presuming, as well as indecent, to contend with one of that sex in altercation. For I never was so mean a creature as to commit my anger against a lady to paper, though but in a private letter. But soon after, her denial of it was brought to me by a noble person of real honour and truth. Your Lordship indeed said you had it from a lady, and the lady said it was your Lordship's; some thought the beautiful bye-blow had two fathers, or (if one of them will hardly be allowed a man) two mothers; indeed I think both sexes had a share in it, but which was uppermost, I know not. I pretend not to determine the exact method of this witty fornication; and if I call it yours, my Lord, it is only because, whoever *got* it, you brought it forth.

Here, my Lord, allow me to observe, the different proceeding of the ignoble poet, and his noble enemies. What he has written of *Fanny*, *Adonis*, *Sappho*, or who you will, he owned, he published, he set his name to. What they have published of him, they have denied to have written; and what they have written of him, they have denied to have published. One of these was the case in the past libel, and the other in the present. For though the parent has owned it to a few choice friends, it is such as he has been obliged to deny in the most particular terms, to the great person whose opinion concerned him most. Yet, my Lord, this epistle was a piece not written in haste, or in a passion, but many months after all pretended provocations, when you were at full leisure at Hampton Court, and I the object singled, like a deer out of season, for so ill-timed and ill-placed a diversion. It was a deliberate work, directed to a reverend person, of the most serious and sacred character, with whom you are known to cultivate a strict correspondence, and to whom it will not be doubted but you open your secret sentiments, and deliver your real judgment of men and things. This, I say, my Lord, with submission, could not but awaken all my reflection and *attention*. Your Lordship's opinion of me as a *poet*, I cannot help; it is yours, my Lord, and that were enough to mortify a poor man; but it is not yours alone. You must be content to share it with the gentlemen of the Dunciad, and (it may be) with many more innocent and ingenious men. If your Lordship destroys my *poetical* character, they will claim their part in the glory: but, give me leave to say, if my *moral* character be ruined, it must be wholly the work of your Lordship: and will be hard even for you to do, unless I myself co-operate.

How can you talk (my most worthy Lord) of all Pope's Works as so many *libels*, affirm that *he has no invention* but in *defamation*, and charge him with *selling another man's labours printed with his own name?* Fye, my Lord, you forget yourself. He printed not his name before a line of the person's you mention; that person himself has told you and all the world in the book itself, what part he had in it, as may be seen in the conclusion of his notes to the Odyssey. I can only suppose your Lordship (not having at that time *forgot your Greek*) despised to look upon the *translation;* and ever since entertained too mean an opinion of the translator to cast an eye upon it. Besides, my Lord, when you said he *sold* another man's works, you ought in justice to have added that he *bought* them, which very much alters the case. What he gave him was five hundred pounds: his receipt can be produced to your Lordship. I dare not affirm that he was as well paid as some writers (much his inferiors) have been since; but your Lordship will reflect that I am no man of quality, either to buy or sell scribbling so high, and that I have neither place, pension, nor power to reward for *secret services*. It cannot be, that one of your rank can have the least envy to such an author as I: but were that possible, it were much better gratified by employing not your own, but some of those low and ignoble pens to do you this mean office. I dare engage you will have them for less than I gave Mr. Broom, if your friends have not raised the market. Let them drive the bargain for you, my Lord; and you may depend on seeing, every day in the week, as many (and now and then as pretty) verses, as these of your Lordship.

And would it not be full as well, that my poor person should be abused by them, as by one of your rank and quality? Cannot Curll do the same? nay, has he not done it before your Lordship, in the same kind of language, and almost the same words? I cannot but think the worthy and discreet clergyman himself will agree, it is improper, nay unchristian, to expose the *personal* defects of our brother; that both such perfect forms as yours, and such unfortunate ones as mine, proceed from the hand of the same Maker, who fashioneth his vessels as he pleaseth, and that it is not from their shape we can tell whether they are made for honour or dishonour. In a word, he would teach you charity to your greatest enemies; of which number, my Lord, I cannot be reckoned, since, though a poet, I was never your flatterer.

Next, my Lord, as to the *obscurity of my birth*, (a reflection copied also from Mr. Curll and his brethren,) I am sorry to be obliged to such a presumption as to name my family in the same leaf with your Lordship's: but my father had the honour in one instance to resemble you, for he was a younger brother. He did not indeed think it a happiness to bury his elder brother, though he had one who wanted some of those good qualities which yours* possessed. How sincerely glad could I be, to pay to that young nobleman's memory the debt I owed to his friendship, whose early death deprived your family of as much wit and honour as he left behind him in any branch of it. But as to my father, I could assure you, my Lord, that he was no mechanic, neither a hatter, nor, which might please your Lordship yet better, a cobbler, but, in truth, of a very tolerable family; and my mother of an ancient one, as well

* Carr, Lord Hervey.

born and educated as that Lady, whom your Lordship made choice of to be the mother of your own children; whose merit, beauty, and vivacity (if transmitted to your posterity) will be a better present than even the noble blood they derive only from you; a mother, on whom I was never obliged so far to reflect, as to say she spoiled me; and a father, who never found himself obliged to say of me that he disapproved my conduct. In a word, my Lord, I think it enough that my parents, such as they were, never cost me a blush? and that their son, such as he is, never cost them a tear. . . .

How unhappy is it for me, that a person of your Lordship's modesty and virtue, who manifests so tender a regard to religion, matrimony, and morality; who, though an ornament to the court, cultivate an exemplary correspondence with the clergy; nay, who disdain not charitably to converse with, and even assist, some of the very worst of writers (so far as to cast a few conceits, or drop a few antitheses, even among the dear joys of the *Courant*); that you, I say, should look upon Me alone as reprobate and unamendable! Reflect what I was, and what I am. I am even annihilated by your anger: for in these verses you have robbed me of *all power to think*, and, in your others, of the very *name* of a *man!* Nay, to show that this is wholly your own doing, you have told us that before I wrote my last Epistles, (that is, before I unluckily mentioned *Fanny* and *Adonis*, whom, I protest, I knew not to be your Lordship's relations,) *I might have lived and died in glory*.

What would I not do to be well with your Lordship? Though, you observe, I am a mere *imitator* of *Homer, Horace, Boileau, Garth*, &c. (which I have the less cause to be ashamed of, since they were imitators of one another), yet what if I should solemnly engage never to imitate your Lordship? May it not be one step towards an accommodation, that while you remark my *ignorance in Greek*, you are so good as to say, you have *forgot your own?* What if I should confess I translated from Dacier? That surely could not but oblige your Lordship, who are known to prefer French to all the learned languages.

But allowing that in the space of twelve years' acquaintance with Homer, I might unhappily contract as much Greek as your Lordship did in two at the university, why may not I forget it again as happily?

Till such a reconciliation take effect, I have but one thing to entreat of your Lordship. It is, that you will not decide of my principles on the same grounds as you have done of my learning; nor give the same account of my want of grace, after you have lost all acquaintance with my person, as you do of my want of Greek, after you have confessedly lost all acquaintance with the language. You are too generous, my Lord, to follow the gentlemen of the Dunciad quite so far, as to seek my utter perdition; as Nero once did Lucan's, merely for presuming to be a *poet*, while one of so much greater quality was a *writer*. I therefore make this humble request to your Lordship, that the next time you please to write to me, speak of me, or even whisper of me, you will recollect it is full eight years since I had the honour of any conversation or correspondence with your Lordship, except just half an hour in a lady's lodgings at court, and then I had the happiness of her being present all the time. It would therefore be difficult even for your Lordship's penetration to tell, to what, or from what principles, parties, or sentiments, moral, political, or theological, I may have been converted, or perverted in all that time. I beseech your Lordship to consider the injury a man of your high rank and credit may do to a private person, under penal laws and many other disadvantages, not for want of honesty or conscience, but merely perhaps for having too weak a head, or too tender a heart. It is by these alone I have hitherto lived excluded from all posts of profit or trust: as I can interfere with the views of no man, do not deny me, my Lord, all that is left, a little praise, or the common encouragement due, if not to my genius, at least to my industry.

Above all, your Lordship will be careful not to wrong my moral character with THOSE* under whose protection I live,

* The King and Queen.

and through whose lenity alone I can live with comfort. Your Lordship, I am confident, upon consideration will think, you inadvertently went a little too far when you recommended to THEIR perusal, and strengthened by the weight of your approbation, a libel, mean in its reflections upon my poor figure, and scandalous in those on my honour and integrity: wherein I was represented as "*an enemy* to the human race, a *murderer* of reputations, and a *monster* marked by God like *Cain*, deserving to wander accursed through the world."

A strange picture of a man, who had the good fortune to enjoy many friends, who will be always remembered as the first ornaments of their age and country; and no enemies that ever contrived to be heard of, except Mr. John Dennis, and your Lordship: a man, who never wrote a line in which the religion or government of his country, the royal family, or their ministry, were disrespectfully mentioned; the animosity of any one party gratified at the expense of another; or any censure passed, but upon known vice, acknowledged folly, or aggressive impertinance. It is with infinite pleasure he finds, that some men, who seem ashamed and afraid of nothing else, are so very sensible of his ridicule: and it is for that very reason he resolves (by the grace of God, and your Lordship's good leave)

> That, while he breathes, no rich or noble knave
> Shall walk the world in credit to his grave.

This, he thinks, is rendering the best service he can to the public, and even to the good government of his country; and for this at least, he may deserve some countenance, even from the GREATEST PERSONS in it. Your Lordship knows of WHOM I speak. Their NAMES I shall be as sorry, and as much ashamed to place near yours, on such an occasion, as I should be to see you, my Lord, placed so near their PERSONS, if you could ever make so ill an use of their ear as to asperse or misrepresent any innocent man.

This is all I shall ever ask of your Lordship, except your

pardon for this tedious letter. I have the honour to be, with equal respect and concern,

>My Lord,
>>Your truly devoted servant,
>>>A. POPE.

ℂ From Preface to the Works of Shakespear

. . . The *power* over our *passions* was never possess'd in a more eminent degree, or displayed in so different instances. Yet all along there is seen no labour, no pains to raise them; no preparation to guide our guess to the effect, or be perceiv'd to lead toward it; but the heart swells, and the tears burst out, just at the proper places. We are surprised the moment we weep; and yet upon reflection find the passion so just, that we should be surprised if we had not wept, and wept at that very moment.

How astonishing is it, again, that the passions directly opposite to these, laughter and spleen, are no less at his command! that he is not more a master of the *great* than of the *ridiculous* in human nature; of our noblest tendernesses, than of our vainest foibles; of our strongest emotions, than of our idlest sensations!

Nor does he only excel in the passions: in the coolness of reflection and reasoning he is full as admirable. His *sentiments* are not only in general the most pertinent and judicious upon every subject; but by a talent very peculiar, something between penetration and felicity, he hits upon that particular point on which the bent of each argument turns, or the force of each motive depends. This is perfectly amazing, from a man of no education or experience in those great and public scenes of life which are usually the subject of his thoughts: so that he seems to have known the world by intuition, to have looked through human nature at one glance, and to be the only author that gives ground for a very new opinion, That the philosopher, and even the man of the world, may be *born*, as well as the poet.

It must be owned that with all these great excellencies, he has almost as great defects; and that as he has certainly written better, so he has perhaps written worse, than any other. But I think I can in some measure account for these defects, from several causes and accidents; without which it is hard to imagine that so large and so enlightened a mind could ever have been susceptible of them. That all these contingencies should unite to his disadvantage seems to me almost as singularly unlucky, as that so many various (nay contrary) talents should meet in one man, was happy and extraordinary.

It must be allowed that stage poetry, of all other, is more particularly levelled to please the *populace*, and its success more immediately depending upon the *common suffrage*. One cannot therefore wonder if Shakespear, having at his first appearance no other aim in his writings than to procure a subsistence, directed his endeavours solely to hit the taste and humour that then prevailed. The audience was generally composed of the meaner sort of people; and therefore the images of life were to be drawn from those of their own rank: accordingly we find, that not our author's only, but almost all the old comedies, have their scene among *tradesmen* and *mechanics:* and even their historical plays strictly follow the common *old stories* or *vulgar traditions* of that kind of people. In Tragedy, nothing was so sure to *surprise* and cause *admiration* as the most strange, unexpected, and consequently most unnatural, events and incidents: the most exaggerated thoughts; the most verbose and bombast expression; the most pompous rhymes, and thundering versification. In Comedy, nothing was so sure to *please* as mean buffoonery, vile ribaldry, and unmannerly jests of fools and clowns. Yet even in these our author's wit buoys up, and is born above his subject; his genius in those low parts is like some prince of a romance in the disguise of a shepherd or peasant: a certain greatness and spirit now and then break out, which manifest his higher extraction and qualities.

It may be added, that not only the common audience had no notion of the rules of writing, but few even of the better sort piqued themselves upon any great degree of knowledge or nicety that way. . . . To judge therefore of Shakespear by Aristotle's rules, is like trying a man by the laws of one country, who acted under those of another. He writ to the *people*, and writ at first without patronage from the better sort, and therefore without aims of pleasing them; without assistance or advice from the learned, as without the advantage of education or acquaintance among them: without that knowledge of the best models, the ancients, to inspire him with an emulation of them: in a word, without any views of reputation, and of what poets are pleased to call immortality: some or all of which have encouraged the vanity, or animated the ambition, of other writers.

Yet it must be observed, that when his performances had merited the protection of his prince, and when the encouragement of the court had succeeded to that of the town, the works of his riper years are manifestly raised above those of his former. The dates of his plays sufficiently evidence that his productions improved, in proportion to the respect he had for his auditors. And I make no doubt this observation would be found true in every instance, were but editions extant from which we might learn the exact time when every piece was composed, and whether writ for the town or the court.

Another cause (and no less strong than the former) may be deduced from our author being a *player*, and forming himself first upon the judgments of that body of men whereof he was a member. They have ever had a standard to themselves, upon other principles than those of Aristotle. . . . By these men it was thought a praise to Shakespear that he scarce ever *blotted a line*. This they industriously propagated, as appears from what we are told by Ben Jonson in his 'Discoveries,' and from the preface of Heminges and Condell to the first folio edition. But in reality (however it has prevailed) there never was a more groundless report, or to the contrary of which there are more undeniable evidences—as the comedy of the 'Merry Wives of Windsor,' which he entirely new writ; the 'History of Henry VI.,' which was first published under the title of the 'Contention of York and Lancaster;' and that of 'Henry V.,' extremely improved; that of 'Hamlet,' enlarged to almost as much again as at first, and many others. I believe the common opinion of his want of learning proceeded from no better ground. This, too, might be thought a praise by some, and to this his errors have as injudiciously been ascribed by others. For 'tis certain, were it true, it could concern but a small part of them; the most are such as are not properly defects, but superfœtations; and arise not from want of learning or reading, but from want of thinking or judging: or rather (to be more just to our author) from a compliance to those wants in others. As to a wrong choice of the subject, a wrong conduct of the incidents, false thoughts, forced expressions, &c., if these are not to be ascribed to the aforesaid accidental reasons, they must be charged upon the poet himself, and there is no help for it. But I think the two disadvantages which I have mentioned (to be obliged to please the lowest of people, and to keep the worst of company), if the consideration be extended as far as it reasonably may, will appear sufficient to mislead and depress the greatest genius upon earth. Nay, the more modesty with which such a one is endued, the more he is in danger of submitting and conforming to others, against his own better judgment.

But as to his *want of learning*, it may be necessary to say something more. . . . I am inclined to think this opinion proceeded originally from the zeal of the partizans of our author and Ben Jonson, as they endeavoured to exalt the one at the expense of the other. It is ever the nature of parties to be in extremes; and nothing is so probable as that because Ben Jonson had much the more learning, it was said on the one hand that Shakespear had none at all; and because Shakespear had much the most wit and fancy, it was retorted on the other, that Jonson wanted both. Because Shakespear borrowed nothing, it was said that Ben Jonson borrowed everything. Because Jonson did not write extempore, he was reproached with being a year about every piece; and because Shakespear wrote with ease and rapidity, they cried, he never once made a blot. Nay, the spirit of opposition ran so high, that whatever those of the one side objected to the other, was taken at the rebound, and turned into praises; as injudiciously as their antagonists before had made them objections.

Poets are always afraid of envy; but sure they have as much reason to be afraid of admiration. They are the Scylla and Charybdis of authors; those who escape one, often fall by the other. . . . But however this contention might be carried on by the partisans on either side, I cannot help thinking these two great poets were good friends, and lived on amicable terms, and in offices of society with each other. It is an acknowledged fact, that Ben Jonson was introduced upon the stage, and his first works encouraged, by Shakespear. And after his death, that author writes *To the memory of his beloved Mr.* William Shakespear, which shows as if the friendship had continued through life. I cannot for my own part find anything *invidious* or *sparing* in those verses, but wonder Mr. Dryden was of that opinion. He exalts him not only above all his contemporaries, but above Chaucer and Spenser, whom he will not allow to be great enough to be ranked with him; and challenges the names of Sophocles, Euripides, and Æschylus, nay, all Greece and Rome at once, to equal him; and (which is very particular) expressly vindicates him from the imputation of wanting *art*, not enduring that all his excellencies should be attributed to *nature*. It is remarkable too, that the praise he gives him in his 'Discoveries' seems to proceed from a *personal kindness;* he tells us that he lov'd the man, as well as honoured his memory; celebrates the honesty, openness, and frankness of his temper; and only distinguishes, as he reasonably ought, between the real merit of the author, and the silly and derogatory applauses of the players. Ben Jonson might indeed be sparing in his commendations (though certainly he is not so in this instance), partly from his own nature, and partly from judgment. For men of judgment think they do any man more service in praising him justly than lavishly. . . .

Having been forced to say so much of the players, I think I

ought in justice to remark, that the judgment, as well as condition, of that class of people was then far inferior to what it is in our days. As then the best playhouses were inns and taverns (the Globe, the Hope, the Red Bull, the Fortune, &c.), so the top of the profession were then mere players, not gentlemen of the stage. They were led into the buttery by the steward, not placed at the lord's table, or lady's toilette; and consequently were entirely deprived of those advantages they now enjoy, in the familiar conversation of our nobility, and an intimacy (not to say dearness) with people of the first condition.

From what has been said, there can be no question but had Shakespear published his works himself (especially in his latter time, and after his retreat from the stage), we should not only be certain which are genuine, but should find in those that are, the errors lessened by some thousands. If I may judge from all the distinguishing marks of his style, and his manner of thinking and writing, I make no doubt to declare that those wretched plays, 'Pericles,' 'Locrine,' 'Sir John Oldcastle,' 'Yorkshire Tragedy,' 'Lord Cromwell,' 'The Puritan,' and 'London Prodigal,' cannot be admitted as his. And I should conjecture of some of the others (particularly 'Love's Labour's Lost,' 'The Winter's Tale,' and 'Titus Andronicus') that only some characters, single scenes, or perhaps a few particular passages, were of his hand. It is very probable what occasioned some plays to be supposed Shakespear's was only this—that they were pieces produced by unknown authors, or fitted up for the theatre while it was under his administration: and no owner claiming them, they were adjudged to him, as they give strays to the lord of the manor: a mistake which (one may also observe) it was not for the interest of the house to remove. . . .

I will conclude by saying of Shakespear, that with all his faults, and with all the irregularity of his *drama*, one may look upon his works, in comparison of those that are more finished and regular, as upon an ancient majestic piece of Gothic architecture, compared with a neat modern building: the latter is more elegant and glaring, but the former is more strong and more solemn. It must be allowed, that in one of these there are materials enough to make many of the other. It has much the greater variety, and much the nobler apartments; though we are often conducted to them by dark, odd, and uncouth passages. Nor does the whole fail to strike us with greater reverence, though many of the parts are childish, ill-placed, and unequal to its grandeur.

❦ From Thoughts on Various Subjects

PARTY is the madness of many, for the gain of a few.

To endeavour to work upon the vulgar with fine sense, is like attempting to hew blocks with a razor.

To pardon those absurdities in ourselves which we cannot suffer in others, is neither better nor worse than to be more willing to be fools ourselves than to have others so.

The best way to prove the clearness of our mind, is by shewing its faults; as when a stream discovers the dirt at the bottom, it convinces us of the transparency and purity of the water.

To be angry is to revenge the fault of others upon ourselves.

Some old men by continually praising the time of their youth, would almost persuade us that there were no fools in those days; but unluckily they are left themselves for examples.

The world is a thing we must of necessity either laugh at or be angry at; if we laugh at it, they say we are proud; if we are angry at it, they say we are ill-natured.

People are scandalised if one laughs at what they call a serious thing. Suppose I were to have my head cut off to-morrow, and all the world were talking of it to-day, yet why might I not laugh to think, what a bustle is here about my head?

The greatest advantage I know of being thought a wit by the world is, that it gives one the greater freedom of playing the fool.

Wherever I find a great deal of gratitude in a poor man, I take it for granted there would be as much generosity if he were a rich man.

Some people will never learn any thing, for this reason, because they understand every thing too soon.

There are some solitary wretches who seem to have left the rest of mankind, only as Eve left Adam, to meet the devil in private.

The difference between what is commonly called ordinary company and good company, is only hearing the same things said in a little room, or in a large saloon, at small tables or at great tables, before two candles or twenty sconces.

Many men have been capable of doing a wise thing, more a cunning thing, but very few a generous thing.

Authors in France seldom speak ill of each other, but when they have a personal pique; authors in England seldom speak well of each other, but when they have a personal friendship.

Whoever has flattered his friend successfully, must at once think himself a knave, and his friend a fool.

It is observable that the ladies frequent tragedies more than comedies; the reason may be, that in tragedy their sex is deified and adored, in comedy exposed and ridiculed.

A king may be a tool, a thing of straw; but if he serves to frighten our enemies, and secure our property, it's well enough: a scarecrow is a thing of straw, but it protects the corn.

LETTERS

ℂ To Henry Cromwell

April 27, 1708.

I HAVE nothing to say to you in this letter; but I was re-
solved to write to tell you so. Why should not I content myself with so many great examples of deep divines, profound
casuists, grave philosophers, who have written, not letters
only, but whole tomes and voluminous treatises about nothing? Why should a fellow like me, who all his life does nothing,
be ashamed to write nothing; and that to one who has nothing to do but to read it? But perhaps you will say, the whole
world has something to do, something to talk of, something to
wish for, something to be employed about: but pray, sir, cast
up the account, put all these somethings together, and what is
the sum total but just nothing? I have no more to say, but to
desire you to give my service (that is nothing) to your friends,
and to believe that I am nothing more than your, &c.

ℂ To John Caryll

LONDON, *April* 30, 1713.

DEAR Sir,—I think it very happy for me that the circumstances of our friendship are so much changed since I first
knew you, as it now requires an excuse when I do not write
to you, no less than it once required one when I did. I can
assure you, dear sir, nothing less than the pardon you freely
promised me when last I saw you, in case of such omission on
my part, could have made me satisfied so long without accost-
ing you by way of letter. I have been almost every day employed in following your advice in learning to paint, in which
I am most particularly obliged to Mr. Jervas, who gives me
daily instructions and examples. As to poetical affairs, I am
content at present to be a bare looker-on, and from a prac-
titioner turn an admirer, which is, as the world goes, not very
usual. Cato was not so much the wonder of Rome itself in his

days, as he is of Britain in ours; and though all the foolish industry possible has been used to make it a party-play, yet what the author once said of another may be the most properly in the world applied to him on this occasion:—

> Envy itself is dumb, in wonder lost,
> And factions strive who shall applaud him most.

The numerous and violent claps of the whig party on the one side the theatre were echoed back by the tories on the other, while the author sweated behind the scenes with concern to find their applause proceeded more from the hand than the head. This was the case too of the prologue writer,* who was clapped into a stanch whig, sore against his will, at almost every two lines. I believe you have heard that, after all the applause of the opposite faction, my Lord Bolingbroke sent for Booth, who played Cato, into the box, between one of the acts, and presented him with fifty guineas, in acknowledgment, as he expressed it, for his defending the cause of liberty so well against a perpetual dictator. The whigs are unwilling to be distanced this way, as it is said, and therefore design a present to the said Cato very speedily. In the meantime they are getting ready as good a sentence as the former on their side. So, betwixt them, it is probable that Cato, as Dr. Garth expressed it, may have something to live upon after he dies.

The play was published but this Monday, and Mr. Lewis tells me it is not possible to convey it to you before Friday next. The town is so fond of it, that the orange wenches and fruit-women in the park offer the books at the side of the coaches, and the prologue and epilogue are cried about the streets by the common hawkers. But of all the world none have been in so peculiar a manner enamoured with Cato as a young gentleman of Oxford, who makes it the sole guide of all his actions, and subject of all his discourse. He dates everything from the first or third night, &c., of Cato: he goes out

* Pope.

of town every day it is not played, and fell in love with Mrs. Oldfield for no other reason than because she acted Cato's daughter. . . .

ℂ To Joseph Addison

October 10, 1714.

I HAVE been acquainted by one of my friends, who omits no opportunities of gratifying me, that you have lately been pleased to speak of me in a manner which nothing but the real respect I have for you can deserve. May I hope that some late malevolences have lost their effect? Indeed, it is neither for me nor my enemies to pretend to tell you whether I am your friend or not; but, if you judge by probabilities, I beg to know which of your poetical acquaintance has so little interest in pretending to be so? Methinks no man should question the real friendship of one who desires no real service. I am only to get as much from the whigs as I got by the tories, that is to say, civility; being neither so proud as to be insensible of any good office, nor so humble as not to dare heartily to despise any man who does me an injustice.

I will not value myself upon having ever guarded all the degrees of respect for you; for, to say the truth, all the world speaks well of you, and I should be under a necessity of doing the same, whether I cared for you or not.

As to what you have said of me, I shall never believe that the author of Cato can speak one thing and think another. As a proof that I account you sincere, I beg a favour of you,— it is that you would look over the two first books of my translation of Homer, which are in the hands of my Lord Halifax. I am sensible how much the reputation of any poetical work will depend upon the character you give it. It is therefore some evidence of the trust I repose in your good-will, when I give you this opportunity of speaking ill of me with justice, and yet expect you will tell me your truest thoughts, at the same time that you tell others your most favourable ones. . . .

❡ To Teresa and Martha Blount

Thursday [1715?].

DEAR LADIES,—You have here all the fruit Mr. Dancastle's garden affords, that I could find in any degree of ripeness. They were on the trees at eleven o'clock this morning, and I hope will be with you before night. Pray return, sealed up, by the bearer, every single bit of paper that wraps them up; for they are the only copies of this part of Homer. If the fruit is not so good as I wish, let the gallantry of this wrapping paper make up for it. I am yours.

❡ To Edward Blount

Jan. 21, 1715-16.

DEAR SIR,—I know of nothing that will be so interesting to you at present, as some circumstances of the last act of that eminent comic poet, and our friend, Wycherley. He had often told me, as I doubt not he did all his acquaintance, that he would marry as soon as his life was despaired of. Accordingly, a few days before his death, he underwent the ceremony, and joined together those two sacraments which, wise men say, should be the last we received; for, if you observe, matrimony is placed after extreme unction in our catechism, as a kind of hint of the order of time in which they are to be taken. The old man then lay down, satisfied in the conscience of having by this one act paid his just debts, obliged a woman who, he was told, had merit, and shown an heroic resentment of the ill-usage of his next heir. Some hundred pounds which he had with the lady discharged those debts; a jointure of four hundred a-year made her a recompense; and the nephew he left to comfort himself as well as he could, with the miserable remains of a mortgaged estate. I saw our friend twice after this was done, less peevish in his sickness than he used to be in his health; neither much afraid of dying, nor, which in him had been more likely, much ashamed of marrying. The evening before he expired, he called his young wife to the bedside, and earnestly entreated her not to deny him one request, the last he should make. Upon her assurances of consenting to it, he told her, "My dear, it is only this, that you will never marry an old man again." I cannot help remarking, that sickness, which often destroys both wit and wisdom, yet seldom has power to remove that talent which we call humour. Mr. Wycherley showed his, even in this last compliment, though I think his request a little hard; for why should he bar her from doubling her jointure on the same easy terms?

So trivial as these circumstances are, I should not be displeased myself to know such trifles, when they concern or characterise any eminent person. The wisest and wittiest of men are seldom wiser or wittier than others in these sober moments: at least, our friend ended much in the character he had lived in; and Horace's rule for a play, may as well be applied to him as a playwright:—

> Servetur ad imum
> Qualis ab incepto processerit, et sibi constet.

> I am, &c.

☾ To Teresa and Martha Blount

[Sept. 13, 1717].

You cannot be surprised to find him a dull correspondent, whom you have known so long for a dull companion. And though I am pretty sensible, that if I have any wit, I may as well write to show it, as not; yet I will content myself with giving you as plain a history of my pilgrimage, as Purchas himself, or as John Bunyan could do of his *walking through the wilderness of this world*, &c.

First then I went by water to Hampton Court, unattended

by all but my own virtues, which were not of so modest a nature as to keep themselves, or me, concealed: for I met the Prince* with all his ladies on horseback coming from hunting. Mrs. B. and Mrs. L. took me into protection (contrary to the laws against harbouring papists), and gave me a dinner, with something I liked better, an opportunity of conversation with Mrs. H[oward]. We all agreed that the life of a Maid of Honour was of all things the most miserable: and wished that every woman who envied it, had a specimen of it. To eat Westphalia ham in a morning, ride over hedges and ditches on borrowed hacks, come home in the heat of the day with a fever, and (what is worse a hundred times) with a red mark in the forehead from an uneasy hat! all this may qualify them to make excellent wives for foxhunters, and bear abundance of ruddy-complexioned children. As soon as they can wipe off the sweat of the day, they must simper an hour, and catch cold, in the princess's apartment: from thence (as Shakespear has it) to *dinner, with what appetite they may——* and after that, till midnight, walk, work, or think, which they please. I can easily believe, no lone house in Wales, with a mountain and a rookery, is more contemplative than this court; and as a proof of it, I need only tell you, Mrs. L[epel] walked with me three or four hours by moonlight, and we met no creature of any quality but the King, who gave audience to the vice-chamberlain, all alone, under the garden-wall.

In short, I heard of no ball, assembly, basset-table, or any place where two or three were gathered together, except Madam Kilmansegg's; to which I had the honour to be invited, and the grace to stay away.

I was heartily tired, and posted to —— park: there we had an excellent discourse of quackery; Dr. S[hadwell] was mentioned with honour. Lady [Arran] walked a whole hour abroad without dying after it, at least in the time I stayed, though she seemed to be fainting, and had convulsive motions several

* Afterwards George II.

times in her head. I arrived in the Forest by Tuesday noon, having fled from the face (I wish I could say the horned face) of Moses, who dined in the midway thither. I passed the rest of the day in those woods where I have so often enjoyed a book and a friend; I made a hymn as I passed through, which ended with a sigh, that I will not tell you the meaning of.

Your doctor is gone the way of all his patients, and was hard put to it how to dispose of an estate miserably unwieldy, and splendidly unuseful to him. Sir Samuel Garth says, that for Radcliffe to leave a library, was as if an eunuch should found a seraglio. Dr. S[hadwell] lately told a lady, he wondered she could be alive after him: she made answer, she wondered at it for two reasons, because Dr. Radcliffe was dead, and because Dr. S[hadwell] was living. I am your, &c.

ℂ To Lady Mary Wortley Montagu

Sept. 1, 1718.

. . . I have a mind to fill the rest of this paper with an accident that happened just under my eyes, and has made a great impression upon me. I have just passed part of this summer at an old romantic seat of my Lord Harcourt's, which he lent me. It overlooks a common-field, where, under the shade of a haycock, sat two lovers, as constant as ever were found in romance, beneath a spreading beech. The name of the one (let it sound as it will) was John Hewet; of the other, Sarah Drew. John was a well-set man about five and twenty, Sarah a brown woman of eighteen. John had for several months borne the labour of the day in the same field with Sarah; when she milked, it was his morning and evening charge to bring the cows to her pail. Their love was the talk, but not the scandal, of the whole neighbourhood; for all they aimed at was the blameless possession of each other in marriage. It was but this very morning that he had obtained her parents' consent, and it was but till the next week that they were to wait to be happy. Perhaps this very day, in the intervals of their work, they were talking of their wedding clothes; and John was now matching several kinds of poppies and field-flowers to her complexion, to make her a present of knots for the day. While they were thus employed (it was on the last of July,) a terrible storm of thunder and lightning arose, that drove the labourers to what shelter the trees or hedges afforded. Sarah, frighted and out of breath, sunk on a hay-cock, and John (who never separated from her) sate by her side, having raked two or three heaps together to secure her. Immediately there was heard so loud a crack as if heaven had burst asunder. The labourers, all solicitous for each other's safety, called to one another: those that were nearest our lovers, hearing no answer, stepped to the place where they lay: they first saw a little smoke, and after, this faithful pair; —John, with one arm about his Sarah's neck, and the other held over her face, as if to screen her from the lightning. They were struck dead, and already grown stiff and cold in this tender posture. There was no mark or discolouring on their bodies, only that Sarah's eyebrow was a little singed, and a small spot between her breasts. They were buried the next day in one grave, in the parish of Stanton Harcourt in Oxford-shire; where my Lord Harcourt, at my request, has erected a monument over them. Of the following epitaphs which I made, the critics have chosen the godly one: I like neither, but wish you had been in England to have done this office better; I think it was what you could not have refused me on so moving an occasion.

> When Eastern lovers feed the funeral fire,
> On the same pile their faithful fair expire;
> Here pitying Heaven that virtue mutual found,
> And blasted both, that it might neither wound.
> Hearts so sincere th' Almighty saw well pleas'd,
> Sent his own lightning, and the victims seiz'd.

I.

Think not, by rigorous judgment seiz'd,
    A pair so faithful could expire;
Victims so pure Heaven saw well pleas'd,
    And snatched them in celestial fire.

II.

Live well, and fear no sudden fate:
    When God calls virtue to the grave,
Alike 'tis justice, soon or late,
    Mercy alike to kill or save.
Virtue unmov'd can hear the call,
And face the flash that melts the ball.

ℭ To Lord Bathurst

September 23, [1719].

. . . That this letter may be all of a piece, I will fill the rest with an account of a consultation lately held in my neighbourhood about designing a princely garden.* Several critics were of several opinions: one declared he would not have too much art in it; for my notion, said he, of gardening is, that it is only sweeping nature: another told them that gravel-walks were not of a good taste, for all the finest abroad were of loose sand: a third advised peremptorily there should not be one lime-tree in the whole plantation: a fourth made the same exclusive clause extend to horse-chestnuts, which he affirmed not to be trees but weeds: Dutch elms were condemned by a fifth; and thus about half the trees were proscribed, contrary to the paradise of God's own planting, which is expressly said to be planted with all trees. There were some who could not bear evergreens, and called them nevergreens; some who were angry at them only when cut into shapes, and gave the mod-

* The garden of the Prince of Wales at Richmond.

ern gardeners the name of evergreen tailors; some who had no dislike to cones and cubes, but would have them cut in forest trees; and some who were in a passion against any thing in shape, even against clipped hedges, which they called green walls. These, my lord, are our men of taste, who pretend to prove it by tasting little or nothing. Sure such a taste is like such a stomach, not a good one, but a weak one. We have the same sort of critics in poetry; one is fond of nothing but heroics, another cannot relish tragedies, another hates pastorals; all little wits delight in epigrams. Will you give me leave to add, there are the same in divinity; where many leading critics are for rooting up more than they plant, and would leave the Lord's vineyard either very thinly furnished, or very oddly trimmed. . . .

ℂ To the Hon. Robert Digby

December 28, 1724.

It is now the season to wish you a good end of one year, and a happy beginning of another. . . . They tell me that at Coleshill certain antiquated charities and obsolete devotions are yet subsisting: that a thing called Christian cheerfulness, (not incompatible with Christmas-pies and plum-broth,) whereof frequent is the mention in old sermons and almanacks, is really kept alive and in practice: that feeding the hungry, and giving alms to the poor, do yet make a part of good house-keeping, in a latitude not more remote from London than fourscore miles: and lastly, that prayers and roast beef actually made some people as happy as a whore and a bottle. But here in town, I assure you, men, women, and children have done with these things. Charity not only begins, but ends, at home. Instead of the four cardinal virtues, now reign four courtly ones: we have cunning for prudence, rapine for justice, time-serving for fortitude, and luxury for temperance. Whatever you may fancy, where you live in a state of ignorance, and see nothing but quiet, religion, and good-humour, the case is just as I tell you where people understand the world, and know how to live with credit and glory.

I wish that heaven would open the eyes of men, and make them sensible which of these is right; whether, upon a due conviction, we are to quit faction, and gaming, and high-feeding, and all manner of luxury, and to take to your country way; or you to leave prayers, and almsgiving, and reading, and exercise, and come into our measures. I wish (I say) that this matter was as clear to all men as it is to your affectionate, &c.

ℂ To Jonathan Swift

Oct. 9, 1729.

IT pleases me that you received my books* at last; but you have never once told me if you approve the whole, or disapprove not of some parts of the commentary, &c. It was my principal aim in the entire work to perpetuate the friendship between us, and to show that the friends or the enemies of one were the friends or enemies of the other. If in any particular any thing be stated or mentioned in a different manner from what you like, pray tell me freely, that the new editions now coming out here may have it rectified. You will find the octavo rather more correct than the quarto, with some additions to the notes and epigrams cast in, which I wish had been increased by your acquaintance in Ireland. I rejoice in hearing that Drapier's-Hill is to emulate Parnassus. I fear the country about it is as much impoverished. I truly share in all that troubles you, and wish you removed from a scene of distress, which I know works your compassionate temper too strongly. But if we are not to see you here, I believe I shall once in my life see you there. You think more for me and about me than any friend I have, and you think better for

---

* Copies of the Dunciad.

me. Perhaps you will not be contented, though I am, that the additional 100*l*. a-year is only for my life.

My mother is yet living, and I thank God for it. She will never be troublesome to me, if it but please God she be not so to herself: but a melancholy object it is, to observe the gradual decays both of body and mind, in a person to whom one is tied by the links of both. I cannot tell whether her death itself would be so afflicting.

You are too careful of my worldly affairs; I am rich enough, and I can afford to give away a 100*l*. a year. Do not be angry; I will not live to be very old; I have revelations to the contrary. I would not crawl upon the earth without doing a little good when I have a mind to do it. I will enjoy the pleasure of what I give, by giving it alive, and seeing another enjoy it. When I die, I should be ashamed to leave enough to build me a monument, if there were a wanting friend above ground.

Mr. Gay assures me his 3000*l*. is kept entire and sacred. He seems to languish after a line from you, and complains tenderly. Lord Bolingbroke has told me ten times over he was going to write to you. Has he, or not? The doctor* is unalterable, both in friendship and quadrille. His wife has been very near death last week: his two brothers buried their wives within these six weeks. Gay is sixty miles off, and has been so all this summer, with the Duke and Duchess of Queensberry. He is the same man. So is every one here that you know: mankind is unamendable. *Optimus ille qui minimis urgetur*. Poor Mrs. [Blount] is like the rest; she cries at the thorn in her foot, but will suffer nobody to pull it out. The court-lady I have a good opinion of. Yet I have treated her more negligently than you would do, because you like to see the inside of a court, which I do not. I have seen her but twice. You have a desperate hand at dashing out a character by great strokes, and at the same time a delicate one at fine touches. God forbid you should draw mine, if I were conscious of any guilt; but if I were conscious only of folly, God send it!

*Arbuthnot.

for as nobody can detect a great fault so well as you, nobody would so well hide a small one. But after all, that lady means to do good, and does no harm, which is a vast deal for a courtier. I can assure you that Lord Peterborough always speaks kindly of you, and certainly has as great a mind to be your friend as any one. I must throw away my pen; it cannot, it will never tell you, what I inwardly am to you. *Quod nequeo monstrare, et sentio tantum.*

ℭ To John Gay

Aug. 18, 1730.

DEAR GAY,—If my friendship were as effectual as it is sincere, you would be one of those people who would be vastly advantaged and enriched by it. I ever honoured those popes who were most famous for nepotism. It is a sign that the old fellows loved somebody, which is not usual in such advanced years. And I now honour Sir Robert Walpole for his extensive bounty and goodness to his private friends and relations. But it vexes me to the heart when I reflect, that my friendship is so much less effectual than theirs; nay, so utterly useless, that it cannot give you anything, not even a dinner at this distance, nor help the general,* whom I greatly love, to catch one fish. My only consolation is, to think you happier than myself, and to begin to envy you, which is next to hating you—an excellent remedy for love. How comes it that Providence has been so unkind to me, (who am a greater object of compassion than any fat man alive,) that I am forced to drink wine, while you riot in water, prepared with oranges by the hand of the Duchess of Queensberry? that I am condemned to live by a highway side, like an old patriarch receiving all guests, where my portico, as Virgil has it,

Mane salutantum totis vomit ædibus undam,

---

* General Dormer.

while you are rapt into the Idalian Groves, sprinkled with rose-water, and live in burrage, balm, and burnet, up to the chin, with the Duchess of Queensberry? that I am doomed to the drudgery of dining at court with the ladies in waiting at Windsor, while you are happily banished with the Duchess of Queensberry? So partial is fortune in her dispensations! for I deserved ten times more to be banished than you, and I know some ladies who merit it better than even her grace. After this I must not name any, who dare do so much for you as to send you their services. But one there is who exhorts me often to write to you, I suppose, to prevent or excuse her not doing it herself. She seems,—for that is all I will say for a courtier,—to wish you mighty well. Another, who is no courtier, frequently mentions you, and does certainly wish you well. I fancy, after all, they both do so.

I writ to Mr. Fortescue, and told him the pains you took to see him. Dr. A[rbuthnot] for all that I know may yet remember you and me, but I never hear of it. The dean is well. I have had many accounts of him from Irish evidence, but only two letters these four months, in both which you are mentioned kindly. He is in the north of Ireland, doing I know not what, with I know not whom. Cleland always speaks of you. He is at Tunbridge, wondering at the superior carnivoracity of the doctor. He plays now with the old Duchess of M[arlborough], nay, dines with her, after she has won all his money. Other news I know not, but that Counsellor Bickford has hurt himself, and has the strongest walking staff I ever saw. He intends speedily to make you a visit with it at Amesbury. I am my Lord Duke's, my Lady Duchess's, Mr. Dormer's, General Dormer's, and your, &c.

ℂ To Jonathan Swift

April 2, 1733.

You say truly, that death is only terrible to us as it separates us from those we love, but I really think those have the worst of it who are left by us, if we are true friends. I have felt more, I fancy, in the loss of Mr. Gay, than I shall suffer in the thought of going away myself into a state that can feel none of this sort of losses. I wished vehemently to have seen him in a condition of living independent, and to have lived in perfect indolence the rest of our days together, the two most idle, most innocent, undesigning poets of our age. I now as vehemently wish you and I might walk into the grave together, by as slow steps as you please, but contentedly and cheerfully. Whether that ever can be, or in what country, I know no more, than into what country we shall walk out of the grave. But it suffices me to know it will be exactly what region or state our Maker appoints, and that whatever is, is right.

Our poor friend's papers are partly in my hands, and for as much as is so, I will take care to suppress things unworthy of him. As to the epitaph, I am sorry you gave a copy, for it will certainly by that means come into print, and I would correct it more, unless you will do it for me, and that I shall like as well. Upon the whole, I earnestly wish your coming over hither, for this reason among many others, that your influence may be joined with mine to suppress whatever we may judge proper of his papers. To be plunged in my neighbour's and my papers, will be your inevitable fate as soon as you come. That I am an author whose characters are thought of some weight, appears from the great noise and bustle that the court and town make about any I give: and I will not render them less important, or less interesting, by sparing vice and folly, or by betraying the cause of truth and virtue. I will take care they shall be such as no man can be angry at, but the persons I would have angry. You are sensible with what decency and justice I paid homage to the royal family, at the same time that I satirized false courtiers, and spies, &c., about them. I have not the courage however to be such a satirist as you, but I would be as much, or more, a philosopher. You call your satires, libels: I would rather call my satires, epistles. They will consist more of morality than of wit, and grow graver, which you will call duller. I shall leave it to my antagonists to be witty, if they can, and content myself to be useful, and in the right. Tell me your opinion as to Lady [Mary]'s or Lord [Hervey]'s performance. They are certainly the top wits of the court, and you may judge by that single piece what can be done against me; for it was laboured, corrected, pre-commended, and post-disapproved, so far as to be disowned by themselves, after each had highly cried it up for the other's. I have met with some complaints, and heard at a distance of some threats, occasioned by my verses. I sent fair messages to acquaint them where I was to be found in town, and to offer to call at their houses to satisfy them, and so it dropped. It is very poor in any one to rail and threaten at a distance, and have nothing to say to you when they see you. I am glad you persist and abide by so good a thing as that poem, in which I am immortal, for my morality. I never took any praise so kindly, and yet I think, I deserve that praise better than I do any other. When does your Collection come out, and what will it consist of? I have but last week finished another of my epistles, in the order of the system; and this week, *exercitandi gratiâ*, I have translated, or rather parodied, another of Horace's, in which I introduce you advising me about my expenses, housekeeping, &c. But these things shall lie by, till you come to carp at them, and alter rhymes, and grammar, and triplets, and cacophonies of all kinds. Our parliament will sit till midsummer, which, I hope, may be a motive to bring you rather in summer than so late as autumn. You used to love what I hate, a hurry of politics, &c. Courts I see not, courtiers I know not, kings I adore not, queens I compliment not; so I am never like to be in fashion, nor in dependence. I heartily join with you in pitying our poor lady for her unhappiness, and should only pity her more, if she had more of what they at court call happiness. Come then, and perhaps we may go all together into France at the end of the season, and compare the liberties of both

kingdoms. Adieu. Believe me, dear sir, with a thousand warm
wishes, mixed with short sighs, ever yours.

ℭ To Jonathan Swift

Jan. 6, 1734.

I NEVER think of you, and can never write to you now,
without drawing many of those short sighs of which we have
formerly talked. The reflection both of the friends we have
been deprived of by death, and of those from whom we are
separated almost as eternally by absence, checks me to that
degree that it takes away in a manner the pleasure, which yet
I feel very sensibly, too, of thinking I am now conversing with
you. You have been silent to me as to your works; whether
those printed here are, or are not genuine. But one, I am sure,
is yours; and your method of concealing yourself puts me in
mind of the Indian bird I have read of, who hides his head in
a hole, while all his feathers and tail stick out. You will have
immediately by several franks, even before it is here published, my Epistle to Lord Cobham, part of my *Opus Mag-
num*, and the last Essay on Man, both which, I conclude, will
be grateful to your bookseller, on whom you please to bestow
them so early. There is a woman's war declared against me
by a certain lord.* His weapons are the same which women
and children use, a pin to scratch, and a squirt to bespatter.
I writ a sort of answer, but was ashamed to enter the lists
with him, and, after showing it to some people, suppressed
it,—otherwise it was such as was worthy of him and worthy
of me. I was three weeks this autumn with Lord Peterborough,
who rejoices in your doings, and always speaks with the greatest affection of you. I need not tell you who else do the same;
you may be sure almost all those whom I ever see or desire to
see. I wonder not that B—— paid you no sort of civility
while he was in Ireland. He is too much a half-wit to love a

* Hervey.

true wit, and too much half-honest to esteem any entire merit. I hope, and I think, he hates me too, and I will do my best to make him. He is so insupportably insolent in his civility to me when he meets me at one third place, that I must affront him to be rid of it. That strict neutrality as to public parties, which I have constantly observed in all my writings, I think gives me the more title to attack such men as slander and belie my character in private to those who know me not. Yet even this is a liberty I will never take unless at the same time they are pests to private society, or mischievous members of the public, that is to say, unless they are enemies to all men as well as to me. Pray write to me when you can. If ever I can come to you, I will: if not, may Providence be our friend and our guard through this simple world, where nothing is valuable, but sense and friendship. Adieu, dear sir; may health attend your years, and then may many years be added to you.

P. S. I am just now told, a very curious lady intends to write to you to pump you about some poems said to be yours. Pray tell her that you have not answered me on the same questions, and that I shall take it as a thing never to be forgiven from you, if you tell another what you have concealed from me.

ℂ To Jonathan Swift

Aug. 17, 1736.

I FIND, though I have less experience than you, the truth of what you told me some time ago, that increase of years makes men more talkative, but less writative, to that degree, that I now write no letters but of plain business, or plain how-d'ye's to those few I am forced to correspond with, either out of necessity or love. And I grow laconic even beyond laconicism; for sometimes I return only Yes, or No, to questionary or petitionary epistles of half a yard long. You and Lord Bolingbroke are the only men to whom I write, and always in folio. You are indeed almost the only men I know, who either can write in this age, or whose writings will reach the next. Others are mere mortals. Whatever failings such men may have, a respect is due to them, as luminaries whose exaltation renders their motion a little irregular, or rather causes it to seem so to others. I am afraid to censure any thing I hear of Dean Swift, because I hear it only from mortals, blind and dull: and you should be cautious of censuring any action or motion of Lord B[olingbroke] because you hear it only from shallow, envious, or malicious reporters. What you write to me about him, I find to my great scandal repeated in one of yours to ———. Whatever you might hint to me, was this for the profane? The thing, if true, should be concealed; but it is, I assure you, absolutely untrue, in every circumstance. He has fixed in a very agreeable retirement near Fontainebleau, and makes it his whole business *vacare literis*. But tell me the truth, were you not angry at his omitting to write to you so long? I may, for I hear from him seldomer than from you,—that is, twice or thrice a year at most. Can you possibly think he can neglect you or disregard you? If you catch yourself at thinking such nonsense, your parts are decayed: for, believe me, great geniuses must and do esteem one another, and I question if any others can esteem or comprehend uncommon merit. Others only guess at that merit, or see glimmerings of their minds. A genius has the intuitive faculty: therefore, imagine what you will, you cannot be so sure of any man's esteem as of his. If I can think that neither he nor you despise me, it is a greater honour to me by far, and will be thought so by posterity, than if all the house of lords writ commendatory verses upon me, the commons ordered me to print my works, the universities gave me public thanks, and the king, queen, and prince crowned me with laurel. You are a very ignorant man; you do not know the figure his name and yours will make hereafter. I do, and will preserve all the memorials I can that I was of your intimacy; *longo, sed proximus, intervallo*. I will not quarrel with the present age; it has done enough for me, in making and keeping you two my friends. Do not you be too angry at it, and let not him be too angry at it. It has done and can do neither of you any manner of harm, as long as it has not, and cannot burn your works. While those subsist, you will both appear the greatest men of the time, in spite of princes and ministers; and the wisest, in spite of all the little errors you may please to commit.

Adieu. May better health attend you than I fear you possess: may but as good health attend you always as mine is at present,—tolerable, when an easy mind is joined with it.

BIOGRAPHICAL DATA

[These entries are not meant to provide a "background" to Pope's verse. They merely offer a little information and an occasional anecdote about a certain number of Pope's more interesting or consequential contemporaries. Excluded, on the one hand, are people so famous in history or literature— British monarchs, the Duke of Marlborough, the Earl of Chesterfield, Swift, Addison, Prior, Gay, &c.—that comment is scarcely required; excluded, on the other hand, are people so buried under the deposits of Time that they scarcely exist outside the pages of Pope. Excluded, beyond that, are a number of people who just don't seem to me either very interesting or very important—Broome, Henley, Lyttleton, Parnell, Radcliffe, &c., &c.]

ALLEN, Ralph (1694-1764), grew rich through improving the postal system, and turned philanthropist and patron of the arts. He helped finance the "authorized" edition of Pope's *Letters* and was often host to Pope at Bath. The two were for a time estranged, and Pope in his will was rather snide about Allen's generosity. Allen was Fielding's model for Squire Allworthy in *Tom Jones*.

ARBUTHNOT, John (1667-1735), a much-loved and respected man, was one of Queen Anne's physicians and one of Pope's and Swift's closest friends. The three of them were the backbone of the famous Scriblerus Club; and Arbuthnot and Pope collaborated on Gay's notorious farce, *Three Hours After Marriage*.

ATTERBURY, Francis (1662-1732), Bishop of Rochester; seized as a Jacobite, imprisoned in the Tower, tried before the Lords (where Pope testified stutteringly in his behalf), found guilty and banished the country. He corresponded with Pope from abroad.

BENTLEY, Richard (1662-1742), the greatest of all English classical scholars; a redoubtable figure who lived a tempestuous life. For many years Master of Trinity College, Cambridge, he was at length expelled for high-handedly breaking rules and violating traditions; but just as high-handedly ignored his expulsion, and went on being Master of Trinity. Pope had good cause to dislike him, if only for Bentley's famous comment on Pope's translation of Homer: "A pretty poem, Mr Pope; but you must not call it Homer."

BLOUNT, Martha (1690-1762), a member of a good Catholic family, whom Pope knew from early youth, presumably loved, and was plainly devoted to. Educated abroad, "Patty" Blount lived in England with her mother, and with a sister whom Pope disliked and suspected of being his enemy. Martha Blount was the cause of Pope's falling out with Ralph Allen. She received, in Pope's lifetime, the dedication of the *Epistle on Women;* and at his death, a very handsome legacy.

BOLINGBROKE, Henry St John, Viscount (1678-1751), a Tory statesman of noble birth, notable talents, and boundless ambitions. Under Queen Anne he became second to Harley in the Administration; and, wishing to be second to no one, got Harley ousted, and for a brief moment headed the Government. But having conspired with the Pretender, Bolingbroke was attainted on the accession of George I, and fled to France, where for a time he was the Pretender's secretary of state. Eventually pardoned, he returned to England in 1723 and joined the Opposition to Walpole, but was asked to withdraw from its ranks as harmful to its cause. In 1735 he once more removed to France.

Eminently a grand seigneur, notoriously a rake, a polished writer and a resplendent orator, Bolingbroke forfeited most of his lustre by reason of his lies, duplicities, and thirst for power. His professions of high-mindedness, and his real appreciation of the finer springs of conduct, only make him out the greater scoundrel. His most brilliant contemporaries, however—Swift, Pope, Voltaire—admired him extravagantly; and Mr Pitt put at the head of all vanished things he would most wish to recover, a speech by Bolingbroke. Pope owed him two great literary debts: Bolingbroke supplied the philosophy of the *Essay on Man*, and suggested the idea of the *Imitations of Horace*.

BURLINGTON, Richard Boyle, third earl of (1695-1753), a states-man who held office in England and Ireland, but is better known as a patron of the arts and friend of artists (including Pope). At a time when massive baroque dominated English architecture, Burlington helped popularize Palladio, and remodeled Burlington House in the Palladian style.

CAROLINE, Queen of England (1683-1737), by birth a German princess, by education something of a bluestocking, by destiny the wife of George II. The impetuous, irascible, anything but courtly George thought no other woman worthy of buckling Caroline's shoe, yet be-devilled her in a hundred minor ways, and in such odd ones as seeking her advice in the matter of his mistresses. In all that counted, however, Caroline's hold over George II was absolute; and because she was a firm supporter of Walpole (with whom she used to talk filth by the hour) he was retained as Prime Minister after the death of George I. Her own death yields a famous and fantastic anecdote. When George II learned, what she had forborne from telling him, that Caroline was about to die, he was convulsed with tears. Caroline urged him to remarry, whereupon he sobbed out, "No! No! I shall have mistresses." "God knows," sighed the Queen, "*that* needn't prevent you from marrying!"

CIBBER, Colley (1671-1757), celebrated actor, playwright (his *Love's Last Shift* was once translated into French as *La dernière chemise de l'amour*), poetaster, Poet Laureate, adapter of Shakespeare ("Off with his head! So much for Buckingham"), entertaining autobiographer (*Memoirs of My Own Life*). Having imprudently cast some aspersions on Gay's *Three Hours After Marriage*, in which Pope had a hand, he became one of Pope's targets, and ultimately the most famous target of all: Cibber replaced Theobald, in the later *Dunciad*, as King of the Dunces.

COBHAM, Sir Richard Temple, Viscount (1669?-1749), a distinguished soldier during—and after—the Marlborough wars, and a member of the Opposition during Walpole's ascendency. He rebuilt Stowe to make it, with its gardens, one of the great show-places of England; and was the friend and patron of literary men.

CURL (or CURLL), Edmund (1675-1747), a scoundrelly, piratical publisher who lost no chance of turning a dishonest penny, and had no dislike of smutty or scandalous literature. He ascribed to Pope the authorship of some inglorious poems; then, much later (see Introduction) printed the P.T. letters. Pope's dislike of most of Curl's authors was an additional reason for his constantly abusing the publisher. Yet, despite everything unsavory or unscrupulous about him, Curl did publish a number of creditable books.

DENNIS, John (1657-1734), was expelled from Caius College, Cambridge, for stabbing a fellow-student, and thereafter became a Whig hanger-on, an unsuccessful playwright (whose *Appius and Virginia* Pope ridiculed for its bombast) and a fairly acute but extremely acrimonious critic of his contemporaries. He and Pope went for each other during a great many years. Pope resented Dennis bitterly, and got in the final licks in *The Dunciad*.

FREDERICK, Prince of Wales (1707-51), the famous
Fred
Who was alive and is dead
was cordially detested by his parents, George II and Caroline (she ex-

pressed the desire that he might drop dead of an apoplexy). Like his father before him under George I, Frederick was a sort of rallying-point for the Opposition, and head of an Opposition court. Very likely he has been over-maligned. He pre-deceased his father by some years, and the throne eventually passed to Frederick's son (George III).

HERVEY, John, Baron (1696-1743), favorite of Queen Caroline, friend of Lady Mary Montagu, husband of "beautiful Molly Lepel," Member of Parliament and Lord Privy Seal, author of the valuable and vivacious *Memoirs of the Reign of George II*. An effeminate fop who once refused beef, saying: "Beef? Don't you know I never eat beef, nor *horse*, nor any of those things"; yet an undoubtedly intelligent and able man. Pope, after they fell out, hounded Hervey relentlessly, first in the prose *Letter to a Noble Lord* (q.v.); then frequently in verse as "Lord Fanny"; and pre-eminently in the *Epistle to Dr Arbuthnot* where, as Sporus, Hervey is the object of the most terrible piece of abuse in the English language.

KNELLER, Sir Godfrey (1646-1723), famous German-born portrait painter who spent the last fifty years of his life in England, enjoying the patronage of a succession of monarchs, and painting virtually everybody who was anybody. A country neighbor of Pope's, he asked on his deathbed that Pope compose his epitaph: which Pope did, but not very dazzlingly.

MANSFIELD, William Murray, first earl of (1705-1793), an immensely able lawyer and extremely eminent orator who held many Government posts and ultimately became, for more than thirty years, Lord Chief Justice of England. As every reader of Boswell knows, in his youth he "drank champagne with the wits" and "was the friend of Pope." In later life he was harshly assailed by Junius.

MARLBOROUGH, Sarah Churchill, Duchess of (1660-1744), wife of the great Duke. She was brought up with the Princess Anne, and on Anne's becoming Queen, enjoyed her confidence and closest friendship. But Sarah forfeited her position through excessive rudeness and high-handedness. Once the Duke of Marlborough had ceased being indispensable to the nation, Sarah was haughtily dismissed; presently went with her husband into exile; returned to England to inhabit Blenheim Palace, and to quarrel with almost all her friends and almost all her family. An able, arrogant, high-mettled, ill-tempered woman whom Pope pretty much characterized as Atossa, Sarah was for all that a not unworthy consort of the great and courtly Duke. She was, moreover—in spite of all her faults—a free-moving personality in an age of guarded behavior; and a relatively honest woman in an age of endless double-dealing.

MONTAGU, Lady Mary Wortley (1689-1762), a duke's daughter who eloped with Edward Wortley (later Montagu), a Whig politician who became ambassador to Constantinople. There Lady Mary penetrated the harem, and was inoculated in the Turkish fashion for smallpox, a practice she subsequently introduced into England. In later life she lived apart from her husband, moving all over Europe and writing her brilliantly personal and picturesque letters to her husband, family and friends. Lady Mary was a woman with a keen mind, a sharp tongue, a taste for highborn bohemianism and little interest in the proprieties. She was habitually hard, and often mentally coarse and physically unclean. (On somebody remarking to her at the opera, "Your hands are dirty," she is said to have answered: "You should see my feet.") She and Pope were at first great friends; but following their famous quarrel, he hounded her—principally as "Sappho"—throughout the rest of his career.

PETERBOROUGH, Charles Mordaunt, Earl of (1658-1735), soldier and sailor, general and admiral, with notable exploits in Spain during the Marlborough wars; First Lord of the Treasury under William III, ambassador under Anne, patron of letters, friend of Pope, Swift, Arbuthnot and Gay.

PHILIPS, Ambrose (1675?-1749), a poet and dramatist who allied himself with Addison and by his *Pastorals* won the resentment and presumably the jealousy of Pope. His rhymed compliments earned him a nickname—Namby Pamby—that passed into the language.

RICH, John (1682?-1761), theatrical manager, at Lincoln's Inn Fields and Covent Garden, who did much to develop the pantomime. He received the dedication of Theobald's *Shakespeare Restored*, with its censures of Pope; and is perhaps best known for having produced *The Beggars' Opera*, "which made Gay rich, and Rich gay."

SHIPPEN, William (1673-1743), a Jacobite M.P., notable in a treacherous and vicious age, for probity. "I will not say who is corrupt," remarked Walpole, "but I *will* say who is not, and that is Shippen." His reward was to be linked with Montaigne in a famous line of Pope's
(*As downright Shippen or as old Montagne*)

THEOBALD, Lewis (1688-1744), writer, scholar, well-known editor of Shakespeare (who out of a jumble of words "created" the famous description of Falstaff on his deathbed: "His nose was as sharp as a pen, and a' babbled of green fields.") His *Shakespeare Restored* was a sharp and competent criticism of Pope's *Shakespeare*, which blasted Pope not as a poet but only as an editor. That was enough to gain him, however, a role he far from merited: that of King of the Dunces in the early version of *The Dunciad*.

WALPOLE, Sir Robert, first earl of Orford (1676-1745), leader of the Whig party under George I and George II, and Prime Minister of England from 1721 to 1742; the legal though possibly not actual father of Horace Walpole; the Macheath of *The Beggars' Opera*. A bluff, hearty man who originated the Parliamentary week-end so that he might indulge his love of fox-hunting, Walpole made England prosperous by keeping her peaceful, and philistine by making her prosperous. An able and highly cynical administrator (who is credited with the famous remark, "Every man has his price," but actually said of particular men, "All these men have their price"), Walpole had grave limitations and indulged in politically discreditable practices. All the same, much of the bitter scorn and antagonism he aroused was owing to envy of his ability and of his success; for however shabby his political methods (nepotism, bribery and the like), they were superior to the back-stabbings and closet conspiracies of Stuart politicos. Since most of Pope's best friends and advisers were Walpole's political opponents, Walpole does not fare very well at Pope's hands; yet even Pope paid tribute to his likeableness:

> *Seen him I have, but in his happier hour*
> *Of Social Pleasure, ill-exchanged for Pow'r;*
> *Seen him, uncumber'd with the venal tribe,*
> *Smile without Art, and win without a Bribe.*

(Epilogue to the Satires).